THE SPIRIT OF
Adventure Calls

a compass for life, learning and leadership

Inspired by the life of Mark Auricht

Wayne B Enright

Paperback first edition published by UNESCO-APNIEVE Australia Publishing 2017
ISBN: 978-0-99464121-1-3

EBook ISBN: 978-0-646-97362-3 Published 2017 by Wayne Enright 2019

Second edition (POD) published by Wayne B Enright 2019
ISBN: 978-0-99464121-1-3

All Rights Reserved
© 2017 Wayne B Enright

This work is copyright and may not be reproduced without the written consent of the author, in accordance with the Australian Copyright Act 1968. To seek consent or to order copies, please contact the author: wayne@freespirittruenorth.com.au

A copy of this book is held by the State Library of South Australia and The National Library of Australia. National Library of Australia Cataloguing-in-publication entry:

Author:	Wayne B Enright
Title:	The Spirit of Adventure Calls: A Compass for Life, Learning & Leadership
ISBN:	978-0-9946121-1-3
Topics:	Leadership Development Personal Growth Adventure Biography Business Success

Edited by:	Jennie Bickmore-Brand and Gabrielle Enright
Cover Design:	Openbook Howden Print and Design, and Greg Wilson—Probiz
Cover Photo:	Mark Auricht on Lobuje East, 1998—taken by D. Chessell
Printed By:	Openbook Howden Print and Design—Adelaide, South Australia

Disclaimers:

The material in this publication is of a general nature, expressed as opinion by the author and does not represent professional advice. It is not intended to provide specific guidance for any individual or organisation and should not be relied upon as such. Readers should seek professional advice on matters pertaining to their personal circumstances. The author and publisher accept no responsibility or liability for the use or misuse of information in this publication.

The designations employed and the presentation of material throughout this publication do not imply the expression of any opinion whatsoever on the part of UNESCO concerning the legal status of any country, territory, city or area or of its authorities, or the delimitation of its frontiers or boundaries.

The author is solely responsible for the choice and presentation of the contents of this book and for the opinions expressed therein.

Among the foundation stones of our life
we sometimes find gems of immeasurable value.
If they slip through our fingers after awakening our heart,
shall we leave them hidden in the dust of our past,
or hold them up to the light for all to see their beauty?
Surely these gems are too valuable to become lost treasure.

WB Enright

ABOUT MARK AURICHT

Mark Auricht was one of the early adopters of adventure-based learning used for organisational development in Australia.

In 1995 he was the first Australian, with his climbing partner David Hume, to summit Mt Makalu - the fifth highest peak in the world at 8463 metres. Tragically, David Hume fell to his death as he and Mark descended from their triumphant moment on the summit. Mark survived to tell the story of his arduous and heart-breaking journey back to safety. The triumph and tragedy of the Makalu Expedition was to become a prophetic moment that would lead Mark to a similar fate on Everest six years later.

This book covers the story of these two expeditions and takes the reader on a personal journey into Mark Auricht's inspiring life and the impact of his legacy beyond the mountains.

DEDICATION

To my dear friend Mark Auricht,

This book is dedicated to you, a peaceful servant, a man who had the unique ability to make people feel special. You always encouraged others without fail, praised every risk and celebrated every triumph no matter how small. You laughed with and empowered people, rather than have the attention for yourself. You were generous, caring, inspiring, humble and loyal. I loved that about you.

Richard Bach says that *meeting again after moments or lifetimes is certain for those who are friends.* I trust that this is true, and look forward to seeing you in the mirrors among the mountains and sky.

What the caterpillar calls the end of his lifetime,
the master calls the butterfly.
Richard Bach—Author of *Jonathon Livingston Seagull* and *Illusions*

ABOUT THE AUTHOR

Wayne Enright specialises in leadership, team and personal development through the design and facilitation of memorable learning experiences drawing on his 25 years experience as a life and business coach, corporate facilitator, professional speaker and adventure guide.

Wayne has worked with large corporations, government and small businesses around Australia and internationally, assisting them to improve the self-management, leadership and team skills of their staff. After meeting Mark Auricht while doing post-graduate studies in counselling, Wayne continued to study accelerated learning methodologies and collaborated with Mark on the delivery of experiential learning programs. In the year 2000, Wayne and his wife Gabrielle established their own business to assist individuals and organisations to improve their quality of life and performance.

In 2003 Wayne was diagnosed with a neurological condition that affected his speech. It was during this year that he first walked the Kokoda Trail which led to the establishment of an adventure travel business with Gabrielle. This took them on adventures around the world including places such as Kilimanjaro, Kokoda, the Inca Trail in Peru, and as far as Patagonia in Southern Chile. Closer to home they guide treks in New Zealand, Tasmania, Central Australia and the Kimberley.

Wayne also volunteers as a Team Leader for 'youth at risk' adventure therapy programs with the *Operation Flinders Foundation* and speaks regularly on the topic of *Leading Teams Through Challenging Terrain.*

Wayne's belief is that the mindsets, skills and character traits required to meet the challenges of 'new world chaos' are not developed in classrooms, but by learning to navigate the challenges of experience. He attributes much of what he shares in this book, to the legacy of his friend Mark Auricht to whom this book is dedicated.

A COMPASS FOR LIFE, LEARNING AND LEADERSHIP...

The world's social and economic landscape has dramatically changed in the last 50 years. We've experienced an explosion of consumerism, the social revolution of the 60s, the formation of networks and the booming information age. We now operate in a highly competitive global marketplace.

The type of leadership necessary to survive and thrive in this new frontier is vastly more demanding. Recent generations are challenging the old paradigms of leadership and now expect a different kind of leader who must earn the right to lead rather than rely on their title.

This book explores how to make the transition to a new way of leading and the role that professionally facilitated experiential learning can play in developing teams and leaders who can adapt to the challenges of the new frontier.

Drawing on Mark's wisdom, together with his own experiences of leading teams through challenging terrain, the author provides a guide for living, learning and leading in an unpredictable future.

PEER REVIEW

Stories are a time-honoured way of passing on the legacy of those who have walked this way before us, leaving a trail of treasure behind them that we would otherwise be blind to. Artists and story-tellers often use metaphor, parable, poetry and symbols to articulate concepts beyond the boundaries of language and time. This tale includes a collection of stories, adventurous anecdotes, inspiring quotes, user-friendly visuals and thought-provoking insights to paint an engaging picture of profound but simple principles for life, learning and leadership.

Universities and other places of learning prepare us for the technical skills of a profession; they challenge us to think; solve-problems; create and innovate; and perhaps most importantly they provide us with the tools and experiences to become all we can dream to be. I like to think of this book as a valuable companion for those of us on this journey of exploration, growth and pursuing a meaningful purpose.

This book is written for a broad audience including the young person starting out in life seeking their True North; the university student who understands the need for personal development in addition to mastering the knowledge and skills of their field; the eager entrepreneur who has a creative, brilliant mind and yet knows that growing a viable business requires a special kind of leadership and resilience. It is also written for mature leaders, parents, mentors and teachers who recognise the value in expanding their toolkit for nurturing the next generation. This story is also for the solo adventurer who desires to take the road-less-travelled to discover the universe of their potential.

Every heart has a story to tell and this one has been beautifully crafted as a tribute to a friend but also as a resource that will stand the test of time for everyone who desires to live more authentically, learn more potently and lead others in challenging endeavours. I have a hardcopy on my desk as a ready reference when I need a compass to guide me or I am seeking inspiration. I also have a copy of the e-book that I take with me on trips as a travelling companion. This book is one of those rare finds that may be dog-eared, underlined and highlighted throughout as it is re-read and consulted on more than one occasion. It may become old and tattered over time, but I suspect for me, will be akin to a well-worn coat or a favourite pair of boots that will always have a place in my home by the fire. I recommend it to all who have a love of learning, adventure and personal growth.

Sidney Arthurson
Friend, Mentor and Guide.

TESTIMONIALS

"I have had the pleasure of working with Wayne, delivering programs to organisations since 2005. His passion, authenticity, attention to detail and ability to help individuals and teams to grow and perform through adventure-based experiential learning is incredibly outstanding. Wayne has been a wonderful teacher to me and a very good friend. I highly recommend reading this book if you are dedicated to living, learning and leading with excellence. I encourage you to be a part of the ripple effect that Mark Auricht began and Wayne so gracefully continues."

Katrina Webb-Denis OAM
Director of *Silver 2 Gold High Performance Solutions,* Triple Paralympic Gold Medallist

"Following Wayne's journey into the power of adventure and experiential learning will take you on a magical path of discovery, where building resilience, self-responsibility, emotional intelligence and improved teamwork, become obvious solutions to critical personal, workplace and global challenges. This book opens up a whole new way to look at the world, how we learn best and what it takes to cultivate engaging workplace environments. This invaluable *Compass for Life, Learning & Leadership,* is a must read manuscript for current and future leaders."

Grant Donovan PhD
Managing Partner—*Workplace Global Network*
Partner—*Paradigm Learning Asia Pac*

TESTIMONIALS

"While reading Mark's incredible story, I couldn't help but think that it could have been me that died that day on the mountain as we were both climbing Everest at the same time. Mark's death made me hug my girls tightly and hope that they will also long to explore the world around them and the limits of their ability. Nature for me is like a human laboratory filled with thrilling experiments of self discovery. We all have *Everests* to climb in our lives and this book can help us prepare for that challenging, beautiful and inevitable journey."

Todd Sampson
Award-winning documentary-maker (*Redesign My Brain, Body Hack, Life on the Line*), Television presenter (*Gruen* and *The Project*), co-creator of the *Earth Hour Initiative*. Award-winning CEO. Summited Everest in 2001.

"Wayne has mastered the art of parable. He has woven the dramatic, perilous, and at times funny anecdotes of his mentor Mark Auricht, together with his own frank self revelation, to create a gripping account. This alone could suffice as riveting reading. However, Wayne has garnered the treasures of his craft in assisting people and organisations to explore their dreams and outwork their potential over decades. *A Compass for Life, Learning & Leadership* is not only a manual for self exploration, leaders and facilitators will find many tools and insights into how to build healthy foundations in teams and organisations. A book full of wisdom I believe I will keep returning to time and again."

Jennie Bickmore-Brand PhD, MEd, MA, Grad Dip Ed BEd, DipT
Investing in Learning Communities

ACKNOWLEDGEMENTS

It is with much gratitude that I acknowledge a number of people who have helped me to bring this project to fruition.

My Family
First and foremost I would like to thank my family for supporting me through the ups and downs of this journey. My wife and life partner Gabrielle, and my two sons Peter and Jesse, have loved and supported me emotionally, physically and spiritually over the last fifteen years as I have taken a sometimes manic ride in and out of the writing zone. Gabrielle has taught me much about service, unconditional love and forgiveness, and how to face life's challenges gracefully. Peter has shown me how to go after dreams courageously and to voice one's truth fearlessly. Jesse has taught me that silence is sometimes the most supreme speech and that mastery of self, not others is the summit of bravery. My family has kept me grounded and reminded me that I am not an expert on everything I have written, but merely a fellow traveller who still gets lost in the forest occasionally. I thank them for their encouragement when at times my courage was fragile. I also thank my parents for their influence and my siblings for the adventures we shared when we were young. Their love from a distance is always with me.

Mark's Family
I thank Mark's wife Catherine Auricht-Crease for trusting me, encouraging me and being patient over such a long time, not knowing whether I would ever deliver on my declaration to her that I would write this tribute to Mark. Thank you to Mark's father Clive Auricht for giving me his blessing to write a book about his son. I know from my own parents' experience of losing a son, that the connection between a parent and the soul of their offspring is like a precious jewel and that the stewardship of their life story and legacy is not a responsibility to be taken lightly. Thank you Clive for the chats we've had about Mark and about the art of writing a book. Your advice and guidance have been invaluable. Thanks also to Geoff (Mark's brother who sadly is no longer with us) for always being an enthusiastic encourager. I would also like to thank Mark's other siblings - big brother Richard and his wife Merrilyn, Mark's sister Elizabeth and Mark's younger brother David. Thank you all for trusting me to share part of your brother's story and message. I hope that I have done it justice.

Acknowledgements

I gratefully acknowledge the contributions of the following people to helping me produce this book. I couldn't have done it without you.

Publisher: Joy de Leo – Director of UNESCO-APNIEVE Australia
Thank you Joy for your generosity, positive attitude and valuable guidance.

Printing: Openbook Howden Print and Design.
Thank you Dora and Sarah for your coaching and priceless advice. Dealing with your team has been a pleasurable and stress-free process.

Editors: Jennie Bickmore-Brand & Gabrielle Enright.
Thank you for your wise guidance, your patience, tireless dedication and loving respect for this project.

Book Cover: Greg Wilson (Probiz) and **Openbook Howden Print and Design.**
Thanks Greg & Jen for your generous support of this project and for your contribution to the Auricht Gift event in 2002. Thanks also to Openbook Howden for building on Greg's early work to design the final cover.

Foreword: Allan Keogh
Thank you Allan for your kind words, for all that you teach through your example, for your generous support and encouragement of Mark's endeavours and for always being 'on belay' for him and for me.

Todd Sampson
Thank you Todd for sharing your thoughts about the value of adventure.

Thank you to those who generously supported the launch of the first publication of this book in Adelaide 2017.

Rod Buchecker, Jennie Bickmore-Brand, Chris Hodge, Light Regional Council, Nova Systems and Ouwens Casserly Real Estate, Allan & Elizabeth Keogh, Auricht Family and Deb and Thomi Sigrist, Cathy and Steve Grace, Valda and John Baker-Wells, Helen Robinson, Marion Leggo, Katrina Webb, Cindy Pellas and David Lamperd, Openbook Howden Print and Design.

Grant Donovan
Thanks Grant for allowing me to share the learning I gleaned from you about the psychology of business and leading self-managed teams.

Duncan Chessell
Thanks for providing the cover photograph and others within the book. Thanks also for allowing me to share your Everest interview.

Zac Zaharias, Brian Laursen, Tim Robathan, Bob Killip and Peter Maiden
Thanks Zac, Brian, Tim and Bob for your willingness to be interviewed and for what you and the Army Alpine Association (AAA) team did for Mark. Thanks Peter for allowing me to use extracts from your book about the AAA Expedition - it helped to fill a lot of the gaps in my understanding.

Katrina Webb OAM – Paralympic Gold Medallist, professional speaker and mother of three beautiful boys.
I am grateful to you and Ed for your friendship, kindness, encouragement and example. Your dedication to excellence and to teaching others to embrace their unique gifts and challenges is inspiring.

Joanna Flavell – Speech therapist.
Thank you for helping me to learn how to work around the challenges of my speech disability and to find my true voice.

David Griggs – Facilitator of the 'Beyond Words' program and professional speaker coach.
Thank you for teaching me that story telling is more about communicating from the heart and soul rather than words alone.

Rob Young – Vision Quest Guide.
Thank you Rob for leading me to discover my truth, reclaim my voice and honour the foundation stones of my life. Your egoless guidance is a gift I will always see as an example for me.

The Buna Boys – Our friends, brothers and guides from Papua New Guinea.
Thanks for helping us to take people on the life-changing Kokoda journey over the years. You've taught me much about life and leadership for which I am eternally grateful. PNG will always have a place in my heart as it does for Mark's family.

Other Teachers, Mentors and Authors
There are so many other teachers, mentors, authors and speakers that have shared their wisdom with me and inspired me to explore my potential. In addition to Mark Auricht there were many other influencers in my life, some of whom I write about in the pages of this book. These range from my art and history teachers at school; mentors in the martial arts and in business; masters in the art of facilitation, counselling and personal growth; those who have taught me about leadership and guiding young people; and all of the inspiring authors and presenters who have influenced my thinking.

What was at first an emotional response to the death of a close friend, has become much more than a tribute to his inspiring life. In the end it has evolved into a book that aims to guide whoever reads it to live, learn and lead in a way that makes a positive difference in the world.

Proceeds from the sale of this book will be donated to support programs for young people at risk and to a scholarship supporting the development of emerging leaders in Nature-based Adventure Therapy.

Operation Flinders Foundation.
Thanks for all that you do for young people at risk and for providing me with the opportunity to contribute to their lives and learn some valuable lessons about the harsh realities of leading in challenging terrain.

Will Dobud – Adventure Therapist & Founder of True North Expeditions. Thanks for having the courage to go out on your own to make a difference to the lives of young people at risk and for teaching me through your example some of the finer points of adventure therapy.

Wayne Enright wishes to pay respect to Elders past and present, and to acknowledge the Traditional Custodians of the lands upon which the stories and events contained in this book have taken place.
Please also note that his book contains some stories about deceased people.

All quotes, figures and photographs contained in this book are the creation of WB Enright unless otherwise attributed. Contributions by other authors have been acknowledged and every attempt has been made to locate the copyright holders. Any person or organisation that may have been inadvertently misattributed or overlooked, please contact Wayne Enright.

CONTENTS

About Mark Auricht	1
Dedication to Mark Auricht	2
About the Author	3
A Compass for Life, Learning and Leadership...	4
Peer Review and Testimonials	5
Acknowledgements	8
Foreword – Allan Keogh	15
Preface – A Compass for Life, Learning and Leadership	17
Prologue – My Awakening	21
Introduction – Fulfilling a Promise	25

Part I – The Spirit of Adventure Calls – The Inspiring Life of Mark Auricht

1. Facing the Truth of Impermanence — 33
2. Himalaya Calling — 49
3. The Challenge of Chomolungma — 55
4. Triumph and Tragedy on Everest — 67
5. Tributes to a Magnificent Human Being — 83
6. The Path of His Happiness — 89
7. Discovering the Treasure Within — 99
8. The Gift of His Legacy — 105

Part II – Exploring the Inner Landscape – Our Learning Journey

9. Metaphor and Mythology — 109
10. Parallel Lifetimes — 113
11. Organisational Wellness — 119
12. Venturing into the Learning Zone — 125
13. The Day my Voice Broke — 135
14. Learning – a Daring Adventure — 139
15. The Art of Facilitation — 151
16. Secret Destinations — 161

Contents

Part III – The New Leadership Frontier – Navigating Uncharted Horizons

- 17. The Evolution of Leadership — 169
- 18. The Business Biologist — 171
- 19. Mountains of Gold in a Silver Landscape — 177
- 20. Exploring the New Frontier — 183
- 21. The Journey to Self Management — 193
- 22. Transition to a New Way of Leading — 209
- 23. Loosening the Grip on Autocracy — 213
- 24. The Power of Leverage — 223
- 25. Encouraging the Heart — 227

Part IV – The Spiral Journey – Rites of Passage

- 26. Finding True North — 237
- 27. Waking Up in the Jungle — 241
- 28. Kokoda – a Journey of the Spirit — 247
- 29. Vision Quest — 253

Part V – True North Leadership – A Compass for Leaders

- 30. The Four Directions — 267
- 31. True North – the Internal Compass — 271
- 32. Resilience — 293
- 33. Responsibility — 311
- 34. The Art of Influence — 327

Part VI – Apogee – Reaching the Summit of Your Potential

- 35. Renovating the Inner Landscape — 365
- 36. Fulfilling Your Significance — 373
- 37. The Journey Home — 381

Epilogue – Circle of Stones — 385

Appendices and References

- Appendix A: Animal Instincts Profile — 391
- Appendix B: Emotional Intelligence Profile — 392
- Appendix C: Developing Self-managed Teams — 393
- Notes — 396
- List of Figures — 403
- References — 405
- Index — 409
- Services — 415

FOREWORD
By Allan Keogh

Life is a daring adventure or nothing! Mark's story is just that—a bold, audacious and exhilarating exploration of courage and determination, and an inspiration. Wayne's tribute is a testament to Mark's far-reaching legacy.

My association with Mark began back in 1990 after he participated in *Money and You,* a Robert Kiyosaki personal development program designed to stretch and take participants outside their comfort zone. Our close personal and professional relationship evolved as our businesses: *Keogh Consulting* and *Venture Corporate Recharge,* delivered some groundbreaking work for clients such as Santos, Woodside, BHP Billiton, and Motorola.

Mark's academic credentials in Physical and Outdoor Education, Counselling and Psychology, together with his professional membership of the *Australian Institute of Training and Development,* complimented his pioneering spirit for adventure learning. Remembered in the "Adventure Hall of Fame" along with such greats as Karl Rohnke and Derek Lucas, Mark's contribution to the value of adventure in our lives was outstanding. His transformational work continues through colleagues that he worked with and mentored, such as Darren Williams, Vanessa Walker, Travis Kemp, Charles Manning, and the quiet achiever Wayne Enright.

To write this narrative, Wayne has travelled far, surmounting many obstacles, and facing his own demons along the way. This story is a triumph of the soul and evidence that we are, after all, human *beings.* We all have an Everest challenge to face in life, some like Mark Auricht and Duncan Chessell, take on the highest mountains in the world, some never climb, but we are all confronted daily with what appear to be unattainable challenges. Mark's story and Wayne's journey to bring it to these pages, is proof that the impossible can become possible.

The day before Mark left for the Himalayas, I asked him whether he was sure that he wanted to climb Everest, his answer still rings true—*Yes, it is what I'm meant to do!* He said. I dare say too, that Wayne was meant to write this story. I encourage you to read it with an open heart and be inspired by a man that had the courage to BE! It is a provocative, high voltage playbook for those who aspire to be extra-ordinary leaders. I highly recommend it as a must-read for any leader who has the ticker to be all they can be.

Allan Keogh—Executive Principal Consultant and MD Keogh Consulting

PREFACE

Roger Rosenblatt, author of *Unless it Moves the Human Heart – The Craft and Art of Writing* said that writers write from who they are, what they fear and what they love. Some write from their beliefs and how they want the world to be and some secretly wish to just make a difference without being too obvious about it. I am not an author by profession, but this story I feel compelled to share, not only as a tribute to a friend but also to share his treasure with you. My secret wish is that you will see, beneath this stream of words, a message from this friend of mine whose life has made a difference to me and many others.

> *Some people, art, experiences and stories, disturb people.*
> *They stir our heart and spirit… Sometimes just enough to change our course!*

I hope that this story stirs your heart and spirit and helps you to appreciate some of what Mark had to share with the world. This is my personal tribute to a dear friend and I share these words with you, trusting that you will find some 'fish beneath the surface.' I believe his legacy is too valuable to become lost treasure.

A Compass for Life, Learning and Leadership

Our world shall never be well understood by theory alone: life experience is much more valuable; but surely it is of great use to a young person, before they set out on their journey through a life full of twists and turns, mountains and mazes, to at least have a map and compass to guide them, made by an experienced traveller. Inspired by *The Letters of the Earl of Chesterfield to His Son.*

The journey of personal growth requires us to explore and find our own path. At the same time it is helpful to have some guidance along the way. May this book also provide a compass for life, learning and leadership.

Navigating the Landscape of this Book

As you travel through the changing terrain of these pages, you will accompany me on my writing journey of the last fifteen years where I take you back to stories from Mark's past, including his early years and subsequent adventures; then to his and my learning years together; and forward to my own journey since his death. I also refer back to stories from my personal past; and to thoughts about the future. So you'll be doing some time travel as you read. Following is an overview of the territories we will be exploring to help you navigate the landscape.

Part I – The Spirit of Adventure Calls – The Inspiring Life of Mark Auricht
I start this tribute to Mark by sharing some of what I know about his life and adventures and I write about my reflections on his life's legacy.

Part II – Exploring the Inner Landscape – Our Learning Journey
Here I reflect on my relationship with Mark, the learning journey we took together and how he taught me to leave my comfort zone in search of my potential as a teacher and guide, and more importantly as a human being.

Part III – The New Leadership Frontier – Navigating Uncharted Horizons
After Mark's death I continued on with my own journey, which has had some interesting twists and turns, including some adventures of my own. I share some of what I've learnt about life, learning and leadership, and explore its application to the challenges of what I call *New World Chaos*.[3]

Part IV – The Spiral Journey – Rites of Passage
In this part of the book I share some of the more challenging parts of my personal journey to illustrate the rites of passage that we all have to move through at different stages in our lives to discover the truth of who we are.

Part V – True North Leadership – A Compass for Leaders
Here I bring together what I learnt from Mark and what I've discovered while continuing on the trajectory we travelled together. This is summarised in a simple model to provide a compass for leading in challenging terrain.

Part VI – Apogee – Reaching the Summit of Your Potential
In this final part of the book I explore questions about self-mastery, fear and freedom and I share suggestions for those who may be on a quest to find their own *True North*.[4] In the end I trust that this journey will guide you to the summit of your potential.

Compass Checkpoints and Trail Markers

The overview of the landscape is intended to provide you with a map to indicate the main route we will follow, but this journey, like any good adventure, takes many detours, so be prepared to go off the beaten track from time to time. Below I have provided some checkpoint and trail markers to serve as a guide.

If you've ever trekked an unfamiliar trail that has many sidetracks, you'll know the feeling of security you get when you see a trail marker. It provides a point of reference as if to say, "keep going you're on the right track". The checkpoint symbols and the trail markers below will help you to make sense of the journey as I go back and forth in time. If you get lost don't panic—just keep taking the next step and you'll eventually come to more easy going terrain.

The other option to take if you're lost is to sit calmly, have a cuppa and be still for a while (every good survival kit has a tea bag in it for this reason). While waiting with a warm cup of tea nestled between two hands, a little steam rising to meet your face, insight comes and enlightens the way. Never underestimate the value of a tea break to calm and clear the mind.

I wish you well on your travels through this book and trust that the following navigation aids will be helpful. I also encourage you to stop along the way at a comfortable place among the trees, beside a lake or at the top of a peak in the silence of the snow. Listen for what is true for you, rest a while and reflect on your own journey. My hope is that you will find many treasures scattered among the hills and along the shoreline, as you comb these pages—some may be obvious and familiar, others perhaps more subtle and profound. Whatever you discover along the way, I hope you enjoy the journey and find what your soul is seeking.

Compass Checkpoints

When navigating across land, sea, sky and life, it is often helpful to stay on course by using checkpoints. They provide us with waypoints, rest stops, a place to check our location on the map, space to reset our compass and our intention for the next part of the journey. In the context of this book they are the spaces between the six parts or territories we will travel through. A chance to reflect, catch your breath and be introduced to the next place we will explore.

The Writing Journey
These are pieces I have written while at the desk, reflecting on my writing journey, sharing my thoughts and feelings as I typed away in a flurry of inspiration, insights and emotions that arose as I sat quietly waiting for words to come. Sometimes I've included a short narration of what was happening in my life while I ebbed and flowed with my commitment to writing.

Personal Stories
These are personal stories from different times in my life, sometimes just a slice to use as an analogy or to set the scene for a chapter and other times I have shared longer stories to explain how I learnt something, why I have a particular point of view or simply to illustrate a key lesson that I think may be of value for the reader.

Personal Reflection Exercises
At the end of some chapters I offer some personal reflection questions which may be helpful for you to contemplate. Reflection is an often neglected part of learning from experience, and the experience of reading stories or knowledge imparted by someone else is no exception. *How does this apply to me? How can I put this lesson to use in my own life?* These are good questions to ask. Otherwise intellectual understanding alone will fall short of making a difference.

Tools for Living, Learning and Leadership
Tools are things we use to simplify our life, to make our trade easier, more effective and user-friendly. I like to illustrate ideas with stories, visual models and practical experiences or journeys. As we go along I'll share some of these learning tools with you, including some easy to remember visual diagrams and some suggested processes that can be practically applied in your world. I encourage you to take them with you as you journey on in your own life with a spirit of adventure.

I've prepared you as best I can. Now let me take you to the start of this trail.

PROLOGUE

My Awakening

WHACK!!... in an instant my world is pitch black and silent...

I reach out for consciousness but it eludes me.

Darkness... silence... numb... nothingness...

In this eternal timeless space I find myself quietly floating in a still, quiet black hole.

Then after what seems like an eternity... I come up from the deep and find my way back... a breathless diver breaking through the surface, gasping for air...

I orientate myself slowly to my surroundings, eyes blinking back into the light.

How long have I been asleep to this world?

I find myself lying awkwardly on my back, legs dangling through cables, cold water cresting to meet my feet.

Strangely, I feel no pain but the right side of my face is numb and I feel stunned and confused.

Then I feel strong hands pulling me to safety.

I see snapshots of people cringing as they survey the damage...

My vision is blurred and I taste blood in my mouth, a warm trickle through my fingers as I hold my face in my hands.

Drifting in and out of darkness, there is chaos around me as those who escaped my fate struggle to regain control...

**There are moments in life that wake us up and change our course.
This was one of those moments for me.**

 It is now ten days since I found my way back to consciousness and I am sitting at my desk silently reflecting on this close encounter which woke me up from a long slumber. I hear a bird singing to me from the garden as if to celebrate my renewed focus and commitment. After months of neglect I have resumed writing a story which has taken far too many years to write.

> **The responsibility to share a story of importance often starts with fear and doubt, not knowing where or how to begin. Enclosed in a cocoon of silence, I wait patiently for inspiration to breakthrough.**

Ten days ago I was out on the water with friends. It wasn't the best day to go sailing but the conditions were neither beyond the boat, nor us, as we sailed out into the blue. On board were a handful of people I'd sailed with before, most of them experienced and confident sailors.

We had been out on the water for about an hour and noticed a change brewing... As the wind and waves grew stronger we headed for the safety of the marina about 40 minutes sailing time from where we had turned for home. We were running with the wind behind us which sounds easy but proved to be challenging as the sea became unpredictable. After half an hour we were being tossed around in the sea like a toy boat in a giant washing machine, indiscriminant waves pushing us up, forward and sideways with chaotic timing. One minute we were rounding up into the wind, the next we were surfing a wave in the opposite direction with the mainsail and boom threatening to swing across the deck without notice.

As we approached safe harbour the wind was gusting over 20 knots while the waves continued to manoeuvre our boat into a precarious position between two rock walls that guarded the narrow passage between us and calmer waters. Finding a path to safety was becoming increasingly risky.

We had about 100 metres to go when I looked out to the west to see a huge wave stalking us over my right shoulder. I was sitting on the port (left) side of the boat just in front of the helm with my head and shoulders about boom height. I remember pointing to a wave that was about to engulf us, when all of a sudden my world went pitch black and all I could hear was silence... As I pause to recall this moment, I am back there on the deck in the darkness...

Waking Up

 *I wake up lying awkwardly on the deck with my legs dangling over the side of the boat about a metre forward of where I'd been sitting. Although I am dragged to safety, we are far from safe at this moment.*

We come close to disaster as our out of control boat heads for a wall of rocks after our unscheduled jibe. Fortunately the quick thinking of our skipper prevents a collision with the rocks as we head back out to sea with the mainsail flapping ferociously like a restrained wild horse that wants to be set free.

At this stage our safe entrance into the calmer waters of the harbour is not looking likely, as the crew continues to struggle against menacing wind and waves, while attempting to thread the boat through the eye of a needle without smashing into the rocks on either side of the narrow passage.

The crew considers dropping the sail but fear that it will be blown overboard and become an anchor. After more failed attempts at tackling the entrance head on, this insanity is abandoned for a safer plan. The skipper decides to sail further north until he can achieve a more predictable tack across the entrance by sailing closer to the wind. This manoeuvre requires precision timing as our boat hurtles towards the rock wall with waves crashing into its starboard beam and winds straining its rigging to breaking point.

Despite the chaos and the impending collision with the rocks, the skipper and crew maintain their composure as they focus on the exact moment at which to turn the boat and trim the sail, allowing us to slot through the tenuous gap between the rock walls.

While this is happening all I can do is hope and pray, holding my face as it starts to throb and swell in my hands. I am feeling a mixture of shock and anxiety, not knowing what facial bones I've fractured, whether I'll be able to see out of my right eye and what damage has been done to my neck or brain matter… but first we all have to get to safe harbour without drowning!

Relief comes eventually when the crew manages to get the boat into calmer waters where they can control the sail more easily by positioning the boat behind a large moored ship that provides shelter from the strong winds. This windless haven enables them to get the sail down, preventing any further drama. At this moment my body starts to shake uncontrollably as the reality of the situation hits me. I notice blood trickling through my fingers as I hold my swelling face in cold shivering hands and come to the realisation of what has happened…

~~~~~~~~~~~~~~~~~~~~

The rogue wave I had been watching as it pursued us, had tossed the boat sideways to windward and allowed just enough wind to get behind the sail causing it to jibe (a manoeuvre which is normally conducted safely by pulling the mainsail into a central position and then letting it out slowly as the boat changes direction in relation to the wind, until the boom is safely positioned on the opposite side of the boat). This technique for changing direction while the wind is behind the boat is normally performed in a controlled manner and with the crew fully aware of what is about to happen, so they can take evasive action by keeping their heads down as the boom swings across the deck with ferocious speed and power.

In this case, the boom, which had been fully released to the starboard side of the boat so that we could run with the wind behind us, had suddenly been pulled across the boat in a clockwise arc by the sail which had now adjusted itself for the new wind direction. The boom travelled about 8-10 metres in a fraction of a second, from one side of the boat to the other, crashing into anything in its path; including my face. I just happened to be turning back to face it as it came sling-shotting through the air to meet me with a whipping action that should have taken my head off but somehow managed to spare me a sudden death.

After I realised what had happened, I remember thinking, *Why am I still conscious or even alive?* after being hit in the face at horrendous speed with a metal object many times bigger and heavier than a baseball bat. *How did I manage to survive this and how close had I come to not being here?* The fraction of an inch that made the difference between being dead or alive was very sobering. I thought about all sorts of crazy things... *How would my family cope with the news, all the things I had planned to do with my life that would no longer be possible, all the people that I cherish so much that I would not get to say goodbye to or hold again.* It's interesting what comes to mind when we have a close encounter with our own mortality.

I can't explain logically how I was spared from more serious injury. Even a week later after thinking my face would be left with a scar, all of the swelling, burnt skin and bruises disappeared without a trace. I have come to call this moment in time 'My Awakening'.

Ten years earlier I had left my job to pursue some projects in collaboration with my friend Mark Auricht. This decision had largely been inspired by his encouragement of me. After his death I slowly lost touch with my deeper purpose and a promise that I had made for him. I had fallen into a slumber until this day on the boat when I received a 'slap in the face' from the Universe. Regardless of the origins of this rogue wave that culminated in my 'awakening', I am eternally grateful for this 'slap'. It woke me up and caused me to start writing again.

INTRODUCTION

This book was written over a period of 15 years—not a sprint by any means, more like an ultra-marathon punctuated by lots of detours along the way. Fortunately I am no stranger to endurance events but this one has taken longer than I expected. The first part of this book, covering Mark's journey to the top of the world and the aftermath of the tragedy on Everest, was written between 2005–2010 but the majority of the book was still un-penned up until 2010.

Then I had the encounter with a rogue wave from the ocean, a slap in the face that caused my awakening... a reminder to get on with it! The remainder of this book was written between 2010–2016 during which time it has had a number of re-writes and new thoughts or information added as I have reflected more deeply on how best to honour Mark Auricht's memory. So the finishing line has been a long time coming after detouring over peaks and through hidden gorges that led me away from the horizon I saw in the distance. I had planned to finish this many years ago but discovered after a number of false starts there was more to be added to these pages. Some of this story was written by Mark himself; in the life he lead, the principles he shared, the lives he influenced along the way, and in the legacy he so poignantly punctuated by the way he graduated from this life.

His story and legacy were captured in the memories of those who were touched by his presence in their life and played out in the subsequent paths they have taken, even in some small way, because of his influence. Mark influenced people's attitudes, authenticity, persistence, perspective, courage, compassion and in some cases their sense of humour and capacity for kindness. Without knowing it, he taught me to schedule meetings with him at least thirty minutes ahead of when I actually wanted to meet. Time management and fastidious administration skills were not his greatest strength. Mark had far more time for people than for admin and watches. I like to think that his unique non-attachment to punctuality was a consequence of giving his time generously to the previous person or purpose he was serving. When it came to dealing with people, effectiveness was more important than efficiency.

Mark had many close friends, those he shared adventures with, worked with and served through his profession and his propensity to give to others. His ability to listen, encourage and validate people for who they were, left a lasting impression on those who had the privilege to meet him.

My friendship with Mark began back in the late 1980s when we were studying counselling together. We kept in touch and started collaborating on corporate and personal development programs during the 1990s. Ten years later we embarked on a major project together after I had left my job and started my own business in a similar field to Mark. This was to provide more opportunities for collaboration given that we enjoyed working together and had become close friends. Unfortunately we only had a short time to enjoy this informal partnership before the 'Spirit of Adventure' called him to Everest.

As the departure date for Everest came closer, I remember spending more time with Mark to work on the project we had embarked on, to discuss our future visions in life and business, and of course to talk about how he was feeling, leading up to Everest. In those last few weeks I sensed a combination of excitement and apprehension in his mood as the time drew closer. I remember the night of his farewell, hugging him and, with some bravado in my head but fear in my heart, telling him that I had every confidence in his ability to make the right choices. It was difficult to say goodbye, not knowing whether I would ever see him again. I'm sure that is how a lot of people felt.

Heartbreaking News

I remember the day that I heard of his death on Everest. I was in the reception area of a client's office when I picked up the phone and heard the voice of Mark's colleague, Darren Williams, on the other end. I expected Darren was going to give me the news that Mark had summited but instead it was bad news.

"How bad?" I said.
"As bad as it gets... Mark died this morning..."
and the rest was a blur.

I dropped everything in my hands and made a bee-line for the lunchroom where I locked the door behind me and proceeded to sob for half an hour as my mind screamed with disbelief. Eventually I recovered enough to leave the building and drive to my wife's place of work. That night I met with numerous friends of Mark's who had planned to celebrate the culmination of his Everest expedition. Instead it had turned into a wake. So many people were grieving in the one place together. It was a memory that will be etched in my mind and heart forever.

Twenty three years earlier I had lost my older brother in an industrial accident during my last year of school. I remember the last time I saw my brother... he was sleeping after another night shift and I was about to head off to school. I kicked his bed and said *Get up you lazy bugger.* I so wished that my last words to him could have been more loving.

I wish too, that I had not taken for granted the last moments I had with Mark before he left for Everest. We never know when someone will disappear from our lives.

It took several years to get emotionally clear after my brother's death. The death of a loved one is so hard to bear, especially if it is unexpected. Mark's death was equally painful for me and I can only imagine how agonising it must have been for his wife and family. Families often have a bond of the heart and spirit that cannot be severed by geography, time or even death but the unexpected loss of someone so close can be the worst kind of pain.

Fulfilling a Promise
We all respond in different ways to the loss of someone close to us. My response was to grieve in waves that seemed to keep coming unpredictably until I was eventually empty of highly charged emotion. I then began a process of reflection by writing my thoughts and feelings in a journal. During this reflection process I asked this question:

If everyone we meet is our teacher and Mark came into my life for a reason before leaving just as quickly as he appeared, what did I learn from my relationship with him and how can I honour this in the way I live my life from here on?

The answer to this question lead me to make three promises to myself and to Mark:
1. To support Mark's wife Catherine in whatever way I could to ensure his business and its mission would continue.
2. To organise a memorial adventure challenge called the *Auricht Gift* to raise money for a respite care facility named in Mark's honour.
3. To write a book in tribute to his life and the wisdom he shared through his life's work, so his teaching would continue beyond his 'graduation' from this life.

Between Mark's death and the sale of his business I assisted Mark's wife Catherine to continue his mission and organised the *Auricht Gift* event.

During the year after Mark's death, proceeds from the *Auricht Gift Memorial Challenge* contributed to the completion of Centacare's *Auricht House*[5] which provides respite facilities to support families and carers of intellectually disabled young people. *Auricht House* has since won an award for excellence in service to the community. I continue to become aware of ways in which Mark gave to many causes close to his heart, sometimes financially and often through the gift of his time, particularly with young people at risk and those less fortunate.

Sixteen years on from Mark's passing, his business – *Venture Corporate Recharge* is in new hands and no doubt has influenced numerous business leaders, teams and young people. The people Mark worked with at the time have moved on, but I suspect that they continue to follow *Venture's* statement of purpose in some way: *To enhance quality of life by providing opportunities for growth through unique learning experiences.*

Promises from the heart are like waves that spring from deep in the ocean, having the persistence to cross vast seas until reaching their intended shore.

The first two promises I made have been fulfilled. The writing of this book, although belated, fulfils the last promise. In some ways it has been the hardest promise to keep because I didn't want to take the task lightly. I wanted to do justice to Mark's life and the lessons he taught. I also needed time to gain some perspective and time to complete the task with the focus it deserved. Many times I have sat down to write and then been distracted by other priorities. Until recently I had almost allowed this promise to quietly drift away into unconsciousness as Mark did that day on the mountain. Then one morning I went sailing and was reminded that genuine promises from the heart are like waves that spring from deep in the ocean, having the persistence to cross vast seas until they reach their intended shore.

I have shared the sailing story to acknowledge the significance of that moment in re-igniting my commitment to writing this book. I believe that it was not an accident but a message… a message to *wake up and get on with it!* It has caused me to reflect once more on how fleeting our existence on the planet can be, and about what is really important in the scheme of things. That day on the water impacted me in ways I did not expect and reminded me of what Mark taught me and many others about the value of adventure: *It wakes us up and urges us to live with more urgency and passion. We don't have to seek danger and unreasonable risk but we do need to leave our comfort zone if we are to grow and learn to live a more valuable and fulfilling life.*

Life is a Daring Adventure
I've come to learn that adventure, although risky at times, is essential to living a life beyond mere survival to one of experiencing the highest of human needs… self-actualisation. Helen Keller once said,

> *Security does not exist in nature.*
> *Avoiding danger is no safer in the long run than outright exposure.*
> *Life is either a daring adventure or nothing.*

Mark's philosophy was that adventuring into unknown territory takes us out of our *comfort zone* and into the *learning zone*, where we have the opportunity to test our personal resources and challenge the inner rules we live by. Going on an adventure puts us to the test. Although it can be uncomfortable and we may even fear it, at a deeper level we yearn to be challenged and to know that we have what it takes. In the wilderness of life we find wisdom and a deeper connection to our spirit.

Todd Sampson, who climbed to the summit of Everest in 2001 and was on the mountain at the same time as Mark, says that he has always been drawn to adventure and spending time in nature, which he describes as a *human laboratory filled with thrilling experiments that lead to self discovery*. Todd's belief is that *exploration (although at times considered undeniably selfish) is not only how we understand the world around us, but also how we come to understand ourselves.*

Mark understood this as he followed the path of his happiness to find the learning he had chosen for this lifetime. He believed that we should all take full responsibility for the consequences of our choices. He knew the risks that went with his choices and he played his heart out in the arena of life, not in the stands where, as Theodore Roosevelt said, *the critics and timid souls know neither victory nor defeat.* Although Mark's loss brought pain to those who love him dearly, I respect his choice to follow his dream. Mark's wife Catherine said that *he took all of his dreams and fashioned them into a life.* It is my hope that this book will inspire you to do the same.

Time to Rest and Reflect
Before we embark on the adventurous journey into Part I of this book, let us briefly recap where we've been thus far. I have endeavoured to provide you with some background on my motivation for writing this tribute and my intention to share some of Mark's legacy, together with a few lessons I have learnt from my own journey. I have also provided some guidance to help you navigate your way through the landscape of these pages and introduced you to the underlying themes I will be sharing with you, particularly about the value of adventure as a pathway to self-discovery.

 This might be a good place to take some time to reflect on your own relationship to adventure, your comfort with exploring the limits of your potential, and how familiar you are with your internal compass and your dreams. Here are some challenging questions to contemplate before we step off into the mountains:

Reflection Questions

1. What have been your most memorable adventures and how have they impacted the way you see and live life?

2. How comfortable are you with taking risks and exploring your potential?

3. Do you have a strong sense of inner guidance and do you follow it?

4. What dreams are you passionate about?

5. How aligned is your life with your passions?

When you are ready to move on from this resting place, come with me into the mountains of the Himalaya, where we encounter Mark trudging along in the snow as he makes a precarious descent to safety on Mt Makalu at 8000 metres above sea level, with only the moon to guide him as he comes face to face with the *truth of impermanence*.

PART I
The Spirit of Adventure Calls
The Inspiring Life of Mark Auricht

Mark Auricht—Ama Dablam, Himalaya 1998

Overland Track—Tasmania, 2008

Chapter 1   Facing the Truth of Impermanence

...By now my torch was almost out and the moon had gone behind the Makalu Ridge, so it was really quite dark. This made it difficult to pick up the trail of my footprints that were now barely visible between the shadows cast by odd shaped bits of snow, threatening to lead me astray. I seemed to walk for endless hours down this ice field and I remember distinctly two voices, one on each shoulder: one saying "you've gone too far, you've gone too far... you're lost," and the other voice saying "you're doing fine just keep going, you're doing fine, just keep going." These two voices were just battling... I don't even know the time frame but had I lost my way then it would have been all over.

Eventually I was enormously relieved to find the fixed rope which led back to Camp 4 so I knew then that I was still on track and almost home. I clipped onto the fixed rope which cut diagonally across this large ice field and began abseiling down. Previously on the trip I had damaged my left ankle, twisting it quite badly. As I abseiled across the ice field with all my weight on my left foot, my ankle gave way and I tumbled off the slope and around the ice face, a sheer wall of blue water ice dropping down into a dark abyss. In my mind I could see myself falling off the ice field in slow motion, swinging sideways on the rope for what seemed like eternity before smashing into this hard cold wall of ice which brought me to an abrupt and painful halt. My life was now literally hanging in the balance by an ice screw which the rope was fixed to above me.

In the forefront of my mind I could see this image of the ice screw tenuously holding the rope and I thought: "Will it hold?... or will I fall helplessly into the darkness?" Then a strange thing happened in that moment... I reached the point where I completely let go... I had no fear and I didn't care whether it went one way or the other... I distinctly remember that feeling...

Excerpt from a story told by Mark Auricht about his Mt Makalu Expedition, 1995

~~~~~~~~~~~~~~~~~~~~~~~

In horror of death, I took to the mountains.
Again and again I meditated on the uncertainty
of the hour of death, capturing the fortress
of the deathless unending nature of mind.
Now all fear of death is over and done.
Milarepa—Tibetan Yogi and Poet

In *The Tibetan Book of Living & Dying*, Tibetan Lama, Sogyal Rinpoche tells us *the fear that impermanence awakens in us, that nothing is real and nothing lasts, is, we come to discover, our greatest friend because it drives us to ask the question: If everything changes, then what is really true? Is there something behind the appearances, something boundless and infinitely spacious, that we can depend on, that survives what we call death?*

Sogyal Rinpoche goes on to say that *impermanence has already revealed to us many truths, but it has a final treasure still in its keeping, one that lies largely hidden from us, unsuspected and unrecognised, yet most intimately our own.* He says that *with continued contemplation and practice in letting go, we come to uncover in ourselves, something we cannot name or describe, something that lies behind all the changes and deaths in the world. Over time our obsessive grasping to permanence begins to dissolve and fall away. As this happens we catch glimpses of the vast implications behind the truth of impermanence, we begin to experience a new dimension of freedom and we come to uncover a depth of peace, joy and confidence in ourselves that fills us with wonder and gradually breeds within us a certainty that there is 'something' that nothing destroys, nothing alters and that cannot die.*[6]

Perhaps this 'something' is what Mark experienced in that moment on Makalu or what Canadian mountaineer, Jamie Clarke referred to when he said after his first summit of Everest: *On the other side of fear, is freedom.*[7] The truth of impermanence then is a double-edged sword: the edge of loss and all of the pain and fear that human beings experience because of it, and the edge of freedom, peace and truth that we experience when we let go.

> **Our deepest fears are like dragons guarding our deepest treasure.**
> Rainer Maria Rilke—*Letters to a Young Poet*

Mountaineers, I suspect, must come face to face with the truth of impermanence and slay their dragons in order to discover the treasures that lie beyond the veil of their fears. Those of us who don't understand why people risk their lives to climb mountains like Everest are perhaps unlikely to face this truth by choice but more likely when the inevitable tide of life brings it to our shores.

Mark contemplated this truth prior to climbing Makalu in 1995 and came face to face with it during the climb to the summit and during his arduous and heartbreaking descent to safety. Makalu is the fifth highest mountain in the world at 8463m, just 385m lower than the summit of Everest. This was the first time that Mark had attempted to climb a peak above 8000m.

There are fourteen mountains on earth that are more than 8000m (26,247ft) above sea level. The first recorded successful ascent of an eight-thousander was by Maurice Herzog and Louis Lachenal, who reached the summit of Annapurna on June 3, 1950.[8]

When Mark returned from Makalu in June 1995 I remember meeting him in the Adelaide Botanical Gardens to hear about his experience. I hadn't seen him for over three months and was excited to hear the story but also mindful that he had come face to face with a 'dragon' and needed an empathic ear to help unravel the knots he carried within his heart and mind. His story was inspiring, confronting, and as it turns out, a prophetic glimpse of what was to come.

A year before the Everest climb I invited Mark to share the Makalu story with a group of leaders I had been working with. The introduction to this chapter and the following summary of the Makalu story is based on a transcript of Mark's words that were recorded during this presentation.

Mark's Makalu Story—Told by Mark Auricht
The plan was for us to climb Makalu without supplementary oxygen and without the assistance of climbing Sherpas on the mountain. This was a minimalist and more purist approach but also more challenging compared to the other two teams (the French and Spanish Basque teams) who were on the mountain at the same time as us and had more significant Base Camp support.

Prior to the trip I experienced a lot of doubt... I knew I was capable of getting to the top but wasn't sure how things would pan out? A whole lot of factors have to come together to allow you the rare opportunity to stand on the summit of an 8000 metre peak. For a start there is a very narrow window of opportunity to climb at this altitude. There is a jet stream of wind that blows across Asia at about 8000 metres and above. The big planes flying across Asia get up into the jet stream which helps them to fly across the continent more efficiently. This jet stream blows at about 80-100 knots and makes climbing very difficult and dangerous above 8000 metres.

At this time of year however, in late April to early May, you'll see plumes of snow being blown off the top of the mountain as the warm air of the monsoon arrives, forcing the jet stream off the mountain top and creating a window of opportunity where summiting is more possible. Then once the monsoon is in full swing the opportunity is lost. The exact timing and duration of this window is unpredictable but usually provides 2-3 weeks of optimal opportunities to reach the summit successfully. Many weeks of preparation and establishing camps at stages up the mountain to provide a launching point, need to be completed successfully to position climbers high up on the mountain, ready to go for the summit as soon as the jet stream is gone. So everything is geared around getting your body acclimatised properly and having the mountain kitted up with gear ready for summit day. We needed to be healthy, fit and ready when the favourable weather window opened to allow us our little piece of time on the top.

We had seven climbers in our Australian Makalu Expedition to start with but eventually only two of us were in a position to try for the summit. You never know who is going to get sick, who will pull out or if indeed you or a member of your team will come back alive from an 8000m peak. We all knew the risks and were prepared to face them.

Most expeditions will establish six staging points on Mt Makalu

1. Base Camp - 4800m (4500-5000m)
2. Advanced Base Camp - 5700m (5500-6000m)
3. Camp 1 - 6350m (6000-6500m)
4. Camp 2 - 6670m (6500-7000m)
5. Camp 3 - 7400m (7000-7500m)
6. Camp 4 - 7600m (7500-8000m)
    Summit - 8463m

This provides a sequence of camps at which climbers can acclimatise and leave gear as they establish a route to the top for the ascent and descent.

Figure 1.1 Makalu Camps—Mark Auricht, 1995

The Death Zone

There are very few civilisations that live above 5500 metres due to the long term impact of low oxygen levels on the body. The body compensates by producing more red blood cells but is also breaking down over time at this altitude, so there is a trade off.

Above Camp 3 at about 7500 metres is termed 'The Death Zone'. If you die up here this is where you stay. The reason for that is that choppers can't fly or land in this environment as the air is so thin so it's very, very hard to stage a rescue and it's pretty much an unspoken agreement that if you die above 7500 metres that's where you stay. I was provided with a confronting reminder of this as we came over the rise onto the long ridge of snow above Camp 3. Looking across to my right there was a man sitting in the snow, his hips and legs were buried in the snow but his torso was exposed, wearing a red jacket. He was a Polish climber who had actually been sitting there for three years like a statue. As it turns out, he was later to become my saviour.

The Closing Window

As the window of opportunity came closer, all the climbing teams started to funnel towards the summit at pretty much the same time. The Basques arrived at Camp 4 not long after us, the French were already there, and were all looking to summit at around the same time.

When the Basques arrived at Camp 4 they made an unexpected discovery. All of the gear they had dropped at Camp 4 prior to going back to Base Camp for some rest while they waited for the right time to summit had been blown off the mountain. While they were down at Base Camp the jet stream must have dipped and scoured the mountainside and it was all gone; their tents, sleeping bags, food, stoves; everything they needed for their summit push was gone!

They approached us for help and despite their poor command of the English language, their intention was very clear... and that was... 'We're getting in your tent!' It was difficult to say 'No' to them because we'd been quite co-operative on the mountain, we'd shared fixed ropes and they'd been quite friendly at Base Camp.

At this altitude and this close to the opening and closing of the window, everybody starts to get incredibly summit focussed. There's only so long you can stay high and there's only so many goes you get at it so at this point everybody basically wants to get up there. There is a tension between the need to give up on the summit and turn back if the odds are not in your favour and the will within that wants to push on despite the odds. We all understood this.

So now there are six people in the same tent... not only six... but we've only got one stove. The most important thing you need to do the moment you get your tent up is to bundle inside and get the stove going to melt ice. That's the only way you can get water. You have enormous water loss from breathing and sweating so you need to drink 5 litres or more each day to keep your fluids up. So we got the stove going but it was just hopelessly inadequate to provide enough water for all six of us.

We had two conditions for the Basques sleeping in our tent... we said "You run the stove and we'll have the sleeping bags!" By about 11pm we'd filled a litre of water for the next day, and we'd all had a reasonable drink but neither of those was enough. We hadn't rehydrated properly from the previous day and a litre certainly wasn't enough for our push to the summit. We put a bowl of noodles on and we passed that around which brought us to about 11.45pm. Our plan was to get up at midnight and start getting ready to go to the summit around 12.30am. It was a shocking night... the big moment... the day before the huge event... and it was just diabolical!

In the tent that night I experienced the strangest feeling... the only way I can describe it was selfishness mixed with reliance. It took about 95% of my energy to look after my own needs... I couldn't put any focus on anyone else... I was just making sure that I was OK and doing what I needed to do. It just felt very desperate... I knew that everyone else in the tent was doing the same thing and yet we were also relying on each other so there's this strange insular experience.

Reaching for the Summit

At midnight we started to get organised. Now bear in mind I'm wearing a down suit like a sleeping bag turned into a pair of overalls... I'm sleeping with my harness on, my full suit and my inner boots. All I had to do in that half hour was pull my two pairs of boots on, my gaiters and then strap on my crampons. Sitting here I would probably do that in five minutes but at Camp 4 above 7500 metres, where the oxygen level available is a third of what it is at sea level, it's a half hour job. Just struggling to push a boot on and lace it was exhausting... so you'd lie back gasping for breath, trying to recharge your energy and then dig around to find the next boot... pull that on... lace that up... lie back and breathe some more... dig around... find a gaiter... that would go on and on. In between every small thing we did, we needed to rest. We finally got out of the tent at 12.40am and started plodding to the top.

For the first time we were climbing without packs, so we had a rope between the two of us, our head torches, an ice axe, a litre of water and a little bit of food (Mars bar, muesli bar and nuts) and that was basically our kit for the climb to the summit. The air temperature here is around minus 35°C... so frosty, sweat freezing on my face... but I was buzzing with excitement.

I remember at Camp 3 looking up and actually seeing our way to the top and I thought... "This is possible, I know this is possible." This morning as we plodded our way toward the summit from Camp 4 was an incredibly exciting moment... I was just buzzing... my skin was crawling with excitement. It was the first time during the entire trip that I thought "I'm actually going to get there, I'm going to do it today!"

Although our bodies were under a lot of stress, I felt quite okay and strangely elated. This of course was probably due to the fact that our bodies were also producing a large amount of endorphins which is like a natural morphine.

On Makalu there is a false summit and a true summit. As we were walking along that long summit ridge leading to the false summit we met the Basques who'd climbed past us and were now coming back from the summit. We shook their hands and congratulated them before continuing to climb.

Chapter 1—Facing the Truth of Impermanence

A Critical Decision
We got to the false summit right on 4.00pm which was our deadline for turning around. We said we'd climb and hopefully get to the summit around 2.30 or 3.00pm. At 4 o'clock no matter where we were we'd turn around and head back down. So it's now 4 o'clock and we're on this false summit. The true summit was about 200 metres away and only maybe 20 metres higher than where we were. So now David and I had to make a critical decision. We decided we would press on... the weather was fine, we were 200 metres from our goal and we felt okay. Feeling okay is actually not a criteria for making that kind of decision, but the truth is that we had the bit between our teeth and we were going to keep going.

So we were plugging fresh snow all the way to the summit. In fact, quite strangely, we noticed that there were no other footprints between the false summit and the true summit. This confused me and made me question whether the Basques had gone all the way to the true summit or not?

The last 50 metres along this ridge was like a knife edge... my ice tools were punching right through the top of it and I could see through the holes in the snow and down into Tibet. This was the most extraordinary, exposed climbing I've ever done. I'm not normally an overly courageous climber. I know that when I get onto a mountain it takes me a little while to feel confident and start to feel safer but this day I was just charging with so much courage.

We reached the summit of Mt Makalu at 6.00pm on the 8th of May 1995, *eighteen hours after leaving our high camp. The sun on the horizon was casting a perfect shadow of the pyramid shaped summit upon which we were perched, onto the snow capped mountains to the east of us. The summit of Makalu at 8463 metres, is about as wide as a horse's back, leaving just enough room for us to straddle it, facing each other with one leg in Nepal and the other in Tibet. On the Tibet side there is a 1500 metre drop to the snow, ice and rocks below.*

So here we are, a couple of proud Aussies sitting at about eight and a half thousand metres above sea level where jet planes fly. I felt an incredible sense of privilege at getting this half hour on top of the world. All the factors had come together for us and we were finally there.

I remember feeling a great variety of emotions. One just of relief at having finally got there, after all the preparation we'd done at home and in the mountains, all the lugging of gear up the mountain and dealing with the hardship of actually just functioning at this altitude. There is an enormous amount of relief knowing that going down will be significantly easier.

The next feeling I remember was an enormous sense of appreciation for my physical body for getting me to this incredible spot. I'd punished it unmercifully beyond anything I'd done before and it had done everything I'd asked of it.

And then the next more overwhelming emotion was anxiety, just an incredible amount of anxiety. We were way too late to be sitting on this mountain at this time. We still had to get back to Camp 4 and there was only about an hour of daylight left so I knew it was going to get dark and I knew that descending, despite being physically easier, was the most dangerous thing we had yet to do. The unfortunate thing about summiting any mountain is that you know that the moment you get there your head's thinking about heading back down.

Time started to go incredibly quickly now... the hands on the clock just took off... we were on the summit for about half an hour and in that time took a photograph of each other, panned the video around and that was a half hour gone. We were already starting to move a bit more slowly due to the altitude and fatigue as well. The last thing I remember doing was standing up with my arms outstretched above me (as per my company logo[9]) and then I quickly sat back down and we made our way off the summit.

Makalu Shadow at Sunset—Mark Auricht May 8th, 1995

Descending Into Darkness
We got back to the false summit and it was dark. We'd been climbing with our head torches all that morning, which is an okay way to climb on the snow and ice... your torches just glow beautifully... but now our torches were down to a dull glow on the ice. We had to traverse back along the summit ridge and find the steep gully that would bring us back onto the ice field above Camp 4. It was incredibly important that we found the correct gully because we had a couple of ropes there leading us back to Camp 4. Had we gone down the wrong gully we would have had no idea of the terrain we'd come into.

At about 9 o'clock that night we found the head of the gully and our footsteps. We were relieved to know that we were back on track. I remember sitting down at the top of this gully to have a rest... imagine now a big slippery dip of ice with a vertical rock step of about 50 metres, then another ice field... another rock step... then another ice field leading down onto the glacier below... all of it about 350 metres in height. Here we sat resting for a moment, not talking, hardly wasting an ounce of energy on a thought.

One of the things I remember about altitude is that there's no daydreaming. I could focus on a thought... I knew what I was doing... I was absolutely clear on what I was doing... but there were no extraneous thoughts happening at all... no extra conversations... so I don't remember talking to David as we sat there.

We then got up and I started heading down. I'm facing out now, and I'm walking down with my crampons gripping the ice and David behind me. All of a sudden this incredible impact took my feet out from under me. It was David sliding out of control down this ice slope. Fortunately he hit me low enough that my legs flipped out from under me but I was able to spin around and use my ice axe to stop my fall... just in time to look over my shoulder at David going like a steam train over this rock ledge that was maybe 20 metres below me... and just like that he was gone!

It was shocking and unreal... "is this really happening?" It felt unreal but again my mind did not waste thoughts. It was immediately very clear that I just had to do what I had to do to get down. In hindsight it was surprising that I wasn't overwhelmed with panic... I got very nervous though and instead of facing out I turned around and used my tools to back down, which is the safer way to go but much slower. I got down to the rock step where we had a piece of rope only 20 metres away. This piece of rope may or may not have saved his life. I might have been in control of him... but when I think about it, had we been tied together I would have gone with him. It's incredible the speed at which the 'what if's' go through your head but it can't change what has happened and I must focus on what I have to do now in this moment.

I abseiled down this rock step and saw the eeriest thing that still sticks in my mind... when you carry an ice axe, you have a lanyard that runs up and sits around your wrist in case you drop your axe so that you won't lose it down the mountainside. When David fell and landed on the ice below his axe must have caught on the ice and skun his glove off while he kept going. So you can imagine an ice axe just hanging out of the ice with the lanyard and a bare glove on the end of it... just swinging. When I abseiled down I was confronted by this ice axe just hanging there... it was an awful sight... but it also set my mind crazy thinking for a moment that maybe he was alive?

I'd actually come to the conclusion by then that he was already dead before he went over the edge. What I think happened was that he had a cerebral oedema... an accumulation of fluid on the brain. Cerebral Oedema is a condition caused by high altitude where fluid starts leaking from cells into spaces it shouldn't be and squashes the brain, causing the victim to lose consciousness which is often closely followed by death as the brain stops functioning. I think David just passed out after he stood up and started walking. He might have already been dead when he fell over and took off down the slope. The reason I think that was because he was on his back and your initial response as a mountaineer is to roll straight onto your front and use your axe to stop... but he was on his back... and he said absolutely nothing... he was completely silent. So I hope that he was unconscious when he went over the edge and I really believe that was the case. However when I saw his axe I thought for a moment... "Was he alive?... did he try to stop himself?"

Then I continued down to the bottom of this 350 metre gully. It was quite obvious where he landed, and he continued off down the glacial field and ended up in a crevasse that would have been some 150-200 metres down the glacier. Now that I was at the bottom of that gully I had to cut across the glacier to get to Camp 4 but the path of his descent had continued down the glacier... so then I sat and thought... "Do I go and look for him, or do I go home?" Fortunately I made a good decision at that point and I went for home. I figured there was a one percent or less chance that he would have survived that fall, and if he had done, there was nothing that I could have done for him.

In my head I remember thinking (and maybe this was just to help me make the decision) "I'll come back... I'll go to Camp 4 and rest up then come back to try and find him"... not expecting to find him alive, but expecting to put him into his sleeping bag. We'd had a conversation in the Blue Mountains about death and as a group we decided that if a person died we'd put them in their sleeping bag and lower them into a crevasse... so all that was going through my head was "I'm going to get a sleeping bag, come back and put him in it..." so I continued back across the glacier.

Following the Inner Compass

By now my torch was almost out and the moon had gone behind the Makalu Ridge, so it was really quite dark. This made it difficult to pick up the trail of my footprints that were now barely visible between the shadows cast by odd shaped bits of snow, threatening to lead me astray.

I seemed to walk for endless hours down this ice field and I remember distinctly two voices, one on each shoulder: one saying "you've gone too far, you've gone too far... you're lost", and the other voice saying "you're doing fine just keep going, you're doing fine, just keep going" and these two voices were just battling... I don't even know the time frame but had I lost my way then it would have been all over.

Eventually I was enormously relieved to find the fixed rope which led back to Camp 4 so I knew then that I was still on track and almost home. I clipped onto the fixed rope which cut diagonally across this large ice field and began abseiling down. Previously on the trip I had damaged my left ankle, twisting it quite badly. As I abseiled across the ice field with all my weight on my left foot, my ankle gave way and I tumbled off the slope and around the ice face; a sheer wall of blue water ice dropping down into a dark abyss. In my mind I could see myself falling off the ice field in slow motion, plunging sideways on the rope for what seemed like eternity before smacking into the hard cold wall of ice which brought me to an abrupt and painful halt.

My life was now literally hanging in the balance by this rope I was attached to and the ice screw that secured it tenuously to the mountain side. As I pictured the knot attached to the screw I thought "will it hold or will I fall helplessly into the darkness?"

Then a strange thing happened in that moment... I reached the point where I completely let go... I had no fear and I didn't care whether it went one way or the other... I distinctly remember that feeling.

This timeless moment is like the void between the trapeze bars where the outcome is uncertain – faith, hope and trust are all we have to rely on. All we can do is let go and be at peace with it.

Then... "nup, it hasn't gone... great... I'm still here!"

After feeling the rush of survival I realised now that the rope was anchored at the top and anchored again at the bottom of the ice field. Because I'd swung sideways down the side of this wall of ice, I had fully loaded the rope putting tension on the whole system and I was now jammed on the rope... locked off... hanging over this black abyss.

Letting Go

I've been on the go now for about 25 hours and into my second night without sleep with only a litre of water, a handful of nuts, some muesli. Again I just 'let go' and relaxed, thinking "Okay, I've got to solve this."

Then came an answer from the silence... the only way I could solve this was to turn myself upside down and haul myself diagonally down the rope, feeding it into my abseiling device... like abseiling upside down basically. I did this with painstakingly slow progress until I eventually made it back onto the snowfield and collapsed. After recovering from this exhausting ordeal I got back onto my feet and completed the journey to the safety of Camp 4 where I collapsed into the tent that I'd left 27 hours earlier.

Then I spent this incredible 12 hours waiting for David to turn up... it was the strangest thing... I was now also on my third night either above or just below 8000 metres. Above about 5500 metres your body is gradually just shutting down and the higher you go the more your body just can't survive as the oxygen level goes lower and lower. No one to my knowledge has survived longer than 4 days at 8000 metres... I was now on the end of my third day and was still thinking foolishly "I'll go back and find David." So I spent that whole day and night there before loading David's sleeping bag into my pack after which I left the tent and started to head back up towards where he was.

I climbed for about an hour and probably only covered a distance of 20 metres. There was just no way that I was going to get back... so again I made a good decision... I had to get off the mountain. So I turned around... went back... dumped David's gear in the tent and headed back towards Camp 3.

Fortunately it was that big bowl type section and after a bit of steep stuff I was onto some reasonably good snowfields. This was fortunate because I couldn't walk further than about 20 paces without falling over. To keep myself going I started counting steps... I'd get up to 18..19..20 and fall flat on my face in the snow. Then I'd lie there and think "I've got to get more than 20"... so I'd stand up... 18..19..20..21... doof (a face full of snow)... and then get up and do it again. I was in no pain... I felt fine... I was warm... it was bizarre... I just felt great... probably the endorphins charging through my body again.

The Temptation to Sleep
Anyway, I was almost back at Camp 3 when I've fallen over again and I'm lying in the snow drifting in and out of delirium, thinking, "It would be so nice to stay here... warm... peaceful... blissful sleep..."

And then as my gaze follows the moonlight across the surface of the snow, I find myself looking directly at the frozen Polish guy with the red jacket flapping in the breeze about 200 metres away. So then, still lying there in the snow I remember suddenly thinking "Get up Mark... get up Mark!" It was probably good timing seeing that guy. In a way he just may have saved my life, as I was about to surrender to the snow... but the 'Icey Pole' reminded me of what would happen if I stopped for too long. So I got up and kept going, eventually making it to Camp 3.

In the same way as the Polish guy had turned up when I most needed it, another incredible thing happened on my way down to Base Camp. As I recall it, there happened to be some Sherpas who were trekking with some other people up around the Makalu region who had heard about what happened.

These three guys who I didn't know from a bar of soap, didn't have any gear or anything... they put some food and some gear in a pack and climbed all the way up to Camp 1 to meet me. They made me some soup and then guided me down in the dark that night with a torch... it was just sensational! I got back to Base Camp and these guys disappeared. I never saw them again!

Spiritual helpers are often anonymous
Anon

I remember feeling really different now. I was having these incredible swings between this great excitement at having achieved what we'd set out to achieve, and this incredible upset and anger about what had happened to David. I was blaming the Basques... I guess I had attached his death to them and that was the way it was in my head... so I was quite angry and my moods were swinging radically. I had also lost 10kg in bodyweight... mostly muscle digested by my own body to keep me alive. I was by now this skinny, ravenous rake.

Into the Arms of the Bear
I'm almost home now... walking into Base Camp when the Basques leap out of their mess tent... "aahhhh come in!"... I've caught them at their summit celebration meal... so they're all sitting around this table with all this food and grog... and I haven't eaten a decent meal in a week... I've had one night's sleep... gone for three without... had one ravaged night on the mountain... I've turned up in the Basque tent... whisky straight into my hand as I sit down... "Strong Man... Strong Man" the Basques say as they pat me on the back... and this plate of food arrives with a mound of rice, chicken and lentils... so that's gone... phoom... disappeared down the gullet in about three seconds. I managed to get down another two plates full in succession.

As I scoffed down all the food and drink I was picking up this mood in the tent...so I asked one of the Basques who could speak reasonable English, what the leader of their expedition was saying... "What's Juanito saying?" He started to shuffle in his seat and was getting quite uncomfortable. I asked again "Tell me what he is saying?" His reply was astonishing...

"He thinks you should've shared your sleeping bags with us at Camp 4," he said. In a flash, all the hair on the back of my neck just stood up... and I'm out of the chair screaming at this guy. As I head around the table toward him, he leaps out of his chair and just grabs me...

He gives me this big bear hug and says, "That's it, we're not going to mention it again". He then put me back down in my seat... and he sat down. It didn't get mentioned again... but boy I was volatile... so I finished my meal... staggered back down to Base Camp... walked in and it was just elation... I said "I'm home... Thank God."

The New Comfort Zone
... I've collapsed in my tent... and lo and behold... at about 3 o'clock in the morning the alarm bells go off in my tummy! So I leap out of bed... bear in mind the toilet tent is about 30 metres across all this rocky terrain... so I've put my ugg boots on... thermal underwear... and I'm sprinting!... across these rocks and I just wasn't going to make it... I'm trying to get my pants off... and it was just too late... all this stuff just poured down into my ugg boots... down my legs and through my pants.

So there I am standing there with all this shit everywhere... full moon in a clear night sky shining down on me like a spot light on a stage... and I remember just thinking... "what have I become?"... "how basic is this?"... so I pulled it all back up and got back into my sleeping bag and went to sleep... that's how basic things had become... "I'll fix it in the morning"... my comfort zone was different now!

David Hume on Makalu's Summit—Photo by Mark Auricht

On May 8th, 1995 David Hume and Mark Auricht became the first Australians to climb to the summit of Mt Makalu. David will be remembered for his happy disposition, strong leadership and sense of humour.

MARK'S LESSONS FROM MAKALU

1. A strong and clear vision

It is not enough to have a goal. You have to have a vision that inspires you to get out of your comfort zone and keep persisting despite the obstacles. The vision must be stronger than the temptation to retreat into your comfort zone when the going gets tough and clear enough that you can see a vivid picture of what you want to achieve.

2. Breaking down your goal into tangible chunks

Mountains provide very tangible goals in terms of distance and altitude. The big picture goal is to reach the summit and return safely but this can be overwhelming mentally. Having the ability to break down the overall goal into smaller chunks that you can focus on each day, each hour, each minute, each step or each breath, can help you to handle the mental overwhelm that can happen if you are not focussed on the present moments. Goals should not only include the more tangible physical goals but also goals related to health, morale and relationships.

3. Physical and mental preparation

Being well prepared with short-term and long-term preparation benchmarks both physically and mentally is a key to getting to summit day in good shape. Long term physical preparation such as running, cycling, bushwalking in the hills and preparation climbs, is followed by shorter term preparation including acclimatisation treks and climbs in the Himalayas, together with the staged establishment of camps, and further acclimatisation on the mountain, closer to summit day. Mental preparation is a by-product of the physical preparation but can also include reading about other people's experiences and how they dealt with them in similar conditions and circumstances to the ones you could face. Thinking about and discussing possible scenarios and how you might deal with them, is also important for mental preparation. This includes physical, mental, emotional and social challenges.

4. Willingness to take risks and take responsibility for consequences.

To venture toward any goal is to risk failure. To persist is to risk failing again and again in the pursuit of eventual victory. When we fail in the pursuit of a goal or dream, we must also be prepared to take responsibility for our choices. We must do what we can to minimise controllable risks but there are no guarantees in life and especially in nature. When it comes to climbing mountains, success is rarely possible without taking a risk.

5. Being prepared to put up with discomfort

This includes not only the discomfort of climbing a mountain for days and weeks on end in sub-zero temperatures and rarefied air, together with rough living conditions and unpredictable weather, but also includes putting up with the discomfort of training, the sacrifices you need to make in preparing for the expedition and time away from loved ones. Adventures often require you to embrace difficult group dynamics as people get stressed, or differences in personality and culture. The desire to achieve a dream must win the battle over the discomfort experienced in pursuing it.

6. Willingness to lead and be lead

My strategy on Makalu was to follow as close as I could in the footsteps of David Hume. He had the experience on an 8000m peak before and was a good leader and climber. I also had to be prepared to lead when it was required of me and to trust my own internal guidance system.

7. The importance of family

My experience on Mt Makalu led me to a profound realisation about the importance of family. My relationship with my family became deeper and stronger after Makalu. Their willingness to support me and allow me the freedom to pursue my dream was essential to my success. Sometimes it is difficult to know where the line is between the relentless pursuit of a goal and the health of our relationships.

From an interview with Mark Auricht by Wayne Enright—March, 2000

Reflection Question

Which of the above lessons are most relevant to you in pursuing your goals and dreams?

Mark after losing 10kg on Mt Makalu

Chapter 2   Himalaya Calling

The Himalaya is an immense mountain range which runs 2,400 kilometres east-south-east in a great curve between the Tibetan Plateau to the north and Indian sub-continent to the south. *Himalaya* is derived from the Sanskrit for *Abode of Snow* and Mt Everest, at 8848 metres above sea level, is the jewel in its crown. The Tibetans call this sacred mountain *Chomolungma* which means *Mother Goddess of the Universe*. The Nepalese call her *Sagarmatha*, which loosely translated from Sanskrit means *Goddess of the Sky*. These inspiring names highlight the spiritual significance of this famous mountain for the people of the Himalaya.

To the Western World this, then relatively unknown mountain, once known as *Peak 15*, was re-named Mt Everest in 1865 after Sir George Everest, a British surveyor who was the first person to record her height at 8839m. Although the mountain was formed over 60 million years ago, the forces of nature continue to increase her height by a few millimetres every year.

The fascination with Everest goes back to 1852 when the Great Trigonometric Survey of India determined that Mt Everest had been officially identified as the world's highest mountain. This announcement captured the international imagination, and soon the idea of reaching the summit of the 'roof of the world' was viewed as the ultimate challenge. Attempts to climb Everest, however, could not begin until 1921, when the forbidden kingdom of Tibet first opened its borders to the outside world.

On June 8, 1924, two members of a British expedition, George Mallory and Andrew Irvine, attempted the summit. Mallory had already failed twice at reaching the summit but persisted in trying a third time. The two climbers were last spotted 'going strong' for the top until the clouds perpetually swirling around Everest engulfed them. They then vanished.

Mallory's body was found 75 years later, in May 1999. No evidence was found on his body to clear up the mystery of whether these two Everest pioneers made it to the top before dying on the mountain. After Mallory and Irvine's attempt in 1924, ten more expeditions over a period of thirty years failed to reach the summit, with 13 lives being lost in the process.

**On May 29th, 1953
Edmund Hillary of New Zealand and Sherpa Tenzing Norgay, became the first to reach the roof of the world.**

Hillary and Norgay, 1953

Both of their sons, Peter Hillary and Jamling Norgay have followed in their father's footsteps, climbing to the summit of Mt Everest since then. Tashi Tenzing, grandson of Norgay Tenzing followed the family tradition, also attempting Everest in 1993 but did not make it to the top. He had to turn back about 90 metres from the summit due to snow blindness and his uncle, who was also on the mountain at the time, fell to his death on the descent. Tashi's second, third and fourth attempts were successful.

Tashi Tenzing says of Everest... *This great peak is like a member of my family. I have always felt we have a special relationship with her. She has not always been kind to us and she has tested our deep faith to its limits. Seven times my grandfather Tenzing, tried to reach the summit and only once did she permit it. She was more lenient on me for I reached the top on my second attempt but she gave way only after extracting the ultimate price... the life of a much loved family member.*

Tashi continues, *You never conquer Everest. It's not a conquest, it's more a spiritual thing. You have to be very courageous and strong in the mind. The mountain permits you stand up there for a few minutes if you're lucky.*

High Altitude Risks
Although not considered one of the most technically challenging mountains to climb (K2, the world's second highest mountain and Makalu, the fifth highest, are considered more technically difficult) the dangers of Everest include avalanches, crevasses, ferocious winds up to 200kph, sudden storms, temperatures of minus 40°C, and oxygen deprivation. In the *Death Zone* (above 7500m) the air holds only a third as much oxygen as at sea level, heightening the chance of hypothermia, and the high-altitude illnesses of pulmonary and cerebral oedema where fluid swells in the lungs and brain.

Even when breathing bottled oxygen, climbers experience extreme fatigue, impaired judgment and coordination, headaches, nausea, double vision and sometimes hallucinations. Expeditions spend months acclimatising and usually attempt Everest in May each year, avoiding the winter snows and the summer monsoons.

In 1978 Reinhold Messner and Peter Habeler were the first to climb Mt Everest without supplemental oxygen. Messner later described his summit experience: *In my state of spiritual abstraction, I no longer belong to myself and to my eyesight. I am nothing more than a single narrow gasping lung, floating over the mists and summits.*

The above information about the Himalaya and Everest is a summary of facts sourced from Wikipedia.[10]

Mark Auricht and David Hume summited Mt Makalu in 1995 without supplementary oxygen. When Mark was asked whether he would use it on Everest, he said: *I might use it on the way up to the high camp if required and then decide from there whether I use oxygen for the summit push, depending on how strong I feel.*

Once you start climbing consistently with supplementary oxygen, you become more reliant on it and this can become a problem if you get held up. If you run out of bottled oxygen at high altitude, it's like experiencing a sudden increase in elevation of about 1000m.

Mark Auricht—From a Q&A Session facilitated by Wayne Enright—March, 2000

The Cost of Climbing Mt Everest

The permit from the government of Tibet or Nepal can range from $7-11,000 USD per person, depending on the number in a group of climbers. Add to that:- equipment, Sherpa guides, additional permits, transport, food, oxygen and other essentials, and the cost per person can be well over $60,000 USD.[11]

The human cost of climbing Everest is even higher for up to 10% of people who attempt it. This loss cannot be measured in dollars. Since the first successful summit in 1953, more than 4,000 people have successfully climbed Mt Everest where more than half of these would be Sherpa who have done multiple summits, bringing the number of total summits up until the year 2013 to a total of 6,871 by 4,042 different climbers.

2014-2016 have been difficult years for the local Sherpa people, causing the average yearly statistics to depart from the norm. As at 2016 there have now been just over 7,000 successful summits of Mt Everest.

Unfortunately, due to the hazards and rigors of climbing such a dangerous mountain, over 200 have died attempting the climb. Since 1990, the deaths as a percentage of summits have dropped to 3.6% due to better gear, weather forecasting and more people climbing with commercial operations. However, this does not take into account all of the people who die on Everest who do not make it to the summit, one of which was Mark.

Overall 248 people (161 westerners and 87 Sherpas) have died on Everest from 1921 to 2013. The worst year for clients (or 'members') on Everest was 1996 when 98 climbers made the summit and 15 died. For the 2013 climbing season, the Himalayan Database showed that 658 climbers made the summit (539 from the south side—Nepal and 119 from the north side—Tibet). There were eight confirmed deaths in 2013.

Statistics above, from the Himalayan Database.[12]

Recent Events on Everest
More recently the Everest region has been the scene of even greater tragedy. In 2014, twenty-five people were hit by a gigantic avalanche of ice while making the treacherous journey through the infamous *Khumbu Icefall*. This is a maze of unstable chunks of ice, crevasses and overhanging cornices that climbers must pass through on their way up to the South Col of Everest. Climbing Sherpas must take this high risk journey up and back through the icefall many times more than the 'members' they support as they establish camps and fix ropes and ladders to assist climbing teams. So it was not surprising that all sixteen of those who died during the avalanche were Nepali working for guided climbing expeditions. This lead to the eventual cancellation of all expeditions on the mountain that year. Then in 2015, as if life had not gotten hard enough for the Nepali people who have come to depend on the money they earned from doing the high risk work of supporting commercial climbing expeditions, there were a series of earthquakes which killed 9,000 and injured over 22,000 people, devastating many of the communities in the mountains of Nepal.

On April 25th, 2015 when the first major quake happened, members of Mark's family were at Kathmandu airport. They had planned to trek to the Tibetan Base Camp to place a plaque in memory of Mark but sadly were unable to do so. *Watching Kathmandu collapse in front of us was surreal, shocking and sad to witness*, said Mark's sister Lil in a recent email. She and her brothers Richard and David, returned to Tibet in April this year (2017).

Chapter 2—Himalaya Calling

Fifteen Years Earlier—2001

The recent tragedies that have impacted the people of the Everest region were yet to happen in 2001. Most of the western media attention about the dangers of Everest back then was primarily focussed on the risk to climbers. Every climber that considers the challenge of Everest must confront the sobering facts about its dangers and prepare as well as they can to minimise the risks which threaten to thwart their dream of standing on top of the world.

Although I have climbed Mt Kilimanjaro and done some moderately challenging trekking at altitude more recently, back then my personal understanding of the dangers of high altitude climbing was based on what I'd gleaned from Mark and from several books I'd read and documentaries I'd seen. The first book I read about mountaineering was an autobiography written by Australian climber Michael Groom, called *Sheer Will*, which was published in 1997. Michael Groom has been fortunate enough to survive avalanches, losing toes to frostbite, and the circumstances on Mt Everest during May 10-11, 1996 when eight climbers died in a blizzard. Two other well known guides, New Zealand climber Rob Hall and American Scott Fischer, together with their clients, were not so lucky.

I read about the story of the 1996 Everest Tragedy in Jon Krakauer's book *Into Thin Air*. Krakauer was a writer for *Outside* Magazine, participating in Rob Hall's expedition. He was fortunate enough to reach the summit and descend safely before the 'perfect storm' hit the mountain. In 1996 *Imax* had also mounted an expedition on Everest and were caught up in the events of May 10-11, which were later made into an Imax movie in 1998 called *Everest* (A more recent version of the story was released in a movie of the same title in 2015). I remember going to see the Imax movie with my wife Gabrielle, together with Mark and his wife Catherine, before having dinner together one night in 1998. The next day I broached the subject of death with Mark.

In the year or two before he departed for Everest we would often catch up for lunch across the road from his office in Rundle Street, Adelaide. Inevitably the conversation would lead to a discussion about his upcoming expedition. I would usually avoid talking about the risks because I didn't want to reinforce any fear-based thoughts that he might already have vying for attention in his mind. I wanted to be encouraging and for the most part I was actually quite confident and optimistic about his ability to achieve his dream. The day after we saw the Imax Movie, I felt curious about Mark's thoughts on the risk of dying on Everest.

Mark's Thoughts on Fear and Risk

I asked Mark if he gave much thought to the possibility of dying in his attempt to achieve his dream. He said yes, as if it was an obvious question to contemplate, and yet he was not full of fear about it. He said that he had studied the mountain, its hazards and difficult spots, and had examined the stories of tragedies that had happened and what contributed to them. He knew the mountain's history well and this seemed to be as much a part of his preparation as the physical conditioning, planning the logistics and raising the money to finance the expedition.

Mark's philosophy on fear was that it was like being a bird in a cage with the door open. *We can be imprisoned by our fear, not realising that we have the power to fly to our freedom. We can either stay in fear's cage or choose to fly free of it,* he would say. For Mark, a life lived in fear was a life half-lived. Adventurous challenges were not about ignoring fear; they were about feeling it, facing it and pushing one's boundaries in spite of it, not in a reckless manner, but putting yourself on the line and experiencing the satisfaction of knowing that you have the skills, determination and makeup to overcome the odds.

When Mark was asked by Adelaide journalist Peter Hackett if he believed he would stand on the summit of Mt Everest, he apparently gave the journalist a reprimanding look and replied: *Yes, absolutely! We are confident that we have prepared well and that we are fit enough and strong enough in mind and body to make it to the top.*

On the summit of Makalu in 1995, Mark remembers looking across to Everest and thinking "I could do that." The truth is, he could 'do that' if the dice fell favourably for him as they had on Makalu.

Mark on Ama Dablam, 1998

Chapter 3   The Challenge of Chomolungma

Mark's desire to climb began as a kid climbing trees around his childhood home in Adelaide. His brothers tell the story of how he abseiled from a tree in the backyard using a harness made from an old seatbelt. Throughout his younger years, his family went on regular hiking and camping trips which led to his love of adventure. After climbing St Mary's Peak in South Australia's Flinders Ranges at the age of eight he developed a passion for mountains and exploring the limits of his potential. As he got older he went on to test his limits on more serious mountains and achieved a number of successful summits on his way to taking on the ultimate challenge of Mt Everest.

Mark Auricht had successfully climbed the following peaks leading up to his expedition to Mt Everest.

Mt Cook (Aoraki)	3754m	New Zealand
Chulu Far East	6059m	Nepal
Lobuje East	6129m	Nepal
Pachermo	6371m	Nepal
Ama Dablam	6856m	Nepal
Mt Makalu	8463m	Nepal/Tibet

Figure 3.1 Mark's Successful Summits—Mark Auricht, 1998

Prior to 2001, Mark had successfully climbed to the top of five Himalayan peaks, including Makalu, the fifth highest and one of the most challenging peaks above 8000 metres with steep climbing, exposed ridges, and rock climbing on its summit pyramid. The mountains of the Himalaya were now about to test the absolute limits of his endurance, tenacity and courage.

> *For as long as I can remember, I have always wanted to climb big mountains and put my skills and ability to the test in the ultimate way.*
> Mark Auricht

Mark had dreamt of climbing Everest for a number of years leading up to 1994 when he and fellow adventurer, Duncan Chessell decided on a more serious plan to climb to its summit. In 1995 they ventured up Mt Makalu (8463m) which was their first attempt at an 8000m peak. This served as a valuable learning experience for taking on the challenge of Chomolungma.

Whilst Mark was fortunate enough to summit Makalu with expedition leader David Hume, he then came face to face with death, watching helplessly, as David slid into the darkness at 8200 metres. Prior to summit day on Makalu, Duncan Chessell had already decided that the circumstances were not favourable for him to go all the way to the top on that expedition and so made the decision not to continue.

Three years later, on December 5th 1998, Mark and Duncan successfully climbed to the top of Ama Dablam (6854m) and stood upon her summit together. If everything went to plan and Chomolungma gave them her blessing, they expected to do the same, to stand together arms outstretched on top of the world!

Mark and Duncan on the summit of Ama Dablam, 1998

South Australian Everest Expedition 2001

The Team for the South Australian Everest Expedition of 2001 included Mark Auricht and Duncan Chessell, the two climbers who planned to be the first South Australians to summit Mt Everest, their Expedition Doctor, David Tingay and their two climbing Sherpas, Tshering Palden Bhote and Pemba Sherpa (the Clan of Sherpa people can have last names such as Sherpa, Bhote and Lama). Other members of the team were Gyanu Shresthra, the Expedition Cook and Alex Robey, another climber from Queensland who shared a tent with Mark during the acclimatisation phase and was there to document their progress on film. Compared to some other teams on the mountain that season, the South Australian team was relatively small and lean, although there were some other trekkers who accompanied the expedition team for the acclimatisation trek in the Annapurna region and some sponsors who joined them for the journey to Base Camp in Tibet.

Routes to the Summit

Mt Everest's two main climbing routes are: the *South Col Route* via the Southeast Ridge from Nepal (taken by Hillary and Norgay Tenzing), and the *North Col Route* via the Northeast Ridge from Tibet (taken by Mallory and Irvine). The *South Col Route*, although more popular, requires climbers and Sherpas to take the risky journey through the *Khumbu Icefall*[13]. It was the route across the Tibetan north face that was to be used by the South Australian Expedition in the Himalayan Spring of 2001.

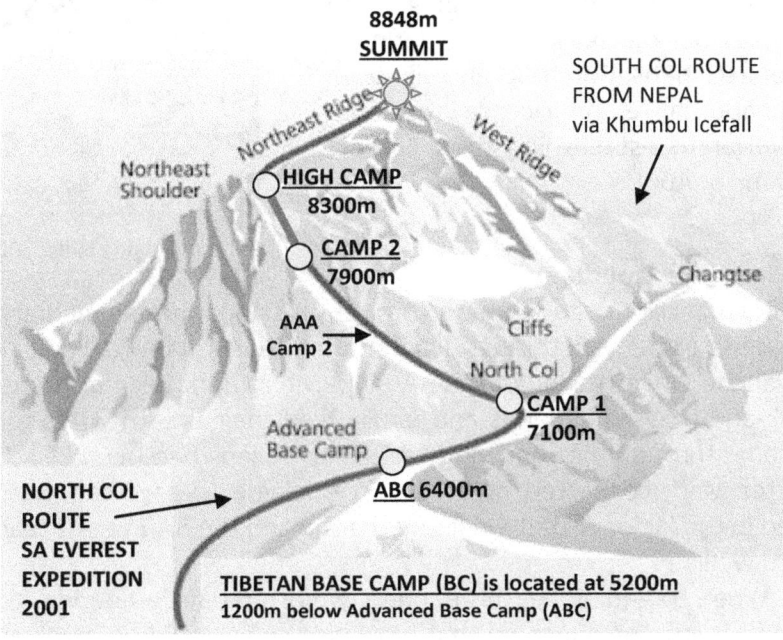

Figure 3.2 SA Everest Expedition Climbing Route—SA Expedition Diaries, 2001

The above map[14] shows the route taken by the 2001 SA Everest Expedition via the *North Col*, starting from *Base Camp* (*BC*) located in Tingri County, Shigatse Tibet, about 19km north of Mt Everest. Some expeditions have an extra camp between *Camp 2* and the *High Camp* located at the bottom of the Northeast Ridge. The South Australian's had three camps (including *High Camp*) above *Advanced Base Camp* (*ABC*) as underlined on the map with altitudes shown for each of their camps. The *South Col Route* is not visible on the map as it is on the opposite side of the West Ridge of Everest.

Later in this chapter I will share with you the *SA Expedition Diaries*. You may like to refer back to this map while you follow the journey of the SA climbers, as they zigzagged their way up and down the mountain.

Preparing for the Climb

Mark and Duncan spent several months building their fitness by cycling hundreds of kilometres each week, training for many hours in the Flinders Ranges and Adelaide Hills during their initial preparation before departing for Nepal on February 27th, 2001.

They commenced preparation for the steeper and more challenging, high altitude terrain of the Himalaya during a series of acclimatisation treks and climbs in the Annapurna region over a six week period prior to establishing their Everest Base Camp in April.

Adelaide Hills, 2000

Omen from the Mountains

During their acclimatisation phase through the Annapurna Sanctuary in late March, news came back to Australia that three Australians had been killed in an avalanche while trekking in the Annapurna region. Back at home, many of Mark and Duncan's friends and family held their breath when the initial news came through, not knowing which Australians had been killed. It was only after Mark contacted his family in Adelaide to say that he was not involved in the incident that we knew that he and the SA Everest team were safe and well.

When tragedies like this happen, we often have a fleeting feeling of anxiety as it crosses our mind that our loved ones could be involved. Then there is a collective sigh of relief when we discover that it happened to someone else. The reality is *that* 'someone else' has family and friends too. For them it is heart-breaking news, while for those who escape the tragedy there is relief that they were lucky enough to dodge the bullet.

It was reported that the three were part of an Australian Army expedition preparing to climb Everest. They were identified as RAAF Squadron Leader Peter Szypula, his partner Flight Sergeant Michelle Hackett and their 8yr old daughter Kathleen. An Israeli trekker was also killed in the avalanche. These particular people and their story recently became more familiar to me when I spoke to Zac Zaharias, the leader of the Army Alpine Association (AAA) team who met Mark on Everest. Zac was impacted by this tragedy more than most and has graciously provided me with details about his 2001 expedition in a phone interview and has also sent me a DVD that was produced and a book that was written about it.

The following abbreviated account of the Annapurna tragedy is sourced from the book: *Anzac Day on Mount Everest* written by Peter Maiden, together with some observations from the DVD: *Everest 2001—Tragedy & Triumph AAA Tenix Expedition*. I will later refer to more information from this book and from interviews with members of the AAA team regarding their involvement with Mark on Everest.

Annapurna Avalanche
The *AAA Tenix Everest Expedition* consisted of 14 climbers and 6 support staff, one of which was Peter Szypula who was to serve as the Expedition's video documentary producer. His partner Michelle Hackett and her bright and enthusiastic daughter Kathleen Cassandra (KC), together with two other trekkers, accompanied the expedition team for the acclimatisation trek in the Annapurna region, after which they planned to return home.

By March 23rd, the group had trekked to *Maccapucchre Base Camp* (MBC) where they enjoyed a beautiful 360 degree panoramic view of the surrounding mountains at 3700 metres. Those who were acclimatising for Everest, set off the next morning for a trek to *Annapurna Base Camp*, returning to MBC for a second night. Over the following two days they were to do a long trek down the valley to Birethanti from where they could go by bus back to Kathmandu and then onto Everest.

Instead of taking the extension trek to *Annapurna Base Camp* with the others, Peter Szypula, Michelle Hackett and KC decided to take a more leisurely three day trek to Birethanti and would meet the others along the way. Peter was looking forward to the next few days walking with Michelle and KC as a family unit. As they trekked down to the Modi River they were met by some Israeli trekkers who walked with them for awhile and later gave account of the last time they saw them, which was near a stream at a stone crossing in the Modi Khola Gorge. Peter was taking photos and Michelle and KC were relaxing by the stream.

That afternoon, as the main group returned to MBC they heard word that there had been an avalanche down in the valley. This had been the first fatal avalanche on the Annapurna Circuit in 13 years and one of monstrous size. The ice-avalanche thundered down from Hiunchuli, nearly 6 kilometres away, and crashed into the Modi Khola Gorge. It was estimated to be 400m wide, 150m high, and up to 500,000 cubic metres in volume.

At first the AAA team thought that their three companions may have already passed the gorge but it became clear by the next day that there was little hope of survival for the three Australians. Despite this, the AAA team dug for two days, hoping for a miracle.

Eventually their search became futile and they reluctantly had to let go. They huddled together near the search area in a cave formed by two enormous boulders. No sunlight reached inside this makeshift chapel, only the cold blue light reflected from the surrounding ice and snow. Nothing but the sound of the river running under the cave floor and small candles flickering inside the cave, soothed the solemn mourners as they gathered silent and still, to remember and pay tribute to their friends.

Despite this tragedy that had befallen their expedition, a final group of nine chose to continue, including Tanya Bylart, an Army Reserve Captain and registered nurse who was particularly affected by KC's death. *It was an amazing expedition,* she said *Sometimes I thought to myself, "What more can happen now?"*

...

Meanwhile, Mark Auricht and Duncan Chessell, were continuing with their own preparation and hoping to become the first South Australians to reach the roof of the world. Little did they know that their paths would cross so significantly with Zac Zaharias and his team two months later on Mt Everest.

~~~~~~~~~~~~~~~~~~~~~

SA EVEREST EXPEDITION DIARIES

The following diary entries were sent to sponsors and supporters of the SA Expedition from the Tibetan Base Camp and whenever the team returned to ABC in between establishing camps higher up the mountain. The diary entries provide a detailed account of what transpired after the Annapurna acclimatisation phase and cover the expedition's journey over the following six weeks, from Kathmandu on April 10th, through to May 19th, during which time the team established ABC at 6400m, Camp 1 on the North Col at 7100m and Camp 2 at 7900m. The last entry includes their thoughts prior to leaving Advanced Based Camp again on May 20th for their final summit push.
(Refer to Map of the SA Expedition route—Figure 3.2 on page 57)

Kathmandu April 10, 2001
Our acclimatisation trek in the Annapurna Region came to a successful conclusion on April 6 as our Twin Otter aircraft touched down in Kathmandu, returning our team back to civilisation temporarily. The group, totalling 24 people, trekked for 34 days, covering over 200km.

We crossed two high passes - Mesokanto Pass (5200m) and Thorung La Pass (5416m), and successfully climbed Chulu Far East (6059m) but cloud prevented us from going higher than 5800m on Chulu West.

We have achieved a significant boost in fitness and have acclimatised to 6000m so far, having spent seventeen days above 4500m, enduring the late winter temperatures (minus 10°C to minus 20°C), while carrying heavy backpacks to build our strength.

The last few days in Kathmandu saw the arrival of our Expedition Doctor, David Tingay and two support trek members, Greg Perks and Justin Hogan who are also sponsors of the expedition. During these final days of preparation all of our team members busied themselves with a variety of tasks. Gyanu the cook has bought large quantities of rice, potatoes and other foods required for seven people to exist in the back blocks of Tibet for up to two and a half months. The result of this shopping spree is about 20 barrels of food, each weighing 25kg; soon to be strapped to the sides of a large herd of yaks. Other tasks included obtaining final permission from the Chinese to enter Tibet (not a straight forward process by any stretch), sorting and packing climbing equipment and corresponding with family, friends and sponsors.

...

It's now 3.00am on the morning of April 10, the truck is packed with loads of gear, the drive to the Tibetan border and the gateway to Everest is only four hours away.

Everest Base Camp (5200m), April 14

On April 10 we left Kathmandu to begin our Tibetan leg of the journey using a Land Rover and truck to transport our 1500kg load of gear, two climbing Sherpas, Base Camp cook and our six expedition members to the Tibetan border where we arrived at midday. We then waited for four hours while negotiations took place to allow us to pass through Chinese immigration.

Having spent the night in the Chinese town of Zhangmu, the following two days involved a spectacular journey across the high Tibetan Plateau in 4WD vehicles. We rapidly gained altitude and sat mesmerised by the vast rocky plains and frozen river valleys. The Himalayan Range with its snowfields and towering buttresses was a stunning backdrop to this high altitude desert. Parts of the journey reminded us of the deserts of northern South Australia, only here they are surrounded by snow top mountains and the air temperatures are normally well below zero.

We passed numerous small villages and yak herders leading their herds toward Base Camp (BC) to sell supplies and to transport the vast amounts of expedition gear from BC to Advanced Base camp (ABC). The rivers in the area are only just thawing out from the cold winter allowing the 4WD to occasionally break through into the river where the ice was thinner.

Arriving at Base Camp (5200m), April 15

On April 12th we established our tiny presence among the rocks and moraine walls below the North Face of Mt Everest. Spread across the river flat were hundreds of tents in small clusters, the only indication of a record number tackling Everest this year. The official count is 30 expeditions of 400 people, tackling four different routes.

The most obvious thing to strike the team as we sat taking in our first view of Chomolungma was how devoid of snow the mountain was. Instead of vast white snowfields, there was mostly black rock covering the mountain. This prompted much discussion about our intended route and the selection of climbing gear required. Despite the best plans, we have had a few unforeseen difficulties. Upon arrival at Base Camp, the Chinese liaison officer revealed that the rules regarding yaks had changed and the 23 we were promised, each to carry 50kg, was reduced to 15 only carrying 40kg. The result, not surprisingly, was a hefty increase in cost to the tune of 1200USD!

Everest Base Camp is a meeting place for adventurers from every country on Earth and the mess tent became a Mecca for all sorts of 'disparate characters.' We were here on Easter Sunday and after three days of preparations and a spot of cricket as we camped amidst the rows and rows of tents pitched on the snow and ice, the yaks are loaded and we are setting out for our next goal, Advanced Base Camp (ABC) at the foot of the North Ridge (6400m). This journey will take two days, covering 22km and gaining 1200m as we hike up, down and across a glacier vulnerable to avalanches at any time. Memorial headstones for dead climbers are a stark reminder of these ever-present dangers. All of our expedition members are in good health.

Advanced Base Camp (6400m), April 27

Our SA Everest team arrived at ABC on the afternoon of April 16th. During the past 11 days, the Sherpas have established Camp 1 on the North Col (7100m). All the group equipment required for the remainder of the climb has been carried to the Col in readiness to establish Camp 2 (7900m).

We have completed a successful climb of four peaks adjacent to Base Camp, including the spectacular Lhakpa Peak (7043m). This critical stage in the acclimatisation program proved a difficult, tiring but highly rewarding day. Both of us found the going surprisingly easy in comparison to previous climbs at the same altitude and as such, the day not only provided a huge confidence builder, it confirmed that we are both ready to tackle Everest.

We have spent an additional day at Base Camp due to our involvement in an emergency with a very ill climber from another expedition. The climber was struck with a severe case of high altitude cerebral oedema; a condition where the brain swells with potentially deadly consequences.

His condition was soon complicated by pulmonary oedema where the lungs fill with fluid and can drown the person in a short space of time. Fortunately, with the assistance of our Expedition Doctor David Tingay, we were able to save the man's life when death looked almost certain. David's expertise in specialised drugs, oxygen and a specially designed altitude chamber bought the victim a few extra hours of life. The Tibetans and Sherpas then literally ran down the mountain carrying the victim on a makeshift stretcher. An express jeep took him to the Nepal border town of Kodari where a Medivac helicopter carried him to Kathmandu. His outlook is now reasonably good.

On April 28, we will climb to Camp 1, spend one day sorting gear and making preparations to establish Camp 2 and then continue up the mountain to put in Camp 2 at 7900m. Camp 2 will provide the launch point for our first summit attempt. May 1st could see us heading for the top. This will obviously depend on weather conditions (most importantly the cessation of the jet stream winds) and our fitness and health. Our goal of being the first South Australians to reach the highest point on Earth is close to becoming a reality! We remain focused on the goal, looking forward to a possible early summit.

Everest Base Camp, Saturday May 5
The team has now established Camp 1 (7100m) and Camp 2 (7900m). We spent several nights on the North Col and Mark ascended to 7900m. We had hoped to climb further, weather and health permitting but unfortunately, Duncan has developed a cough and is in need of some rest to recover. On Thursday May 3, the whole team returned to Base Camp to rest and recuperate. We expect to be heading back up to ABC and beyond by about May 9th.

Advanced Base Camp, Thursday May 10
Having spent 4 days resting down at the Rongbuk Base Camp (5200m), we returned to ABC on the 9th of May. Whilst at Base Camp we all ate well, enjoyed the denser atmosphere, caught up on sleep and have recovered from various coughs and sore throats. All of our camps on the mountain are now stocked with food, fuel and oxygen, and the team is poised for a summit push. We are in a very good position to take advantage of the next weather window.

Above 8000m, the winds at present are 25 to 40 knots with air temperatures hovering around -30°C and as such it is too cold to summit in the next two days. The weather report for the 12th of May is for easing winds so we plan to leave ABC for our summit bid then. This would see us at the North Col (7100m) on the 12th, Camp 2 (7900m) on the 13th and our high camp—Camp 3 (8300m) on the 14th. We plan to have a shot at the summit on the 15th of May.

Excitement and anticipation is building throughout ABC with most teams preparing for summit attempts within the next two weeks. It has been reported that two Korean climbers reached the summit from the Nepal side on the 7th May. As yet no one has reached the summit from the Tibetan side.

Mark and his diary at Everest Base Camp—Tibet, 2001

A Letter to Home—Saturday May 12
Hi Dad and Helen, I hope you are both well... Duncan and I have returned to Advanced Base Camp and are in good health. All of our higher camps are now well established, thanks mostly to our strong Sherpas. So we are now ready to go for the summit when the weather allows us to and are currently playing the waiting game. The good news is that the jet-stream winds have moved south, so the high wind speeds have eased, but the bad news is, we are getting a lot of early monsoonal snow. This has made some slopes unstable, so we have to wait for it to consolidate. It also means more hard work up high, wading through knee to waist deep snow. We had hoped to leave ABC today for a go at the summit on the 15th but will now be here for an extra two days, thus hoping for a summit attempt on the 17th or 18th... I have decided to use oxygen above high camp, which has not been an easy decision, as I would rather have a go without the bottle and am quite sure my body can do it. The sponsorship commitments, including video footage, mean that we will be carrying more weight and moving more slowly than we would otherwise. I am also aware that an oxygen-less ascent costs brain cells (and I sure can't afford to lose too many more!)... I hope you are both well and look forward to sharing the expedition stories when I return.

Thanks for all your love and support, I couldn't go on without it!
Love from Mark in Tibet!

THE LAST TWO EXPEDITION DIARY ENTRIES

Everest ABC, Tuesday May 15
We returned to a snowy Advance Base Camp last night (14th May) after aborting our first summit push due to heavy snow falls. We reached a high point of 7600m but with high cloud rapidly approaching the decision was made to turn around. With both of us in good health and well acclimatised, it was a difficult but good decision. The ensuing snow fall and cloud has blanketed the mountain for the last 24 hours with no sign of improvement. All other teams have returned to ABC as the forecast predicts a further five days of snow falls and poor visibility.

On the 14th of May a large and very experienced American expedition failed to reach the summit ridge due to deep snow and dangerous avalanche conditions, from their high camp at 8300m. This would have been the first expedition to have reached the summit from Tibet this year.

The route above high camp has not been established yet so a strong large team will be required to force its way through the deep snow and fix the necessary rope. The general consensus in ABC is that if anyone summits this season, it will be late May. A couple of expeditions have self-destructed and have packed up and left already. Most other expeditions plan on waiting out the weather until the end of May and into early June. We hope to mount a second summit bid in a few days time.

Everest ABC, Saturday May 19
Our latest plan is to leave tomorrow morning at 6.00am for our second summit push. The weather forecast has been totally wrong today and instead of 40-50 knot winds with heavy snow falls as we have had for the last week, the day dawned clear and windless. Two American climbers and four climbing Sherpas, the only people on the mountain, were able to make good use of the unexpected clearance and summited at 10.00am today. These fortunate six people are the first to summit Everest from Tibet this year. Well done to the Sherpas and the American climbers. This caught the rest of the expeditions off guard as everyone else was in ABC or BC waiting for the clearance expected in 4 days time.

A full scale exodus from ABC to the Nth Col is now underway in expectation that the good weather will last for a few more days. Another storm is predicted for the 24th of May so everyone is aiming for the 22nd or 23rd. Let's hope the weather holds and the mountain allows us a chance to climb.

This was to be Mark's final diary entry.

The Final Push
On Sunday May 20th the SA Everest Expedition left their Advanced Base Camp (6400m) for their second summit attempt. This would see them at Camp 1 on the North Col (7100m) that night, then Camp 2 (7900m) on the 21st and at High Camp 3 (8300m) by the 22nd, which would see them ready for their shot at the summit (8848m) on May 23rd, assuming Chomolungma and the weather gods allowed it.

A Prayer to the Moon
Three days later, on the 23rd of May, news came through that Duncan had made it to the summit and that Mark had about 200 metres to go. This was great news for Duncan and there was a sense of optimism mixed with anxiety for Mark.

I remember that night calling Mark's wife Catherine to see how she was going. She was reluctant to say much and I sensed her anxiety.

I went for a walk in the park after the phone call. The moon was out and as I walked I remembered a conversation I had with Mark about his night alone on Makalu, trying to get back to his high camp after David Hume fell to his death. He spoke of how he used the moon to keep his bearings until it became obscured by the Makalu Ridge. Then he had to focus on the positive voices in his head to guide him home. As I recalled this I looked up at the moon and said a prayer as I wondered whether the moon would be there for Mark this time?

**And now these three remain: faith, hope and love.
But the greatest of these is love.**

1 Corinthians 13:13

Chapter 4   Triumph and Tragedy on Everest

Full Moon on the Kokoda Track—Jesse Enright, 2009

I imagined that night as I looked up at the moon, that Mark would somehow find the strength to inch his way, breath by breath to the summit. Part of me was excited at the prospect that he was so close to achieving his dream but like many of those close to Mark who knew how quickly triumph can turn to tragedy on high mountains, I did not sleep well that night.

Climber from SA Reaches Pinnacle of His Career
On the morning of May 24th, 2001 the local South Australian newspaper announced that Duncan Chessell had reached the pinnacle of his career by becoming the first South Australian to reach the summit of the world's highest mountain at 9.30am on May 23rd. It was reported that his climbing companion Mark Auricht, was poised to emulate Duncan's accomplishment. Mark was less than 200 metres from the summit when the Media asked his wife to comment. Catherine said that Duncan had begun his descent and that her last information was that Mark was on his way up. *It might be an hour or as we speak* she said. *We'll certainly be very relieved to hear when they are down.* Dr David Tingay, the expedition doctor was also cautious, warning that Mark would be exhausted and dehydrated as he strove to climb the last few hundred metres to reach the summit.

Two hundred metres doesn't sound like much, but at the cruising altitude of a jetliner; where the oxygen levels and air pressure are not conducive to survival, let alone climbing through knee deep snow while exhausted, dehydrated and dis-orientated; two hundred metres can take hours... precious hours of life that is draining out of the body as the irrational mind says *keep going, I'm almost there.* Mark's success was far from assured when the news broke.

Meanwhile on the Mountain
As most South Australians were reading the news about Duncan reaching the summit and that Mark was soon to do the same, they were unaware that Mark had already passed away that same morning, May 24th between 7.00—7.30am. Most of Mark's family and friends received the shocking news of his death by phone during that day before it was reported in the news. It's strange, but I can even remember the tiles on the floor where I was standing as I listened to the words I did not want to hear.

A Difficult Message to Send
The following day (Friday May 25th) a message via the SA Everest Expedition website from Duncan Chessell's wife, Jo Arnold, confirmed early details.

> Dear Friends,
>
> I am deeply saddened to report the death at breakfast time yesterday, Thursday 24th of May 2001, of our good friend Mark Auricht, at camp two (7900m) on Mount Everest. It seems too early to speak about Mark, as the news is so recent.
> Few details are available at this stage but the Australian Army Alpine Association Team was extremely generous in extending all assistance to Mark. We wish them luck with their own summit attempts. Scott Ferris at Advanced Base Camp and expedition doctor, David Tingay have been an invaluable help at this difficult time.
> Duncan Chessell reached the top of Mount Everest early on Wednesday, 23rd of May, as did Tshering Sherpa. Duncan, Tshering and Pemba Sherpa, have now returned to Advanced Base Camp and are tired but well.
>
> Jo Arnold

The last email I received from Mark was sent some weeks before on May 3rd while he rested in Base Camp after climbing to 7900m. As I tried to grapple with my disbelief, I hung onto the last words he shared with me:-

Hi Wayne, hope all is going well in Adelaide for you...
Thanks once again for your support, I think about you, your farewell words and your support often. Say hello to Gab and the kids and I look forward to sharing the stories with you in Adelaide.
Cheers Mark

Pieces in the Puzzle

Like many of Mark's family and friends we never got to hear his stories, only snippets from the expedition diaries and what little was reported in the news. In the days following Mark's death it was unclear what had happened, but as days passed into weeks, the details of what happened that day on the mountain gradually emerged and the pieces of the puzzle for Mark's family and friends became clearer. The two parties that know most about what happened are the SA Expedition members who were with Mark between the summit and High Camp (8300m) and the Australian Army Expedition members who looked after him during the morning of his death at Camp 2 (7900m). The following interviews bring to light some of these details.

INTERVIEW WITH DUNCAN CHESSELL
By Julian Burton—September 17th, 2004

Everest is so hard to climb because of the lack of oxygen and the cold. You are looking at about 30% of available oxygen compared to that at sea level. The temperature on its own wouldn't present so much of a problem. It's about minus 40-45, depending on the day which is not too bad if you have the right gear but if there is a lot of wind that is not good. The wind chill factor can kill you pretty fast. The lack of oxygen is the real problem. It slows everything down, including your thinking. The oxygen level in your blood stream drops considerably. So much so that if you were in a hospital in Australia and they tested your blood they would put you in intensive care.

There is an incredible amount of effort required for each step at high altitude; which is the physical part of climbing, but then there is the mental part as well. Your physical and mental capacities need to match each other. That is the trick with climbing and mountaineering. If you have two columns and one has mental toughness and the other physical toughness; in climbing you want physical toughness to be slightly higher or equal to your mental toughness. If mental toughness is higher you will push yourself and push yourself to the point where you can't go on and on a mountain you have to go on. You have to not only have enough to get to the summit but also enough in reserve to come back.

On the way up a mountain you break your walking down. You might walk for 50 steps, then stop and breathe, focus again and then breathe as hard as you can for 30 seconds and keep going. Your lungs are just trashed, because you're respiration rate is so high. By the time you get to the last five minutes from the summit of Everest you are down to focusing on taking 10 steps and then 8 steps. As soon as you start to go more than a very slow pace, you get straight into oxygen debt and you can't maintain it.

In front of you, you are looking at the snow ridge where the summit is. You keeping looking up at it every 30 seconds or so, take those 8 steps, then look again to your goal.

When I finally got to the summit of Everest with my Sherpa - Tshering Pande Bhote, it was pretty weird... I remember going "Oh, I guess this must be it then". No bells or whistles went off when I arrived. The summit is about 3 metres long and about 1 metre wide with three faces converging at the top; one very steep and the other two moderately steep; with a patch of snow that is fairly flat on top. You end up on this tiny perch at the very top of the world where there are prayer flags, pictures and rocks that have been left by other people. I sat down and looked around for about an hour and twenty minutes. We came from the Tibetan side but now all of a sudden I could see the other half of the mountain and down into Nepal where there were tiny villages that I recognised in the distance below.

At first it wasn't too emotional... at the time you are focusing on what you have to do. For years you have been imagining it and visualising it and you pre-program what you will do when you get there. 'If this happens I go to plan B, or this I use plan C'; so you have worked out what you need to do on summit day and are just rolling it out.

It wasn't until I called Base Camp on the radio that it first started to sink in. I said "Base Camp, this is Duncan calling from the summit; do you copy?" and the response came from Base Camp, "we copy." I could hear in the background all these chants and cheers. I then thought to myself, "I have climbed it!" It was then that I realised that all the guys that had helped us get to the top were as happy, if not happier, than we were. I was tired and buggered from the climb, so I didn't fully take it in but I thought "I'm finally here, I have been waiting to do this for 10 years."

Base Camp called Australia and the rest of our team on the mountain, they were all stoked. Everyone had put in such a big effort. I realised then that now that we'd actually gone through with our dream and I'd become the person standing on the summit, there were all these other people who shared in the dream with us: our fellow climbers and Sherpas; the base camp people; our sponsors and our families who had supported us on our way there. It was a victory for everyone and I assumed that Mark would soon be joining me.

I guess what I had achieved did not really sink in for about a week, partly because Mark and I had planned the whole expedition together and I had visualised a summit photograph with Mark, and our arms around each other's shoulders, thumbs up, smiling and grinning... 'Beauty, well done, off we go, let's walk down now.' So I had that picture in my mind and I sat there and waited for Mark for one hour and twenty minutes.

I looked at my oxygen bottle and it was going down and down and I knew I could not wait too much longer. I had to go. It wasn't the completion that I had pictured. I hadn't visualised it just being me standing up there without Mark, going 'yahoo!' I was always anticipating it to be at least the two of us and our Sherpas there together. That is what we had worked on for years before that day.

Picking Mark up on the way down was the greatest feeling of disappointment. He was pretty happy for the two of us who got there but for Mark, this was probably going to be his one and only shot at Everest. It wasn't an option for him to come back in another year, so he was bitterly disappointed at having to turn around.

I remember on the way down we were talking about how we could set up another summit bid for him to get another shot in a few days time but we kind of all knew deep down that the season was about to close, the bad weather was about to come in and it was going to be pretty unlikely that he would get another shot at it. It would have been our third summit bid on that expedition. On our first try the weather came in half way up and we didn't get anywhere near it so we came back down and rested for a few days and then the second attempt was when I and my Sherpa friend Tshering Pande Bhote made it to the top. For Mark, it was very improbable now.

Mark's mental toughness was very strong and his physical ability was usually very strong too but on this day, having had a slight cold which may have reduced his physical capacity to cope with high altitude, his physical strength wasn't able to match his mental strength and will to get to the top.

When Mark got down to the high camp at 8300m with us he was very tired. We all were, but Tshering and I were in a better state than Mark was. With this in mind we asked Mark if he wanted to go down to the lower camp where the impact of altitude would be significantly lessened. It's always the best option to get down to a lower altitude where there is more oxygen, especially if you are already experiencing early signs of altitude sickness.

Tshering and I who had been to the summit were low on water and needed to stop at the high camp to melt snow and re-hydrate... and since Mark wasn't feeling so good we offered him the option to continue down to the lower camp where there was also more tent space, a support Sherpa with another oxygen bottle and a radio. Had we all gone down, there wouldn't have been much room in the tent at the lower camp at 7900m.

It was about a one hour walk on fixed lines down to the lower camp. The rope actually went passed the door of our tent and we had our support Sherpa in the tent below with a radio so that if Mark needed to call for assistance he could do so on his radio. All of our radios were on standby if he needed a hand. So we thought that everything was covered.

My best guess as to what had happened on the way down, was that Mark's altitude sickness had started to affect him later in the day as he descended and he was so fatigued and disappointed that he no longer had the energy that had been driving him up. I'm pretty sure this was the case, based on a lot of other expeditions and seeing people in a similar place. I think he probably sat down on a rock just before sunset and just went to sleep. When he woke up he would have been out of oxygen and his altitude sickness would have gotten worse, to the point where his thinking would have been affected. This might explain why he didn't use the radio and why he missed our camp as he continued down the rope.

He must have walked straight past our tent and kept going before he bumped into the Army expedition's tent at about 1.00am. It had taken seven hours to walk down something that should have taken an hour. He must have been out for a long time so I knew his oxygen had run out.

It is my understanding that he bunked in with the Australian Army Expedition for the night and they didn't think too much about it. They thought he was just tired and a bit out of it. The next morning they said "Right mate we're heading off to go up to the summit." According to them, Mark was a bit slow and floppy and not too together. He got out of their tent and was sitting against a rock and just put his head down and stopped moving.

Up until the tragedy of Mark's death, every other aspect of the expedition went pretty well - we nailed all of our small and medium goals for the expedition and everything rolled out pretty well as planned. We'd already had a very fulfilling expedition prior to summit day. The one person who was missing at the top was Mark and he got within 150 metres which is an amazing achievement in itself.

Interview shared with permission from Duncan Chessell[15]

Duncan's achievement was bitter-sweet. He said to me recently that he had lost more guide friends and climber mates over the last 15 years, but come May 24th each year, he still thinks about Mark and all that could have been.

> **There isn't a year that goes past without a quiet tear and a raise of the glass to 'Marko'**
> Duncan Chessell

 **Understanding Leads to Healing**
In my personal experiences with grief and loss, it eases the heart and mind when we have more understanding about an event that disturbs us. With this in mind, I hope to shed some more light on what happened to Mark and perhaps, in the process, provide some catharsis for myself and others.

Readers are often poorly served when an author writes as an act of catharsis, but I hope something will be gained by spilling my soul in the calamity's immediate aftermath.
John Krakauer—Author of *Into Thin Air* and *Into the Wild*

Unfortunately, Duncan Chessell wasn't with Mark when he died, so he could only piece together the events after Mark left their High Camp in the late afternoon of May 23rd, from accounts provided to him by the Army expedition members who looked after Mark the next morning. When I first wrote a draft of this manuscript 10 years ago, I felt that it would be helpful to include excerpts from media interviews done with the *Army Alpine Association (AAA)* team members to fill some gaps in my mind and the minds of others who wanted or needed to know and understand more.

I recently decided however, that it would be more accurate to get first-hand accounts from those who were involved. Even though some of the memories have faded after 15 years, those who were on the spot have some vivid memories etched in their minds. I interviewed Zac Zaharias, Brian (Henri) Laursen and Tim Robathan, who all played a significant role in looking after Mark on the morning of May 24th, 2001. I also had a chat with Bob Killip who helped with the return of a precious item to Mark's family.

Following is a summary of their recollections, sewn together with details about the events of that day and May 25th, that were published in 2006 by Peter Maiden in his book, *Anzac Day on Mt Everest*. I have not used military titles with the names of the AAA team members, most of who were serving in either the Australian Army or Air Force, because rank was irrelevant on the mountain where all humans are equalised by the laws of nature. Leadership though, was tested many times in the case of Zac Zaharias, the Leader for the AAA Expedition.

It was a tough expedition, having to deal with death on numerous occasions.
Zac Zaharias

AUSTRALIAN ARMY ALPINE ASSOCIATION EXPEDITION STORY

The AAA team members had gotten to know Mark and Duncan quite well as they shared space at their base camps. Despite being on different schedules while setting up their higher camps and going for the summit, they spent quite a bit of time together. Brian (Henri) Laursen—pronounced 'Lawson' (hence the nickname Henri), told me that the South Australians were welcome and regular visitors to the Army Mess Tent.

Tim Robathan also shared his recollections of meeting Mark and Duncan and becoming friends as they spent time together at BC and ABC.

I met Mark at Everest Base Camp, along with Duncan and the rest of their team. We all became instant friends. We were all Aussies about to climb Mt Everest. We spent most days at Base Camp hanging out together, and I recall chatting to Mark a lot and really liking him. I was 23 at the time, so I was fascinated by the climbs that Mark had done, particularly Makalu. Some nights I'd be in Mark and Duncan's tent watching movies on their laptop with them, while other nights they'd be in our mess tent playing cards, chatting, or having a drink. We became good friends.

Unexpected Rendezvous
Prior to his unexpected rendezvous with members of the *AAA Expedition* down at 7900m (AAA's Camp 3 / SA's Camp 2), Mark was descending with Duncan as we know, down the North Ridge which lead from the summit of Everest to their High Camp at 8300m. Along the North Ridge, all climbers have to negotiate three so-called 'steps' which are steep and technically difficult rocky sections that must be scaled slowly and carefully, leaving ascending climbers bent over double and breathing like a fish out of water, and descending climbers feeling anxious as they inch their way down to safety.

As if their journey back to the shelter of their High Camp wasn't long enough, Mark and Duncan had to wait in line behind other climbers for over an hour in two places as they climbed down narrow ledges. When they finally got back to their High Camp, we know that Mark decided to continue down to lower altitude, while Duncan and Sherpa Tshering Pande Bhote stopped to re-hydrate and rest. It was 5.00pm and the walk down to Camp 2 at 7900m should have taken Mark only 60-90 minutes. Eight hours later, at 1.00am, the Army's Zaharias, heard something outside his tent...

Members of *AAA Team One* that were camped there that night, were Zac Zaharias and Tim Robathan who shared a tent, and the other pair were Michael Cook (Cookie) together with Brian (Henri) Laursen. These four were to be the first of three *AAA Expedition* teams to attempt the summit for their expedition and had planned to get as restful a night as possible, in preparation for climbing to their Top Camp the next day.

At 1.00am Zac Zaharias remembers hearing someone outside the tents. The night was pitch black and super windy as Zac stuck his head out of the tent into the chill. Spindrift threatened to fill their tent with snow. Zac was concerned enough to get his boots on and went out into the freezing conditions to discover that it was Mark Auricht stumbling around, trying to find his tent. Fortunately the wind had blown the fixed rope over the top of Zac and Tim's tent, so he bumped into it as he followed the life line.

Mark looked knackered and confused, Zac recalls. *He wasn't sure whether his tent was above or below ours and I didn't have a clue, so we thought it best to take him into our tent and help him warm up and re-hydrate with a cuppa. Perhaps then we could help him back to his tent.*

A certain Samaritan came upon him.
He felt compassion... brought him in... and took care of him.
Luke 10:33-34

Mark was completely exhausted, said Tim. *We were trying to understand what he was doing. It was really crowded in the two-man tent with the three of us on a not-so-level snow slope. I crouched at one end, while we got Mark into a sleeping bag for warmth*, Tim said... *I started the stove up to begin melting snow to get water for Mark. At sea level this is an easy process, but at our altitude and in the temperatures we were in it was hard work. It took about an hour to get 1 litre of water. As I was getting water heated we'd sit Mark up and get him to drink. Zac gave him his water as well. We were all suffering from altitude, and at the time Mark appeared to be more exhausted than anything else. He managed to explain to us that Duncan had made it to the summit but that he had to turn around and he left Duncan and the Sherpa at their High Camp at dusk I think. It should have been maybe a two hour descent at the most, but he'd been going for maybe 7-8 hours and had run out of oxygen.*

No Silent Night
Zac reports that while they were giving Mark a cuppa and he was relaying his story, he seemed lucid and there were no obvious signs that he was critically ill.

He was exhausted, dehydrated and talking slowly but that was to be expected at that altitude, especially after what he'd been through. At the time we thought he'd be okay after warming up, re-hydrating and having a good rest, said Zac. *I remember him going back outside again to have another go at finding his tent. He staggered and fell over, so I suggested he spend the night with us in our tent, even though there was little room. He had a better chance of finding his tent safely in the morning,* said Zac.

So they rode out the rough night in the cramped tent together, with Mark wedged between Zac and Tim. There was no 'heavenly peace' that night!

The Dawn of Silence

When sunrise came, Zac and Tim began the slow process of getting their boots and other gear on, so they could let Henri and Cookie know what was going on. Hopefully Mark was feeling better and they'd be able to start the climb to their Top Camp.

Zac got out of the tent first, said Tim. *Then we moved Mark to the entrance of the tent and stuck his legs out so we could get his boots and crampons on. He was a bit incoherent and just wanted to lie down.*

Mark was leaning on his elbow, talking slowly and drifting in and out a bit as he was trying to get dressed, Zac said. *I was saying to him, 'Here's your glove, make sure you put it on'... He was responding and doing things under his own steam, but kept drifting off to sleep. While I was glancing down, putting on my boots, I talked to him but got no response. I looked up to see that he was lying down with the top half of his torso inside the tent and his legs outside,* Zac said. *I checked him for a response but there was none.*

Tim recalls getting a bottle of oxygen set up and putting the mask on Mark to see if it would help him but he was lifeless. *At the same time we yelled out to Henri and Cookie for assistance,* said Tim.

Henri remembers having no time to cover his own hands, so he had difficulty detecting a pulse, whether Mark had one or not. *My hands were like cold hard plastic,* he said. *I checked Mark's pupils too but they were not responsive. It was difficult to determine whether he was still alive, so I started compressions, while Zac took care of Mark's airway,* said Henri.

After some time trying to revive him it was obvious that Mark wasn't coming back and so I had to 'call it.' I think it was about 0700 or so.
Tim Robathan distinctly remembers the moment:

We were holding Mark when he passed.
It was pretty devastating as we sat there with him in silence.

Shockwaves

Despite other tragedies that Zac Zaharias had experienced previously, he said he was taken aback by Mark's death. *I was shocked because I'd never seen this happen. I've seen all sorts of accidents in the Himalayas but I've never seen someone die in front of me before,* he said.

Tim and Zac then commenced communications with the other team members further down the mountain. Tim asked his Base Camp to see if they could communicate via the SA Base Camp to get a message to Duncan on the radio but wasn't sure if they were able to reach him.

The first that the rest of the expedition heard about the drama unfolding 1000 metres above them, was when Tim Robathan rang down to Bob Killip at Camp 1. It was just after 7.30am when Bob took the call. He shook his head with sorrow as he relayed the message to the others—*Mark from the South Australian Expedition just died at Camp 3 in the arms of our boys... He slipped into unconsciousness fifteen minutes ago.*

As a flurry of questions went back and forth between team members around him, Bob was kneeling like a silent statue inside his tent, staring into space in disbelief. Bob was clearly moved by Mark's death, as were most of them who had gotten to know Mark. Tim said that when he made the call to ABC he was deeply upset but tried not to show it. *I got to know Mark pretty well during the trip and I really liked him, so it was a difficult moment,* he said.

The issue now was whether to try and bring Mark's body down or leave him on the mountain as was the usual practice at that altitude where it is very difficult to bring someone down without risking the lives of those who attempt the task. *We really couldn't take any decisive action until we heard from Mark's family, so we wrapped Mark in a tent-fly and waited for Duncan to arrive or to hear from the family,* said Zac. *There wasn't much more we could do.*

Henri Laursen and Michael Cook were ascending above the tents where Zac and Tim were with Mark, when Duncan Chessell came down with his Sherpa looking for Mark. Henri gave Duncan the distressing news of Mark's death. According to Henri, Duncan was having a hard time processing it at first. *He'd heard some of the radio chatter but didn't seem to be fully aware of the gravity of the situation until I told him,* said Henri.

Duncan was in shock and disbelief as he continued down to find Mark. *When Duncan arrived at about 0800, he was just stone-faced. I guess he had the shutters up,* said Zac. *He sat down next to Mark and spent quite some time grieving.* Duncan had now seen for himself that Mark was gone. *We just sat there in silence and cried.*

Eventually contact was made with Mark's family and the decision was made to lay him to rest among the mountains he so loved. Both Zac and Henri told me that there really wasn't anywhere to bury Mark at that location, so the best they could do was move him off the main ridge onto the western face of the mountain, where he could be placed in a rock fissure not to be disturbed by passing traffic.

Becoming One with Chomolunga

I recently spoke to Bob Killip who had taken the radio call at the lower camp that morning and was on his way up the next day. Bob said that he didn't remember much about those few days, except for the sad task of having to remove Mark's wedding ring from a necklace he was wearing, so that it could be returned with other personal effects to his family. Bob said that he found this difficult. He also remembers being there when a group of Sherpas from Russel Brice's team helped to move Mark to his final resting place.[16]

Mark was laid to rest on the western face, in the direction of the setting sun. He would over time, become at one with the mountain, covered in snow or taken by an avalanche back into the arms of Mother Nature. Like a burial in the ocean or ashes taken by the wind, his spirit would become one with *Mother Goddess of the Universe*.

> *I took to the mountains to find myself.*
> *In fear of death I did my best. Now all fear is laid to rest.*

The Ascent of Angels

Those who attended to Mark at 7900 metres on Everest would probably squirm with embarrassment at being referred to as angels but I think it is an apt description for those who put their own needs aside to help others, especially in extreme circumstances.

According to those who know him, it seems that Zac Zaharias rarely participates in an expedition where he does not help somebody in distress. He left himself seriously dehydrated after giving his drinking water to Mark, and as the rest of the team continued up the mountain after doing what they could, Zac remained with Mark to keep vigil over him until Duncan arrived. He arrived quite late at his Top Camp where for the second night he had almost no sleep. The AAA Team's readiness for the summit was less than ideal.

Later that night they prepared to leave for the summit but delayed their departure due to misgivings about the weather. Henri Laursen and his two Sherpas (Chhewang Nima and Ngima Nuru) eventually led the group into the night, after initially climbing with Michael Cook until Cookie was set back by a problem with his head torch. Cookie and Zac ended up behind Henri, with Tim Robathan following a short distance behind them.

It is not uncommon for high altitude climbers to end up being spread apart due to differences in how they feel on the day, variation in pace, frequency and duration of rest stops, issues with gear, and having a staggered departure due to the fact that just suiting up and getting out of the tent takes time. At that altitude you can't stand around waiting for too long, you need to get moving, saving oxygen and time for stops later.

Pivotal Decisions
Tim wasn't happy with his rate of ascent and didn't like the look of the weather when he got to the first step and saw that Zac and Cookie had already climbed it. His intuition told him that he needed to turn back. He had set a turnaround time for himself and knew that he wasn't going to make it... *I really wanted to reach the top but wasn't prepared to risk my life,* he said. As Tim took his decision to abort his ascent, the other three continued up over the second and third step. It is very technical climbing at that altitude when the mind is not sharp and fatigue is setting in, not to mention the weather. Cookie said the second step is possibly the most daunting obstacle on the north side of Everest, at the top of which is a vertical face.

As Cookie continued winding up through the rocks and snow on the ridge, he stopped to wait for Zac to catch up. Time was ticking away as they were about to start climbing the final snow slope to the summit. They had slowed down now, the weather was deteriorating and it was getting close to their time limit. There was still a long way to go as they wondered whether they should continue. A night on Everest near the summit without a tent and sleeping bag or negotiating the rock steps in the dark where they might get caught on the ridge in a storm, were not probabilities they were prepared to dismiss lightly.

By now they were the last climbers on the higher stretch of the North Ridge after Henri Laursen had passed them on his way down from the summit, and they felt very isolated. Cookie was sitting there at over 8,700m, the highest man on earth at that time, and Zac was climbing up to him. They were no more than 150m from their goal, which was about where Mark was when he turned around after Duncan came down from the summit.

As Cookie sat in this spot, so tantalisingly close to the summit, he had already realised a dream (what was another 150m in the scheme of things!). He may not appear in the historical records as an 'Everest Summiter,' but he had overcome the three most technically difficult sections that confront climbers on the North Ridge and he was still alive. To continue might put him in the history books but would probably kill him. He had made up his mind that this would be his summit today.

Zac hadn't quite got to the same pivot point yet and wanted to push on. *Let's just go on for one more hour, we're so close*, he said. By then it would be 3.00pm and even if they did reach the summit, they would face hours of difficult descent. Cookie agreed for the moment, but remained where he was at the edge of the snow slope, as if it were a shoreline to deeper waters. He watched as Zac waded into the waist deep snow.

After 20 minutes Zac had only managed to make about 5 metres of progress. Cookie pulled his oxygen mask off and yelled out to Zac to come back. They both kept looking up at the summit... it was so close. *Come back to the rock, please Zac, and let's talk. It's not for us today mate.* After assessing their situation as rationally as you can with impaired thinking and summit fever, they reluctantly turned around and headed back to safety.

The Challenge of Morality

There is more of this tale to tell but you'll have to read Peter Maiden's book *Anzac Day on Mt Everest*, to get the whole story. The point of sharing this much of AAA Team's push for the summit after helping Mark, is to illustrate the challenges of decision making, teamwork and leadership in extreme environments, and also to acknowledge that these four men somewhat sacrificed their own chances of reaching the summit to look after Mark as best they could. Unfortunately they couldn't save his life but at least they did what they could and delayed their departure long enough to ensure that he was laid to rest with some semblance of dignity. There are other bodies on Everest that have not been offered such respect.

> *We climb by ourselves, by our own efforts, on the big mountains...*
> *Above 8,000 metres is not a place where people can afford morality.*[17]
> Japanese climber Eisuke Shigekawa

There is probably some truth to the above statement, in circumstances where trying to help someone else in such a challenging environment would threaten one's own survival, but for me, Zac Zaharias, Brian Laursen, Michael Cook, Tim Robathan and other members of the AAA Team, together with Sherpas from Russell Brice's American *Himex Expedition* who helped to lay Mark to rest, demonstrated that there are moments when morality can indeed survive on high mountains.

In Part IV of this book, I tackle this question of morality and values in more depth, with regard to leadership. It seems that it is not as straight forward as we'd like to think, especially when competing priorities prevail.

One and All
Brian (Henri) Laursen was the only one from the AAA Team to physically reach the summit with his climbing Sherpas Chhewang Nima and Ngima Nuru. When Henri arrived at the top at 11.30am on May 25th, there were eight other climbers there who had summited from the south side. Henri had 35 minutes on the summit so after the others left, he did get some time alone on the patch of snow at the highest place on earth.

While his two Sherpa friends watched silently, he knelt down and gently placed a sprig of wattle on the snow. After the Annapurna tragedy, the AAA Team had been given this wattle from Governor-General William Deane's garden in Canberra. A small white card with the names of the three who were killed in the avalanche, signed by Sir William Deane with his condolences, was attached to the wattle sprig by a green ribbon. The Governor-General suggested that the expedition could take it with them up the mountain and place it at the highest point that they were able to reach.

It was decided the night before the group of four departed from their Top Camp that Henri would be the one entrusted to carry it because he had been moving well up the mountain. Back at Base Camp the whole expedition team had previously had a discussion about the composition of their teams, during which Henri essentially said: *If some of us get to the top, we all get there. We're all part of the summit team.*

> ***When one man climbs, the rest are lifted up.***
> *When We Were Kings*—Brian McKnight.

As it happened Henri was the 'one man' to get there in the end and managed to take Peter, Michelle and KC with him all the way to the top. He fulfilled his commitment to them and the rest of the team when he placed the small but significant memento on the summit of the world.

To have reached the top was a very emotional experience. *It was a huge relief,* he recalls. *Physically and emotionally, I was drained.* The emotion that he felt on the summit was a mix of relief and elation, for having finally arrived there after a 9 year journey, and grief for the lives lost.

Henri sent a heartfelt message of thanks to the support teams below him, before sticking his axe in the snow, then hanging his backpack, water bottle and camera over it. He could then finally take in the moment he had been dreaming of for almost a decade. The depth of emotional intensity that Henri experienced during those few minutes of solitude at 8,850m must have been palpable by his two Sherpa friends, as they too had experienced the journey of tragedy and triumph.

When Henri returned from the summit, weary and euphoric, his emotions were up and down as he recounted his experience. He was asked if he would come back. *I would think hard before coming back,* Henri said, as he visibly choked back his emotion. *This mountain throws everything at you; horrendous weather, deep snow, and rock climbing all the way to the summit. You've gotta have your wits about you to make sure you get back to your tent,* he said. *At 8000m it is a different game. To have finally overcome all of that is a pretty good feeling... climbing mountains is an emotional thing,* he said as his voice broke.

When I finished interviewing Henri on the phone, he said he had two young boys now and he had given up climbing big mountains. *I couldn't put them through that,* he said. Tim also said that the 2001 Everest expedition had a huge effect on him. *It totally changed my life,* he said. *It took me two years before I went back into the mountains. The psychological scars have an impact. The hardest thing was coming home. No one can really understand what you've been through. One minute you're below the summit of Everest struggling for life and 2 weeks later you are in suburbia. You think you're okay but small things can bring it all back,* Tim Said. *I still think about Mark now and again, usually May 24 each year. Mark's passing had a pretty big impact on me.*

Sacred Mother Mountain of old
Keep loving care of our brother's soul.
Wayne

Chapter 5   Tributes to a Magnificent Human Being

I remember Mark's memorial service as if it were yesterday...

As I sat in the Chapel of St Peter's College, with hundreds of others who came to pay their respects and celebrate Mark's extraordinary life, I saw an assortment of adventure gear and other symbols on the stage together with photographs of Mark that represented his essence. I sat in silence and looked at the 'Order of Service' booklet that I held in my hands. As I looked at his smiling face and read the words beneath it, my heart overflowed with gratitude for having known him and with grief for having lost this most precious friend.

The words beneath his photograph said it all.

Courageous   **Compassionate**
Inspiring   **Loving**
Strong   **Honest**
Caring   **Understanding**
Open Hearted   **Unassuming**

A number of people spoke at Mark's memorial service, including friends, family, clients and expedition members.

Mark's brother Geoff spoke of Mark's strength and fearless spirit
Mark was capable, skilled, and strong in body and mind. He was an inspiration to all who knew him and many who didn't. Mark would be humbled at the 100s of tributes which have poured in over the last few weeks and for the number and diversity of people who were here to honour and remember him today. We feel that Mark would not want us to mourn his death for too long but would wish us to celebrate his life and to remember the values he stood for. If he thought that in some way he had changed our lives for the better and inspired us to extend ourselves, rise to a challenge, or realise a dream, he would be delighted.

David Tingay, the expedition doctor, represented the SA Everest Team
In a lot of ways, I resent that mountain but I understand what it meant to Mark. During the expedition Mark displayed a quiet confidence and a settling manner. These were exciting days for us. The freedom and sense of purpose was very apparent but there was always that sense of apprehension, and yet Mark would always come in smiling when he returned to Base Camp. He was never tired. Somehow he managed to show us the qualities we thought we didn't have. He showed us the way things should be.

Allan Keogh, represented corporate clients and colleagues
Mark profoundly affected all those who came into contact with him. His lessons were simple, subtle and profound. Mark's philosophy included 'honouring the ordinary because that will encourage the extra-ordinary' and 'acting out of choice, rather than need or ego', said Allan.

During the week after Mark's death numerous tributes were also reported in the local media. The tributes that follow are a few of many that emphasised Mark's qualities of character over his achievements.

Comments from Mark's Family
Mark rests in peace, embraced by the mountains that fascinated and challenged him... Mark was always true to, and cared for, his mates in life, and we all admired him for this... We congratulate Duncan and his Sherpas, who achieved their joint goal for which Mark had worked so hard.

The Advertiser—May 26, 2001

Appreciation from a client group—A Tribute from ATSIC[18]
Mark, you encouraged us to look at our own fears and to face each challenge with courage and belief. You inspired so many people with your own courage, belief and vision so that we could succeed as individuals if we were prepared to believe in ourselves and have the determination to succeed. Courage is a special kind of knowledge. From this knowledge comes an inner strength that inspires us to do what seems impossible. Your courage and achievements are testimony to a man in pursuit of an inner vision with spiritual awareness. Your passion for life and the land, and your empathy with indigenous Australians made your work with us all the more meaningful. As a caring, understanding, passionate and sensitive man, you inspired us to stretch ourselves that little bit further. We cherish the moments we shared together. You shall remain an inspiration to us all.

The Advertiser—June 1, 2001

Words from the Outdoor Education Association SA
Following, are some of the words read out by Scott Polley at the *OEASA* Presentation Dinner on June 1, 2001 before presenting the inaugural *Mark Auricht Award* for Outstanding Achievement in Year 12 Outdoor Education.

Mark's contributions to the South Australian Outdoor Education and Recreation community were significant... but Mark was remarkable not only for his deeds but for the person that he was. He was an extraordinary person and yet an ordinary person also. He was a person of principle who listed among his associates those with little and those with substantial means. He always had time for you even when he didn't have time for you. He was strong and yet vulnerable. Courageous and yet scared, pragmatic but deeply caring. He was passionate about fostering the development of others and has been a mentor to many outdoor education leaders in South Australia.

Journal of the Outdoor Educators Association SA—August 2001

The Bluff—Victor Harbor, SA

Mark's memorial service was followed by the unveiling of a plaque at the *Auricht Adventure Tower* in the Adelaide Hills where he conducted many of his adventure-based learning experiences with corporate and 'youth at risk' groups. The plaque simply reads:-

In memory of Mark Auricht.
***When the spirit of adventure calls to our hearts,
we must go.***

Every now and then I have the opportunity to take a group to the high ropes course or the adventure tower at Woodhouse, facilities that were both established by Mark. Whenever I am there I always take a moment to silently acknowledge him and say a prayer of gratitude for this most magnificent human being.

Alive Among the Mountains

I once asked Mark what made him want to go back to the mountains of the Himalaya after the tragedy he experienced on Makalu. He had this to say:-

It's difficult to answer that question with much of a rational explanation, given the risks that are involved in climbing Everest. I love the mountains and the physical challenge involved in exploring my personal potential. I've always had a fascination with standing on top of the highest point on the globe. Perhaps because it represents the ultimate in what's possible? Makalu gave me a heightened appreciation of life and a gratitude for being alive. I remember abseiling down from Camp 3 to Camp 2 after surviving the ordeal on Makalu and literally feeling the oxygen coming back into my body. I guess it makes no sense to those who would ask why I would risk my life again.

As I stood on the ledge on my way back to safety on Makalu, I remember how beautiful the day was. I could see white puffy clouds below me; they looked so close that I could reach out and touch them.

All I can say is I just love the mountains. They are one of the most beautiful places on earth and I feel so alive when I am amongst them.

May Mark rest in peace in the arms of Chomolungma—Mother Goddess of the Universe.

Chapter 5—Tributes to a Magnificent Human Being

Among the Glorious Mountains—Lobuje East, 1998

At the end of Mark's memorial service his family played Andrea Bocelli's *Time to Say Goodbye*.

Whenever I hear it I remember him, as if he were sending a message across the mountains.

Mostra a tutti il mio cuore
Show everyone my heart

La luce che, hai incontrato per strada
The light you encountered on the street

Tu mia luna tu sei qui con me
You, my moon, are here with me

Time to Say Goodbye

Andrea Bocelli

AURICHT FAMILY PHOTOGRAPHS

In the path of our happiness,
we shall find the learning for which we have chosen this lifetime.
Adapted from Richard Bach,
Illusions: The Adventures of a Reluctant Messiah

Chapter 6 The Path of His Happiness

While Mark was perhaps best known by most people as an Adventurer or Mountaineer, he had many facets, some less well known and quite possibly more important. In this chapter I share a brief summary of Mark's life beyond the mountains, including some family history, some memories of his early adventures and other aspects of his multi-faceted life.

It is often said of those who die pursuing a dream or a passion, that *they died doing what they loved,* as if this would provide some comfort to those who suffer the loss of their loved one. It has become somewhat of a cliché, but the truth is that Mark followed *the path of his happiness* for most of his life, marching to the beat of his heart's drum until it could beat no further. Perhaps having learned the lessons that his soul had chosen for this lifetime, it was time to complete his journey, surrounded by the mountains he loved.

The renowned mythologist Joseph Campbell, author of *The Hero with a Thousand Faces,* encourages us to follow our bliss... *the path of our happiness,* you might say.

The goal of life is to make your heartbeat match the beat of the Universe, to match your nature with Nature.
Joseph Campbell

Mark certainly did this by following his adventurous and sometimes audacious dreams. His name can be found on most of the cairns on peaks throughout the Flinders Ranges where his love for the South Australian outback, for camping, hiking, and getting to the top of mountains was first nurtured. He would often sign off his letters with... *Yours in adventure, Mark.* such was his identification with living an adventurous life and inspiring others to explore their potential, including those less fortunate.

Snow and mountains always held a fascination for Mark. He was a keen cross-country and down-hill skier, and an expert in the construction of igloos and snow shelters, although his brothers would say he preferred to sleep outside of them.

Mark's cousin Chris Hodge recalls a trip with Mark and his brothers to the Gammon Ranges. *Mark had a plan to spend 3-4 days hiking into the park and surviving on whatever we could carry. One night, we pitched camp at the top of a ridge overlooking the Gammons.*

Mark was keen to see the sun rise before anyone else, so he got as close to the cliff edge as possible and then tied himself (in his sleeping bag) to a sturdy bush. We thought he was crazy but even back then, Mark was prepared to go that little bit further than anyone else to experience something wonderful.

Chris has fond memories of family adventures and credits Mark with inspiring him to pursue a more adventurous life. *We spent wonderful times together exploring and usually climbing something high. We learned a lot from Mark's father, my uncle Clive, and together we developed a love for the outdoors. We did some excellent bike rides, cross country skiing through the Victorian High Country and hiked the Overland Trail at the end of year 12. Mark got me involved in scuba diving and we did a brilliant dive off the Blow Hole near Pondalowie on York Peninsula,* says Chris.

I'll never forget the day my phone rang to tell me that Mark had died on the mountain. The sense of loss was utterly overwhelming, but in the years since, I've reflected a lot on Mark's philosophy and have been inspired by his adventurous spirit. I've since gone on to do a number climbs and treks in Africa, the Himalayas, Borneo and Europe. I've also pursued the family connection to PNG, trekking the Kokoda trail a couple of times. I've no doubt that Mark's influence has changed my life... I am eternally grateful, said Chris.

A Father's Words about his son – Clive Auricht

Mark was such a special son who touched the lives of so many people and who was making such an impact on industrial relations throughout Australia, to an extent that we had not previously comprehended. His goal was much bigger than Mt Everest. He was set to conquer the mountain of life in all its manifestations. The family has erected a fitting memorial to Mark, located at the site of his Great Grandfather's memorial in the Langmeil Church Cemetery in Tanunda. The family has a tradition of tending these sites, then going for a picnic on the Tanunda oval, so it has great significance to us.

As part of the dedication of Mark's Memorial at Langmeil on July 1, 2001, Clive shared the following details of the Auricht Family history.

Family History

Mark was the son of Clive and Ruth Auricht. (Clive remarried some years later to Helen). It all began with Mark's great–great grandfather Christian Auricht, born at Klastawae east of Berlin, in 1806. He was a blacksmith and Elder of the Lutheran Church with a presumed historical link to the town of Auricht in West Germany near the North Sea. In 1839 Christian Auricht, together with hundreds of other refugees took a 4-5 month voyage from Hamburg to Australia on a ship called the *Catharina* to escape religious persecution in Germany.

Christian Auricht's 2nd son, Johann Christian, later became a Pastor at the Langmeil Church in Tanunda where he now rests in peace. Mark's memorial was placed nearby in July 2001.

The village of Hahndorf was named after Captain Hahn, who sailed one of the ships from Hamburg. The old family home established by great great uncle Theodore Auricht who was the doctor at Hahndorf still stands in Hahndorf on the corner of Echunga Road and Auricht Road, the street named after Dr Theodore Auricht.

Mark's Grandfather was the Reverend Canon Ernst Oswald Auricht, born in 1901. After becoming an Anglican priest Ernst served at Angaston in the Barossa Valley. According to Mark's father Clive, Ernst was the most selfless, caring person he ever knew.

By Faith, Not Arms
The Auricht Coat of Arms appears on the first page of the book: *From Persecution to Freedom – A History and Family Tree of Christian Auricht*. The motto on the Coat of Arms reads: **Fide non Armis** which means *By Faith, not Arms*.

The colours of the Coat of Arms also have meaning.
RED: *fortitude, valour, patriotism, creative power*
WHITE: *nobility, serenity and peace*
GOLD: *celestial light, joy and honour*
BLACK: *resolve to live a more responsible life*

Through Faith not Arms

These characteristics reflect the values of the Auricht family and were certainly values that Mark strove to live by. He is among the family's 6th generation in South Australia—a family with involvement in a wide spectrum of careers, many that involve caring for and helping others to strive for and achieve meaningful purpose in their life—*By Faith, not Arms*.

Medicine Beyond Kokoda
In later chapters I will share a few of my own stories about Papua New Guinea (PNG). It wasn't until some years after Mark's death that I discovered that his family also had a strong connection with PNG. Mark's father Clive wrote a book first published in 2011 titled *Medicine Beyond Kokoda*. In it he writes about some of the family history and his early life as a doctor bringing up a family in Papua New Guinea. I found this fascinating reading and it gave me a greater appreciation for the 'adventure' genes that Mark and his siblings had obviously inherited.

Mark's father, Clive was born in 1935, four years before World War II. His early years were spent watching the advance of the German and Japanese armies. The Japanese advanced all the way from Japan to Papua New Guinea which at that time was a territory of Australia. Our regular army was fighting in North Africa and our country was poorly prepared for war. A Militia Army (Army Reserve) was hastily cobbled together and young 19-year-olds with next to no training bore the brunt of the defence of Australia along the Kokoda Track until the regular soldiers could arrive to join them at Isurava, a day's walk from Kokoda.

When Clive was a young man he was awarded the Queen's Scout Badge at Government House which was scouting's highest award. It is not surprising then that Mark became a keen outdoors man and took on many of the values of his father. After matriculating Clive gained a Commonwealth Scholarship in Medicine at Adelaide University and later spent 5 years in Papua New Guinea as a doctor attending to the local communities from Kokoda to the northern coast. He first went to PNG in December 1956 as a 4th yr medical student. He returned to PNG after his 5th yr of studying medicine and again in 1959. His experiences forever changed how he would practice medicine and embedded in him a very deep respect for the complexities facing indigenous people and those living in rural and remote areas. Mark too had a deep appreciation of indigenous cultures and connection to the land, both here in Australia, and also in Nepal and Tibet.

After Clive Auricht's post graduate year he was posted to PNG to continue his work there as a doctor from 1961 to 1963. Both of Mark's older brothers, Richard and Geoff spent their earliest years living in PNG and when Mark came along in August 1963, the decision was made to settle back in South Australia to take care of their growing family. Mark's younger brother David and sister, Elizabeth, were later born in Adelaide—and so the Auricht brood began!

The Auricht Brood—Mark, David, Richard, Lil, Geoff

Chapter 6—The Path of His Happiness

THE MANY FACETS OF MARK

The path of Mark's happiness lead him in many directions. He became a multi-faceted man with a deep compassion for people and a passion for personal development. I've heard some stories from friends, but his family summed up the various facets of his life best, when they shared their cherished memories at Mark's memorial service.

An Active Lad
Mark was active from the very beginning with energetic kicks from the womb forewarning his mother of what was to come. As a toddler he was restrained in shops with a chest harness attached to a lead. None-the-less his exuberance inevitably lead to the rearrangement of the contents on the shop shelves. Messing around at home with his siblings as a young lad, Mark was a key partner in the construction of go-karts, skate boards, model aeroplanes and joined in enthusiastically with activities such as catapulting fruit into neighbouring properties.

School Days
Mark's formal education started at Westbourne Park Primary School and then from year 5 to year 12 at St Peter's College. Amongst many stories from his years at Saints, Mark's lunchtime activities included piggyback fights, red rover games and big brother baiting. A fearless Mark would often return home with torn or grubby shirts and the occasional slight burn on the back of his legs from being held down on a classroom heater by one of his brothers.

Mark returned to St Peter's College many years later to address the next generation of young men. He shared his mountaineering exploits, lessons on leadership and his plans for his forthcoming Everest Expedition. His talk was well received and inspiring. The whole school was keen to follow his progress.

A Keen Sportsman
In school sports Mark was best remembered for his rugby. Active but by no means large in stature, he was a natural half-back. Mark represented the school in this role for many years, including First 15 and he represented the State at the Under 18 level.

During his school years and at Flinders University Mark trained in the martial arts of Tae Kwon Do and Judo (rest assured his brothers stopped sitting him on the heater after that). Like Kato from the Pink Panther movies, Mark would stalk his younger siblings Dave and Lil at home and wrestle them to the floor as part of his training.

Mark was also into running, cycling, triathlons and rogaining: the sport of long distance cross-country navigation involving route planning and prioritising. Water sports were always a favourite of Mark's. He was keen and highly competent at swimming, water polo, sailing and canoeing but his most favourite water sport was water skiing at which he excelled. Camping trips to Morgan on the Murray River with friends and the family boat 'The Oracle', gave Mark the chance to develop spectacular stunts, such as barefoot starts from a height in overhanging gum trees. Mark's strength and fearless spirit made for spectacular viewing, and nightmares for his mum.

A Leader in a Crisis

A university friend, Marion Leggo, also speaks of Mark's ability to stay calm in a crisis and to take leadership in difficult circumstances...

Mark was an adventurous, popular and lovable man. He approached life with enthusiasm and moulded his life according to his plan. I will be forever grateful for Mark assisting me after a serious water skiing accident where he demonstrated his specialist skills in first aid and his ability to take control of a challenging situation. His survival skills also came to the fore during a hiking trip to the Grampians where we had veered off course and had to make a treacherous journey back to safety. All the while he kept our spirits up and maintained his sense of humour while leading us home. I am privileged to have known such a magnificent man.

Mark the Scholar and Business Person

After finishing Year 12 in 1980, Mark attended Flinders University where he completed a Bachelor of Education majoring in Physical Education in 1984. From there he went on to work at the 'Royal Society for the Blind' for three years, followed by a stint with 'One-on-One Executive Fitness,' before establishing his own business, 'Venture Corporate Recharge' in 1989-90.

While working, Mark studied part-time to complete a Graduate Diploma in Counselling at UniSA and completed a Graduate Diploma in Psychology at Deakin University. He also constantly pursued personal and professional development as his business grew to become one of South Australia's most respected companies.

Outdoor Education Advocate

Mark's contribution to the South Australian Outdoor Education community included being treasurer, assessor and board member of the 'Rock Climbing Education Association,' an advisor and assessor for 'Bushwalking Leadership SA,' and a member of the 'Outdoor Educators' Association.'

Philanthropist

Much of Mark's study and work was focused on helping others. Apart from his work in the corporate world, he also ran programs for 'at risk' young people and quietly gave of his time and money to other causes that very few people knew about. His father speaks of his reticence to talk much about himself and what he was up to, *It was on rare occasions that I was able to grasp an awareness of Mark's activities.* At one time when there had been a lot going on in the media about the street kids in Adelaide at night, Mark quietly said to his father—*Dad, I can walk anywhere around Adelaide at night and I know I will be looked after.* Mark confided in his father that he would sometimes invite a 'street lad' along on one of his adventure trips, such as canoeing on the Murray River or hiking in the Flinders Ranges. *Sometimes he would persuade a business to help him fund this activity, but mostly he financed it through his own business,* Clive said. *He must have helped rescue many young homeless people that way and made Adelaide a safer place at night.*[19]

> **Climbing to the summits of our success in life are often fleeting moments in the bigger picture of our soul's journey. That which endures most is not what we achieve at any point in time, but what we learn and who we become, as we journey across life's horizons in pursuit of our dreams.**

Mark the Homely Man

While Mark was more widely known for his more manly adventures, he was also a lover of family and other interests that made him a well-rounded person. Among Mark's other interests were cooking, gardening and carpentry. He was also a reader of poetry and a musician. His musical tastes ranged from The Angels to Mozart. He loved to play the clarinet and those who have camped with him will likely have heard the wail of his harmonica late in the night as he enjoyed a few quiet moments around the campfire.

Mark and his wife Catherine, shared a loving life together for over 10 years, enjoying a deep, rich and fulfilling relationship. They recognised and explored in each other the broad boundaries of themselves and their world and were wonderful and supportive companions for one another.

Mark was very proud of Catherine and her son Tom, to whom he was a loving stepfather, friend and an inspiration. To his nephews and nieces too, he was a special uncle, whether he was setting them up with ropes and climbing gear in his backyard tree, twirling them over his shoulder or just listening to what they had to say, he'd always be present for them and was very much loved. Mark recognised so much of himself in his dearly loved parents and was truly grateful for the values they'd instilled in him.

Soul Mate

> *A true soul mate is someone who causes your soul to grow.*
> *That is what we did for each other.*
> Catherine Auricht-Crease

To those outside family I am known as Catherine Auricht-Crease but Mark always called me Cass. He and I were soul mates—a term that is a bit of a cliché perhaps. We caused each other's soul to grow and for that I am eternally grateful.

Mark had a quiet strength about him. I was with him for about ten years before I realised how stubborn he was. He was so gentle, so even tempered and reasonable, such a great listener, and so it never occurred to me that he also had such a strong will when he wanted to do something. What I came to know about Mark was that he was someone who was absolutely going to live his dreams. A lot of us talk about our dreams and things we might do one day—Mark lived them and from a young age was always going to climb Everest. He knew the risks, like all mountaineers do and was prepared to accept them responsibly. He had climbed so many mountains, it was a natural progression that he wanted to climb the highest.

Mark took his dreams and fashioned them into his life, which was wonderfully full and successful. Perhaps his biggest challenge was finding the time to do all the things he loved. In the media he was known as an adventurer but he also loved practising the clarinet, listening to Mozart and reciting poetry. Mark was a busy person. He completed three university degrees, was an advocate for the outdoor education community, ran a successful business and yet still found time for family and friends, and for giving to the less fortunate. He would always make time for people—if someone walked into his office they would never know that he was highly stressed with workload pressure. He would most often take the time to sit and have a chat even though he really did not have the time. He was a magnificent human being who had such a special empathy for people and touched something in everybody he met.

I knew Mark had done a lot of fabulous things in his business, but I didn't realise how creative he was until I got more involved and saw what he had created. He invested so much back into the business and could have made more money if he worked alone and consulted from home. However, he had a different purpose—he wanted to provide employment and enjoyed giving young people opportunities for growth. Mark wanted the ten years that he'd invested to be of sustained value beyond his own input, into the future. I really wanted to honour Mark and do justice to what he'd created, so I spent the year after his death doing my best to keep his business running until it could be sold.

Mark and I had many plans and then suddenly they were gone. It was like I had a map of where we were headed and then suddenly it was taken from me. I had to somehow redraw another map that provided some sense of purpose to me. Losing Mark has been the hardest thing that has happened to me in my life. The pain was indescribable—like someone had driven a truck through my heart. I struggled to breathe every day. Some nights I would go to bed and really not care whether I woke up but for some reason I knew I would be ok.

There is so much growth that happens with pain and loss. I have realised that the important aspects of life are our relationships, having love in our life, growing, learning and giving. The constant challenge is to stay clear about what is important and the most important aspect for me is love. Mark was a wonderful step-father to Tom, who said that Mark was the most genuine person he'd known and that he would have been the perfect human being, if only he had not climbed mountains and worked so hard. Tom found the loss of Mark's love and guidance as hard as the rest of us.

In a way Mark did not leave me. I climbed Black Hill recently, for the first time since his death. Mark and I used to go there while training for his expeditions. It was beautiful actually, I felt his spirit there... I really felt his spirit. There are times when I catch myself, and it's not that I am Mark, but it's like, well... there is a sense that we are one.

During the second night after he died, I went to bed and felt him arrive... I actually felt him arrive in my being and stay. He would say *I love you Cass.* I would not hear the words but I felt the vibration of them in my heart and knew he was with me. Since then he has been with me every day and that will forever sustain me.

Excerpts from Interview with Catherine by Katrina Webb, 2004

Cass and Mark—Skydiving together

The Mountain of Life

Mark's original business logo depicted a person getting out from behind their desk and climbing a mountain, standing tall with arms outstretched to the sky, reaching for their highest potential. This reflects the endeavour required to achieve one's purpose in life. On his memorial stone at Langmeil there is a picture of a mountain too. It represents *the mountain of life* which he strived to climb and to help others to climb as well. He now lies at rest in peace amidst the beauty of the mountains.

Auricht Family lay a plaque for Mark at Everest Base Camp Tibet May 2017

This short summary of Mark's life includes some extraordinary achievements and talents by anyone's standards. At the same time it only scratches the surface of the value he brought to the world in which he lived for such a short time. His greatest achievements, I believe, were the quality of the relationships he had with his wife, his family, his friends and those he served so generously and authentically.

Mark gained a lot of valuable knowledge through his education and devotion to personal and professional development but he didn't just have an intellectual understanding of his profession, he also had an extraordinary depth of innate wisdom about people and how to inspire and nurture them to become the best they could be. His way with people came from the heart and not from the ego. It was his authenticity, vulnerability and humble example that earned him the right to be known as a masterful teacher and facilitator. Perhaps his greatest teaching was the subtle influence he had by setting an example for others as he "fashioned his dreams into his life" as his wife Catherine so eloquently put it. The final words on his memorial service booklet capture this truth.

And the Master said unto the silence,
"In the path of our happiness shall we find the learning for which we have chosen this lifetime. So it is that I have learned this day, and chosen to leave you now to walk your own path, as you please."
Richard Bach—*Illusions*

Chapter 7   Discovering the Treasure Within

*I climbed a mountain and I turned around
I saw my reflection in the snow covered hills*
Stevie Nicks—*Landslide*

 This morning I've been reflecting on a movie I saw last night called *Into the Wild*, based on the book of the same title, by Jon Krakauer[20]. It was one of those movies that seemed to speak directly to me, a movie about following a dream. Often dreams come and go in our sleep, some having a deeper meaning than we can fathom. Then there are the dreams that have our name on them. As if implanted in our heart, they call us from the deep. Those of us who have been brave enough to follow a dream that calls to our heart without being certain of the outcome, will often discover treasures where we least expect to find them.

As I reflect on the power of dreams, a parable comes to me and I begin to write…

Parable of 'The Treasure'—Written November, 2007
It was one such dream that called a young man to the mountains, encouraging him to take a journey to a distant land. The journey would take many weeks and would involve overcoming unexpected obstacles that would stretch his inner resources and test his spirit.

In the dream, his journey lead to a golden castle in the sky on top of a snow covered mountain peak. The castle on the summit would not be his destination however, it would only be a beacon marking the way to a bridge on the path below the summit. Under the bridge in this dream, a treasure would be waiting for him that would change his life.

'A strange but inspiring dream' he thought, after waking from it the first time. To begin with, he didn't believe he should follow the dream but after years of having the same dream night after night he decided to heed its call and to set off on the journey. On his journey he met other pilgrims who had similar dreams but theirs made no mention of a bridge, only a gold castle at the summit.

When he finally arrived at the bridge on the mountain, he dismissed it in favour of following the others who were seeking the shining castle of gold on the summit. After all, the bridge was old and weathered, with sagging boards heavy with snow. There was no sign of any treasure beneath it.

As he drew closer to the summit he heard the call once more in his heart "come back to the bridge and you will find the treasure." A battle began to rage between his mind that wanted to keep climbing to the castle and his heart which called him back to the bridge. In the end his heart won and he turned around to follow the mountain trail back to the bridge.

When he arrived at the bridge exhausted, there was no-one there and no treasure to be found. He sat disheartened on the step of the bridge looking out across the endless mountain landscape as the sun was setting across the snow. He thought about his family... how could he go home without the treasure? Should he have kept going to the Golden Castle in the sky and return as others did to a hero's welcome or was following the dream that called him to the bridge in the first place, the right choice? Did God have a greater purpose for him or was this just his ego's dream? His head struggled with these questions while his heart felt a longing to become one with the landscape.

There in the silent still solitude of the snow surrounded by the pink and purple hues of a glorious sunset he saw his reflection mirrored in the ice. He reflected on his life journey and all that he'd achieved along the way. After a long period of stillness in his mind he came to the realisation that the treasure was not a chest full of material wealth and trophies. He realised in that moment that he did not need to do anything more than to simply stay connected to his heart and allow his authentic self to fully shine in the world.

He suddenly felt free, free to listen to his inner desires and let go of the expectations of others. Credentials did not determine his identity. His life path was determined by expressing his deepest longings and passions without ego. This is what he had always done when he was living authentically. For a time he had lost his way, pursuing a different kind of treasure.

His love of and connection to the landscape of the mountains was the real treasure he was seeking. It reflected the landscape within him. This was the treasure under the bridge where he sat, the treasure he came in search of, the golden truth that he knew deep in his heart. He reclaimed his treasure at the bridge on the snow laden peak as the light faded behind the mountainous horizon, and there on the bridge holding the treasure in his heart, he fell into a deep sleep.

While he slept he had another dream... an old bearded man dressed in tattered saffron robes, skin as tough as leather, eyes peeping through weathered lids, sat beside him in the snow and spoke to him in Tibetan tongue. Though the pilgrim's mind could only understand some words, his heart understood with much clarity...

"Your journey is not uncommon," said the old man. "Many hear the call of the wild. For some it's a return to childhood dreams, for others it's a test to know that they have what it takes. Many seek the golden summit without being aware of the secret destinations of a sacred journey, but a few like you will discover the hidden treasures along the way," he said.

"To reclaim one's heart and soul, one needs to get away from the noise and distraction of daily life and head into the silence and solitude of the wilderness for time alone, where hidden treasures can come to the surface and be remembered..." he said, bowing his head respectfully.

"What matters most on the journey, are not achievements measured by worldly expectations but how deeply you see, how attentively you hear and how richly your experience is felt in your soul. These are the real treasures that matter in the end, treasures that can only be discovered by the heart... treasures that must be shared with the world to be of value." With that, the sage with no name disappeared.

Along the path, one must turn back in order to seek oneself.
Meng Zi

Into The Wild

The message shared by the old sage in the above parable, is highlighted in the movie *Into the Wild*, which is based on the true story of Christopher McCandless, a young man who leaves his suburban life in North America, to take a two year journey up to the Alaskan wilderness. He dreams of living alone in the wild, surviving off the land, attuned to the rhythms of nature. He is transformed by the experience and writes in his journal each day about the beauty of nature with all its challenges and peak experiences that transcend the noise, facades and man-made rules of the civilised world that disconnect us from our soul. There he finds his soul's true strength.

> ***I also know how important it is in life, not necessarily to be strong but to feel strong. To measure yourself at least once. To find yourself at least once in the most ancient of human conditions. Facing the blind deaf stone alone, with nothing to help you but your hands and your own head.***
> Christopher McCandless (AKA—Alexander Supertramp)

McCandless is inspired by his experience alone in the wild but realises that he will not be truly happy unless he has someone to share it with, so at the end of the winter he attempts to return from the wild only to find that the river he crossed at the beginning of winter on his way into the wilderness, is now a raging torrent fed by thawing ice and snow. His attempts to cross the river lead to a near-drowning in the fast moving current. After recovering from his near-death experience he decides not to tempt fate any further and returns to his camp (an abandoned old bus he calls 'The Magic Bus'). He then makes the mistake of eating some seeds, unaware that they have toxic side-effects, ultimately leading to his death. The last words in his journal describe his impending death and the insights he gained from his time in the wilderness. His most poignant revelation is that the freedom he enjoyed and the beauty of life he experienced is worth nothing without the opportunity to share it.

> *Solitude is where we learn, what we can only learn alone.*
> *To share our learning for the benefit of others is a precious gift.*

In Mark's life and death and in these stories that I have shared, there lies a beautiful and yet sometimes tragic truth for all of us—that is, that we often seek self-actualisation, truth and life's treasures outside of ourselves, only to discover that they are really part of our inner landscape, waiting to be revealed. Solitude helps us to find our treasure and to learn what we can only learn alone. At the same time, our treasure is of little value without someone to share it with. This is the blessing and the challenge of relationships, a balance that requires a love beyond understanding.

Among the Solitude
Fortunately Mark had already explored vast areas of his inner world and had the generosity to share a lot of his treasures with others before he graduated from this life, and yet, part of me feels that he had more to share about the deeper connection he had to the wild places he loved and the personal journeys that he experienced. In my mind, one of the tragedies associated with his loss was that he didn't get to share more about this. I do recall one story though, shared by a friend, of a time when Mark was alone in the mountains after taking a detour to an old trapper's hut by himself

while others walked on. In telling the story, Mark shared how amazing he felt during that time alone in the silence of the snow and expressed that his underlying passion for mountains was not just about summiting them. While that was a tangible reason for climbing mountains and fulfilled his desire to challenge himself, it was somewhat of a justification for just being 'among them'—in the same way that some people go fishing for the solitude, not the fish!

> *How beautiful a day it was, white puffy clouds below me*
> *as far as the eye could see, so close I could almost reach out and touch*
> *them. These mountains I love are the most beautiful place on earth.*
> *I feel so alive when I am among them.*
> Mark Auricht

I too, remember a day like this earlier this year, just before finishing the first draft of this manuscript. It was in January 2016 while trekking with a group through the *Los Glaciers National Park* in Patagonia Argentina. This beautifully pristine place is just across the border from Southern Chile where the winds from Antarctica gust across the Patagonian Ice Field. During the time we were there though, we were blessed on most days, with glorious clear blue sky.

...We had been trekking for two weeks and on this, the last day of our trek, we had climbed up to a viewpoint on a ridge overlooking a glacier near a place called El Chalten—a popular destination for climbers from all over the world. On every other day I had trekked with others to the summit of a number of hills but on this day I said to myself, "It's not always about getting to the top, I think I'll stay here and just be."

On this day I stayed at the viewpoint while others completed the climb to the summit an hour away, for the 360° view. I instead, sat in solitude on a rock overlooking a glacial lake, back-dropped by snow capped mountains and blue sky. The silence was as pure as the snow, as solid as the granite walls of the huge cliffs and as deep as the freezing lake of ice before me. So beautiful... I cried and cherished this moment of silence and solitude unbroken by the noise of life. I felt within me a deep peace and a connection to this glorious landscape. At peace, calm and silent, I almost felt that Mark could have been sitting alongside me saying, "What a pearler of a day..."

Fitzroy Glacier—El Chalten Patagonia, 2016

Bringing Back the Boon

Sometimes I wish I was around in the Ancient Greek times with Socrates and Plato, where ideas were challenged and philosophies explored. It is often, not until we discuss our opinions, that we discover a deeper understanding.

While reviewing this chapter with Gabrielle, we discussed the apparent contradiction between seeking solitude to 'find oneself', and seeking relationships where we can share our self-discoveries and enjoy shared experiences. Todd Sampson said that *exploration can sometimes be seen as undeniably selfish and yet it is also how we come to understand ourselves.*

Solitude is a place of purification, relationship is a place of sharing.

In Chapter 9, I explore the concept of the *Hero's Journey*[21]—a metaphor for the journeys we all take in life that test us or inspire us in some way. After such experiences we often return with a 'treasure' that we want to share with others. This stage of the *Hero's Journey* is referred to as, 'bringing back the boon' or the blessing, from our travels or challenges. In the next chapter I wish to introduce you to Mark's legacy. Although he didn't get to share the boon of his last adventure with us, I hope to pass on some of the treasures he shared with me and others in his inspiring life.

Adventure is not about conquering nature. It is about the journey within us that takes place when we explore the frontiers of our personal boundaries, taking ourselves to places we normally wouldn't venture to go, and then returning to lead a richer, more colourful life because of our experience!

Chapter 8   The Gift of His Legacy

> *The key to immortality is to live a life worth remembering.*
> Bruce Lee

A Compass for Life, Learning and Leadership
This book is not only a tribute to a friend, as my way of honouring the gifts he shared, it is also a book for those who may not have been fortunate enough to meet Mark, especially young emerging leaders, for which the latter half of this book may serve as a guide. I chose the subtitle *A Compass for Life, Learning and Leadership* because I wanted to somehow provide some continuity of Mark's work in the area of leadership, team and personal development and to share what I see as his legacy.

A *Legacy* is defined as 'a gift handed down from the past'. Its origins come from the word 'legate' which means 'an ambassador or a person sent on a mission'. Some would say that Mark's life was a mission. His work was not just a way to 'make a living,' it was a passion, a gift that he had to share and a higher purpose that he took the risk to pursue. He was indeed an ambassador for all he stood for.

A *Legacy* is also personified as a 'student of a predecessor.' Those who were 'students' of what Mark had to share are also part of his legacy. I for one was heavily influenced by what he taught me. We were colleagues and friends but we were also mentors for each other and his mentorship for me was a significant pillar of my professional and personal development. I suspect that this was the case for many who saw him as a role model and went on to become facilitators, teachers or guides, who continue to live out his legacy today.

It is my belief that when we die, we live on in the lives of others we have touched, as if we were a distant moon influencing their tide. For some this is subtle and hardly measurable, for others it is astounding how much their path is guided by the legacy of those who have influenced them.

Mark, like many of us, may not have been fully aware of the impact that his life had on others, but he had the courage, and some might say, the good fortune, to follow his dreams and fashion them into a life of significance. He was also generous enough to share his treasure for the greatest advantage of others and in doing so lived an inspiring life.

> *Our significance may forever remain obscure to us... but we fulfill it by devoting our talents to the highest advantage of others.*
> Dr. R. Buckminster Fuller

Sharing his Treasure

Today as I write, I look out into the garden and see the trees I planted a few years back. How they have grown and matured, shading me from the sun with their umbrella of leaves. It is summer now and we've had some of the hottest days on record. I notice that one of two young shrubs that I planted back in Autumn has died, while its brother has survived. I wonder about how different our garden will look in ten years with one of these shrubs fully matured and the other no longer part of our garden? This reminds me of my brother Peter, who died when I was in my last year of school, and of Mark. I often wonder about where their trajectory would have taken them if they had lived on. How would they have impacted the world, not only personally but also through the ripple effect of their influence on others? What would they have shared in a book if they'd had a chance to write one?

In the remainder of this book I attempt to explore possible answers to these questions in relation to Mark's life. I express my take on his legacy and I endeavour to share some of his treasure with you. I also write about some of the less obvious ways that Mark has influenced my life journey over the last fifteen years since his passing: some of the directions I have taken; the work I've been drawn to do; and how what I learnt in collaboration with him has evolved to become part of what I too share with the world.

> *A truth or a relationship once experienced, changes our trajectory.*
> *Like one atom colliding innocently with another, changing us forever.*
> *We pay tribute to those who inspire us, not just with words,*
> *but in the way we live our lives thereafter.*

I hope that you find the remainder of this book challenging, thought-provoking and adventurous, but most of all, an authentic sharing of Mark's legacy and some other gems I have found while on the path we once walked together.

PART II

Exploring the Inner Landscape
Our Learning Journey

Brothers Crossing the Dunes—Cervantes, Western Australia, 2005

Part Two of this book tells the story of how Mark and I met after travelling similar paths in our individual lives. It focuses on our learning journey together, as we sought the answers to creating and facilitating optimal learning experiences that influence not only the mind but also the heart.

Life, Learning and Leadership
There are certain lessons that I learned from Mark, together with other influences I have since encountered, that have evolved into what I would collectively call *lessons for life, learning and leadership*. I dare to say that these lessons are valuable gems that are worth sharing with others, and I trust that the following stories will shed light on these gems and serve as an inspiration and a compass for emerging leaders, adventurous souls and anyone interested in personal development.

As the world enters a time of unprecedented change—politically, environmentally, technologically and socially, we must evolve new ways of thinking, living, learning and leading that will help us to navigate the challenging terrain of this new frontier. Through the metaphor of adventure and journey experiences, this book also examines the application of these key lessons to some of the challenges likely to face the next generation.

Writing My Truth

This writing journey has been a challenging experience, as I have sailed ahead through the changing oceans of my own life, while trawling a net behind me in the hope of capturing some truths from the past. The word History provides a clue to the fact that anyone writing about the past is doing just that, telling her or his-story, and I am no different. From here on, I can only speak and write from my own perspective without censoring what I believe to be true. Some people will appreciate these words while others, no doubt, will have a different view. Either way, I have written with honesty and endeavoured to express my truth about what I know of Mark's legacy and how it has played out in my personal experience.

I can't attribute all that I have learnt to Mark alone, as I have been influenced by many other mentors and messengers, together with an interesting mix of life experiences and adventures along the way, but what I do know for sure is that, apart from my wife Gabrielle who has had the biggest influence on my life, Mark was one of a few gracious souls that helped me to explore my inner landscape and discover a unique way of using my gifts to make a difference in the world—he helped me to find what the Native American Indians would call, my *Medicine*.[22] This book is an expression of that *Medicine*, a gift that I pass on with gratitude.

Chapter 9   Metaphor and Mythology

 Most mornings before I write, I'll go for a walk in the bush or along the beach. In summer when the early morning water is calm and warm, I'll dive into the clear blue millpond of the gulf and float for a while, then emerge refreshed and alive as I walk across the cool sand with the morning sun on my face. There is a favourite bench upon which I sit and meditate for a moment, listening to the morning magpies and the rippling reach of the tide swishing along the shoreline. This well worn bench has been there for a few years—in memory of Bert and Elsie, an elderly couple I've not had the pleasure to meet in person, but feel that I have come to know. They loved long strolls along the beach too. This morning, as I sat in silence after my lazy swim, I imagined Bert and Elsie walking arm in arm along the shore and was reminded of a familiar story that is perhaps worth retelling.

MAKING A DIFFERENCE

One morning there was a young boy sitting on a sand hill looking out to sea. The boy noticed an old man strolling along the shore-line. Every now and then the elderly man would bend over and pick something up from the sand, hold it to his heart and then throw it out into the water.

After some time, the boy's curiosity got the better of him and he plucked up the courage to walk up to the old man and asked him what it was that he was throwing into the sea? The old man smiled and pointed along the shoreline in front of him. As far as the boy could see there were hundreds of little starfish washed up on the high tide and baking in the morning sun. The old man explained to the young boy that he was saving the starfish from drying up in the sun and dying there on the beach.

The boy shook his head and said... "How can you possibly think that you're going to make a difference... there are so many of them?" The old man's reply was to pick up another starfish, hold it to his heart and then throw it is far out into the ocean as his elderly arm could manage. With a smile on his face he then said to the boy... "Sure made a difference to that one!"

Adapted from *The Star Thrower*—an essay by Loren Eiseley.
Published in *The Unexpected Universe*, 1969.

I wonder if Bert and Elsie were starfish throwers too… people who inspired others enough to have a bench placed at the beach in their memory. And on this bench as each day passes, strangers sit, not knowing who these elders were but perhaps feeling their presence as they breathe in the morning air or watch the sun setting in the west.

While Mark was not an elderly gentleman like Bert or the old man on the beach, he inspired many people and, for some, made a significant difference to their lives that has rippled on and on. I am certain that I was not the only starfish on the sand, as he took his stroll along life's shore before returning to the deep.

A Deeper Way of Learning
Like the *starfish thrower*, I believe that Mark wanted to make a difference in the world in whatever way he could. His way was humble and he was in some ways covert about what he had to teach. He taught mostly through the mode of adventure-based experiences which served as potent metaphors for life. *Adventure-Based Experiential Learning* (ABEL) was not a new idea at the time—Outdoor Educators had been using it for decades, but I had not realised the power of its 'metaphorical learning' potential until I worked with Mark.

Learning through metaphor can also include experiences beyond the sphere of adventure, such as: simulation games; problem-solving; and the use of music, art or story-telling—the 'Starfish Story' is a good example. Stories and rituals used in religious or indigenous ceremonies also use metaphor to convey a level of understanding that is beyond the rational, linear thinking mind.

> *Metaphor and myth capture the essential nature of things,*
> *somehow by-passing the brain's logical filter,*
> *embedding their insights deep within us.*

Like children, most adults learn less obviously but more deeply from the metaphors in nature, play, fairytales, mythological movies, and life experiences. Unfortunately many of the latest generation have been somewhat insulated from these *metaphorical learning opportunities* in favour of safety, technology-based training and social media. Although most Baby Boomers and Gen-X adults were lucky enough to have a more raw connection with nature and play, we were also brought up with a more strict and formal education system, followed by workplace training which, until recently, was mostly dominated by instruction, flipcharts and 'death by power point.'

Chapter 9—Metaphor and Mythology

> **Becoming an adult can be a wonderful adventure
> if we have not forgotten how to learn.**

In the eighties and nineties many organisations tasted an entrée of adventure-based learning but most of it was an over-emphasis on activity, 'wow' experiences and team bonding at the expense of deeper and more sustainable learning outcomes. Many of us have missed out on artfully facilitated metaphorical learning experiences which reveal the hidden treasures of our inner landscape. Memorable learning experiences such as these, stir our hearts and spirits in ways that can change our inner and outer worlds not just for a fortnight, but forever. This was Mark's gift and passion.

> *I have experienced no greater joy than to witness a person's renewed desire to discover, to learn, to grow, to accept challenge, to risk—just as we did when we were children.*
> Mark Auricht

Mark was an ambassador for metaphorical learning through adventure experiences and I would go so far as to say, was one of the pioneers for its more serious application in the areas of team, leadership and personal development in Australia. Filled with imagination, emotional charge and powerful symbolism, this type of learning impacts us on a gut level that we are yet to fully understand.

Metaphor and mythology are timeless and tap into our innate wisdom. Joseph Campbell's concept of *The Hero's Journey*, referred to in his book—*The Hero with a Thousand Faces*, describes a mythology that most of us are familiar with, where an ordinary person or 'reluctant hero' is called to take an extra-ordinary journey to another world where they must face a series of trials and be tested beyond the edge of their limits. After overcoming adversity they eventually return with a treasure to share with the world. *The Hero's Journey* is often used as a scaffold for good story telling, especially in movies such as *Star Wars* and *Lord of the Rings*. It can also be a metaphor for any individual who takes on the challenges of life, learns from their adversity and shares their wisdom with others. Well designed and facilitated metaphorical learning experiences will often follow this familiar pattern, and subconsciously tap into this mythology which is embedded deep within the human psyche.

Mark Auricht was somewhat of a 'natural' when it came to facilitating metaphorical learning experiences. He certainly wasn't a slick Anthony Robbins type. He engaged people more through his authenticity than 'personality-based charisma.' Those who knew him well would probably say that he was often torn between the priorities in his life and sometimes had an internal struggle between his authentic self and the person that others wanted him to be, but this vulnerable authenticity made him real and relatable. He was thus, a modest and sometimes uncomfortable teacher and his unassuming persona betrayed the truth of his deep wisdom. Mark's use of mythology and metaphor in his ABEL programs opened my eyes to the power of this unique learning methodology.

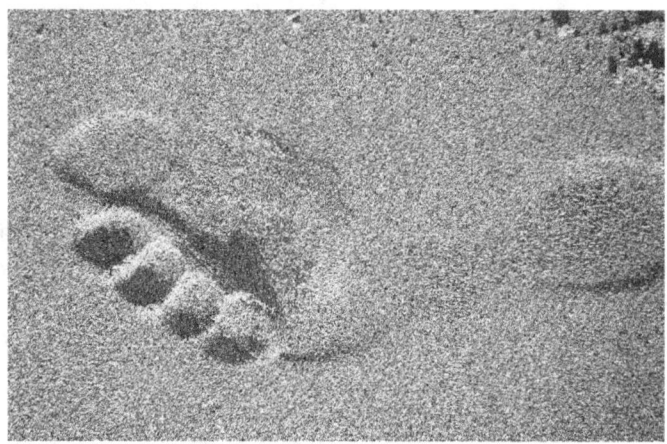

Footprints in the Sand

A question to contemplate

If the footprints you leave on the sand during your walk across life's shore were to make a difference to others, what treasures would your footprints leave behind before death's tide washes them away?

Sometimes the most challenging questions provide valuable answers—this one is worth contemplating next time you walk along a beach.

Chapter 10   Parallel Lifetimes

*Meeting again after moments or lifetimes
is certain for those who are friends.*
Richard Bach—*Illusions*[23]

Before Mark and I met, we both studied a Bachelor of Education majoring in Physical Education at different universities, graduating in the same year—1984. From university, Mark went to work for the *Royal Society for the Blind* (RSB) for three years, while I ventured into the health and fitness industry after graduating with a double major in Physical Education and Biology.

It wasn't until 1987 that Mark and I first met whilst doing post-graduate studies in *Counselling and Group Work*. During the two years that we studied together with my wife Gabrielle, and some fifty others doing the course, we would often discuss how what we were learning in theory might apply in practice within the context of the fields we worked in. This lead to many practical ideas that we could apply more immediately, and some visionary ideas that we would collaborate on some day in the future.

Gabrielle was specialising in *Educational Counselling* whilst working as a teacher. Mark specialised in *Group Work* and was to later work with corporate teams and leaders, as well as young people. I was studying *Health Counselling and Group Work*, which is where Mark's subjects and mine overlapped. In the first year of the course I worked as a manager of a health and fitness facility in Adelaide and facilitated corporate retreats on Kangaroo Island. This gave me ample opportunity to trial some of the knowledge and skills I was learning, including what didn't work!

In that first year of studying together, Mark was still with RSB but was soon to start working as a personal trainer with Indra Reinpu and Darren Williams at *One on One Executive Fitness*. He later started his own company to provide business people with outdoor recharge experiences. At this time I had also moved to a company called *Corporate Health Group*, working in corporate health promotion. After the counseling course, Gabrielle and I went on to study Psychosynthesis[24] and later Mark studied Psychology. The similarities between the paths we had followed during the 1980s and beyond was a little uncanny and Mark's family link to Papua New Guinea, together with my connection to Kokoda, was also synchronistic. It seems that we were destined to meet and work together. Perhaps Richard Bach was right when he wrote that *meeting again after moments or lifetimes is certain for those who are friends*. I like to think so.

Outbound
In 1989 Mark started his fledgling business—*Outbound Corporate Recharge*. I'm sure he sensed that he was onto something that would make his heart sing and had found his calling. His hopeful beginnings evolved over ten years into something that few others might have imagined. Mark's business not only thrived but the impact of his programs left an indelible footprint on the hearts and minds of thousands of people and inspired other like-minded individuals to become experiential learning facilitators and more authentic leaders.

Mark came close to mastering the art of facilitation more than most people I have worked with, not in a polished and seamless style but in his unassuming, humble and authentic approach to 'drawing out' from people what they already had within them and were yet to discover. He was masterful at creating unique and memorable learning experiences that stimulated imagination and drew on metaphors that paralleled life in a subtle but profound way. His ability to question, listen, pause for reflection and wait patiently for answers to come from 'ah hah moments,' was intuitive and yet mindfully used in response to the learner's readiness to hear. Mark made it safe for people to be vulnerable, to be open, to take risks, to share their unrehearsed thoughts, feelings and insights. He was not only able to do this with people for whom he was contracted to teach, but also for those whom he may have interacted with outside of his professional role. He spawned a significant number of other facilitators, teachers, guides and leaders over the decade that he spent mastering his craft.

> *A true master is not the one with the most students*
> *but the one who creates the most masters.*
> Neale Donald Walsch—*Conversations with God*

From Agnostic to Believer
After finishing our studies together in 1988, Mark and I kept in touch, but did not start collaborating with each other on a professional level until Mark invited me to participate in one of his corporate team programs a couple of years later. This was to be my first taste of his chosen method of teaching. I had been introduced to the theory of *Experiential Learning* (EL) as a teaching method, while studying components of outdoor education within my teaching degree, but had not yet 'experienced' it as a participant or observed it being used in a corporate context. Up until this first encounter, I would have to say that I wasn't fully aware of the potential potency of experiential learning, especially when delivered by a skillful facilitator.

The importance of learning through experience had been highlighted as far back as 1938, by John Dewey, in his publication, *Experience and Education*,[25] and by others such as Kurt Lewin and David Kolb. For professionals in the field of outdoor education, adventure therapy, and some early adopters in the corporate training arena, it was familiar. For others though, it was still a bit 'out there,' a bit too playful, some considering it unorthodox and even questionable as a valid method of influencing culture change in organisations or personal development within individuals.

Despite my degree in physical education and my graduate studies in counselling, psychotherapy and group work, I could, to a certain extent, still understand why some might be skeptical, particularly in the corporate world where training in the 20th Century was more linear and logical. Plenty of companies had tried some form of *adventure-based training* but most had not experienced the true power and relevance of *metaphorical learning* when conducted by a professional facilitator who is highly skilled in the art of translating experiences into meaningful learning that has specific and practical application to the real world. The lifeless theoretical world of some classrooms and the impotency of outdoor activities that are poorly designed and facilitated, can often be an inadequate preparation for the dynamic and complex world of reality. I certainly enjoyed adventurous activities, playing games, group problem-solving, and other fun ways of learning, but I hadn't fully understood the depth of learning that could occur, nor seen any strong evidence of the effectiveness of this type of learning in the business world until I participated in my first program run by Mark, and his co-facilitator Vanessa.

Lost in the Forest
The year was 1990 and we were near Mt Crawford Forest in the Adelaide Hills of South Australia. It was here that I learned some uncomfortable, but life changing lessons about myself.
On this summer evening, in the forest, more than 25 years ago, my agnostic attitude toward this fun but somewhat 'airy fairy' teaching methodology, literally changed overnight.

It was 9.00pm and the sun had just settled behind the trees for the night. We had experienced a long day participating in various group activities and discussions which, as I learned later, were a 'setup' for what was to happen next. We'd just had dinner and completed a discussion on the subject of fear, when we were asked to step outside of the cabin that doubled as our meeting room and overnight accommodation. As Mark closed the door to the cabin, we heard the latch click into its locked position. His next words were:

"The key to a good night's sleep is the key to this door, and that key is hidden in the middle of Mt Crawford Forest 10kms from here. Your mission, should you choose to accept it, is to find the key and bring it back to this location, then open the door in the presence of all team members. There is no time limit but the sooner you find it, the sooner you'll hit the sack."

The first clue was a short drive away at an old cemetery in the middle of nowhere. It was dark and difficult to see, so it took quite a while to find a plain white headstone, indistinguishable from hundreds of others like it among the overgrown bushes, trees and rocks. Except for a particular name that provided confirmation of its unique identity, we would never have found it.

After some initial excitement, followed by a frustrating half hour of searching, we eventually found the headstone and another clue under a rock at its base. The next clue gave us a grid reference at Mt Crawford which would lead us into the forest. Then we'd be on foot again searching for the next clue inside an even bigger 'haystack.'

By now it was after 10.00pm and we were navigating with map and compass to a particular knoll in the middle of the forest. When we got to the small area of high ground among the pine trees, we were to search for a treasure chest at the grid reference given.

At that time I was 30 years of age and had a little more experience with maps than most of the others in the group who were younger than me, so I was pretty confident that we had the right spot on the map and that it wouldn't take long to find this treasure. We didn't know what it looked like, how big it was and whether it was hidden in a tree or buried in the ground, so all we could do was scan the general area within twenty metres or so of what we thought was the knoll on the map. I say 'we,' but in truth it was 'I' who declared with confidence that we were at the right location based on my self-professed navigation experience.

After a half hour of searching, one of the other group members suggested that we could be mistaken about where we were in relation to the knoll feature on the map. I disagreed, thinking to myself that this was certainly the spot and we just had to search more carefully. I dismissed his suggestion, knowing he had little experience with navigation compared with me.

So this time we lined up and did a very thorough grid search of a wider area, back and forth several times until inevitably, frustration sabotaged our commitment to the cause. Expletives followed and slowly but surely we all became despondent to the point of giving up. I kept saying "this has to be it!" All other suggestions were not worth pursuing... I was so sure of myself.

By now it was after midnight and in desperation I gave in to the better judgement of others in the group. "Let's go to this other spot and have a look if it makes you feel better... then at least we can rule it out," I said, with covert hostility in my voice.

We re-orientated ourselves with the compass and headed off to find a small creek line that we'd walked over on the way in. This was also on the map, so it was a reasonably reliable strategy to confirm our position. From there we headed to another stretch of high ground about 100m away, hoping to find a treasure chest among the trees, if we could find it in the now very dark forest. We shivered in the early morning chill among the pines, our discomfort compounded by frustration and fatigue. As we walked heads slumped solemnly and stumbling through the darkness to our new destination, I could feel the edge of anger in the group. They were pissed off and resigned to the fact that we would never find this bloody treasure.

At the distant perimeter of my fading head torch's search light, I noticed a flash of red among the trees to my right. At that same moment I heard someone yell out. "That's it, I can see it, it's f...ing huge." There among the trees, sitting in a small clearing was a big red treasure chest!

While others celebrated around me, my heart sank as I came to terms with the fact that I had so arrogantly dismissed other people's suggestions and had delayed this triumphant moment for more than two hours as we searched over and over in the same spot to no avail.

They say that doing the same thing over and over, expecting a different result is the definition of insanity. At that moment I felt insanely embarrassed and guilty for being such an arrogant and stubborn, so-called leader. I could feel the daggers in my back and they were certainly justified.

At this point we had found the treasure but then noticed a note taped to the top of it, which said "congratulations, you've found the treasure. Now you need to retrieve the key from within a container which is surrounded by a moat at grid reference... ." We couldn't believe that we still had more to do and it took all of our failing energy to regroup and refocus for the next stage of our mission. Suffice it to say, we eventually got the key and after a belated celebration, returned to our warm beds at approximately 2.00am exhausted.

Upon returning to work the next day, I gave serious consideration to resigning from my management position after reflecting on my attitude and behaviour. Of course this was just a simulated, 'non-business critical' activity that had no consequences back at work but I felt that I was not fit to continue as a manager after discovering such a significant blind spot.

~~~~~~~~~~~~~~~~~~~~~

After some initial soul searching, I fell in love with the methodology of experiential learning. This enlightening experience had a profound impact on me and left me wondering whether Mark and I could combine our expertise to deliver a program that addressed both the individual and the organisation.

The following year we had the opportunity to co-facilitate our first *Treasure Challenge*[26] together, and over a quarter of a century later, I am still using versions of the concept because I have found it to be one of the most effective experiential learning activities that I learnt from Mark. It is not only fun and challenging but also serves as an engaging metaphor for teams in the real world, who need to work collaboratively to overcome obstacles in the pursuit of a common goal. It also has the potential to provide deeper insights for individuals about how they operate in their personal and professional life. For me it confronted my sense of who I was, what I was good at and how others saw me in the context of my role at work. I discovered a more realistic measure of my strengths and weaknesses and was motivated to improve myself.

One of the other metaphorical lessons from the Mt Crawford story, apart from the importance of considering all suggestions regardless of people's level of experience or apparent confidence, is that we must not only look where we least expect to find treasure, but we also need to have the key to unlock it. This is one of the fundamental truths about learning—every person has their own wisdom locked inside, they just need to learn how to access the key to the treasure within them.

Accessing Your Treasure

In the Appendix I have listed all of the activities referred to in this book. Whether you are seeking to discover your own personal treasures, or accessing the treasures within teams that you are part of, some of the key questions that we discuss in the debrief of the *Treasure Challenge* activity are perhaps worth pondering before we move on.

1. What attitudes and behaviours impact your ability to get the most out of each team member, when pursuing a common goal?
2. What 'blindspots' (strengths or areas for improvement) have you discovered by experience and/or feedback from others, and how can you use them more wisely?
3. How do you usually respond to obstacles and challenges and what can you do more or less of, to improve your ability to problem-solve?

Chapter 11   Organisational Wellness

Not long after the Mt Crawford experience and the subsequent shaking up of my personal snowdome, I started to take a different direction. Up until then I was in a comfort zone at work, doing lots of health assessments, some basic seminars on illness prevention and a little bit of health counselling but I had not yet explored the deeper questions of how one's psycho-emotional state impacts one's health and performance. I hadn't discovered the keys to a more valuable treasure—*how to live one's best life personally and professionally?*

My work was mostly focused on illness prevention rather than wellness promotion. The *Workplace Health Promotion* team I worked with, primarily considered the health of the individual and not the wider context of workplace relationships and culture. As I read more and came into contact with thought leaders in the field of Organisational Health, I began to explore these new areas of interest with enthusiasm. My change of direction evolved from experiences and discussions that I had with Mark and from my new interest in what it meant to live well, rather than just how to avoid illness. I began to look into the wider landscape of wellness in organisations which inevitably lead to learning more about the secrets behind high performance team cultures and highly effective leadership.

During my health counselling studies in the late 1980s I came across a book written by John W Travis MD and Regina S Ryan called the *Wellness Workbook*. This book was a ground breaking read for me as I was working in the field of health and wellness at the time, but I also became increasingly interested in its application to developing healthier organisations. One of the key concepts covered in the book was the *Illness/Wellness Continuum*.[27] I have adapted it here to include its application to *organisational health and performance*, as well as *personal health and quality of life*.

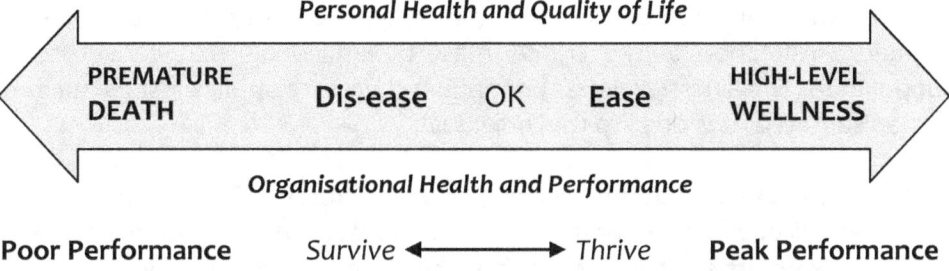

Figure 11.1 The Illness/Wellness Continuum—Adapted from John Travis, 1988

Organisational Health and Performance

In Travis' model (originally conceived in 1972) he puts *Premature Death* on the left hand end of the continuum and on the right hand end is *High Level Wellness*. I have added *Performance* as a measure of *Organisational Wellness*, but you could also include *quality of relationships, job satisfaction, culture, productivity, leadership effectiveness,* or any number of other parameters to express the health of an organisation or business.

In terms of personal health and quality of life, the continuum is perhaps more obvious. For example—when we are stressed, out of balance, living an unhealthy lifestyle or exposed to health risk factors, we are more likely to experience a lack of ease, with subsequent signs and symptoms of 'dis-ease' leading to illness. I have come to see illness as a barometer—a red flag, urging us to treat ourselves more lovingly or to explore ways of healing the dis-ease we feel. Illness can therefore be viewed as a gift that provides valuable feedback. If we don't listen to the feedback, and the red flags go unheeded, this can sometimes lead to chronic illness or premature death.

> ***Love your disease, it's keeping you healthy.***
> Dr John Harrison MD

Many of us are fortunate enough to avoid illness most of the time, but if we are not mindful, self-caring and open to learning, we can sometimes drift around the middle of this continuum with no discernible illness or wellness, in somewhat of a comfort zone, but be unhappy, ill-at-ease, stressed or producing mediocre results in our life. In this 'OK Zone' we may occasionally experience peaks of wellness and bouts of illness as we go in and out of balance in our life, but for the most part we are only surviving, not thriving.

Over the years I have contemplated the implications of this concept in my own life and its relevance to organisational health and performance. *The microcosm is reflected in the macrocosm*—this phrase, used by philosophers, physicists and ancient cultures alike, underpins my belief that the health of an organisation, a community, a country and our planet is indeed a reflection of the critical mass of individuals that constitute its population. The *Illness/Wellness Continuum* therefore applies just as much to organisations as it is does to the individual.

> ***The health and performance of an organisation is dependent on the physical, mental, emotional, spiritual and social health of its people and the environment within which they survive or thrive.***

Beyond Treating Symptoms

The allopathic health system has primarily been based on a *treatment model*, which brings people to the neutral point on Travis' *Illness/Wellness Continuum*, where signs and symptoms of illness are alleviated. This does not necessarily help people to learn from their illness and advance toward *High Level Wellness* which is characterised by higher levels of energy, resilience, happiness, fulfilment and contentment. The same applies for sick or dysfunctional organisations. We need to look beyond just treating symptoms with a 'quick fix', to exploring continuous improvement in the environments, culture, processes and relationships that help organisations to function well and thrive.

The Wellness Model is a more holistic approach, in that it can work in harmony with the treatment model, taking people beyond alleviating symptoms, to a more consistent experience of high level wellness by addressing underlying causes of illness and helping people to learn from the lessons inherent in their bio-feedback.[28]

Self-Awareness, Learning and Personal Growth

When Gabrielle is not co-facilitating corporate programs and guiding adventures with me, or conducting her own personal development programs, she also runs her *Natural Therapies Clinic* and provides a counselling and life coaching service. Through a combination of approaches, she assists clients to explore the causal factors which may be triggering their symptoms or feelings of unease. These can be physical, emotional, mental, social, spiritual, environmental, or a combination of factors that one may or may not be aware of. Her *Wellness Model* approach combines treatment, self-exploration, education and personal growth.

In the *Wellness Workbook*, Dr Travis emphasises the fact that achieving and sustaining wellness is not just a matter of being informed, it requires an ongoing process of *awareness, education and growth*. The relevance of this to the concept of developing *Learning Organisations* and businesses that are focused on the pursuit of wellness in all aspects of their people and operations, prompted my interest in the early 90s, to find ways of helping people and businesses to take the journey from just surviving to growth and thriving.

Although the company I worked for back then, was often engaged to help clients solve 'health and performance challenges' with a more treatment orientated approach, I was keen to take them beyond this, to a place over the horizon, in the direction of wellness and peak performance.
As I started to take people and organisations on this journey to wellness and improved performance, I became interested in how best to educate them,

not only for awareness and intellectual understanding, but further out from the shore of their comfort zone, to a more challenging place where they could grow as a people and sustain the improvements in thinking and behavior that made their life more fulfilling, joyful and well. This would have obvious benefits for their businesses and for their relationships at home. In my experiences with Mark I saw a potent way of achieving this.

Wellness Advocates
As part of the new direction I was taking back in the early 90s, I began pursuing further studies in organisational health with Grant Donovan, who had been working as a sport psychologist with the *Kookaburra Campaign* in the 1987 defence of the *America's Cup* in Perth. Following his commitments with this elite sailing team, Grant ran a program called the *Wellness Advocates Network*[29] in which I was trained to be a facilitator. He also ran a *National Wellness Conference* throughout the 90s, which subsequently evolved into the *Self-Managed Work Teams Conference*.[30] Grant and Mark were significant mentors for me over that time and it was through their influence that I began to concentrate more and more of my energy into the area of organisational wellness. I explored questions and found answers as to how I could assist individuals, teams, leaders and businesses to improve their wellness and performance and I was convinced that one of the best ways of achieving this was through the modality of experiential learning.

Complementary Medicines
In American Indian culture, the term *medicine* is used to describe a person's healing powers or more broadly, the gifts or expertise that they share with the world to bring about transformation, growth or healing. I like to think that the *medicines* that Mark and I were learning to develop and share, were complementary. During the early years of our collaboration, I drew on his expertise to complement what I was trying to do with clients as a corporate health consultant and I also shared my new learnings with him. We began to co-facilitate programs whenever the opportunity arose.

One of the programs we collaborated on while I was working as a corporate health consultant, was a three day course for the *SA Ambulance Service* called the *Wellness Retreat*. Many of the themes explored in the course were inspired by what I had learnt from the *Wellness Workbook* together with my personal experience and studies over the previous ten years, and the more recent work I had done with Grant Donovan and Mark. I was also heavily influenced by the humourous style of other role models such as John Tickell, Patricia Cameron-Hill, Don Ardell and Patch Adams.[31] Humour became an important part of my experiential approach to wellness.

The first half of the *Wellness Retreat* was focused on stress management, life balance and personal development. Then Mark would join me to co-facilitate the second half of the retreat which would transition to a focus on teamwork, leadership and organisational wellness. This is where I learnt a lot of practical skills from Mark, both consciously and unconsciously, as we began to work more closely together.

The Task/People Balancing Act
We would start with a relatively simple group problem-solving task which would require the group to get through an obstacle using limited resources and the collective initiative of the group. There would usually be a set of rules that limited their options, making it more or less difficult depending on how challenging we wanted to make it, and of course there would be a time limit which could also be varied to change the degree of pressure.

To the uninitiated eye, these tasks just looked like a bit of fun, a bit of a pointless challenge and perhaps a bit cliché! The key distinction that I learnt early on from Mark, was that the task itself was merely a means to an end, and therefore somewhat irrelevant. The end itself was not to see how quickly or successfully they could accomplish the task, but to notice the attitudes and behaviours exhibited by individuals and the group during the 'people process' involved in solving the problem.

And so it was this distinction between *task process* and *people process* that became a foundational concept underpinning all of the experiential learning activities that Mark introduced to me and all of the activities and experiences I was to design into the future.

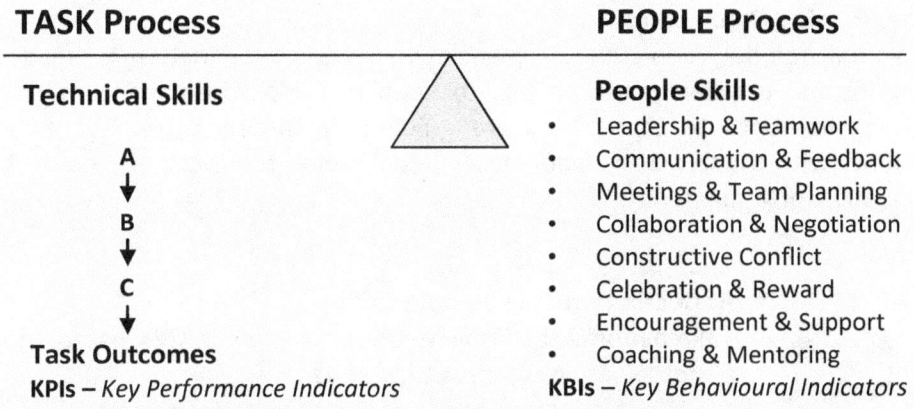

Figure 11.2 *Task/People Model*—Evolved from Mark Auricht, 1990

The *task* side of the scale refers to the hard skills or technical tasks involved in achieving outcomes which are often measured by *Key Performance Indicators* (KPIs). The *people* side of the scale refers to the soft skills or people-processes involved in getting tasks done efficiently and effectively, thus leading to better outcomes. I like to differentiate performance indicators by using the term *Key Behavioural Indicators* (KBIs) when referring to these soft skills or people skills. These skills are more about how we behave in a team or in a leadership role while achieving a task.

Most trades and professions employ people based on their *task competencies* or technical qualifications to begin with, and then *people skills* and attitude will often sort the wheat from the chaff. Many of those who are experienced 'experts' end up in management positions but don't always have the soft skills of leadership as well honed as their technical skills. In service industries and people orientated businesses where technical skill may not be as essential, it tends to be the other way around—recruitment of staff is more focused on people skills in these industries.

People skills, attitude and emotional intelligence far out-weigh intellect when it comes to leadership, teamwork and customer service.

Even when staff are selected on the basis of their people skills, my personal experience is that many of us can still lose sight of the *people-process* side of the equation when we are under task pressure. This can often tip the scales out of balance, leading to poor performance, conflict, stress and dis-ease. Being mindful to be balanced in our focus on both task and people-process, is relevant in business, family, social and political relationships.

Maintaining Connection

This balance between task and people is also a key distinction for leaders, facilitators, teachers and coaches to keep in mind when mentoring and giving feedback to those they are guiding. Maintaining connection and affinity with those we are leading, while delivering feedback and guidance, is a skill worth mastering.

Reflecting on Your People Skills
Take a moment to review the examples of KBIs, listed under *People Skills*, in *Figure 11.2* (page 123).
1. Which of these would you say are your strengths?
2. Which skills do you think you need to improve?

Chapter 12   Venturing into the Learning Zone

Throughout the years of our collaboration I was invited to attend regular professional development days that Mark ran for his staff. In these sessions we shared the latest thinking on learning methodology, leadership and team dynamics, business success principles and organisational development research. We also explored different ways of presenting this material in a way that was engaging and thought-provoking. We brainstormed creative ways of achieving learning outcomes using group problem-solving challenges; indoor and outdoor games; business simulations; adventure activities and deeper reflection processes.

Many of the learning activities and personal development processes we developed arose from an eclectic mix of ideas drawn from: accelerated learning technologies; group counselling and psychotherapy processes, that we learned while studying together in the 80s; physical and outdoor education methodology, which we both studied at University; indigenous rituals, that we had been exposed to; and our own creative ideas.

It was exciting to take a simple idea out of a book such as *Silver Bullets*[32] and then re-engineer it to create a metaphor that could provide insights into leadership or team behaviours in the workplace that either helped or hindered performance. Designing better and better learning experiences became our mission.

We soon learned after experimentation with different activities and the way we framed, facilitated, and debriefed them, that it wasn't so much the activity that was important but the way it was facilitated and debriefed to draw out potential learning. It was the skill of the facilitator that was the key, and so this became our primary focus—how could we improve ourselves as people and as facilitators, and in so doing, improve the quality of our facilitation and subsequent learning outcomes for clients?

By the late 90s *Outbound Corporate Recharge* had evolved in to *Venture Corporate Recharge*. Mark's original entry into outdoor activity programs to help businesses recharge, had developed into something much more sophisticated than just the activities he used. He continued to learn more about himself and about the science of learning, which lead to his growing expertise in facilitation and his advocacy for *Adventure-Based Experiential Learning (ABEL)*. This was to become one of Mark's most enduring legacies.

To discover the limits of the possible, one must venture to do the impossible.
Adapted from Arthur C Clarke

Mission Venture

To 'venture' is to take a daring journey or begin an audacious undertaking. One of the most daring things we can do is to venture beyond our perceived limitations to the outer reaches of our unexplored potential. The mission of *Venture Corporate Recharge (VCR)*, later known as *Venture*, was to assist individuals and organisations to realise their full potential. Mark and his team achieved this by providing highly effective training programs to enhance individual and team effectiveness. Their methodology, based on experiential and *Accelerated Learning Principles*[33] applied to a balance of indoor and outdoor management exercises, maximised the learning opportunities for all participants. They recognised that individuals had different learning styles and created an environment where individuals were encouraged to take responsibility for their own learning.

The Venture Corporate Recharge Team at Morialta—Late 90s

Mark's team at VCR, had extensive knowledge and experience in the design and facilitation of ABEL Programs, and were all tertiary qualified educators who had a commitment to their own personal and professional development. Mark's belief, that the competence of the facilitator was the single most important element affecting the success of any learning program, made the selection and development of his staff one of his highest priorities.

One of the most important agendas in most of VCR's programs was to assist participants to become aware of and improve their *people-process* skills. Mark would often frame a team day by saying, *We're not here to work on the 'technical skills and knowledge' related to your business but to enhance what you do with what you know, by helping you to discover more effective 'People or Team Process skills.'* Again, this distinction between task and process was a key message in all of VCR's programs, and applied just as much to Mark's staff and associates as it did to their clients.

Venture Corporate Recharge—Statement of Purpose and Values, 1990

Mark believed strongly in having a meaningful purpose and being guided by a values compass in business and in life. VCR's purpose was: *To enhance quality of life by providing opportunities for growth through unique learning experiences.* There were 7 values upon which this purpose was founded.

VENTURE CORPORATE RECHARGE—CORE VALUES[34]

1. **Integrity**
   We practice personal discipline by being true to ourselves, aligning our behaviour with our intentions and keeping commitments.

2. **Freedom**
   We value individual uniqueness and seek to provide a nurturing environment in which we may all choose to fulfil our purpose, within the context of our agreements.

3. **Purpose**
   We are committed to our purpose and its ongoing development. We demonstrate our purpose through our actions.

4. **Growth**
   We provide opportunities for people to identify areas for development, exercise their courage and participate in experiences that encourage 'stretch' for the purpose of personal growth.

5. **Interdependence**
   We recognise the power of diversity within relationships. We achieve synergy by encouraging people to work together to achieve a greater outcome.

6. **Self Responsibility**
   We acknowledge and accept that we are responsible for our behaviours and attitudes. We recognise that we are the product of our choices.

7. **Balance**
   We work towards achieving harmony between physical, spiritual, emotional and intellectual areas of our lives for a state of well-being and peace.

Figure 12.1 Venture Corporate Recharge—Core Values, 1990

Mark and his staff were well known for their commitment to these values and to the quality of their design and facilitation of learning experiences.

Learning to Learn

I shared Mark's commitment to professional development and continued to pursue my own passion for learning and development. In the late 1990s I recall participating in a program with Mark called *Learning to Learn* which was convened by an organisation called *Accelerated Business Technologies*. This was the first time that I really started to consciously examine what we'd been doing and why it worked so well. I had a degree in Physical Education but hadn't really made the connection between 'educating through the physical' and 'the art of facilitating experiential learning' in a business or corporate context.

It became obvious to me that teaching students about how the brain works and how to apply learning principles to optimise the brain's capacity for learning and development was, and perhaps still is, a neglected piece in the education puzzle. Ongoing Research[35] into the way we learn and how best to teach is forever unlocking the mysteries of the mind and revealing new approaches to learning every day. Much of what Mark taught me and many others was based on these accelerated learning principles. They are as true today as they were back in the 1980s and 90s when they were taught to millions of people around the world from many walks of life and a broad spectrum of professions, through programs such as *Money & You, Powerful Presentations, Learning to Learn, Landmark Education, Investment in Excellence, Skills for Training Mastery and Facilitation Mastery.*[36]

Some of the trainers, facilitators and consultants we worked with back then, and still do today, have continued to draw on the methodology and skills they learnt from the 'Master Teachers' who shared their expertise during these programs. Some educators and consultants however, are still using ineffective, slow, cumbersome and uninspiring methods of education, compared with the accelerated learning methodologies that are available.

Money And You

Mark's methodology was heavily influenced by his outdoor education background and by the *Money & You* program which was more about 'you' than it was about 'money'. Money, you could say, was one of the possible outcomes or measures of success that can result from a focus on developing one's highest potential and focusing on the people aspects of business and life. Mark put the *Money & You* principles into practice in his business and also used a similar learning methodology in his teaching of others.

The *Money & You* program was a unique 3½ day experiential process run by facilitators such as Robert Kiyosaki who used accelerated learning strategies to enable participants to learn faster and more effectively. The program provided an optimal learning environment with frequent breaks, constant variety and the use of stories, metaphor, imagery, colour, music, challenging games and lots of laughter. All the senses were stimulated, and the *learning domains* of the *head, heart and hands*, were all engaged during the program. These important but often ignored aspects of learning have been extensively explored and defined by educational researchers such as Bloom, Harrow and Simpson.[37]

In the *Money & You* program participants 'played games' which were a metaphor for real-life business situations. The word 'game' in the context of experiential learning can include: game-like activities; group problem-solving tasks; adventure activities or more realistic simulations. I will refer to some examples throughout this book, most of which have evolved from activities which Mark introduced me to (refer to a list in the Appendix). These can be used for personal or professional development and are particularly potent learning experiences for leaders and teams.

During a program like *Money & You*, participants are encouraged to be observant of their own and other's responses during games and interactive exercises. Games almost always reflect people's behavioural tendencies and emotional responses as they are expressed in the real world. This can be very revealing and produce profound insights and revelations for participants. Feedback from such experiences is very immediate. The job of the facilitator is to help the participants to make links between their experiences during a program, the insights that they glean from it and the possibilities for applying these lessons in the real world.

> **A truth believed is only a belief. A truth experienced is truth.**
> Marshall Thurber

During a program such as this and others that I have attended, participants often experience a microcosm of their whole life – their typical patterns of behaviour and previously unconscious blind spots are revealed to them through the experiences of the program. In the end they come away seeing alternative ways to run their organisations, to grow their businesses, and to live their lives. This opens up a whole new world of possibilities and choices.

Marshall Thurber and Buckminster Fuller

The *Money & You* Program was created by Marshall Thurber, one of the pioneers of accelerated learning and the mind behind some of the concepts that Mark shared with me, together with other accelerated learning programs we studied together such as *Learning to Learn*. I have since adapted some of these concepts in the work I do now but it is important for me to acknowledge that the original source of some of this material was developed by Marshall Thurber who was influenced by Buckminster Fuller. It seems that these principles keep getting handed down from mentor to mentor, so who knows where the source of this river really began?

Following Thurber's success in real estate in the 1970s using innovative 'win-win' business strategies that he had developed based on Buckminster Fuller's concept of *Precession*,[38] Thurber co-founded the *Burklyn Business School* in Vermont, which was designed to teach the global principles of cooperation and abundance that he learned from Buckminster Fuller, and to contribute to the personal transformation aims of the human potential movement. The unique teaching methods that Thurber employed at *Burklyn* were designed to create more powerful learning experiences. I respectfully acknowledge Fuller and Thurber's contribution to experiential learning and to the origins of some of the adapted ideas I share in this book.

Facilitation Mastery

Some years after I was introduced to experiential learning by Mark, I also met one of his colleagues who had been working in the field of organisational transformation for a number of years and had developed a network of consultants called *Keonet*, to share ideas and learn from one another. Allan Keogh and his wife Elizabeth, of *Keogh Consulting*,[39] have been valuable mentors for me over the years since Mark's death and I acknowledge them for teaching me even more about the art of facilitation. Having worked with Allan a number of times now, I have learnt so much from observing the way he pays attention to details such as the use of music, books and colourful visuals, the way he walks the space of a learning environment to make sure that everything is in an appropriate place as he 'zens' the room before a program, to create an engaging and inspiring learning atmosphere. Allan's use of humour, stories, theatre and art have also inspired me to expand my repertoire of behaviour as a facilitator and presenter.

One of the professional development programs offered by *Keonet* was called *Facilitation Mastery*, run by Jane Heard of *Heard Consulting*. This program covered many aspects of a facilitator's toolkit and took us on a thorough exploration of our internal world and how we expressed it externally in our work. It was challenging, insightful and very useful for those who were willing to embrace what they had to learn about themselves and how they could be more effective as facilitators, teachers, coaches and leaders.

> *To engage the learning minds of those we teach,*
> *we must first explore our own inner landscape.*

The Learning Mind
A sound understanding of how the *learning mind* works, is the foundation upon which methodologies for accelerated learning have been developed and continue to be applied in the most successful learning organisations such as schools, tertiary education institutions, adult learning environments, corporate learning programs and youth at risk programs.

Learning needs to be: interesting, engaging, inspiring, thought and feeling provoking, colourful, fun, challenging, magical, relevant and adventurous. All of these elements make learning memorable. One of the most powerful factors in education is when we learn on a heart/feeling level. It's not just about intellectual understanding; it is also about a change of heart. The Greek philosopher and world renowned biologist—Aristotle, proposed that the 'mind' was in the heart rather than the brain, a strange concept perhaps, but interesting to contemplate. I like to think of the brain, heart and soul as one 'connected mind.'

Education is often thought of as a process of putting information and understanding into people, but when it comes to personal development and learning life skills, it is more about 'drawing out' of people what they already know innately. The word *education* is related to the Latin word *educere*, which means *to lead forth* or *draw out*. Unfortunately our formal education systems have evolved from a predominant mindset of preparing children to be productive working adults. This benefit of schooling often comes at the expense of nurturing the creative and naturally inquisitive mind of the child, a mind connected to heart and soul.

School children playing at Kokoda, 2004

Educating for the Whole Person
Thomas Moore, author of *Care of the Soul* says that when the classroom becomes just a place for preparing children to become an efficient part of society's machinery, we neglect the needs of the soul. Fortunately more recent educators understand the importance of balancing vocational preparation with nurturing the passions, gifts and wisdom within young people, but I think we still have a long way to go to turn the ship around.

Beyond the Limits of the School Yard
The limits of the school yard for some are like a circus tent full of wonder and daring. For others they are like an unwelcome prison. Whilst the school system worked well for our oldest son Peter, who knew from an early age what path he wanted to take and responded favourably to the learning environment that was geared to his liking; our youngest son Jesse took a different path. This is not uncommon for siblings, despite having the same parents and a similar upbringing. Jesse is an intelligent, strong and wise young man who found that the environment of the formal school system did more to inhibit his enjoyment of learning, than encourage it. He left school wondering where he fitted into society's grand scheme for the many young people who don't have an immediate answer to the inevitable question: "What do you want to do when you leave school?" Some like me have to explore a number of paths to find their bliss or wait patiently for a dream to surface. Others struggle to be their authentic selves until a crisis stirs their soul to fly.

Fortunately after some time incubating, Jesse felt a spark within his heart that lead him to follow a dream, and he began to follow his passion for cycling. It was only when he had found his 'heart song,' that he discovered a new path to learning as an adult. He has just begun studying the Science of Human Movement with a goal to specialise in Sports Psychology which will be a nice fit with his cycling ambitions, and who knows where else it will take him. That is the beauty of the learning journey for the unfolding self. Regardless of the system of education, the student must be ready to learn. Being mindful of the heart and soul will always enhance the learning process and lay the foundations for self-responsible, life-long learning—a gift that we can do our best to bestow on the young.

For adults and children, well-designed and facilitated experiential learning programs focus on allowing participants to learn for themselves, guided by their own discoveries. When we encourage learners to become comfortable with taking risks in a safe, blame-free environment, any mistakes provide feedback and learning opportunities. In a supportive learning space, some participants for the first time in their lives, experience the amazing feeling of *correction without invalidation*. This leads to self-correction and taking self-responsibility for their learning and growth. It is this kind of environment that I wanted to provide for young people and adults aspiring to become all they can be, a place where 'limits' evaporate.

> *Mastery is a function of practice and how quickly you can correct without invalidating yourself or others.*
> Money & You Program

Wilderness Therapy

The concept of *correction without invalidation* is a crucial principle used in wilderness therapy programs with youth at risk groups, where *connection before correction*[40] is one of the key mantras.

People don't care how much we know, until they know how much we care.

It is essential for the wilderness therapist or guide to establish a trusting relationship and rapport with participants before they will be receptive to feedback for the purpose of learning and personal growth. It is also important to understand that it is not the guide that provides the lessons; it is the experience of the journey and the challenges or metaphors inherent in the environment, which provide *teachable moments*. The guide's job is to provide a safe learning environment and to help participants to connect the dots between their experience and their intuitive insights. 'In-Tuition' is our *Inner Tutor* and yet many of us have learnt not to trust it. I had not joined the dots on the underlying meaning of the word *intuition*, until Gabrielle helped me to see it. (*So much to learn you have,* said my Inner Yoda).

In my work as a Team Leader with the *Operation Flinders—Youth at Risk Program* it is considered an imperative that we, as Team Leaders (or guides as I prefer to call us), are not there to be the primary agent of change. It is instead, the environment of the *Northern Flinders Ranges* and the experience of surviving for eight days in the bush while navigating around a 100km expanse of trackless terrain, that is the real teacher, we are just there to facilitate the experience, guide the participants to discover their own lessons and to keep them safe. It took me a while to work this out and to let go of my natural desire to assert influence over the learning outcomes based on what I considered to be important, rather than help participants draw lessons from their experience and in doing so, draw-out the innate wisdom within them.

Some people think that *young people at risk* are all 'clueless' but many I have worked with are highly intelligent, fast learners who have just ended up in destructive circumstances or have made poor choices. Unfortunately past stories can continue to define their future until they are re-written. Some are changed by a chance meeting with a relatable mentor or through the song they hear in the wilderness that reminds them of who they really are; others carve a new path for themselves just by their own sheer will. When we help them to connect with us, and the *teachable moments* that surface when we are flexible enough to trust in the flow, we can free people from the *internal stories* that no longer serve them, and by so doing, help them to start walking in a new direction.

The High Calling of the Teacher
The word 'teacher' is a universal term for any person or experience that enlightens our thinking or behavior. A professional teacher can include a school teacher, university lecturer, tutor, coach, mentor, instructor/trainer, keynote speaker, facilitator, consultant, counsellor or priest. There are also many others in our lives who teach us informally and often without knowing it. Our most powerful teachers are those that help us to find our own truth.

Learning can happen by default through the ad hoc experiences of life or it can be consciously searched for. The purpose of a professional teacher is to create specific learning opportunities for those who seek to expand their knowledge and skills or to change their quality of life. For those in the professions of teaching or facilitating the learning of others, it is not a responsibility to be taken lightly.

Two school teachers that I remember fondly were my History Teacher at high school in Sydney. His name was Thor Svenson. He was also a professional surfing photographer and introduced us to some of the more famous surfers of the 70s. He taught history by putting butchers paper on the walls of the classroom and we spent the whole term doing a mural of the historical events we were learning about.

The other teacher I remember well was my Art Teacher, Paula Vawter who now lives in the USA. She created such a loving, relaxed and friendly atmosphere in the classroom that we all wanted to hang out there, even during recess and lunch times. Thirty years after leaving school I met Paula again. It was great to see her after all those years. Paula taught me to follow my creative passion and to understand the healing power of art.

> *Only the brave should teach;*
> *the men/women whose integrity cannot be shaken, whose minds*
> *are enlightened enough to understand the high calling of the teacher*
> *and whose hearts are unshakably loyal to those with a hunger for learning.*
> Adapted from Pearl S Buck

It takes courage to teach, not only because it's a risky business trying to influence someone else's thinking or behavior, but also because courage comes from the heart and teaching involves giving of oneself not only intellectually but also emotionally. One only has to stand up and speak in front of a small group to feel the eyes of evaluation and experience the deeply personal side of public speaking—for some it is their greatest fear. Yet taking the risk to teach from the heart is one of the keys to being a person of influence, as every teacher and leader must be. Fear of speaking or living one's truth can have a debilitating effect on one's well-being but I know from personal experience, that eventually truth sets us free.

Chapter 13   The Day My Voice Broke

 *One morning in the Autumn of 2002, I woke up and something out of the ordinary happened. As I stirred and tried to have a conversation with Gabrielle, some words stumbled out of my throat while others were soundless or stilted. I found this a bit puzzling at first and then frustrating. As the day went on I found it a little easier to vocalise the words that I wanted to say but certain words I could not say. This went on for some days and at times improved while on other days it got worse. Frustration turned to despair as I became more anxious about speaking, especially in situations where I had to communicate clearly on the phone, with a shop assistant, with clients, and in my business. This became quite stressful as time went on and I eventually went to see a speech therapist about it after my voice had deteriorated to the point where I feared speaking to anyone but my family.*

After a lot of grief and many visits to the speech therapist I gradually learned to manage my voice more often than not but still had no clear answers as to what was happening. I pursued many lines of inquiry, searching for answers and seeking out all sorts of healing modalities, including alternative therapies and deeper psychological exploration. I was eventually diagnosed with a neurological condition called Spasmodic Dysphonia which strangely, are easy words to say despite my speech disability. I have difficulty starting sentences with open vowel sounds which cause my vocal chords to spasm involuntarily, so I have had to learn how to work around this or suffer the embarrassment and frustration of sounding like an idiot. Not good for the self-esteem or confidence. I felt that I had lost the person who was me.

It has been almost 15 years now and I am only just getting to the point where I don't think about it much anymore. I've trained my brain to work around the words I can't say at the start of a sentence by inserting words that I can say, running into those I can't, so that they become kind of a blend of two words. I have mastered this so well now that it happens subconsciously unless I am tired or stressed (a good barometer). Interestingly I have had days while writing where I feel that I have gone back to square one—the voice struggles some days – perhaps revisiting the emotions of the past has something to do with it?

~~~~~~~~~~~~~~~~~~~~

After much exploration into potential physical and psycho-emotional causes of the voice problem, I came to the conclusion that losing my voice was somewhat influenced by grief, together with the fact that on a *metaphysical level*[41] I wasn't speaking my truth!

While learning to speak again, I enrolled in a course called *Beyond Words* which is run by professional speaking coach David Griggs. There I learnt about how our emotional and physical presence impacts the power of our communication. Among many other things that I learnt from David, was that every great presentation communicates three things:

1. **Ethos**—expressing ethics, values or a moral in the story based on principles that the presenter wants to communicate. Ethos is also about communicating integrity and credibility.

2. **Logos**—the message has a clear and logical flow that is easy to understand. This speaks to the rational part of our mind.

3. **Pathos**—this is the passion with which the message is delivered and so we use the term 'speaking from the heart,' This is where inspiration comes from, not from logic or intellect. To 'in-spire' means to 'put spirit into,' Our spirit is moved by a passionate communicator. They do not need to be overtly passionate in an animated, extroverted way; they just have to voice their truth from the heart—even if it comes out awkwardly.

In an article written by Elizabeth Powell, titled *You will have a voice if you find the courage to speak*,[42] she writes about the Oscar-winning film, *The King's Speech*, where the speech coach prods King George with a confronting question: *Why should I waste my time listening to you?* To which the incensed King George exclaims with fire in his belly **Because I have a voice!** The coach then knowingly replies, *Why, yes you do.*

We all have a voice but many of us neglect to use it to speak our truth. *You don't have to struggle with a speech impediment to identify with the terrifying fear of being caught searching for words*, says Powell, *but underneath that frustrating anxiety lies a powerful and authentic voice waiting to emerge.*

**The key to leading with authenticity and courage,
is speaking from the heart, even when your voice shakes.**
Elizabeth Powell

Chapter 13—The Day My Voice Broke

I remember the first time I watched *The King's Speech*. I related to it so much that I think I just about cried all the way through it. But I came away inspired to speak my truth regardless of how fearful I felt. It was challenging at first, as I tried to press on without revealing that I had a speech disability, but eventually I became more honest about what was happening for me as I struggled to speak with confidence again. Once I was open about it, I noticed that people would empathise rather than judge me and I began to relax and be more authentic. It's as if my willingness to be vulnerable, inspired courage in others to be more authentic as well.

Over many years my speech has improved as I learned to speak more from the heart and less from the ego. Sharing one's true self has immeasurable power. Even if the words come out awkwardly, people know when the words stem from the truth of the heart. Most people have good 'bullshit detectors'. They can tell the difference between an inauthentic speaker who is trying to impress to feed their own self-importance, versus one who is genuinely passionate about what they want to communicate. The authenticity and integrity of a teacher I believe, is the number one ingredient in an effective learning relationship.

> ***The character of a teacher always precedes strategy and methodology, leading ultimately to the quality of learning outcomes.***

As I mentioned earlier, Mark often took the risk to be vulnerable while speaking his truth. His authenticity and character were at the heart of his effectiveness and likeability as a teacher, facilitator and mentor. I drew on the reassurance of his example and that of King George, as I took the risk to speak from my heart, even when my voice shook. This has been a significant part of my learning journey and has given me a deeper appreciation of what makes an inspiring teacher.

Wayne introducing an ABEL Program, 2002

Figure 13.1 The Spiral Journey—W&G Enright ©2015

The Learning Journey

The spiral image above can represent our life journey; the journey of a group; different parts of our life; or aspects of self. The circles surrounding the spiral represent the different people, places or events that have influenced the journey, some perhaps subtle, and others more profound.

In the second half of this book I will refer to this concept in more detail with regard to its relevance to leadership development, and I will share more about those who have influenced what I hope to impart in these pages. For now though, let us pause for a moment to reflect on how the spiral applies to one's learning journey—the journey we all take through life as we learn formally and informally through family, school, friends, work, media and other life experiences.

Reflecting on Your Learning Journey

1. Who have been your most significant teachers in life and what did you learn (good or bad) from them?

2. What have been your most significant learning experiences?

3. How do you prefer to learn—through structured instructive education, self-directed learning using technology, practical 'hands on' experience, or a combination of modalities?

4. When have you taken the risk to be more authentic and been pleasantly surprised at the response?

5. What would you say is your 'Medicine'—the gifts, passions, skills or knowledge that you would like to share with others?

Chapter 14   Learning—A Daring Adventure

Mark's passion for using adventure as a teaching tool and a metaphor for life was applied to his work in a broad range of contexts, from corporate teams to school groups and helping to change the hearts and minds of young people at risk. He was a strong advocate for *Adventure-Based Experiential Learning (ABEL)* and was committed to raising the level of understanding among training professionals of its philosophy, methodology and applications. In 1996 Mark wrote an article titled: *Adventure Based Experiential Learning—An Explanation by an Advocate.* In the article he gave a definition of what *ABEL* was and what it wasn't. He also provided an explanation of its fundamentals and expressed his thoughts on what, back then, was an often misunderstood approach to learning and development. Following is a summary of the key points that he expressed in the article:

ADVENTURE BASED EXPERIENTIAL LEARNING
An Explanation by an Advocate.
Written by Mark Auricht

Reasons why ABEL is sometimes a misunderstood training tool
1. Some of the more 'thrill seeking' components of *ABEL* programs have attracted journalists who have a keen eye for an attention grabbing story. Thus, articles and media about *ABEL*, have a tendency to focus on the 'wow factor,' rather than the valuable learning outcomes that can be gained from this methodology.
2. There is a significant lack of research and reporting done with regard to the effectiveness of *ABEL*, despite its considerable history of use around the world and its enormous potential as a vehicle for both individual and team development. Most of the information available is anecdotal.[43]

Adventure Learning (AL) or Experiential Learning (EL)?
AL and *EL* are almost inseparable because *AL* is inherently experiential and *EL* often has an element of adventure associated with it. The word 'adventure' usually conjures up mental pictures of stereotypical adventure activities such as abseiling, but can also be used to refer to indoor problem-solving activities or workplace mentoring, which may not be physically challenging but can still involve an element of psychological adventure. *ABEL* is distinguished from the 'umbrella term' of *EL*, by the specific adventure-based nature of the activities it uses to elicit learning.

Foundations of Experiential Learning

ABEL is founded on the principles of EL, which put very simply is 'learning by doing.' Of course there is more to EL than just doing activities. One of the early proponents of EL, Prussian philosopher and psychologist Kurt Lewin[44] who established a Research Centre for Group Dynamics at MIT/USA in 1935, identified 12 *Principles of Experiential Learning* (summarised in *Figure 14.1*). Lewin's principles are based on the following philosophical foundations.

Group Participation

Fundamental to Lewin's philosophy was his belief that—*learning about the factors effecting group functionality and developing the attitudes and skills required to improve it*—was best achieved through active participation in group activities. His research demonstrated that learning is achieved most productively in groups whose numbers can interact and then reflect on their mutual experiences. (In my experience small groups of 4-6 are ideal for optimum learning, so if we are working with a larger group, we will always have them form smaller activity groups and have learning partners for debrief discussions.)

Action Theories

Lewin describes EL as a learning process based on the systematic development and modification of what he calls *Action Theories*, which are the theoretical assumptions we make about our behaviour and its consequences. This leads to the subconscious construction of a belief that certain actions (behaviours) will achieve desired results (consequences). Most *Action Theories* function automatically, thus we are rarely conscious of the assumptions we make about our actions and their consequences, unless they are brought to our attention through feedback or intentional reflection on our experiences.

The Purpose of ABEL Programs

ABEL programs are essentially a structured process for helping the learner to become more aware of the *Action Theories* that guide their behavior in a group setting. ABEL also provides opportunities for participants to test their assumptions/beliefs against reality, and to learn how they can modify them to improve their effectiveness as a team member or leader. Mark's article includes Lewin's 3 *Stage Experiential Learning Cycle* which combines the Result/Reflection Stages. Kolb[45] proposes a 4 *Stage Cycle* including: Action-Results-Reflection-Adaptation (see *Figure 14.2* p142).

LEWIN'S PRINCIPLES OF EXPERIENTIAL LEARNING

1. Effective EL will affect the learner's cognitive structures (action theories), attitudes and values, perceptions and behavioural patterns.

2. People will believe more in the knowledge that they have discovered themselves than in the knowledge presented by others.

3. Learning is more effective when it is an active rather than a passive process.

4. Acceptance of new action theories, attitudes and behavioural patterns cannot be brought about by a piece-meal approach. One's whole *cognitive – affective* behavioural system has to change.

5. It takes more than information to change action theories, attitudes and behavioural patterns.

6. It takes more than first-hand experience to generate valid knowledge. There needs to be a theoretical system that is tested by experience, followed by reflection on the meaning of the experience.

7. Behaviour changes will be temporary unless the action theories and attitudes underlying them are changed.

8. Changes in perception of one's self and one's social environment are necessary before changes in action theories, attitudes and behavior will take place.

9. The more supportive, accepting and caring the social environment, the freer a person is to experiment with new behaviours, attitudes and action theories.

10. In order for changes in behaviour patterns, attitudes and action theories to be permanent, both the person and the social environment have to change. Team training is more effective than individual training because it changes both individuals and their social environment.

11. It is easier to change a person's action theories, attitudes and behaviour patterns in a group context than in an individual context.

12. A person accepts a new system of action theories, attitudes and behaviour patterns when they accept membership into a new group.

Figure 14.1 Principles of Experiential Learning—Kurt Lewin, 1987

EXPERIENTIAL LEARNING CYCLE

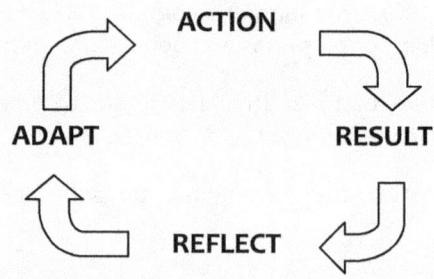

1. **ACTION**
   The learner takes action, trying out the strategies and processes in his or her current *action theory*. (This can happen consciously but is most often done unconsciously.)

2. **RESULT**
   The learner then experiences the consequences/results of their actions. Results usually provide feedback about whether one's actions are helpful or not, but it is not always a given that the learner will notice a *teachable moment*. The learner needs to consciously look for the feedback inherent in the results of their actions or have their attention drawn to it by a facilitator.

3. **REFLECT** (Lewin combines *Stages 2 and 3*)
   Feedback can be from the experience itself (success/failure) or from others observing and interacting with participants. It can also come from self-reflection. In most facilitated programs, the facilitator will provide participants with some specific reflection questions which lead to insights about behaviour and results. Thus the learner discovers what works and what doesn't.

4. **ADAPT** (Lewin labels this as the *Integration* Stage)
   As a result of this process of feedback, examination and reflection on the consequences of their actions, the learner integrates this updated information and experience into a new *action theory*, thus adapting their behaviour for new situations.

It is the last two stages that make the difference between having a learning experience or just having an experience without learning.

Figure 14.2 The Experiential Learning Cycle—adapted from Kolb[45] & Lewin, 1990

The Power of Adventure

One of the fundamentals of *Adventure Learning* is the element of 'risk.' To venture is to take a risk, not knowing what the outcome will be. Risk by its very definition includes the chance to benefit or to experience potentially undesirable consequences. Common examples include learning to walk or learning to drive a motor vehicle. We all live with the chance of unpleasant consequences based on the degree to which we accept and participate in the challenge of life.

ABEL programs provide opportunities for risk taking within a safe and controlled environment where the learner is presented with challenges that they perceive as risky, but in reality do not place them in any danger. This is often referred to as a 'perceived' or 'subjective' risk.

Subjective risks involved in an *ABEL* program may include addressing a group, putting one's ideas before the crowd, accepting a leadership role or abseiling over a cliff—all of which can have potentially uncomfortable consequences, but they are all in the *subjective/perceived risk* category. An important consideration for program designers is that what people perceive as risky varies considerably from individual to individual. Risk is also not a static thing, what was once perceived as risky may cease to be perceived as such in the future or vice versa.

As this discussion demonstrates, *ABEL* programs do not need to include abseiling, a high ropes course or a survival exercise to be an adventure-based program. These activities are possible components of an *ABEL* program to be included or not, depending on the learning objectives of the client and the specific needs of the participants.

Risking the Comfort Zone to Enter the Learning Zone

So why is risk so fundamentally important to learning? Almost every significant transition in life and even many of the small decisions we make, require us to risk something, whether it is security, ridicule, relationships, money or freedom. We always need to learn new things as we mature and grow in all areas of our life. Learning is breaking new ground and new ground almost always involves risk. Entering the *learning zone* requires us to leave our *comfort zone* and this is where getting comfortable with risk taking has its greatest benefit, when we take a risk to achieve something and we eventually succeed, the outcome is not only what we accomplish; it is also accompanied by feelings of joy, happiness, success and love. Embracing the challenge of risk-taking is such an important ingredient in the learning process and yet many adults have become risk-averse due to past conditioning. *ABEL* programs help us to re-engage with the learning benefits of risk taking, which can then be applied across other areas of our life.

*To venture causes anxiety, but not to venture is to lose one's self.
And to venture in the highest senses is... to become conscious of oneself.*
Soren Kierkegaard

Figure 14.3, provides a brief summary of what Mark considered to be the key ingredients that enable an *ABEL* program to have successful outcomes.

KEY INGREDIENTS FOR *ABEL* PROGRAM SUCCESS

1. **Safety**
   The physical, mental and emotional safety of participants is paramount.

2. **Facilitator Competence**
   The competence of the facilitator is the single most important factor in the success of an *ABEL* program.

3. **Challenge by Choice**
   The level of challenge is chosen by the participant, not forced upon them.

4. **A Supportive Environment**
   Trust, respect, support and encouragement are crucial to the quality of learning outcomes.

5. **Opportunities to Venture**
   Providing a variety of opportunities for participants to venture, assists them to expand their comfort zone; develop the confidence to take risks; and to learn from the feedback of their experiences.

6. **Immediate Natural Consequences**
   The consequences of a participant's actions need to be as real and immediate as possible, so that they see more vividly, the connection between their behaviour and its consequences.

7. **Fun and Play**
   Programs that include a sense of fun and play are more engaging, stimulating and memorable.

Figure 14.3 Key ingredients for *ABEL* program success—Mark Auricht, 1996

Dispelling the Myths of Adventure Learning
It was important to Mark to dispel the myths around *ABEL* programs, particularly the 'gung ho commando' image that they had been tarred with due to the media attention given to similar activities that were run by those who were more interested in the challenge aspect of adventurous activities and less interested in using them as a serious learning tool.

As I've already emphasised, professionally facilitated *ABEL* programs are less about the activities and more about the quality of the learning experience and the lessons to be gained that have relevance to the real world. Thus it is how the activities are used and facilitated that is the key.

> *The competence of the facilitator is the single most important factor in the success of an Adventure-Based Experiential Learning Program.*
> Mark Auricht

Mark Auricht was committed to educating people about *ABEL*, partly to clarify misconceptions and help potential clients understand the value of what he was offering, and also to promote *ABEL* as a valid and powerful learning methodology which up until that time, had not only been misunderstood, but also had not fully realised its enormous potential.

Mark held regular *Introduction to Adventure Based Experiential Learning* events to educate people about *ABEL* methodology and its benefits for personal and organisational development. During these events he would share some of the research he had done into the science behind *ABEL*, why it was so effective and how it could be used as a learning tool to improve individual and organisational performance. He would also engage the participants in some practical experiences to give them a taste of his approach. Many of them came away excited and eager to do more.

I was invited to speak from a client's perspective, offering an authentic testimonial by telling the story of my first *ABEL* experience with Mark—the infamous *night in Mt Crawford Forest* (see p115). Apart from Mark's program, I had also participated in a lot of tertiary studies, corporate training programs, personal development workshops and facilitator training, so I was also able to give my opinion on the differences between typical corporate training programs and my experience as a participant on Mark's *ABEL* program. I would then go on to share my experiences as a Corporate Health Consultant delivering workplace health programs, and the conclusions that I had come to about *ABEL*—particularly regarding its suitability as a tool for change, not only in a leadership and team development context, but also for improving *organisational wellness* and workplace culture.

In hindsight, I would have to say that I was far from an expert in this area when I started collaborating with Mark in the early 90s, but I was a keen student of people such as Don Ardell (a specialist in corporate wellness) and his Australian colleague, Grant Donovan. Mark's *Introduction to ABEL* sessions gave me an opportunity to share my growing passion for improving *organisational wellness* and to promote *ABEL* as a unique methodology for achieving this. Ardell also knew that 'hot action learning' was the key.

Superior Training for the Hot Action World

Don Ardell, author of the book *High Level Wellness* and an early promoter of the concept of *Organisational Wellness*, said it best: *Corporate training programs can be long, boring affairs... most participants use them for a little rest and recreation—a day out and a place to catch up on lost sleep!* Ardell calls this type of training—the "Bermuda Triangle" where information is lost for six reasons (listed in *Figure 14.4*, below).

THE TRAINING BERMUDA TRIANGLE
6 Reasons why training information is lost

1. People forget more than they ever learn
2. Their brains selectively eliminate information they don't need or want
3. There is often little opportunity to repetitively use the information
4. Boredom stops learning
5. Most people suffer from information overload
6. Most cognitive learning happens in the first 15 minutes and then decreases rapidly

Figure 14.4 The Training Bermuda Triangle—Don Ardell, 1991

Ardell wrote this back in the 90s and yet there is still a predominance of classroom style learning where intellectual theory is not followed up with the opportunity to practically apply it in the real world. Participants may come away with a greater awareness if their attention has been engaged; more information if they have taken some notes; perhaps a bit of inspiration if the presenter is connecting with the heart—but if this is not followed up with immediate opportunities to put theory into practice, in what Ardell calls the '*hot action world*' of everyday experience; then the opportunity to transform it into sustainable behaviour change is lost.

In the new economy, business success requires us to shrink the gap between learning and doing to the vanishing point.
Don Ardell

This is still true today, as we see a proliferation of professional speakers, workshops and team building programs, some of which achieve excellent outcomes if they are integrated with relevant skill development through ongoing follow up, coaching and mentoring. Unfortunately however, many one-off presentations and programs only offer short–term inspiration and awareness building. Sustainable changes to thinking, behaviour and culture are in most cases not the predominant outcomes.

In the late 90s, Simon Priest, Professor of the *Corporate Adventure Training Institute* at Brock University in Canada, was considered the world's leading authority on outdoor leadership and a leading researcher into the effectiveness of *ABEL*. In 1996 he conducted an evaluation of corporate training outcomes throughout the USA, Canada and the Asia Pacific region and identified implications for the design of *ABEL* courses. (See Figure 14.5 below, for a summary of his findings.) Priest has since authored a number of books on the subject.[46]

In the last 20 years there have been very few evidence-based research studies done in this area—mainly because of the difficulties in conducting scientifically controlled studies with a consistent and large enough sample group, while controlling all the other variables that may impact behaviour change outcomes. Despite this, the anecdotal evidence is overwhelming supportive of *ABEL* as a highly effective training tool.

THE EFFECTIVENESS OF USING *ABEL* AS A CORPORATE TRAINING METHODOLOGY

The key use of *ABEL* by client companies:
- Intrapersonal: increased personal confidence, risk taking and self-esteem.
- Inter-personal: enhancement of teaming, relating and collaboration skills.
- Cultural: helping a company to develop and change its culture.

Research demonstrated the following benefits from *ABEL* training:
- Development of team and leadership behaviours.
- Enhancing risk taking and developing aspects of trust.
- Assisting companies in changing their corporate cultures.

Essential design features should include:
- Pre-briefing and use of metaphors to highlight learning outcomes.
- Appropriately sequenced activities that build on each other.
- Isomorphic framing (mimicking the work place for relevance).
- Specifically focussed and facilitated debriefing.
- Pairing *ABEL facilitators* with company HR personnel.

Figure 14.5. The effectiveness of *ABEL* Corporate Training—S Priest, 1996

The Philosophy of Experiential Education

The Association of Experiential Education regards experiential education as a philosophy that informs many methodologies in which educators purposefully engage with learners in direct experience and focused reflection, in order to increase knowledge, develop skills, clarify values and develop the capacity of people to contribute to their communities and businesses. Source: http://www.aee.org/what-is-ee

John Dewey was a famous proponent of experiential education, writing *Experience and Education* in 1938. He expressed his ideas about curriculum theory in the context of historical debates about school organisation and the need to have experience at the centre of the educational process; hence, experiential education is referred to as a philosophy. Dewey's fame during that period rested on relentlessly critiquing public education and pointing out that the *authoritarian, pre-ordained knowledge* approach of traditional education was too concerned with delivering knowledge and not enough with understanding students' experiences.

For experiential education to be effective, physical experience must be combined with reflection. Our fast moving world does not often allow us the time to slow down and reflect from the 'grandstand of life.' Adding reflective practice, allows for personal introspection of challenges and key learnings. Thus, physical challenges provide a gateway through which we can observe qualities about ourselves and those with whom we interact.

The Organisational Dilemma

The principles of the above philosophy were aptly demonstrated in an activity Mark introduced me to, called the *Organisational Dilemma*. It was essentially a business simulation activity involving a fictitious organisation with different departments and levels of management. The dynamics of a typical organisation were reflected in the simulation, including communication barriers, financial considerations, compliance rules, material and human resources, as well as time constraints. The objective was to run a profitable business and to overcome any obstacles to success. Those with less leadership experience would often be put in leadership roles within the game. Conversely, those with senior positions in the real-life organisation, would be put in the more subordinate positions within the simulated organisational structure. This provided valuable insights for the participants, particularly those that had little empathy for the complex responsibilities of management.

The Business Game Evolution

Over the years I have evolved this idea into a more complex version which we now call *The Business Game*.[47] It has closer parallels with the real-world of business, replicating the complex pressures that challenge teams and leaders who are working together within an organisational structure while trying to achieve business objectives in a pressure-cooker environment. The game includes challenges that businesses need to deal with in the real world such as communication barriers, time, money and resource constraints and requires them to work on tasks such as inter-departmental communication, resource management, budgets, project management and strategic planning. Other considerations, depending on the client, can be: continuous improvement, training, staff transfers, legal compliance, health and safety. Measures of success may include productivity, morale and profitability.

Learning Outcomes from the Business Game

The *Business Game* is a catalyst for questions about things like structure, strategy and the impact of collaboration or competition between inter-dependent departments on relationships and productivity. Issues of staff morale, role ambiguity and ethics are also brought into play. The game generates a lot of thought-provoking questions, insights and sometimes *eureka* moments for participants which often shift their view of themselves and others in the workplace. People who were previously critical of management often have more empathy for those in management positions when they have experienced the pressures of leadership within the game. Conversely, those who are managers in the real world will sometimes get enlightened insights from the game about the strengths and weaknesses of their leadership style or the factors which effect trust and respect between them and those they lead. In order for learning outcomes to be relevant to participants, it is important to design the activity with the client company's specific business context in mind. Consequently, we have run many versions of the original concept over the last 15 years.

> *I can learn more about myself and others in one hour of play,
> than I ever could in a lifetime of conversation.*
> Plato

The Secrets of Experiential Learning

The following summary from the research of corporate psychologists Relly Nadler and John Luckner, provides a good explanation of the reasons why Experiential Learning, particularly simulation type exercises, is so effective. (see Figure 14.6—shared with permission from R Nadler)

SECRETS OF EXPERIENTIAL LEARNING

Activities Reflect Typical Behaviours
Participants project their problem-solving, project management, leadership and team skills onto the experience, which reveals typical behaviours.

Perturbation
The unfamiliarity of challenging experiences places people in a state of perturbation. They can't easily stand behind their normal status and roles.

Removal of Roles and Titles
Unique challenges require people to demonstrate genuine team skills versus relying on their workplace role or title.

Abbreviated Learning Cycle
Time between action and results is compressed, so consequences of decisions can be examined and improved. Time lag in the real world is greater, often delaying learning from experience. *ABEL* provides more immediate feedback.

Greater Learning Intensity
Participants are asked to step back and evaluate their performance during the experience, so issues can be discussed more intensely than they can at work.

Non-business-critical Environment
Participants experience chaos, crisis and unpredictable change, in a safe, non-business-critical environment where consequences of failure are limited. They can develop strategies for managing these critical issues back in the workplace.

Shared Experience
There is a shared experience which can be related back to the work environment. The unique experience helps team members to see each other in a different light.

Risk-Taking is Encouraged
The experience allows participants to take risks, try new roles and make mistakes with no cost. Perceived risk-taking inspires everyone to stretch their comfort zone.

Accelerated Relationship Development
The communication and collaboration required to meet these challenges develops relationships quickly. People often get to know each other better in one day within this context than they would over a year at work.

Figure 14.6 Secrets of Experiential Learning—adapted from Nadler[48] and Luckner, 2004

Chapter 15   The Art of Facilitation

Lessons for Leaders, Teachers, Coaches and Mentors
My experience over ten years working with Mark and during the last fifteen years since his death, has re-enforced to me that the key ingredient for personal and professional development using the modality of experiential or metaphorical learning is indeed the skill of the facilitator. This includes designing and guiding the experience, and then drawing out the lessons that are relevant to the everyday challenges of the participant's real world. To be an artful facilitator of experiential learning, one must possess a range of skills, some of which are obvious and others quite subtle.

I still have video footage of the first programs that I co-facilitated with Mark and have learnt a lot about the art of facilitation from watching him in action, as he facilitates an activity and debriefs the key lessons with participants. His ability to make links to the real world, to draw out insights and to challenge participant's thinking was a great example for me.

I'd like to share some of the key lessons I learnt from Mark about the art of facilitation. These are also lessons that are relevant to the coaching and mentoring roles of leadership, so when I use the term 'facilitator' you can substitute these other terms, as the skills relate to each of them.

Designing 'Games' for the Hot Action World
The first consideration for a facilitator is to design a customised experience that will meet the desired learning outcomes of the client. Activities need to be engaging, relevant and flexible in their design in order to meet the learning needs of a diversity of participants. The term 'game' can literally refer to a game-like experience or any metaphorical activity or real-life simulation that is used to mirror the real world. The design of the game will make a big difference to the quality of the learning outcomes that participants leave with. For example: a fun 'team-bonding' activity that has little obvious relevance to the real world and that has not been thoughtfully designed and facilitated, is a significantly less potent learning experience, compared with a strategically designed activity that is framed clearly, facilitated professionally and debriefed mindfully. It is the facilitator's role to create an experience which by virtue of its design, elicits emotion, engages interest, reveals strengths and weaknesses, stimulates imagination, challenges beliefs and inspires courage in those who participate. A well-designed activity will help the participant to see how their thoughts, feelings and behaviours in 'the game', mirror their reality in the real world.

For an activity or *game* to be really effective, it needs to be an experience which is relevant to the context within which the individual or group is currently operating or in preparation for what they will be doing together, so that the experience becomes a stronger metaphor for their reality. This then makes it a lot easier to see the connections between 'the game' and the real world. It is therefore important for a facilitator to become familiar with the client's *hot action world*, as Don Ardell refers to it.

Opening The Awareness Window
The second phase of experiential learning is about how we open up what I call the 'Awareness Window' of a learning participant. Most of us are not very aware of our habitual behaviours until our attention is drawn to them or unless we go exploring during the process of self-improvement.

After experiencing a number of Mark's group challenges and simulation activities as a participant and then working alongside him as an apprentice facilitator, I soon discovered there was a big difference between being a participant in an activity versus being in the role of the facilitator. There is a very different level of awareness regarding the big picture, and both participant and facilitator experience a learning activity from a different vantage point. The facilitator is more in observation and guide mode whereas the participant is not thinking about these responsibilities; unless they have consciously chosen to take on a role of observer, leader or facilitator within 'the game.' Participants are generally so caught up in their own experience that they will pay less attention to the bigger picture and not be as mindful of their fellow participant's point of view.

Much of the detail about behaviour that happens during an activity, game or simulation, will go unnoticed by participants until they are directed to notice it as they are 'playing the game' or during the debrief. Initially though, we may intentionally not provide much of a briefing or 'framing' for the first activity because we want to see what happens when we just throw people into an 'unprocessed' or raw experience that is not tampered with by an over-zealous teacher. Mark taught me not to draw attention to the psychology behind 'the game' at the beginning of a program by pre-empting what might happen or explaining the science behind the typical ways that groups or individuals might behave when dealing with a challenge. *We want them to do what they would normally do, without too much instruction and interference,* he would say. I found this to be a bit challenging initially, as I had a tendency to rescue, give advice and over-empathise with the frustration of participants who might be struggling with a challenge.

Chapter 15—The Art of Facilitation

The *Johari Window*[49] is a model that was created in 1955 by two American psychologists, Joseph Luft and Harrington Ingham and used to help people better understand their relationship with self and others. I like to call it *The Awareness Window* because one of the goals of experiential learning activities or *games* is to open up the awareness window, thus revealing to self and others the typical attitudes and behaviours that either help or hinder our relationships and performance. Experiential learning provides immediate feedback informing the self-awareness of participants.

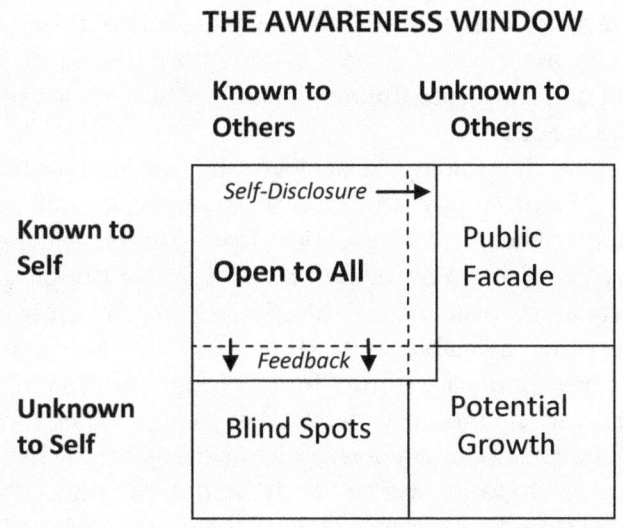

Figure 15.1 Awareness Window, adapted Johari Window—Luft and Ingham, 1955

Feedback and Self-Disclosure

One of the key phrases that Mark would always refer to during the introduction of a program was—*Games reflect typical behaviour.* This is a foundational concept in the field of experiential learning. People have a strong tendency to behave in a *game*, the same way they do in real life. Games provide safe environments where we can get valuable *feedback about our blind spots* that may otherwise remain out of our awareness. We can also choose to share more about ourselves with others, which helps them to get to know us. *ABEL* programs also provide safe spaces for self-disclosure. Openness and authenticity are major pillars for trust.

Games mirror typical behaviour.

Pre-Framing (Pre-brief or Front-loading)
Apart from setting clear expectations for a safe learning environment, 'framing' the context for a specific activity, is not always done in full detail when we want them to have an initial raw experience. However, once participants start to become aware of their typical behaviors and some of their *blind spots* after being thrown in the deep end without much briefing, activities can be specifically framed for desired learning outcomes, providing more opportunities to widen one's self-awareness window.

Framing an activity provides a scaffold to help participants focus on certain things and to reach higher levels of awareness. With a bit of processing and coaching after their initial 'raw experience' they are helped to become more mindful of the experiential learning cycle of *Action→Results→Reflection→Adaptation,* including how to observe their own behavior while in action.

Providing more scaffolding, is achieved by *pre-framing* the activity with suggestions of what to pay attention to, such as: self-talk; emotions that they might experience; communication from others; and behaviours they may not have paid attention to before. This is like pre-programming their perceptual radar to pick up on things they may not have noticed previously. The lessons available from the game happen much more consciously when participants are 'setup' for it through pre-framing.

Sometimes participants will catch themselves doing and saying things they would normally not be aware of but more often than not, the facilitator or other participants will notice it before they do. There must therefore, be a safe, supportive and confidential environment within which participants receive the gift of feedback. This can happen in the middle of an activity during what we call a 'Freeze Frame' or at the end of an activity during the post-activity debrief (discussed on page 157).

Freeze Frames
Freeze Frames can occur at anytime during an activity but usually after a period of settling in where not much upfront guidance has been given, participants have gone through the initial honeymoon phase or minor frustrations and have started to become dysfunctional or have hit a wall. As the term suggests, a *freeze frame* is like freezing a movie while it is running, so it is a bit like a 'time out' in sport, where we take a short break during a game to reflect on progress, challenges we are having, possible solutions to obstacles, improvements we can make and perhaps 'lessons so far' for the team or for individuals. This can also be a time to give some feedback but usually only that which will assist participants to improve their performance in the remainder of the game.

More challenging feedback is best left until after the game, when it can be delivered more safely with more time for conversation. We don't want to mess with the individual's head while they are in *mid-flight* so to speak. This is also something for leaders to keep in mind while coaching people and leading projects or a business venture in the real-world.

We often encourage participants to conduct *freeze frames* in their organisations, especially when everyone is focused on a task, steaming along with their heads down, not noticing the way they are behaving until they come up for air and take a seat in the grandstand with their coach. This is why planning and progress meetings, annual retreats and regular mentoring is so important. Rather than wait for an annual review to give feedback, it is more constructive to provide regular opportunities for communication, including regular *coffee conversations*,[50] as Grant Donovan calls them. When we get to know people on a more human level and have regular informal conversations, it is much easier to give feedback in the context of that kind of relationship. It is still important to choose one's timing and words wisely—asking questions to help a person to reflect on their behaviour is preferable to giving them your opinion. (For example: *If there was something I could tell you that could help you to improve, would you want to hear it? My perception is... was that your intention? Were you aware of how your behaviour was perceived? Can I suggest... ?)*

Guiding the Game
Games and activities can have unlimited boundaries with flexible rules, resources and timeframes, or very tight boundaries depending on the timeframe one has to work with and the learning outcomes requested by the client group. It is best to keep the boundaries flexible, so that the game can be tweaked as it comes alive.

Although there are usually certain learning outcomes we wish to bring to light, not all outcomes of experiential learning are predictable and pre-determined. Sometimes unexpected gems emerge from the mist, which is why the facilitator's approach is usually to allow the game to unfold as organically as possible so as not to inhibit natural behaviours that surface throughout the game. Even when a participant's behaviour seems to be sabotaging desired outcomes, it is helpful to resist the urge to interfere. There is always something to learn from the seemingly inappropriate choices that people sometimes make during a game. One of the most challenging things for a facilitator is to hold back on rescuing participants (in much the same way as a parent or mentor must sometimes allow those they are leading to learn from their mistakes). This allows for *teachable moments* to arrive that would otherwise be lost or concealed.

If a game is well-designed and the facilitator is experienced, all of game's boundaries can be trimmed to achieve a 'sweet spot' of learning with an appropriate level of challenge for the level of the learner and the purpose of the game. Ideally we want to encourage learners to stretch their *comfort zone* in a psychologically healthy way, so that they enter the *growth or learning zone* of their own accord and to the extent they choose to challenge themselves. It is important therefore to set this expectation in the briefing. 'Challenge by Choice' is one of the fundamentals of *ABEL*.

Finding the Sweet Spot

Activities can be a waste of time if the task does not pose enough of a challenge to stretch the participants either physically, mentally, emotionally or socially (if the purpose of an experience is to help participants to find a deeper connection or understanding of the spiritual aspects of self, then this may also be a consideration in how an experience is designed and facilitated).

On the other hand, if a challenge is too difficult, it can create too much stress for a group or an individual participant, which can also be a destructive rather than a constructive learning experience. Thus the facilitator needs to be aware of where the *sweet spot* is in terms of the degree of difficulty that is appropriate for the desired learning outcomes and the receptivity of the learner. The challenge gradient must be enough to keep participants engaged in the *learning zone* and at the same time, not so steep that it is unsafe physically, mentally, emotionally, spiritually or socially.

> ***A master facilitator has the ability to monitor the learner's response to the gradient of a challenge and to make subtle adjustments to that gradient, so the learner stays in the sweet spot.***

Knowing and having a feel for the *sweet spot* and how to stay within it, is much like trimming the sail on a yacht to take best advantage of the changing wind. If the sail is too tight it will luff as the wind starts to pass on the wrong side of the sail, causing it to vibrate. The boat will then lose forward momentum. If the sail is too loose, then there is not enough wind speed across its curved surface and so the amount of lift from the 'wing dynamics' of the sail will drop and the boat will again lose forward momentum. So there is a *sweet spot* in sailing where the sail is just at the right trim to achieve optimal lift through forward speed and momentum. Master sailors develop a feel for this, drawing on experience and instinct. Master facilitators have the same feel for how to 'trim' an experience to get the optimal learning and growth it has to offer.

Multi-Dimensional Awareness

One of the less obvious but crucial skills of a facilitator is situational awareness. They need to be mindful of the big picture and be focused enough to observe behaviour and listen for what people are saying to themselves and others. A good facilitator will pay attention to all the subtle details, including: body language, tone of voice, proximity of people to each other, tensions between people and within individuals, and so on. Then with the 'eyes in the back of their head' they must also keep tabs on safety, time and rule infringements. There is a lot to be aware of. Master facilitators can do this with ease but it takes a long time to get to this level of competence.

Similarly, elite sports people can not only pay attention to the immediate task at hand but are also able to pay attention to team morale, other players who need feedback or support, opposition players who need to be nullified etc! Ice hockey players have a saying: *skate to where the puck is going to be...* this implies that a player needs to anticipate, follow their intuition and be where they need to be before the puck or the ball gets there. Masterful players have a multi-dimensional awareness, as do good facilitators, leaders and guides.

Post-Activity Reflection (Debrief or Review)

The next phase of experiential or metaphorical learning is the post activity reflection phase, often called a debrief. This is where participants reflect on their results and the attitudes and behaviours that either helped or hindered their success. The focus here is not on giving feedback initially but on posing questions that will provide a focus for reflection. The *post-activity* or *program finale* debrief is possibly the most important phase of experiential learning. Mark often told participants that he had no investment in whether they succeeded or failed at a task—he was more interested in what they learned from it. Of course it is always nice to succeed and high-five each other when we achieve a challenging objective but often we learn more from failure or struggling to achieve a goal; this is when we are most vulnerable, most likely to behave in highly functional or dysfunctional ways. So the lessons are more obvious and memorable than they would be if there was an uneventful ease to an outcome.

The experience itself without reflection is not effective in terms of learning.

Reflecting on the experience is a crucial part of the learning process and being able to effectively guide the reflection phase is one of the key skills for an experiential learning facilitator. Participants must be allowed sufficient time to process their experience and the feedback they get from it.

Providing well-framed questions for reflection and well-timed responses to comments that come to the surface in a debrief makes a big difference to the quality of the learning that comes out of this reflection phase.

Translation of Learning, Feedback and Future Application
A good facilitator will be able to guide participants to not only consider productive questions that are more likely to generate insights, but will also be able to help participants translate their insights into conclusions that are relevant in their world and that can be applied to improving future behaviour. Making the links between thoughts, feelings and behaviours that come up during a simulated experience and their relevance to the real world of business or the personal life of an individual, is not always obvious. It is often the skill of an experienced facilitator that will assist participants to discover these connections for themselves. Lessons that are discovered by the learner are much more memorable and powerful than lessons that are delivered from a text book or chalkboard.

> **Learning is caught not taught.**

Translating the learning to reality and helping participants to see how it can be applied in their future with constructive changes in behaviour, is the final objective of the experiential learning facilitator. This can also include providing constructive feedback based on observed behaviour or helping participants to set their own goals for improvement based on the personal insights they may have gained during the experience or from the feedback of other participants.

The End Game
The overall aim of a learning program is to make a difference in the awareness, education and growth of the individual and the group. My belief is that personal and professional development is not about creating something new that does not exist already. It is more about revealing the potential within us and between us that is already there but perhaps laying dormant, like a seed beneath the winter snow. Our challenge is to conduct an 'archeological dig' of sorts, then to polish the rocks to reveal the gems within. When we cut through the cross-section of a tree trunk we can observe the patterns of the past and reveal its rings of growth. To learn through the metaphors of our experience we often need to dig to find the gold, but when we do so, we can find many valuable treasures that we didn't know were there.

Summary of the Subtle Essentials for Experiential Learning Facilitators
After Mark died I assisted his wife Catherine to continue running some of the corporate programs for *Venture Corporate Recharge* (VCR) before completing a handover to the new owner 12 months or so later. During this handover period, there were new staff to be trained and coached in the finer points of facilitating experiential learning activities, which made up a large part of what *VCR* offered to the corporate world. Because I had worked in the corporate arena for more than a decade at that point and had worked as a facilitator with and been mentored by Mark; I was asked by the new owner to design and run a facilitator training program for his less experienced staff. This caused me to reflect on what Mark had taught me and how I had integrated it into my own understanding of the profession. Below in Figure 15.2, I provide a list of 7 *essentials* for *ABEL* facilitators and other experiential teachers to keep in mind. These are more about the subtleties, rather than the technical skills. (For those interested in training for facilitator, coaches, mentors and presenters, please see Services, p415.)

7 Essentials for Facilitators, Mentors, Coaches and Guides

1. Begin with the end in mind—design, pre-frame, guide and debrief the experience accordingly.

2. It's not about you and your ego, it's about them—what's in it for them?

3. Focus on delivering or helping them to discover, small and profound pieces 'chunk it down'.

4. Trust that everything is happening as it should, even when things don't seem to go to plan and people lose the plot or fail miserably—let go of any attachment to the way you think it should go.

5. People 'show up' in the space we provide them with, so make it safe but also appropriately challenging.

6. Be bold and be you... get on with what you're there for—to share your *Medicine* (your gifts) and help them find theirs.

7. Be in the now and allow things to flow, knowing your destination, while being open as to how you get there, or to ending up somewhere else.

Figure 15.2 7 Essentials for *ABEL* Facilitators—Auricht and Enright, 2002

Twenty-five years after my first endeavours in this field of experiential learning, I am still learning and modifying the way I do things, as I continue to distill what Mark shared with me and blend it with my own ideas and the lessons I have also learnt from Gabrielle, as we have co-facilitated programs together since starting our own business in the year 2000.

The 7 Essentials listed in *Figure 15.2* are my summary of the key things that Mark imparted to me through his example and during the many conversations we had over lunch, during a road trip, or in the darkness of a late night observing a group while they struggled to solve a problem... I miss those conversations in the flesh and yet sometimes still, he turns up in my dreams to share some insight with me.

> ***Who dares to teach must never cease to learn.***
> John Cotton Dana

Vision Quest, 2012

Reflecting on your own experiential learning

1. Who are those in your life that you respect as mentors and seek feedback from?
2. How prepared are you to explore your blindspots and to discover your true potential?
3. How often do you take time out to reflect on what you are learning and how you can improve in your work or personal life?

Chapter 16   Secret Destinations

All journeys have secret destinations of which the traveller is unaware.
   Martin Buber

 On a Wednesday afternoon in August 1999, I found myself lying on Doctor Brian Sando's examination table. I worked with Brian for about 12 years at Corporate Health Group. This afternoon I was far from healthy, lying there in pain, overcome by nausea, and at a loss to know why? It wasn't until some days later, after having an endoscopy and another flexible scope stuck up my nose and down the back of my throat to view my vocal cords, that I discovered I was suffering from acute gastritis and had a tumour on my vocal cords.

After some medical intervention, the gastritis was under control and a year or so later the tumour had disappeared. Even though I had some early speech difficulties prior to the more serious voice problems mentioned previously in Chapter 13, it was apparently unrelated to the tumour.

On that Wednesday afternoon, I made a decision…I decided that I should take the risk to leave the security of full-time employment and follow my dream to work for myself in collaboration with Mark. I had numerous discussions with him over the following year about working together more and after discussing it with Gabrielle, who was very supportive of the idea, I ended up not leaving my job until June 2000, almost 12 months after deciding to take this leap of faith. I then started to work with Mark on a casual basis leading up to his departure for Everest. This was to become the foundation of a new direction for me and, although Mark did not come back from Everest, I am grateful to him for helping me to set a new course.

Despite being lost for a while after Mark's death, I was committed to continuing the mission that was spawned from our relationship by developing my own business with Gabrielle, while at the same time supporting Mark's business until it was sold to a new owner. During this time I assisted with training some of the new staff and worked as a casual facilitator for the new owner until things were back on an even keel. It was at about this time that I started to have trouble with my voice again, only this time it had become a major problem and one that threatened to derail me from the new track I was on. Little did I know that it was, ironically, the very thing that may have kept me *on* track with my longer-term purpose!

In search of answers to the challenges I was having with my voice, I commenced a journey that took me to places I had not even imagined. A journey that had many unknown destinations which were later to become blessings. One of these was the Kokoda Track, which became a defining experience and a key turning point that eventually led me to where I am today—working with Gabrielle in the areas of personal and organisational wellness, adventure travel and helping people to live their best life. In Chapter 28 I will share more details of my connection with the Kokoda Track and Papua New Guinea, but for now, let's just say that my inner voice lead me there, and it became a pivotal part of my healing.

After coming back from Kokoda I still had unanswered questions about my voice but I felt that I had 'found myself' again, so I tentatively ventured back into the shore break of public speaking to test the waters. Despite my internal terror, I persevered and slowly but surely regained my confidence. To settle my nerves with groups I hadn't met before, I'd tell them: *I have a steel plate in my head and every time a plane flies over, my voice has a tendency to cut out… so if this happens while I'm talking, don't let it bother you!* I also told audiences that I'd become Gideon's top Bible salesman by asking potential buyers this simple but frustrating question: *W-w-w-would you like to b-buy a B-B-Bible or sh-shall I r-r-read it to you f-first?*

Beyond Words
Before venturing to Kokoda, I did the speaking course *Beyond Words* which seemed like an apt title for me, as I considered what I would be capable of if I continued to have challenges with my voice. During the course I met Katrina Webb who is a Paralympic Gold Medalist and a professional speaker. She introduced me to the *National Speakers Association* where I learnt more about the art of public speaking. Since then we have become good friends and have ended up collaborating together on a lot of projects, some of which I will touch on later. At the time though, I questioned whether I should push on out into the waves to develop a professional speaking career in deeper waters or take an easier path where I didn't risk drowning.

I was told by an 'expert' that my speech would get worse over time and that I should give up any hope of continuing with public speaking. I haven't spoken to that person since, and so far their words have not come true. One gift that I did take away from that consultation was that it caused me to consider my options—one of which was to specialise in *experiential learning* which relied more on my listening and guiding skills, than what I had to tell people. This of course led me to focus on *ABEL* as my saving grace. Perhaps the bush was where I belonged, rather than the stage.

One of the lessons I learned from the *Beyond Words* course and from my time with the *National Speakers Association* was that, whatever path I chose to follow, whether it be a keynote speaker, facilitator, coach or guide; the secret to powerful communication was not just in the message but more so in the messenger. If I was going to be an effective messenger in any form, I had to speak my truth and speak it from the heart. I knew then, that I needed to become more authentic by tapping into my own unique essence when I covered subjects that I had been speaking about for years but had not had the courage to speak about from the heart. This would require me to share more of my own personal stories, beliefs and ideas. I guess this book, in part, is an extension of that commitment to communicate my truth.

The Foundations of Healthy Teams
The upshot of all of this was that I ended up finding that a combination of keynote speaking, interactive workshops and activity-based team programs was a good fit for my skill set and it took me back to the work I had enjoyed doing with Mark. This lead to the establishment of *Healthy Teams* as a trading name which summed up my key areas of expertise at the time (they also happened to be two words I could say on the phone).

Gabrielle came on board with her unique set of skills and together we continued along the path I had hoped to pursue with Mark. Over the next 10 years, *Healthy Teams* became particularly well known for its 'experiential/metaphorical learning' methodology, especially in the areas of team and leadership development. Gabrielle and I developed a number of adaptations to activities I had learnt from Mark and designed a lot of our own. We also created some new models for educating people and businesses about team culture and situational leadership. Some of these evolved out of the programs I co-facilitated with Mark and others from my subsequent experiences working with hundreds of teams from a variety of organisations. Two particular models that we now use are: *The Foundations of Healthy Teams* and the *True North Leadership Compass*.

In Parts III to V of this book I will be focussing on leadership, but for now allow me to give you some background on the *Foundations of Healthy Teams* Model—Seven key elements of successful teams—nothing new, just communicated in a different way and with a subtle salute to Mark who used a similar model with a different look.

All knowledge comes from the same source, there is nothing really new, only a new way of viewing it, communicating it or making it relevant. It is often ancient wisdom dressed in different clothes.

The Seven Team Foundations
During the introduction to most of our programs, we start with an activity called *Blind Line Up*, which is commonly used as a team problem-solving challenge or icebreaker. During this activity, team members must achieve a common objective despite some significant communication barriers and time pressure. (In this book I won't divulge too many details about activities that I refer to in case you haven't done them yet.)

It is possible to spend a whole day debriefing all of the possible metaphors associated with the *Blind Line Up* activity, depending how it is framed and facilitated. As an introductory activity though, it lends itself to generating a good summary of the key elements that impact team success. Over the years we've done this activity many times, leading us to identify seven key factors that we consider to be the foundations for healthy teamwork, whether it be in sport, at work, in a family or in a community organisation. Of course there are other words we could use but these are the most common over-arching themes that always surface as we continue to do our practical research through experience. In 2005 Gabrielle and I developed the *'Foundations of Healthy Teams'* Model (see *Figure 16.1* below).

Figure 16.1 Foundations of Healthy Teams—W&G Enright © 2005

TEAM FOUNDATIONS DEFINED

Vision
A shared vision for the future provides inspiration and sets the direction for the team. Alignment of purpose and flying in formation is essential.

Values
Shared team values reinforce team culture. The way the team works together to achieve their vision. Values provide a compass like guidance and principles to help decision-making.

Responsibility
Everyone is proactive in responding to the needs of the team, regardless of position or title. There is a 'no blame... only solutions' culture.

Trust
Strong bridges of trust are essential for open and honest communication as well as empowering team members to make autonomous decisions. Team mates are reliable, encouraging and consistently supportive.

Diversity
Differences bring a variety of personalities, expertise, perspectives and creativity to a team, giving it more strength. It can also cause conflict but learning to use conflict constructively can produce beneficial outcomes. Harnessing diversity is a team's greatest challenge.

Communication
Open and honest communication is essential to the ongoing health of team relationships and gives a team the ability to adapt, grow and achieve optimum performance.

Leadership
Leadership based on 'position and title' is out—'shared situational leadership' is in. Leadership is central to the establishment and maintenance of all other foundations. Leaders are the architects, builders and maintenance people within teams and therefore, need to be committed to all of the seven foundations.

Figure 16.2 Team Foundations Defined—W&G Enright © 2005

Reflecting on the Team Foundations

It is a useful exercise for teams or team members to evaluate themselves in these seven areas and to ask the following questions:

1. Where are my/our strengths and areas for improvement?

2. What specific behaviours do I/we need to change, that would improve the health of our team/organisation/community/family? (Start / Stop / Do More / Do Less).

Leadership is Central to Success

You'll notice that Leadership is located at the centre of the model. Unlike old hierarchical models of leadership which emphasise a top down approach, leadership in this model is central to all the other foundations. The inference here is that leadership can be taken by anyone, regardless of their position or title in a team. Leadership is framed and supported by a well articulated vision and guiding values. Respected leaders demonstrate a consistent commitment to the vision and values by living their creed.

Leadership is not always about being in charge of other people, sometimes it can be a lone action taken by the initiative of one person who sees something that needs to be done and takes on the responsibility. This can lead to solving a problem or to inspiring others who follow the example. In our model, leadership is more about the *way* we think and behave which is often underwritten by our character. Unfortunately most management training does not pay enough attention to this question of character. Training programs may result in 'management competencies' being ticked off but does not necessarily lead to authentic leadership development which requires emotional intelligence and the ability to:– self-manage; relate to a diversity of people; lead from the heart. When leaders have a willingness to learn and grow, they are more likely to develop confidence in their internal compass, and their ability to adapt to the wilderness of life. The character of a leader is paramount.

In the remainder of this book I provide a potted history of the evolution of leadership and the *new frontier* into which leaders now need to venture—a frontier which challenges old paradigms of leadership and requires leaders to be more authentic, courageous, resilient and creative if they are to be of great influence.

PART III

The New Leadership Frontier
Navigating Uncharted Horizons

Overland Track Tasmania, 2008

As I start to write the second half of this book I've come to a point where Mark's influence although still an underlying current, is less referenced as I begin to write more about what I have discovered since we parted ways.

It is as if we were sailing across the ocean together and he fell overboard. I circled around thinking I could save him but he was gone. All I could do then was to keep sailing. I crossed the horizon never to see him again but the compass heading he put me on, led me to my own *True North*.

Perhaps it is time for you to leave me now to sail your own course, I hear him saying. And so I sailed on into uncharted waters beyond the horizon.

At the Helm, 2010

This next chapter looks at the historical context of leadership and the challenges that leaders now face as they enter into unpredictable waters. Perhaps the metaphor of sailing reminds us that whilst the captain or skipper may be the person at the helm, they will often need to rely on others to take responsibility for their roles in the sailing team and if the skipper falls overboard, every other crew member must be able to take leadership, especially when the seas get rough.

> **When we find ourselves in the most primal of human conditions, facing survival alone, we must know in our gut that we can rely on the head, heart and hands of our own.**

Chapter 17   The Evolution of Leadership

Mother Theresa, Adolf Hitler, Nelson Mandela, Bill Gates, Donald Trump, Indira Gandhi, Henry Ford, Bob Dylan, Abraham Lincoln, and Albert Einstein. What do these people have in common? They are all known as world leaders or people who have had a significant impact on the world—an impact which continues to ripple on.

Not all of these leaders would be considered in a good light, depending on your opinion of their character, what they were passionate about or what they did or didn't stand for. Hitler for example was Time Magazine's *Man of the Year* in 1938 and yet history does not look upon his moral compass favourably. The reality is that they are all considered to have demonstrated strong leadership in some way. Some of them were more influential than others, some left a trail of destruction behind them and some have left the world a better place for having been in it.

They are all very different people with different values, personalities and leadership styles. Some would not see themselves as leaders in the typical sense, with a position and title that formerly grants them the authority to lead others; they have just followed their passion and ended up leading a change in the world. So... what really defines leadership?

Leadership is often talked about in terms of power, either having 'power over' others or being able to 'em-power others'. Leadership can be formal or informal, expressed consciously or unconsciously. The common denominator with leadership is influence (constructive or destructive). On a socio-political level we usually think of leadership in terms of 'who is in power,' who has most influence. Over the course of history there has been a continual shift in the power base of leadership and in the types of leaders that have evolved as humanity's priorities have changed.

The History of Power
Aside from the Elders of indigenous communities, those that have had most power in society from ancient times through to present day, include: royalty, conquerors, the church, law makers, politicians, industry leaders and the medical and education experts. These people still have a great deal of power and influence, but it is fast becoming dependent on whether people are willing to follow their leadership. A desire for more authentic and respectful relationships is making it increasingly difficult to rule with unreasonable authority, while expecting to retain the trust and respect of the majority. Positional power no longer guarantees one's level of influence.

Warrior Leadership

War has always spawned strong leaders, mostly of the authoritarian caliber whose archetype we see in the typical conquerors and warriors throughout history. Leadership development theory has often been influenced by the military thinking of its time, based on the experiences of leaders who succeeded or failed in the theatre of war. Although the principles in Sun Tzu's classic Chinese text *The Art Of War* have heavily influenced military and business thinking throughout history, times are changing and a new style of warrior is evolving—one that is more autonomous and adaptable. In modern theatres of war we rarely see the charging masses of old, blindly following orders from above. Whilst rank structure continues to provide order, this tends to dissolve into a flexible and adaptable small team approach in the field, where 'shared situational leadership' is more effective. Leadership in modern organisations is also evolving to become something quite different from what it once was.

Supervisory Leadership

The Industrial Revolution had a big impact on the evolution of leadership. Many of the books written about leadership since then have been heavily flavoured by the predominant culture of 'command and control' that worked well during the postwar industrial phase of western civilisation where growth industries revolved around mass production. Large organisations developed hierarchical structures to supervise the masses. The business landscape was characterised by authoritarian leaders and big bureaucracies. The markets had not yet gone global and national trade barriers protected local industries, resulting in a relatively stable environment within which they could survive and thrive. Supervisory leadership worked reasonably well in this context and for the most part, employees conformed to expectations and did not question authority or expect to have any input beyond their subordinate role. Current generations expect their leaders to earn the right to lead, rather than rely on their title.

The New Leadership Frontier

The world's social and economic landscape has dramatically changed in the last fifty years. We've experienced an explosion of consumerism, the social revolution of the 60s, the formation of networks and alliances and the booming information age. We now operate in a highly competitive global marketplace within which rapid communication speeds up interactions, resulting in the need for flatter structures that are more responsive and adaptable. The type of leadership necessary to survive and indeed thrive in this new frontier is completely different.

Chapter 18   The Business Biologist

Biology was my other major at university alongside learning to educate through the physical. At times I wondered whether those years of study were wasted, however biology made a valuable contribution to my understanding of wellness and has also helped me to understand *Systems Thinking*—an approach to thinking about solutions or design, from a wholistic point of view that encompasses the inter-dependency of all parts of a system, rather than analysing the parts of a problem or business in isolation, without considering how the parts interact with each other.

The Law of Equilibrium
Nature works on the law of equilibrium which has a reciprocal relationship with the inter-dependently functioning elements of, what biologists call, an ecosystem. When balance is optimal, 'things' thrive, and when the elements are out of balance, the weaker dysfunctional elements either adapt or don't survive, thus allowing balance to be restored. In businesses, communities and some species, this can lead to extinction!

If we wish to conserve something that is struggling to survive such as a garden, our health, a relationship or a business, we must ask the question—*what needs to change in order for it to survive and indeed thrive?* In a health context, we can ascertain the answer to this question through diagnostic testing, then follow with a treatment strategy to improve wellness. Like doctors, business coaches and community leaders need to have a range of skills that not only help them to diagnose problems, but also to bring things back into balance in order to restore and sustain the equilibrium of all elements within the 'business or community ecosystem.'

In a business context, I have often thought of using the term 'Business Biologist.' This idea was inspired by a book I read many years ago called *The Turning Point: Science, Society and the Rising Culture*, written by Fritjof Capra, which started me thinking about how *Systems Theory*[51] in physics applied in other spheres such as biology, psychology, sociology, economics etc. If we think of a business or an organisation as an eco system, what principles can be applied that are common to both a thriving ecosystem in nature and a thriving business? Understanding the biology of a business or an organisation can help guide our development strategies.

> **Knowing the biology of how a garden works
> helps us to nurture its growth.**

Turning Points

In *The Turning Point*, Fritjof Capra discusses how clinging to a mechanistic world view divides us and potentially leads us closer to global disaster. He compares these obsolete mechanistic ideas with what he describes as the *new world view* based on the findings of modern physics as described in his innovative and controversial best seller, *The Tao of Physics: a holistic, systems-based approach*, which in *The Turning Point* he extends to include the areas of medicine, psychology, economics, business, politics and ecology. The new vision of reality that Capra talks about in *The Turning Point* is based on awareness of the essential interdependence of all things—physical, biological, psychological, social and cultural. *It transcends current specialised disciplines and conceptual boundaries and will be pursued within new institutions,* he posits. At present there is no well-established framework that would accommodate the formulation of the new paradigm, but such frameworks are already being shaped by many individuals, communities and networks that are developing new ways of thinking and organising themselves according to new principles.

A Systems View

Capra has since written more about the relevance of this now, more widely accepted paradigm, in a book titled *The Systems View of Life* which he and co-author Pier Luigi Luisi published in 2014. In it, Capra and Luisi offer radical solutions to our 21st century challenges by focusing on the connected world and examining life through its inextricably linked systems.

Capra's *systems view* looks at the world in terms of relationships and integration. Instead of concentrating on individual parts of an organisation as if they were independent silos, the systems approach emphasises basic organisational principles similar to those that operate in nature.

Organisational development experts such as Ackoff, Senge and Covey,[52] also acknowledge the importance of *Systems Thinking*. We need to look at the inter-dependence of all the parts, just as we do in a garden. Systems in nature are intrinsically dynamic, which helps them to maintain their equilibrium in a constantly fluctuating environment. As nature needs to adapt to constant weather and seasonal changes, so too do organisations need to adapt to the local and global environment. We can no longer rely on the mechanistic, hierarchical structures that were born out of the industrial revolution. They were appropriate for their time and for the relatively stable environment within which they were established, but now we live and do business in a very different world.

The Evolution of Life

In 1990 I participated in a program run by Mark where he introduced me to an activity called *Turning Points*. It was a process of personal reflection where we had to identify key turning points in our life journey. It was interesting to see that we continually evolve based on the impact of people, places and events in our lives which sometimes challenge the paradigms we cling to, causing us to adapt to new ways of living and to head in new directions that we perhaps had not previously thought possible. Likewise we evolve in our relationships, communities, countries that we live in, and as a global community living on a constantly evolving planet. The *Gaia Theory*[53] points to the fact that planet Earth is a living, self-regulating organism and that we are part of her garden; ever changing and growing, living and dying. Turning points in life often involve the 'death of what was' and the 'birth of the new.' This requires us to let go of habitual ways of doing things that no longer serve us, and to explore unfamiliar territory and embrace new ways of operating in an evolved environment.

The Disruption Challenge

I read Capra's *The Turning Point* in 1982 while at university. Back then Capra suggested that we were at a 'turning point' in all aspects of our culture. I think his words are as true today as they were back then. It is my experience, and I suspect yours also, that we are always at a turning point as culture and society continues to experience the constant spiral of evolution. Some turning points are more significant than others but the pace of change now is mind numbing, particularly due to the speed of current day communication and the impact of technological evolution, now referred to as 'Digital Disruption.'

Our son Peter, who works as an engineer in Boston USA, recently won an award for an article he wrote about the impact of digital technology as a disrupter to the engineering industry. In it he makes the following point.

As much as digital disruption is about the utilisation of technology, it is also about how digital technology can change social and business interactions. If this is disregarded, it can be easy to misread the bow wave of disruption as a passing technological trend. To rise to these challenges and remain relevant, companies must approach adaptation with proactive vision rather than defensive reaction or casual disregard. Leaders need to be empowered with the authority to act quickly and decisively in response to digital disruption which will continue to be a growing challenge.

The Impact of Digital Disruption in the Engineering Industry[54]—Peter Enright, 2016

The New World Chaos

In a world where there seems to be more disruption and less order, the term 'New World Order' would seem to be somewhat of an oxymoron. Chaos theorists in physics, mathematics, biology and sociology have in the last 50 years become more aware of the unpredictable variables that influence what would otherwise be considered somewhat predictable systems. In reality the world's economies, business organisations and global communities are very dynamic systems that are highly sensitive to small random variables. Small changes in initial conditions can yield widely diverging and unpredictable outcomes. This is popularly known as *The Butterfly Effect,* which is defined as:- *the sensitive dependence on initial conditions in which a small change in one state of a deterministic nonlinear system can result in large differences in a later state.*[55] This unusual term, coined by Edward Lorenz, came from the metaphorical example of a hurricane's path being influenced by minor fluctuations in the air caused by a distant butterfly flapping its wings several weeks earlier. Who would think that such a small and seemingly insignificant event could have such an amplified effect somewhere else?

Modern organisations are increasingly being viewed in a similar context—they are more like the complex adaptive systems in nature which are open and interconnected. Their structures and systems are subject to internal and external forces which may be sources of chaos. Leading organisations are now beginning to acknowledge that they need to be able to rapidly adapt in a world that is becoming ever more chaotic.

The Global Garden

If we view the world as a garden without borders, we can see how interdependent we have become and how much the biological term 'ecosystem' has become applicable to our organisations, the global economy and world politics. The *World Wide Web* is perhaps the most obvious example.

After visiting Japan some years ago with my father who lived there for a time during the Korean War, I fell in love with Japanese gardens and have since created a more 'wild' version in our back yard. A traditional Japanese Garden is highly structured with key elements such as rocks, water, bridges and specific plants that are carefully arranged to imitate nature in miniature and that often reflect ancient mythology. Great efforts are taken to maintain their beauty. Trees, shrubs and lawns are meticulously manicured, and delicate mosses are swept clean of debris. During winter, plants are insulated and straw wraps are used to protect against bug infestations. Whilst Japanese gardens are designed to mirror nature and to provide a sacred space for meditation and contemplation, they are often closed and highly controlled spaces that do not have to adapt to the realities of a wild ecosystem. Ours is a somewhat unorthodox Japanese garden, in that it has evolved more naturally and is a more open system.

A Garden Without Borders

When I look across to our garden from this page I see the abundance and beauty that has grown out of the bare earth since we started planting about fifteen years ago. The garden beds are no longer separated by bamboo edges, stepping stones and bridges. All of the plants flow into each other, but in a strange way they lean one way or another to allow space for their neighbours, and some provide shade for those less fortunate. They have worked out how to co-exist with very little pruning from me.

Similarly the 'garden' of the globalised world in which we now live, no longer has fixed boundaries with neatly pruned plants and manicured edges. Perhaps it never did have, even though some politicians and patriots liked to think so. The boundaries are man-made and we try to control them but they are permeable really—an illusion we have created based on an outdated mechanistic view of the world, which many adhere to for the most part, but which separates and divides us, rather than uniting the whole.

As I proof-read this paragraph, which was written almost a year ago, the USA is inaugurating its new president and there is talk of a wall being built to protect their border. There was another wall built between East and West Berlin in 1961 (the year of my birth) that stood for almost thirty years. I remember the joy I felt in November 1989 when I saw everyday people pulling it down piece by piece. This symbolised the opening up of the boundary between East and West. If only we could learn from history. As I shake my head, Gabrielle reminds me that it is fear that creates walls, but love, like water, is more powerful than bricks and mortar. The desire for freedom will always conquer fear in the end. This sounds idealistic I know, but should we leave idealism to artists, poets and songwriters?

> *Some may say I'm a dreamer but I'm not the only one.*
> *I hope some day you'll join us and the world will be as one.*
> John Lennon

In 1971 John Lennon wrote the song *Imagine*. In his cry from the heart he encouraged us to imagine a world at peace without the barriers of borders or the divisions of religion and nationality, and to consider the possibility that the focus of humanity should be living a life unattached to material possessions. Whilst most of us would love this to be so, the truth is, we do live in a world with territorial borders, religious differences and commercially driven consumerism that doesn't seem to be going in the other direction anytime soon. Despite this, these boundaries are becoming more easily overcome due to technological advances in transport and communication, more international political collaboration, free-trade agreements, global economic inter-dependence and the beginnings of inter-faith tolerance and greater social freedoms. These turning points for the better also bring with them a lot of challenges as we learn to live in a more wild and untamed garden without neatly trimmed boundaries. Many of the challenges we face have solutions, but fear of change and loss of power make progress difficult.

> **There is nothing more delicate to take in hand, nor doubtful in its success, than to step up as a leader of change.**
> Machiavelli

Some would argue that national protection policies may no longer be healthy for all economies in the new global environment—an environment where the opportunity and risk associated with international trade and competition can be a blessing or a curse. Do we respond to the opportunity or the risk? Do we protect inefficient and unprofitable industries that can't compete in the global landscape at the expense of investing in others that can? Do we stick with outdated company structures and leadership models or do we adapt to the new frontier?

Our global garden is now abundant with diversity and overcrowded vegetation competing for resources. The organisations in which we now work are more sensitive to *the Butterfly Effect* and the natural chaos of this more open global community. There is now a greater need for all employees to understand the 'biology' of their businesses, the ecosystems of the organisations they work in and how their role impacts the whole.

Employees in this more chaotic and fast moving environment need to be able to make self-directed decisions without having to wait for an answer from above before they can make a move. The old paradigms of leadership become a liability in this new context and yet it is not easy to change tack overnight. The environment we now live and work in calls for a new approach to leadership which I refer to as the 'New Leadership Frontier.' I believe this is what Capra referred to when he talked about *establishing new types of organisations, developing new ways of thinking and leading according to new principles* (page 172). It is this emerging leadership paradigm and the consequent need for innovative approaches to leadership development that we will explore in coming chapters.

Chapter 19 Mountains of Gold in a Silver Landscape

Mt Salkantay Peruvian Andes, 2013

 *It was late in the day... trudging through drifts of snow, soft and squeaking as its ice crystals crunched under foot, we crossed a saddle nearing 5000m on the Salkantay trail in the Peruvian Andes. Looking back to the east, high up on the snow capped ridges of the silver landscape we could see peaks of gold as the setting sun hit the edge of the mountains within its searchlight rays. This sight captured my eye for beauty!*

I've often wondered why our brain and emotions are stimulated by beauty, inspiration, things and people that stand out from the crowd. Is it because we have a divine urge toward seeking ideals?

Some people's lives are like *a mountain of gold in a landscape of silver*. They stand out as a beacon of inspiration, not only in the qualities of their character but also in the gifts they share with others. When we follow our passions and become the best we can be, we encourage others to pursue their dreams as well.

In the same way, great organisations, causes, works of art, beautiful gardens and breathtaking wonders of nature, all stand out in contrast to the everyday ordinariness of our experience. These *mountains of gold* inspire some of us to seek our own ideal self.

It was for those of us who sought to achieve our potential that Mark would often ask the question: *What are the characteristics of highly effective leaders and teams?* This is a question worth contemplating but then we also need to ask the more important question: *Which of these characteristics are strengths of mine and which would I like to develop?*

Seeking one's ideal self often requires us to answer challenging questions, to set audacious goals and to take the risk of changing some of the habitual ways we live life and interact with others. Some leaders will be open to this challenge if they desire to become the mountains of gold in a landscape of silver. Great businesses, communities, sporting teams and families, require great leadership, not just from those at the helm, but from everyone.

Good to Great
In Jim Collins' book *Good to Great* he researches the key characteristics that lead to some companies making the rare transition from just doing a good job, to fulfilling their greatest potential through continuous improvement and the pursuit of excellence. These 'great' companies, you could say, are like the mountains of gold in a landscape of silver. They stand out, offering an example of what is possible.

Collins believes that one of the characteristics that make companies great is having leaders who are humble and committed to do what is best for the company rather than being driven by ego and purely personal aspirations. I would add that they do even better when 'what is good for the company' is also aligned with the personal values of the leader. Having integrity and a personal vision that is aligned with the vision and values of the company makes a leader more *trust-* and *respect-worthy*, more authentic and more inspiring to follow.

Collins also emphasises that *getting the right people on the bus first*, is a priority before figuring out where to go. This begins with having the right people leading the organisation, and then there is the question of who is the best fit for various roles. *Finding the right people and trying them out in different positions is essential if you want to have people working to their strengths and behaving in alignment with the company culture and the requirements of their role,* claims Collins.

This sounds obvious but often people who are technically brilliant or have been around for a while will rise to positions of leadership without necessarily being the best fit for the team they are leading or having the appropriate people skills, emotional intelligence and humility required of great leadership. In our work with some dysfunctional teams, Gabrielle and I still find this to be the case at times. Not every expert makes a great leader.

Although it can be difficult to implement change when the leadership has the power and are often protective of their positions, sometimes we have to be honest enough and brave enough to call it as it is and recommend 're-assigning' people to environments where they can thrive, rather than allow them to stifle the growth of others.

The Master Gardener

I noticed this one morning in the garden... For two years I had tried to grow a frangipani tree in a pot positioned as the centre piece of my *Zen garden*, without success. After giving up, I'd removed it from the glamorous pot I'd purchased with my life's savings, and unceremoniously thrown it into the corner of the garden among an ad hoc rabble of plants. There to my dismay, it thrived within a few weeks of its stay! It was then that I realised that plants are like people or perhaps people are like plants?—sometimes they have to be removed from the pots that strangle their free expression and planted where they are able to thrive naturally.

Individuals who are motivated by an inspirational mission, working in alignment with their strengths and passions, and collaborating to develop an organisation whose core business taps into those strengths will nearly always perform at a higher level and be happier, healthier and more productive, than those that are restrained by the pots we put them in, or that are in the wrong garden.

On one of my visits to Mark's father, Clive Auricht, to discuss the progress on this book, he took me down to his veggie garden and filled my arms with spinach. I have not seen such a healthy and abundant garden. Clive obviously has a green thumb and is in tune with his garden; knowing the best place to put things, how much to water, when to plant and when to harvest. *Master Gardeners* know such things based on years of experience and some just have an intuitive sense of what works.

The majority of us rely on trial and error, learning from our failures, or we give up altogether and settle for a mediocre garden. The faster we fail the faster we learn, and so it is with teams and organisations—they will often naturally evolve into being highly functional or dysfunctional by trial and error unless there is someone nurturing their growth, tending to the weeds, pruning, watering and fertilising when necessary.

I like to think of *Master Gardeners* as those elders; masters of arts or trades; mentors and coaches; guides and teachers—who know their stuff, how to share it and how to live it. Through years of experience and being a student of their art, these *Master Gardeners* develop an intuitive sense of what works, they allow failure to be their teacher. Trusting their experience and instinct, they become one with the garden and allow it to guide them. If we spend time with them and listen to their wisdom, we can improve our gardens too.

HIGH PERFORMANCE ORGANISATIONS

At the 1993 International Conference on *Self-Managed Work Teams*, many of the researchers and company managers present made predictions of how the best performing organisations would be designed beyond the year 2000. Their predictions were as follows:
1. Self-managed work teams at all levels.
2. A composition of mini-enterprises and strategic business units.
3. Formal partnerships with customers, suppliers, government and competition.
4. Payment for versatility and adaptability.
5. Replace managers and supervisors with coaches.
6. Rotate leadership roles.
7. Develop rapid and open information systems.
8. Create a career development system for all.
9. Provide interpersonal and group process training.
10. Train their customers and their suppliers.
11. Provide at least 30 days per year of education for all workers.
12. Developing financial and business literacy for all staff.

Figure 19.1 High Performance Organisations—SMWT Conference, 1993

World's Best Practice Workplaces

Many of these predictions have come true in most of the top performing businesses around the world. However we have a long way to go before the majority of organisations can tick most of these boxes. This is not to say that all of these predictions are essential or even possible in all organisations but the proof is in the pudding when we look at well-known top performing companies such as *Google, McDonalds, Apple, Disney, Microsoft* and *Netflix*.

Attendees at the *International Conference on Self-Managed Work Teams held* in 1993, hosted by Grant Donovan, also agreed that the characteristics most wanted in graduates from business school were not their intellectual expertise, but their ability to work in teams, having great communication skills and having a real enjoyment of change.

In a more recent article published in the *Harvard Business Review* in May 2013, Professors Rob Goffee and Gareth Jones share their 6 key ingredients for creating the best workplace on Earth (Figure 19.2) and offer a checklist that you can use to assess how close your organisation is to best practice. They also acknowledge the challenges and complexities involved in achieving these ideals and offer tips for helping you to move in that direction. I recommend reading the article[56] (see notes for further details).

THE SIX KEY INGREDIENTS FOR BEST WORKPLACES
1. Authenticity matters and individual differences are nurtured.
2. Information flows freely through the organisation with radical honesty.
3. People are strengthened, as value is both derived from employees while also being instilled in them.
4. The organisation stands for something important.
5. Daily work is meaningful and energising.
6. Stupid rules are eliminated and the few rules that do exist are helpful and vital.

Figure 19.2 Ingredients for the Best Workplaces—Goffee and Jones: HBR May, 2013[56]

A New Paradigm for Leadership and Team Development
To develop great companies, high performance organisations, and the ideal workplaces mentioned above, requires a new paradigm for leadership development and a new type of training to provide team members with the mindsets and skills required to be more self-responsible and innovative. In effect, everyone at all levels of an organisation, can be thinking and behaving as high performance leaders, with the right incentive and support.

Successful organisations that embrace this new paradigm for team and leadership development will be more focused on learning outcomes such as emotional intelligence development, resilience building, innovative thinking and principle-centered decision making. This has already started to happen but more often than not is still delivered in a theoretical classroom setting rather than in a more experiential way where practical application is tested and immediate feedback is available.

> *Leading by principles requires a different kind of training –*
> *the payoff is more expertise, creativity and shared responsibility at all levels.*
>
> Dr Stephen Covey—Author of *Principle Centred Leadership*
> and *7 Habits of Highly Effective People*

Team-bonding days and seminars that provide theoretical input on the latest leadership strategies have their place and yet I don't expect them to yield a long-term change in behaviour and culture. I say this intentionally, knowing that at times we cater for some clients who just want the 'wow' experience, the positive feeling of a team building day or some short-term inspiration from a keynote talk. These are valid ways of breaking the ice or providing an adjunct to a more comprehensive program or conference experience, but significant change usually requires challenging existing ways of doing things.

Developing authentic leaders and self-responsible teams requires changing hearts and minds. The best way to do this, I believe, is through the methodology of experiential learning. This highly practical way of learning, pioneered by the likes of John Dewey, Kurt Hahn, Baden Powell, Robert Kiyosaki and researchers such as Luckner, Nadler, Priest, Lewin and Kolb, has proven to be a powerful and effective pathway for developing the characteristics required to excel in the new leadership frontier.

A Long Way to Go

The early 1990s was a period of exponential learning for me, as I became a student of *experiential learning* and applied it to *Organisational Wellness*. I was also an avid reader of Stephen Covey's work on *Principle–Centred Leadership*, and a mentee of Grant Donovan who was introducing Australian companies to international best practice with regard to the habits of high performance organisations.

In the next few chapters, I share some of what I was learning in this area before and during the time I worked with Mark. It has been almost thirty years since I started my journey in this field and I must say, I have seen a dramatic shift in the way some companies operate, but for others there is still a long way to go before they will look like the *high performance organisations* and *best practice workplaces* outlined in Figures 19.1 and 19.2.

The new frontier is forever unpredictable and constantly moving like a slippery fish in the hands of an overly confident captor.

Questions for Reflection

1. How prepared are you to adapt to the disruption of *New World Chaos*?

2. Are you working in alignment with your strengths and passions?

3. For those currently involved in an organisation or workplace—which of the *Characteristics of High Performance Organisations and Best Practice Workplaces* (listed in Figures 19.1 and 19.2), would be strengths or areas for development where you work?

Chapter 20   Exploring the New Frontier

Rafting the Franklin River—Tasmania, 2008

Inspiration, imagination and innovative thinking prepare us for departures from the comfortable shores with which we are familiar. Then comes the adventurous, yet confronting reality of taking the journey to our imagined destination. These journeys are often full of endless horizons, raging rivers, hills and valleys, detours, unexpected challenges and pleasant surprises along the way. Worthwhile journeys often take much longer than expected and are sometimes littered with failure before eventual success.

It is challenging enough for one person to take such a journey, but to take others with you, all the way to the distant shore, sometimes to find that the winds and tide have changed when you get there—to lead others on a journey such as this, is another matter altogether—one that requires a special kind of leadership.

Pioneering leadership is not for timid souls.
Exploring new frontiers is fraught with exciting danger.

Exploring new frontiers can be exciting and at the same time frightening. It requires a certain hunger to learn what we can from other pioneers, a willingness to be mentored, to ask questions and to seek understanding of things we may not be able to conceive of ourselves. Exploring requires a respect for what we don't know and openness to collaboration. Acquiring the skills to explore new worlds can sometimes take half a life time. It is with this in mind that I share more about the beginnings of my exploration into the new frontier, some of which I did with Mark and much of which I continued with others whom I met along the road less travelled.

Questions, Mentors and Co-conspirators

In the conversations I was having with Mark before he left for Everest, we started to explore the direction we might take with future programs to provide a more innovative approach for team and leadership development that would address the challenges of the new frontier. This included exploring possible answers to questions like:

1. How could we help organisations to improve organisational wellness through the transition to more self-responsible teams?
2. What leadership and team behaviours needed to be developed to get there?
3. And, most importantly for us, what were the best learning methods to use in pursuit of the learning outcomes desired?

We had some exciting conversations about it. Mark was the *ABEL* expert and I was the *Organisational Wellness* specialist (or so I thought). In truth, I was a novice in this field but had experimented a lot, learned a lot through my successes and failures and was a keen student of experts in the field (some of whom I have mentioned already). Much of my thinking was heavily influenced by a number of people, some of whom I was fortunate enough to meet and others who mentored me unknowingly, through their books. In order of their influence on my thinking which subsequently filtered into my work, I gratefully acknowledge the following people:

Gabrielle Enright—Cherished life partner and co-conspirator.
The first person I was fortunate enough to meet and who has had the most significant influence on my life and learning, would have to be Gabrielle. Her partnership in my life has grown beyond anything I could have imagined. I remember the first time I saw her beautiful smile among a group of fifty or so university students who were about to take a four year journey together; her genuine and joyous nature, stood out like a mountain of gold in a silver landscape!

Over the course of the years that we studied Physical Education, Biology and Counselling together, we developed a strong friendship and went on to pursue other areas of personal and professional development together and individually. We've been married since 1986 and went into business together in the year 2000, so we know each other pretty well. Living, studying, parenting and working together has its challenges and at the same time we have been blessed with the opportunity to share our journey of personal growth. Most of what I know about relationships has been fine-tuned and road-tested thoroughly in my relationship with Gab.

It was as if the Universe had conspired to ensure that we would be partners for life and combine our gifts in the pursuit of a common purpose that would make a difference, and at the same time, challenge us to be all we could be. When I look back on the journey we've taken together it's amazing how much we have grown by travelling this road as one.

Gabrielle has enlightened me in many ways, some of which are referred to in other parts of this manuscript but the most valuable things that she has taught me through her example would be: *how to forgive, how to transform wounds into wisdom, how to overcome fear with love, the power of gratitude, the value of serving others, and the importance of spiritual strength in meeting the challenges of life.* Many of these lessons are perhaps not stereotypical of those that are listed under the heading of leadership, however, in my experience, they are the most important; especially for those who wish to lead others through challenging terrain.

In her book—*Living the Light: Discovering Truth and Living in Spirit*, Gabrielle reminds us that we all have a light inside us that is worth sharing with the world if we dare to discover the truth of who we are and allow it to shine. I could write another book about how much Gabrielle has helped me to 'live my light', for now though, I'll finish this reflection on the part she has played in influencing my personal and professional growth, with a piece from a poem called *Angels*, that I will share at the end of this book:

> **Along the way I fell in love with a fellow traveller,**
> **she was like a freshly scented rose, full of laughter and love,**
> **a singing voice that brings tears to your eyes,**
> **a smile that captures everything that is beautiful and warm in this world,**
> **a heart of unconditional love and giving,**
> **a strength like a tree that bends in the strongest of storms,**
> **a generous person of purpose.**

Portrait of Gabrielle—by WB Enright, 1986

Marilyn Ferguson—Author of *The Aquarian Conspiracy: Personal and Social Transformation in the 1980s*.
One of the first authors to shake up my world view was Marilyn Ferguson. Perhaps the best way to describe her influence on me is to share an excerpt from her book: *A great shuddering, irrevocable shift is overtaking us. It is not a new political, religious or economic system. It is a new mind – a turning point in consciousness in critical numbers of individuals, a network strong enough to bring about radical change in the future.* She covered everything from emerging transformations in scientific thinking, business, economics, health and education; to spirituality, environment and more.

I recall sitting on the beach reading her book and being inspired to think that, although there were problems and dysfunction in the world (as we still witness), there was an underlying evolution happening and an invisible mass of like-minded people prepared to look at things differently and to act in whatever way they could, to improve the condition of our world. Thus I became inspired to do my bit within organisations and with each of the *starfish* that I came into contact with. Gabrielle and Mark became co-conspirators in this sense. The world still has challenges and always will, but *from little things big things grow* and a growing number of people are making a difference every day. (It helps that I am an *Aquarian!*).

Fritjof Capra PhD—Author of *The Turning Point and The Tao of Physics*.
I have already covered a lot of what I learnt from reading his books. Like Marilyn Ferguson, he particularly influenced my thinking during my early 20s, in relation to the evolving new world we were and still are entering, where society, culture and business are thought of in terms of open and inter-dependent ecosystems, much like those in nature. This then informs the way we approach our interventions in these areas if we are to be in sync with the true nature of change and chaotic cause and effect.

Dr John Travis MD and Regina Ryan—Authors of *The Wellness Workbook*.
I have referred to this book a number of times already, as it has been a foundational influence on my work in very many ways. I read it while studying counselling with Gabrielle and Mark in the late 80s. Through this book I learnt a great deal about wholistic health, life balance, the difference between the treatment and wellness paradigms and the underlying factors that influence our body, mind, emotions, spirit and relationships. It was in this area of relationships where I saw a connection between the health of organisations and the health of the people who worked together within them. This led to a change of direction as I moved from working in the personal health industry to working in the field of corporate wellness.

Don Ardell PhD—A pioneer in the field of *Organisational Wellness* and Author of *High Level Wellness—An Alternative to Doctors, Drugs and Disease.*
I met Don in Perth at the *National Wellness Conference* in 1991 and was immediately impacted by his intelligent use of humour. I became a keen student of his lectures and writings, which influenced my work as a corporate health consultant during the next decade.

Grant Donovan PhD—Co-author of *Coffee Conversations: The Simple Leadership Secret of High Performance Workplaces.*
Grant is a performance psychologist, corporate coach, speaker and author.
My connection with Grant (previously mentioned on page 122), was through the *Wellness Advocates Network* and the *National Wellness Conference*, which later evolved into the *Self-Managed Work Teams Global Network*. Grant also ran a course called *Manager 2 Coach*, which Gabrielle attended in 2004. I have kept in touch with Grant over the years and gained a lot of knowledge from him about the changing landscape of business, the transition to self-managed teams in progressive organisations and about what I have come to call, the *New Leadership Frontier* which requires managers to become more like coaches. His influence continues to show up in my thinking, even today.

Stephen Covey PhD—Author of *7 Habits of Highly Effective People.*
Whilst *7 Habits of Highly Effective People* is probably Covey's best known publication, he also wrote *Principle-Centred Leadership* and *7 Habits of Highly Effective Families*, both of which I have referred to. Covey heavily influenced my thinking about self-management and leadership.

Patch Adams MD—Healthcare innovator and social revolutionary.
Patch was the focus of a movie starring Robin Williams, which told the story about his dream to create the world's first *Happy Hospital*. I was fortunate enough to meet the real Patch Adams in 1997 while he was touring the world telling his story to anyone who would listen.

After hearing Patch's story I was inspired to implement his ideas while taking a bus load of people to a leadership conference in Brisbane—but this wasn't just any old boring bus trip—one of the conditions of being allowed on the bus was that they had to dress up as a clown. I can't adequately explain the amazing impact that this had on people—we even attracted the attention of the local news in a country town as we had lunch in the park. The next day we were on the front page of the newspaper.

Our visit to the local bank to withdraw some cash, was also fun—I have not seen bank tellers looking so nervous in all my life! It was one of the most fun road trips I have ever taken—one full of laughter and natural endorphins.

I was so impacted by this experience that I started to experiment with wearing a clown nose on the way to work in the car, to see how it affected strangers who caught my nose at the lights—most would stare then smile. I began to use more humour in my presentations and became more of a jester in my daily life. This was such a freeing thing to do for an introvert. I also sought out other role models who were good at presenting and facilitating wellness related material with a humorous style—people such as Dr John Tickell and Patricia Cameron-Hill. I discovered that people much preferred to engage with someone with a sense of humour and joy. I learned that this makes people feel better inside and actually changes our physiology. This was a profound insight for me – someone who previously would receive the not so welcome advice of: "Wayne, if you're so happy, why don't you inform your face?"

Patch Adams re-ignited a spark of joy in me that sometimes still needs a little bit of oxygen to keep it alight but for the most part is glowing brightly within me.

Clowning Around, 1997

Patch demonstrates the courage it takes to be different and to reveal one's wounds. Behind his clown-like persona lies a great deal of wisdom. It often falls to the court jester to speak the truth that those in power need to hear.
Bernie Siegel—Author of *Love, Medicine and Miracles*

Allan and Elizabeth Keogh—Principal Consultants of *Keogh Consulting*.
Allan and his partner Elizabeth have been a significant influence on my personal and professional journey. They were also good friends and colleagues of Mark, and have taught me an immense amount about the art of facilitating organisational transformation and being an authentic teacher.

Katrina Webb OAM—Paralympic Gold Medalist and Professional Speaker
I met Katrina in 2002. Aside from introducing me to the *National Speakers Association* which provided me with more insight into the art of professional speaking, I also learnt from Katrina that telling one's story from the heart can be a powerful way of engaging an audience and reflecting back to them what they may not be able to see in themselves. We often look up to people we admire because we see in them, some truth about our own strengths and vulnerabilities. Katrina is an inspiring person, not only because of what she has overcome to achieve Gold Medals on the track—also because she is a humble, generous and empathic soul who encourages the best in others and teaches us to embrace our unique gifts and differences. Katrina is a great example for me, of a humble collaborative leader.

~~~~~~~~~~~~~~~~~~~~~~

I trust that, in acknowledging some of the other key people who have influenced my thinking in addition to Mark; I have provided you with some foundational understanding of the philosophy behind the themes that I will cover during the remainder of this journey. One thing that motivates me to continue learning, is my belief that we can rarely solve new challenges with out-dated thinking. So what is the latest thinking when it comes to leading in this new frontier of globalisation, technological disruption and chaotic change? Well, it turns out that it is not such new information in terms of the years that have passed since I came across it, but it seems that shifting long-established paradigms doesn't happen overnight.

New Frontier Leaders
In 2001, at a *Self-Managed Teams Conference* in Melbourne, Grant Donovan shared the latest thinking from around the world based on his research of the leading thinkers and doers in the field of business and organisational change. Grant provided a picture of what he saw as the new paradigm for organisations of the future and outlined the key elements necessary for making an effective transition from the old paradigm of *command and control* to what I now refer to as the *New Leadership Frontier*, where transfer of authority and responsibility are a key part of the landscape. With Grant's permission, I have included my notes from that conference in the Appendix. In Figure 20.1, on the following page, I provide a summary of the key differences between *Old Paradigm Leadership* and *New Frontier Leadership*, based on what I've learnt from Grant Donovan, and from my own experience working with a number of organisations at both ends of the spectrum over the last twenty five years.

COMPARISON OF OLD AND NEW LEADERSHIP PARADIGMS

Old Paradigm Leadership—Command and control, authority based on position and title, high dependency on supervision.
- Works in more stable and predictable environments.
- Sometimes appropriate in an emergency/crisis.
- Inflexible and slow to respond to unpredictable change.
- Return on investment is limited due to lack of leverage.
- Often dis-empowering for subordinates.
- Fragile for leaders with big egos who's affinity with followers may be weak.
- Highly dependent on managers/supervisors for decision-making.

New Frontier Leadership—Independent Self-Managing teams, transfer of authority at all levels so that teams become self-responsible, self-directed and autonomous. Leadership is shared and senior staff evolve from managers into facilitators, guides, mentors and coaches.
- ✓ Better for chaotic, fast-changing environments.
- ✓ Much more flexible and adaptable with simplified processes.
- ✓ Empowers more people, leading to leverage.
- ✓ Multiplied return on investment.
- ✓ Better for sustainable long-term success.
- ✓ Leaders need to be humble and to have a strong affinity with followers, to be effective.
- ✓ Supervision is replaced by facilitation, coaching and mentoring.
- ✓ Requires a different set of skills at all levels.
- ✓ The transition to self-managing teams is a challenging and lengthy process, and needs to start at the top.

Figure 20.1 Comparison of Leadership Paradigms—G Donovan and W Enright, 2001

Shared Adaptive leadership

A good example of leadership that is appropriate for the *new frontier* is evidenced by the latest breed of military leaders (in the west at least), who are quite different to their predecessors. The new culture emphasises more mutual respect, zero tolerance for bastardisation, and more initiative-based decision making in the field. In combat situations the traditional rank structure morphs into a less rigid, more adaptive team approach where individuals lead situationally rather than always waiting for orders. Some might say that this has always been the case but it was probably the exception rather than the rule.

Chapter 20—Exploring the New Frontier

This new approach is especially prevalent in *Special Forces* combat troops who operate as small independent, self-managing units. This type of shared leadership approach is fast becoming the norm in progressive organisations.

Shared leadership does not mean that there are no managers. In most teams or organisations with more than a handful of people, it is helpful to have someone who is ultimately responsible for co-ordinating the efforts of the team or at least facilitating the team process to ensure that common objectives are achieved and team values are upheld. The difference is that the manager or leader in this context has a different focus.

> ***A key role for leaders is to guide the direction of the team and remove roadblocks to their success.***

Shared leadership can vary in terms of structure and titles but the common principle is that everyone in the group is thinking and acting as a leader. If they all have the big picture, they can take responsibility for situational decision making and take the initiative to lead where it is appropriate. If there is a manager, their role is more like a coach, mentor, facilitator or guide, and less about command and control. Figure 20.2 below, provides a diagrammatic representation of the transition from the old paradigm of *command and control*, to the *new frontier* of self-management. This does not happen overnight and requires some level of supervised responsibility until teams can become totally self-managing. In the next chapter, we will look at what it takes to make this journey and why most organisations who have tried it have ended up somewhere in the middle.

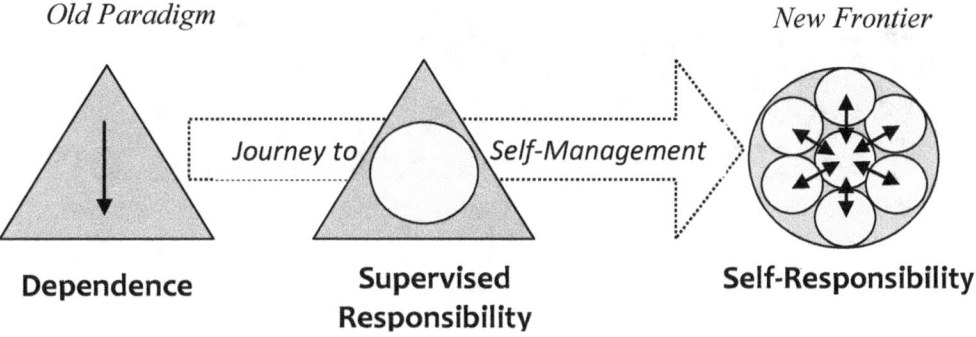

Figure 20.2 The Journey to Self-Management—Adapted from G Donovan, 2001

> ***The transition to self-responsible teams requires time to develop frameworks, culture, mindset, agreements, processes, systems and skills to support self-responsibility.***

Reflection Questions

1. Who have been your leadership mentors and what did you learn from them?

2. If you work in an organisation—where would you say your teams are on the *journey to self-management continuum*? (Figure 20.2)

Army AA Team departing Everest *SA Camp 2* (7900m) May 24, 2001—Z Zaharias

Chapter 21   The Journey to Self-Management

Self-management requires self-responsibility. Making the transition from dependency to self-responsibility requires a number of foundations to be in place before an organisation can fully transfer authority from the old top-down hierarchy to the new structure of self-managing teams or individuals.

Most organisations have ventured out to the new horizon but found the going tough. In the early stages there still needs to be a reasonable level of what could be considered 'supervised responsibility' until all of the necessary foundations are solid. It takes time, patience and persistence to lead this journey over challenging terrain. It also takes a tolerance for failure, a willingness to learn from mistakes, to take unexpected detours and to overcome what sometimes may seem like insurmountable obstacles. This is not a journey for timid souls!

Like the mountains we must climb to bring about organisational change, summiting physical mountains is not for the timid either. Kilimanjaro for me, whilst nowhere near as hard and risky as Everest, was a tough slog up and back, even for a seasoned trekking guide.

I like to think of 'summiting' not in terms of standing on the peak of a mountain but rather in terms of, returning safely after getting to the top. So the 'summit' of the journey is really at the bottom where the climber starts their preparation. This requires courageous leadership, long-term thinking, adaptability, patience, persistence, resilience, teamwork, good fortune, and often some creativity when things don't go as expected.

Even when the goal to stand on top of the mountain has been attained, there is still much work to be done to sustain the achievement. In the case of Everest—getting back to safety is the biggest challenge when one has exhausted their resources getting to the summit.

Leaders of change, like climbers, are at the mercy of the mountain they must climb. They need to be prepared to turn around and regroup when it is unsafe or when the conditions are not favourable. They need a willingness to learn from failure and to have another go, to persist patiently and be prepared to chip away with small steps towards their summit despite feeling as though it is taking forever. As we learned in Chapter 2, Mt Everest is never conquered but rather allows or disallows the climber to get to the summit and back.

Mountains are to be respected and to be climbed accordingly.

Similarly, organisational change often takes more time and effort than we would prefer and requires us to lay foundations, like the progressive setting up of camps and stocking them with resources, as climbers must be prepared to do on Everest. Sherpas, like the leaders of change, take on the bulk of the risk as they carry loads to higher camps, fixing ropes along the route that will keep climbers safe and reduce the energy that those who follow will need to expend. The guides constantly monitor the condition of individuals and the team dynamics, they watch the changing climate and make adjustments to their course of action depending on any number of variables.

Sometimes leaders, guides and climbers get lucky and the way seems to open up favourably. More often than not, the mountains and the weather conditions test those trying to climb to their goal, sometimes pushing them back until they feel like quitting. Like mountains, the process of organisational change is to be respected and approached accordingly.

The Foundations of Change
Some of the foundations that will help teams to climb 'the mountain of organisational change' and make the sometimes treacherous transition to self-responsible teams, will include the following:

1. **Having the Right People in the Climbing Team**

Having the right people in the team who are compatible, collaborative and capable of the *task demands* and *people demands* of the journey, is what Jim Collins refers to as *having the right people on the bus*. This is the foundation stone upon which all other foundations are built. There is no point trying to make the transition to a very different way of operating if the people involved are not committed to it, do not have the ability and willingness to develop the skills required and do not have the right attitude, mindset and emotional intelligence to handle being self-responsible. This includes having managers who are willing to share leadership and to develop the skills required to be a guide, coach and mentor.

Some already have these skills for 'low altitude climbing' but may not have been tested at higher elevations, where self-responsibility is required of all climbers and the guide has less control. In a crisis, we want everyone to be able to think for themselves and make good decisions. Once we have the right people on the team, we then need to involve them in developing the framework within which they can be self-responsible and the skills they will need, in order to operate within a different leadership context.

2. Framework

Creating or re-developing an organisational framework, structure or scaffold upon which the new paradigm can be built takes time, money and energy, so pre-planning is essential. To use the Everest analogy, there must be ladders secured across constantly moving crevasses, ropes fixed across more dangerous high altitude sections, camps set up and stocked with oxygen and other resources. It is imperative to have good quality communication while on the mountain, so that expectations are clear. Without this groundwork the mountain cannot be climbed.

Some frameworks are based on how things have always been done in the past and may not be appropriate for the new frontier we are now entering. Continuous improvement requires us to challenge existing ways of doing things, to simplify over-complicated processes, and to innovate based on the lessons we have learnt from failure or from others who share more successful ways. This is as true in business as it is on Everest. Establishing a framework has many layers, some of which are outlined in *Foundations 3, 4 and 5* to follow, but the layers need to be uncomplicated and flexible.

3. Culture

The importance of the team culture cannot be underestimated. There are numerous stories about teams of technically brilliant climbers who couldn't work as a team and team members who have had a falling out with those who are there to support them. Time invested in building a strong but flexible team culture is an essential part of preparing people for the climb to self-responsible teams.

4. Agreements

Part of establishing a culture that has 'integrity' (i.e. strength and resilience) is having *Team Agreements*. Agreements are the outcome of discussions about group values and acceptable behaviours within a team context. They could be called—*Key Behavioural Indicators* (KBIs) which complement *Key Performance Indicators* (KPIs) as a measure of performance with regard to team success.

If a team or members of an organisation can come to an aligned commitment to a set of agreements about appropriate behaviour that will help the team to be successful, this will minimise dysfunctional behaviour that might sabotage the team's success. There must also be a clear protocol for dealing constructively with behaviour that breaches team agreements.

> *A team's commitment to their agreements is like the mortar that holds a wall of bricks together, giving it integrity.*

5. Systems and Processes

Simple, user-friendly, trustworthy and clearly defined systems and processes assist efficiency, reduce risks and make it easier for people to make decisions and act in accordance with rules that help them succeed safely. This certainly applies to mountain climbing and is accepted as a given in business. The trick is to not over-complicate it and to get rid of unnecessary rules and regulations or processes that sap energy, reduce productivity or make life difficult. Rigidly sticking to a set process or practice is not always a good idea when the conditions change, so flexibility is crucial.

> *Principles should take priority over practices when unexpected conditions in the wilderness call for a compass and an intuitive solution.*

6. Mindset

Like acclimatising for a climb at high altitude, we also need to consider in an *organisational change* context, the need for helping people to stretch their thinking and to acclimatise to a new way of viewing the world into which they are about to enter. This takes time, patience, feedback, support and encouragement. A thorough acclimatisation makes all the difference when people are tested in a more challenging atmosphere. Mental acclimatisation, as with physiological acclimatisation, does not always need to be done in a 'business-critical' environment. It is often safer to stretch people in a more predictable environment first before entering into more risky terrain.

A mountaineering example of this has become common practice for non-Sherpa climbers on Everest. Russell Brice, owner of the company, *Himalayan Experience,* arguably the most experienced commercial operator on Everest, prefers to acclimatise his client team members on less hazardous peaks accessible from Everest Base Camp, so that they don't have to take more than a handful of journeys through life threatening terrain, such as the *Khumbu Icefall* that killed 16 Nepali Sherpas in May 2014.

> *Acclimatisation of the mind is an important foundation when climbing the mountain of organisational change.*

7. Skills

Of course anyone climbing a mountain needs a certain set of skills. If you haven't climbed a mountain before, this may be a steep learning curve. Any shortcuts that are taken in skills training and practice will create potentially catastrophic risks when the going gets steep and slippery or when climbers are fatigued and mentally foggy. Similarly in business, staff need to have good quality training, coaching, feedback and opportunities to learn from failure in non-business-critical environments until the skills become second nature to them. Then they can climb competently and confidently, trusting and relying on each other when the going gets tough.

At the end of the day it is up to the climbers on the mountain or the players on the field to respond to the everyday challenges of their journey, especially when the pressure is on. They all have to look after 'the garden' along the way. But these things don't come about by decree and changing an organisational structure, or writing a new values statement does not affect lasting change. Sustainable change only comes when a critical mass of individuals transform their consciousness (beliefs, values, and thinking). It is my belief that this transformation needs to be guided and facilitated. It very seldom happens by chance.

8. Transferring Authority

Once the key foundations for change are in place, the biggest challenge for leaders who want to develop a self-responsible or ultimately self-managing team culture then becomes the transfer of authority. In a self-responsible or self-managing team culture; guides, coaches and 'manager/mentors' are still important, but ultimately we want team members to be able to take full responsibility as much as possible. This requires leaders to transfer authority gradually which will often include 'supervised responsibility' at first, followed by full responsibility once the guide or mentor is satisfied that all of the foundations are in place and working. Then the leader's role is to *guide the direction of the team, helping them to find a clear pathway to success* (like the 'lead out' rider on a professional cycling team who rides ahead of the rider designated to cross the line for the team, and clears the way for them to perform at their best).

The guidance process in an organisation can be formal or informal; including regular communication opportunities to catch up and ask questions, seek feedback, or discuss ideas or challenges. Strategic objectives, business plans, guiding principles, KPIs and KBIs, systems and processes all provide a framework or a context within which team members can then be set 'free' to be self-responsible. This framework or context is crucial to the successful transfer or authority. When a contextual framework is lacking, it is like not having a map and compass or the resources required to get to the agreed destination. The biggest reason why teams don't do all of this is because it takes time away from 'profitable tasks,' but when time is invested in laying these foundations well, employee engagement, productivity, performance and consequent profits go up. As Kevin Costner said in the movie *Field of Dreams, If you build it, they will come!*

THE SELF-MANAGEMENT TRILOGY

At this point it may be helpful to define the terms authority, responsibility and accountability, to avoid confusion.

Authority is about having the right or power to issue directives and assign tasks. This is usually what managers, parents, teachers and governments do.

Responsibility is usually defined as the obligation to follow through on commitments that are assigned to or volunteered for, by a person or group. Managers and supervisors take responsibility for the tasks they contribute to, but often pass on responsibility to the team as well. Responsibility can also be defined as our 'ability to respond' to situations.

Accountability is about being answerable for the consequences of a decision or course of action. This can be a grey area in that those responsible for doing a task can be considered accountable, and yet they may not have the authority to oppose a management directive.

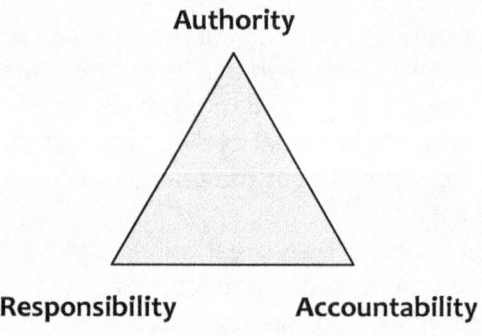

In true self-managing teams, all members share in all parts of the triangle.

Figure 21.1 The Self-Management Trilogy—W Enright © 2015

In teams where managers hold all of the power and authority to give directives and assign tasks to subordinates, the responsibility for completing the tasks usually lies with the subordinates. However, the manager is ultimately accountable for the initial decision and subsequent outcomes. So there can sometimes be a disconnect between authority, responsibility and accountability, which can lead to *blame* when things go wrong.

True *self-managing* teams, as Grant Donovan would refer to them, have the authority to make most of the decisions that affect their ability to complete their responsibilities and are therefore fully accountable for the decisions they make and the results of their actions (e.g. hiring team members, spending money, allocation of resources, strategic and business planning).

I use the terms *self-managing* and *self-responsible* somewhat interchangeably because the reality is that most teams are not truly self-managing unless they are fully autonomous. Typically there is some level of management or leadership that oversees or guides most teams in an organisational or sporting context. So I prefer to use the term self-responsible, as the ultimate aim is for teams to be able to respond to changing conditions without having to defer their decision-making to a higher power much of the time. In this case leadership is informally shared by all team members. When things go wrong, we ask 'what did we learn,' rather than look for someone to blame.

Responsibility is our 'ability to respond.'

To use a trekking analogy—it is the ability to respond to the realities of the wilderness around us as we trek from where we are, to our desired destination. In business, a strategic plan outlines the parameters and big picture objectives that will best help us to achieve our overall purpose and mission. For a trek I would have a strategic plan regarding preparing clients, logistics, risk management, resources, transport, contingencies and so on. I would also have an 'operational plan' which for me would be a more specific plan outlining the route we will take to get from A to B, with checkpoints noted on the map and estimated timeframes between checkpoints. Despite these plans, we must be flexible so that we can adapt to the multi-dimensional reality of the real world which is often different from a 2D map.

Set your goals in concrete and your plans in sand.

Response-ability comes into play once we start to take action on our plans. Even when we have a plan, we must still adapt to unexpected obstacles and weather conditions along the way. We may also have to be adaptable when attending to the needs of the team during the journey—physiological, psychological and social needs that we can't always predict but must be mindful of. So *self-response-ability* is paramount and is best shared between the individuals in the team that are actually crossing the wilderness, not left up to a single designated leader (especially one that is disconnected from the field). Clear communication is a vital part of a team's ability to adapt.

To take this analogy further—I would much rather the whole team be involved in the planning process so that they have intimate knowledge of the map and the thinking behind the plan. In fact it is highly probable they have knowledge and experience the leader does not have, which could make a valuable contribution to the plan, including an appreciation of challenges together with unique solutions that the leader may not have considered.

> ***If we rely on the leader alone, then we limit the valuable input of team members and we set up a dependence on the leader.***

Whenever I am going to take a group out into the wilderness on a remote adventure over several days (e.g. the Kokoda Trail), I will always do some team/leadership development with them in addition to the physical training we must do to prepare for the trip. This will include some wilderness first aid scenarios and a discussion about the protocol to follow if I am the one who is injured or ill. The last thing I want is an over-dependence on me in case I am unable to function. I think the same applies in business. You don't want to set up a dependence on the manager/leader, as this limits the team's ability to respond to the realities of the wilderness, especially in an unexpected crisis where they might need to depend on themselves.

A Wilderness Therapy Example

To be able to transfer responsibility from leader to team members requires not only a clearly defined contextual framework within which team members can take responsibility, but they must also have the skills required to take responsibility for tasks. This takes time to develop and a good dose of patience and trust on behalf of the leader who needs to be a mix of teacher, facilitator, guide and coach.

One of the best examples I can think of where I have experienced the power of transferring responsibility was during an *Operation Flinders* exercise a few years ago. It was probably my sixth exercise as a Team Leader—up until this time I had not had a team that I could fully trust with the responsibility of leading a whole day from dawn to dusk without the guidance of adults (by the way, it is rare that this occurs anyway but for some reason I had a secret wish that it would some day happen for me). On the following page I share a story from the notes I took on that exercise. I have changed names to protect privacy but have left most of the detail in, to give you an idea of the transition that the participants made over the eight days we were together.

Chapter 21—The Journey to Self-Management

Before I take you on this journey, allow me to give some context. As an *Operation Flinders Team Leader*, our job is to provide guidance, support and encouragement, while setting firm and reasonable boundaries that maintain safety and respect. Within this context, we teach participants the skills they need to become self-responsible and reinforce constructive behaviours (at the same time we try not to react to negatives).

Through the journey they take and the feedback they get from the environment, the participants learn about the consequences of their choices and discover new insights about themselves and the world around them. There are many other outcomes such as improved self-esteem, confidence, emotional intelligence, people skills, resilience and more. I would have to say though, that for me, self-responsibility and respect are perhaps the most important take-aways. If they can come away with these two lessons and be inspired to find a more positive direction in life, then I am happy!

A Youth at Risk Journey to Self-Responsibility

Our goal over eight days is to walk over 100kms through challenging terrain in the remote Northern Flinders Ranges. We must navigate across trackless bushland with rocks, creek beds, hills and valleys to test us. If we navigate well and work as a team, we will find basic campsites where there is pre-positioned food and water. There will also be other unexpected challenges and experiences along the way.

Day One
After leaving surplus belongings behind and introducing the boys to their back packs, we headed off into the hills on the edge of the Gammon Ranges. Today was a relatively short walk to get acclimatised and conditioned to the weight of the pack on their backs and the boots on their feet—two parts of the body that were to be tested over the next 8 days walking the rocky landscape that can be so unforgiving, even for the most seasoned of bushwalkers. There was the usual groaning and moaning about heavy packs and sore feet, together with a few well chosen swear words to declare that they had not signed up for this torture, but some were keen to prove themselves in a non-urban environment and were curious about whether I was a good guy or a bad guy—perhaps it was too early to tell.

During some short rest breaks along the way to their first overnight camp we demonstrated how to construct a shelter, how to start a fire with a flint and introduced them to other routine tasks that they would learn to be good at in order to survive in the bush and take responsibility for their daily needs as a team. Pairs were allocated to five key roles which would be rotated at morning tea time every day. During the first 24 hours though, we would give them much more hands-on support, as we coached them and did most of the heavy lifting. This of course was extended by another 24 hours before we were able to get into the swing of things, as the usual protesting, complaining and refusal to take responsibility made it challenging. (Some young people are reluctantly compliant and some instigate drama to distract from having to contribute to the team).

Every Team Leader has their own system for allocating tasks and the titles vary but essentially, the idea is to allocate very clear, simple and relatively easy responsibilities to each team member. I like to have them working in pairs so that they work as a mini-team and these roles can easily be rotated over the eight days. In highly functional teams, we can even get to the point where each pair teaches the next pair what to do, so there is little need for the staff to be involved apart from guidance. By the way, this same principle can operate in adult organisations as well.

OPERATION FLINDERS TEAM ROLES

Fire Chiefs
Collect firewood, start the fire with a flint and maintain the fire to get good cooking coals going within an hour. Clean fire and carry tinder bag.

Greenies
Dig all waste pits, including toilet trench, wash up after dinner, clean up waste, carry shovel and cleaning gear.

Master Chefs
Sort all food into groups for lunch and snacks next day (to be distributed in the morning), have breakfast options ready to go and dinner ingredients laid out ready for cooking. Cook the main meal and tidy up.

Water Carriers
Take care of all needs for water, including topping up water bottles, organising water for cooking and washing up (a rest day really).

Top Dog and Deputy (TD & DD)
Oversee the team, greet visitors, look after the mascot and assist with navigation and radio communication with Base. Lead team discussions when problem-solving and carry First Aid (The keen one's tend to volunteer for this role first).

Figure 21.2 *Operation Flinders* Team Roles—W Enright, 2009

First Night
The Fire Chiefs, as usual, fought over who was going to light the fire with the flint and then required a lot of reminders to keep it going. The Greenies protested the most, as the digging of holes and cleaning up after others challenged their pride. The Master Chefs took on the challenge of preparing food with gusto and made a lot of mess in the process, which then led to a lot of buck passing when it came time to clean up, but they managed to cook a half-tasty meal. The Water Boys spilt quite a lot of water as they hastily and uncaringly filled bottles and washing-up bowls, before promptly forcing their way into the Fire Chiefs territory to steal the flint and demand a ransom for returning it. And the Top Dogs... well they pretty much stood around the fire, not really sure how to be a leader and helped out where they could when asked—their job would get more exciting the next day.

As for the staff, we spent most of our time 'herding cats' and preventing 'spot fires' of aggression from breaking out, as the boys settled into this very foreign place where boundaries and team responsibilities were reinforced in a firm and friendly manner. Some found it strangely comforting as they had rarely experienced being trusted—others didn't want a bar of it!

All of this first night camp activity happened in an atmosphere of organised chaos. Those that displayed their displeasure at having to take responsibility by being aggressive, eventually calmed down as they worked out that aggression wouldn't deter us from supporting them. They realised after getting the basic tasks done, that it wasn't that hard, in fact without all the drama it was achieved quite quickly, allowing lots of spare time to relax and have fun.

I share this portrait of a typical first night on an Operation Flinders Exercise because it is in stark contrast to what can happen in a short time if team leaders are able to persist with a positive and supportive attitude, and praise every small thing that leads to confidence, self-esteem and self-respect. This is not always how it turns out with every group, but is probably not far from the truth for most first nights.

Fire Circle
After finishing the first night meal and cleaning up, we sat around the fire as darkness descended upon us and the chill of the outback came to visit our bones. While waiting for a slow cooking damper and a potential visitor, we had our first fireside chat to discuss expectations for the trip, highs and lows for the day and a few stories. The main message I wanted to get across, was that 'Respect' was my number one value—Respect for self, other team members and the land. "Even when I need to give you feedback, I will always respect you," I said. As if on cue, our visitor arrived to welcome us to his 'Country.'

Day Two
Today was a tough day of walking overall. We started out with an easy walk for about 6 kms across undulating hills, venturing further into the Gammon Ranges, stopping only for morning tea in a creek bed before tackling a steep climb to the top of a big hill where we could see the peak of 'Yudlamoora' in the near distance. After having lunch at the top of this hill we made our way down into a steep gully before climbing up again to the saddle below 'Yudlamoora.' From there most of the boys raced up to the summit in record time where they could see all the way to the distant horizon and watch eagles circling on the warm updrafts from the valley below. I am pleasantly surprised at how good a start we've had after some initial resistance.

Day Three
Today we rose before sunrise and got going early, breaking camp as the sun was rising over the hills in the east and taking our breakfast supplies with us. We navigated cross country to an old bullock trail which led us along 'Thirteen Mile Creek' towards its junction with 'Gammon Creek.'

After an hour or so of walking we found a good spot in the creek bed to put the billy on and have breakfast. The boys enjoyed having breakfast and billy tea on the way and we made good progress over several kilometres to 'Gammon Creek,' before turning north between two hills and on to our 'Night Loc' (a military abbreviation for overnight location). We stopped a few times along the way to strap a couple of ankles and treat some blisters but otherwise made good progress with only the occasional "are we there yet?"

After dinner we had our nightly fireside chat which turned into a discussion on our definitions of 'what it is to be a man' and sharing personal stories about relationships. I was touched by the honesty with which the boys were able to talk about things that obviously meant a lot to them, and the way in which they supported other members of the team during this unplanned but insightful discussion. They were not the same boys I had met a few days ago!

Day Four
Next morning we ventured off to the north-west into some remote country full of spectacular scenery and wildlife. Navigation was a bit more challenging today but the 'Top Dogs' did well to stay on track and we stopped on a saddle between two big hills to see herds of goats climbing to the top of the steep ridges either side of us. We could also see eagles circling on the thermals high in the sky, as well as beared dragons sunbaking on the tops of bushes and the odd kangaroo bounding away after being startled by our presence as we made our way deep into this somewhat unexplored landscape.

We had some tricky navigation to do so that we would not end up in the wrong creek line, as there was a big network of creeks going in all directions through this area. Within an hour or so we'd made it to the wide expanse of the 'Frome River'—a river that floods significantly during heavy rains but is relatively dry the rest of the time. At this time of year the 'Frome' had a few big waterholes at a number of points along its winding banks.

After cooling off and having a good rest, we made our way along the river to our night loc at a place called 'Meriwee.' Tonight we decided that the boys would set up camp and do all the jobs without any direction from the adults. They did a great job and were rewarded with extra time to go swimming again in another waterhole nearby.

I skip forward a few days now, to Day 7 for the sake of brevity. This day was very satisfying because it was the first time that I'd been able to get a whole team to the point of taking full responsibility for everything from 'dawn to dusk.' I haven't written much about the usual behavioural challenges along the way, as they are often just symptoms of fear and with this team, they were overshadowed by a willingness to learn and take more responsibility, so by night six I was looking forward to the next morning when I would see what they were really made of.

Day Seven
Today was Will's day to lead. The extra challenge for him and the rest of the boys was that we gave them full responsibility for getting going in the morning, navigating all day and making decisions about where and when to stop etc. We walked a few hundred metres behind and only communicated with them via radio when necessary, apart from joining them for lunch during the day. They did a great job as a team and Robbie showed his eagerness to lead, as he assisted Will with the navigation.

The boys decided to stop for a long lunch and swim in a great spot with some good waterholes. We enjoyed watching them work as a team and the relaxed way in which they enjoyed the responsibility and the freedom that went with it. Later in the day as we got closer to the night loc, hidden in a valley over some hills, Joel volunteered to do some scouting from hill tops to find the camp and Craig gave some timely encouragement as some team members started to 'fray at the edges' with frustration. They persisted with some challenging navigation toward the end but made it into camp as a team just before dusk. Around the fire circle that night, I sensed a joyous feeling of pride in their accomplishment, as they spoke of the day's highlights and lost themselves in laughter. On the final day it was hard to say goodbye and at the same time rewarding to wave farewell knowing how far they had come!

Successful Transfer of Responsibility

This was probably the most successful exercise I have been part of, if we are measuring success by the extent to which we were able to transfer responsibility to the team. On other exercises I've had to deal with much more difficult circumstances such as violence, serious medical problems and anarchy, but even in those extreme situations there is always an opportunity for success at some level. Later in Chapter 32 on *Resilience* I will share one such story. In this case though, it all came down to setting the context/boundaries within which the participants could be free to take responsibility without feeling controlled. Instead they were respected, trusted and praised, which left them feeling pretty good about themselves and their ability to take responsibility for their lives in the future.

The key is to transfer responsibility gradually by teaching skills in small chunks, providing feedback and coaching and then building on those skills until full responsibility can be taken. The art of delegation is covered in more detail in Chapter 34. Of course when the team gets a curve ball that is not part of their experience, that's when an experienced coach comes in handy to reassure them, guide them, and teach them how to handle the new challenges they might face from time to time. This is as true in the workplace as it is in the wild or at home with a child.

Context vs Control

A good example of a modern company's approach to setting a *framework* or a *context* within which people can be set free to work as self-responsible team members with less supervision and more independence is *Netflix*. In the last ten years they have gone from being a small American company which started out delivering rental videos by post, to now being an international phenomenon that has disrupted the traditional TV industry by streaming movies online. *Netflix* are typical of a *new frontier company* that promotes a culture of freedom, responsibility, high performance and innovation, rather than a culture of strict adherence to complex processes and a dependence on management controls. This is considered one of the key reasons for their ongoing success.

CEO Reed Hastings describes the *Netflix* culture in an excellent slideshow titled: *A Reference Guide on Netflix's Freedom and Responsibility Culture*[57]. Hastings suggests that as companies get bigger there is a tendency to curtail freedom, not intentionally, but because of the complexity of systems and processes, controls and layers of management. He presents the dilemma that companies face if they don't choose to stay small and adaptable—they can either avoid rules as they grow and risk potential chaos, or they can use processes to provide consistency and efficiency in their current business model and risk crippling creativity, flexibility and the ability to thrive when their market changes. *Netflix's* remedy for this dilemma is to recruit and develop high performance people who can think independently and take responsibility. Hastings describes the ideal team member as follows:

QUALITIES OF AN IDEAL TEAM MEMBER

- ✓ Self motivated
- ✓ Self aware
- ✓ Self disciplined
- ✓ Self improving
- ✓ Acts like a leader
- ✓ Doesn't wait to be told what to do
- ✓ Never feels "that's not my job"
- ✓ Picks up the trash lying on the floor
- ✓ Behaves like an owner

Figure 21.3 Qualities of an Ideal Team Member—R Hastings: *Netflix* Slideshare, 2001

Netflix focus on developing managers who use *context* rather than *control* as their leadership tool. This doesn't mean that there are no processes to guide people's behaviour—the paradox is that *systems and processes* are an essential part of providing a clear *context*. The key distinction is the difference between good and bad processes and to avoid an over-reliance on and rigid adherence to processes that can get in the way of being adaptable and creative. Hastings refers to 'good' processes as those that help talented people to get more done and 'bad' processes as those that are designed to control people so that they don't make recoverable mistakes.

The more complex we make our systems, interfaces and processes in an attempt to be more efficient, the more time people waste doing unnecessary or complicated tasks, which leads to less efficiency rather than more. Hastings recommends that when managers are tempted to control people by micro-managing them, they could instead ask themselves: *what context can I set that will allow my team members to become more self-responsible, efficient and less dependent on me?*

Context provides the insight and understanding to enable sound decisions. When one of your talented people does something dumb, don't blame them. Instead, ask yourself, what context did I fail to set?
Reed Hastings—CEO *Netflix*

The reference to *freedom* in the *Netflix* culture is not *absolute freedom*, it is *freedom within a context or boundaries*, much like the freedom that players have on a sporting field. Like *Free Speech*, there are some limited exceptions to *freedom at work*, such as those that I will later refer to as *Below the Line Behaviours*. For example, such exceptions to the freedom of team members to do whatever they like, would be behaviours that are considered unethical, offensive, disrespectful, or any behaviours which do not support the team mission or values. With freedom comes responsibility, it is therefore important for teams to have open and honest communication about expectations and to give and receive feedback to maintain a commitment to the agreements they have made within the context of the team environment.

With the right people and foundations in place, the journey to *self-responsible teams* is made easier. The obstacles that often get in the way, are poor communication, micro-management, dependency and overly rigid rules that curtail freedom and inhibit adaptability. *It is not necessarily the strongest that survive, it is the most adaptable,* said Charles Darwin. *New Frontier Leaders* understand this and are open to leading in a new way.

> **The role of the coach is to create and sustain an environment conducive to high performance.**

Other suggested Reflection Questions

1. In your workplace, family or any team that you are part of, which of the *Foundations of Change* from this chapter (p194-197), have been done well or could be revisited?

2. If you are in a leadership role, either in your work, as a parent or in the community, how well do you set a context for others to be free and self-responsible?
   - Are you a person who likes to have control and therefore have a tendency to impose over-complicated rules, or to micro-manage others?
   - Are you at the other extreme of setting no context, boundaries or framework, which makes it challenging for people to be self-responsible with clarity about their role?
   - or are you like *Goldilocks*—Just right?

I recommend downloading the *Netflix Slideshare* and considering how it may apply in your world: https://www.slideshare.net/reed2001/culture-1798664

Chapter 22 The Transition to a New Way of Leading

The ability to transfer authority or responsibility while still being 'the leader' requires not only setting an appropriate *context* for team members but it also requires a transition in the way one leads as responsibility is progressively transferred. Managers who have relied on their positional power based on the conventions of supervisory leadership will often need to change their mindset and undergo some new skill development so that they can make this transition. This challenge is perhaps best illustrated in the way that a parent's mindset and skill-set needs to change as they help their children become independent, self-determining adults.

One of the most challenging leadership roles in life is being a parent, particularly when guiding children through major transitions in their life. My experience fathering two boys who are now in their 20s, has taught me much about leading people through transitions. Any parent of grown up children knows that the skill-set for parents needs to change and grow as our children change and grow. Babies are very dependent on us for all of their needs, toddlers require constant supervision and some firm boundaries and feedback as they learn to become more autonomous. Teenagers who we want to grow into responsible adults need clear boundaries and expectations to guide them, but less supervision so that they can take more responsibility for their choices. This transition phase during adolescence is often the most challenging time for most parents.

Trusting adolescents enough to transfer more authority to them so they can take charge of their own life, is often a difficult thing to do, especially if we've never done it before and they have never had such a level of autonomy and self-responsibility. For a start, it requires us to be on good terms with them in our relationship, to respect each other and to be willing to give and receive feedback, so that we can become more self-aware.

As with younger children, adolescents also need boundaries and the skills to operate within them. Involving them in the setting of reasonable boundaries and consequences for not respecting them, assists them to take more ownership when the time comes to give them feedback. It is helpful to remember that we are growing adults not children, so involving them in adult level processes as soon as they are capable and being prepared to provide feedback and consequences when they get off track, is one of the more valuable gifts we can give them as a parent. The most important thing is to send them on their own journey knowing that they have our trust, respect and unconditional love.

Ownership of the Rules

In the same way as a parent or teacher involves a child in formulating family or classroom norms and consequences, it is very helpful to involve staff in developing their own team agreements so that they buy into them and have a sense of ownership. Alignment between the organisational values and their own sense of what is acceptable or not, is more powerful than having a set of rules or values that team members have no affinity with. Team agreements not only establish clearly defined expectations for behaviour, they also provide a reference point when people get off track and need to be given constructive feedback.

DEVELOPING TEAM AGREEMENTS

Facilitating the development of team agreements sounds easy however it requires a specific process of consultation with all team members. The 5 step process below helps to ensure that values translate to action.

1. **First come to a consensus on the organisational values.**
   Ask for everyone's top 5 and then circle those that are common and attempt to include others under similar values to come up with the top 10 group values. Then trim them to 5 or 6 if possible.

2. **Clearly define the practical application of values.**
    - How are they demonstrated in practice?
    - What specific behaviours are acceptable/unacceptable?

3. **Educate the team to give and receive feedback constructively.**
   When behaviour is seen to be out of alignment with the team agreements, feedback can improve self-awareness by revealing 'blind spots.' It is essential that this is done constructively.

4. **Develop an agreed process for performance management.**
   A regular process that is fair and respectful, while holding people accountable for their behaviour and supporting them to improve.

5. **Appropriate Consequences.**
   In the event that an individual who has been given feedback and support in a fair and respectful manner, continues to contravene agreements, there need to be clearly defined consequences such as mediation or review of employment contract. Having a clear protocol that staff agree to, will help to ensure accountability.

Figure 22.1 Developing Team Agreements—W&G Enright © 2004

Lines of Acceptability

One of the concepts that Mark shared with me, is the concept of *Above the Line/Below the Line behaviour*, which I will refer to again later in Chapters 33 and 34, when we explore responsibility and influence in more depth.

Above/Below the Line behaviours is a useful concept when defining the practical application of values and the subsequent agreements a team establishes. If we refer back to *Step 2* in the *Development of Team Agreements (Figure 22.1)*, we can use the *Above the Line/Below the Line* concept to sort behaviours into *acceptable* and *unacceptable* groups as we go about clarifying the specific behaviours that demonstrate the values. *Above the Line behaviours* then become the *Key Behavioural Indicators* (KBIs) for the team's performance from a 'People Process' point of view (refer back to page 194—*Foundations of Change*).

Above the Line
Acceptable behaviours that the team wants to see demonstrated more.

Below the Line
Unacceptable behaviours that the team wants to see less of or not at all.

Creating a graphic to illustrate this, perhaps on a poster that is displayed in the workplace, can provide a visual reminder of the behavioural agreements which can then be referred to when giving feedback. Feedback can be in the form of praise or correction. If correction is delivered in a constructive and respectful manner with the intention of helping someone to improve, then it less likely to leave a person feeling invalidated and more likely to help. When people feel judged or criticised, this only reduces rapport and damages their self-confidence.

Grey Areas
Most behaviours are easy to categorise as *above* or *below* the line of acceptability, however sometimes there can be grey areas. There could be a few behaviours that are considered by some to be acceptable and by others not so. For example:- swearing on a construction site might be viewed as normal by some, but considered more offensive in another context. This is why it is useful to discuss the meaning of values with all team members. When a team takes the time to communicate like this, it is amazing how much it helps people to understand each other, to have empathy for differences and prevents mis-understandings.

From Manager to Mentor

The skill set of a mentor or coach is one of many abilities that managers need to be good at to lead in a *self-responsible team* environment. Some managers already have a number of these skills and just need to use them more often by letting go of the need to over-manage people. This is part of the transition we have been exploring and can be easy for some and quite a challenge for others.

The mindset of a coach or mentor is perhaps best demonstrated by using a sporting analogy. Take AFL football for example: The players on the field of play are basically *self-managing*. There is a senior playing group who lead on the field and there are runners who send communication between coach and players, but essentially all players need to be self-responsible.

The framework or *context* within which they play the game is set by the rules of the game, the boundary lines and the team values. There are umpires who give feedback to players when they don't play by the rules and there are penalties for clear breaches of the rules that the players have agreed to play by. The goal posts are an obvious performance objective and kicking the highest score is the common goal for the team. There are other *KPIs* that may be used to measure performance such as tackles, centre clearances, inside 50 entries, marks, kicks, etc. So football like most sports has a very defined framework with clear objectives, rules and boundaries.

Players are generally selected for teams based on performance and are given feedback by the coach to help improve their game. There is a lot of investment in skill development, continuous improvement, psychological resilience, developing fitness, health and wellness, leadership and team development. The return on investment in these areas is significant.

The coach's job is to set the vision, values, culture and boundaries within which team members can be self-responsible, decisive, and perform at their best. Feedback, encouragement and guidance are key skills that coaches need for developing self-responsible team members who can all think and behave as leaders on the field. These coaching skills require a level of empathy, tact and humility that not all leaders have.

In the next chapter we will look at why some managers find it difficult to make the transition to becoming a leader that can let go of control and embrace a more guide/coach/mentor-based leadership style.

Great coaches have high levels of emotional intelligence, a commitment to living their creed, and a masterful understanding of the biology and psychology of the game.

Chapter 23   Loosening the Grip on Autocracy

Gabrielle and I have worked with numerous organisations that have come to us having already invested much time and energy trying to sort out relationship issues in the workplace. Upon further investigation it is interesting to note that many of the issues stem from having people in positions of leadership that are good at managing technical tasks and processes but less skilled when it comes to leading and influencing people. Unfortunately some of these people are not so easy to shift out of their long held positions. They become like rusty bolts that can't be undone.

> *He (she) who innovates will have for their adversary,*
> *all those who are well off under the existing order of things.*
> Adapted from Machiavelli

Rather than take an adversarial approach to managers who are resistant to change or just oblivious to the need for it within themselves, we prefer to take a more subtle but sometimes game-changing tack, by facilitating experiences which provide a mirror to reflect personal truths that would otherwise remain buried beneath the defences of the ego. This is where experiential learning methodology comes into its own. When people 'experience the truth' for themselves and suddenly see the need for change, together with a new way forward, the 'rust' begins to dissolve and a quiet evolution takes place within them. This more 'subtle way' is another skill that I observed Mark employing—A 'Jedi mind trick' of sorts (for those that are fans of *Star Wars*).

Mark was a student of Judo which was a sport derived from the warrior art of Jujitsu (The Gentle Art). The suffix *Do* means *Way*, so Ju-do, apart from being a sport, is a martial art that stresses philosophy with moral and spiritual connotations—the ultimate aim being enlightenment and personal development. The more subtle skills and philosophy of Judo are perhaps a good metaphor for the approach that Mark took when challenging those who wanted to defend their dysfunctional behaviour or character traits. Influencing hearts and minds to change, particularly of those in comfortable leadership positions, is often a subtle process which requires a less confrontational approach, the way of 'non-violence,' Ghandi would say.

Teaching with words of advice, telling people information and trying to force change, in my experience to date, seems to be a consistently unproductive strategy. The saying that *Learning is caught not taught* underpins my belief that experiential learning journeys are one of the best ways to influence a change of mindset, especially when the student's ego is clinging to its rusty thread. A good example of this is the *Fit for Leadership* program, which takes participants on a journey over 3 months and uses experiential activities to subtly challenge their beliefs and to provide personal insights that change their thinking and behaviour.

An Innovative Approach to Leadership Development for Women
Fit for Leadership is a leadership program for women, begun in Adelaide by Katrina Webb in conjunction with the *Adelaide Crows Football Club*. The program has expanded interstate and is being used by innovative Australian companies such as Bendigo Bank. I can highly recommend the program, particularly because Katrina is a master at bringing together people who are experts in their field and has created a program that is truly transformational.

Gabrielle and I facilitate a range of workshops and one-day programs but always find that multi-day programs are the most transformative because we're able to take people on a journey over time and provide them with deeper experiences that help them to see their *blind spots* and awaken to their potential. The *Fit for Leadership* program is a 6 day journey spread over 3 months, which gives participants time to assimilate what they are learning about themselves and to gradually make the internal shifts required to become more effective leaders. During the program there are several opportunities to discover previously unnoticed strengths and areas for self-improvement. This is done using a combination of interactive presentations, honest conversations and experiential activities which provide a mirror for personal reflection. The program is facilitated within a safe space which is confidential and supportive. Participants receive honest but gentle feedback through their experiences and conversations.

There are several contributors to the *Fit for Leadership* program who are highly regarded in their fields; such as Gabe Kelly, former Director of *Adelaide Thinkers in Residence* and now Director of the *Wellbeing and Resilience Centre* which is part of the *South Australian Health and Medical Research Institute*. Gabrielle and I are privileged to be involved in this program and have learnt a lot from Katrina and the other presenters.

The session on leadership includes a business simulation that Gabrielle and I facilitate with Katrina, called *The Business Game* (referred to previously on page 149—see Services p415 for more information). The game can be set up to reflect a more hierarchical business model or modified to reflect a more self-managing team approach but always requires inter-dependent departments to collaborate towards the fulfilment of a common business objective within the constraints of an organisational structure. Events that unfold during the game when departments endeavour to work together within a structure that has inherent challenges, provide a powerful demonstration of the limitations of the old leadership paradigm versus the benefits of a more self-responsible team model. This brings to life a discussion about new frontiers in leadership and what adjustments might need to be made for a business to be run more productively and with more freedom and responsibility at the heart of its culture.

During one of these discussions at a recent *Fit for Leadership* debrief, one of the participants asked this question: *If it is generally accepted that a self-managed teams culture is more efficient and adaptable in the fast changing and chaotic business environment that we now operate in, then why is it that some managers have a resistance to letting go of control and transferring more responsibility to their team members?*

The Confidence, Fear, Trust Equation
While the answer to this question might seem as obvious as Machiavelli's belief that *all those who are well off under the existing order of things become adversaries when their power, control and comfort are threatened,* I think it is not always as simple or as sinister as that. Many managers understand the merits of empowering their staff by delegating, encouraging self-responsibility and developing shared leadership within their teams. They want to transfer more responsibility and authority but may feel that they can't fully trust those that they are passing the baton (either because they under-estimate the skill of their people or their own skills in transferring authority). In my experience, the level of trust I have in myself or others is closely related to the tension between confidence and fear. Our belief in our self and others needs to be stronger than our fear, as the *Tale of Two Wolves* below points out.

A Cherokee Legend—The Tale of Two Wolves

There is a struggle between two wolves, that goes on inside all of us... one is fearful and one is full of confidence, says the Grandfather. *Which one wins?* asks the grandson.

Some might think that the wolf full of confidence wins over the fearful wolf and this is often true, but the wise elder's answer was not what the grandson was expecting...

The wolf that we feed always wins, the Grandfather said. *We can feed one or the other, or guide them both. Fear is only fatal without guidance.*

First Nation Legend—Source unknown

This Cherokee story acknowledges that fear can sometimes be useful and that confidence is not the only ingredient for success. Courage is not the absence of fear but the guidance and taming of it. When we have *butterflies in our stomach*, it heightens our readiness to take on a challenge. The key is to train our *butterflies* to fly in formation!

Passing the Baton
If you have ever participated in a 4 x 100m relay race or watched one, you'll appreciate how important trust and confidence is during the transfer of responsibility. It is important to trust the person you are passing the baton to, as well as your own ability to pass it confidently.

If our confidence is not high and fear gets the upper hand, then trust suffers which in turn starves confidence and feeds fear even further. Fear can become a barrier to performance, especially under pressure and when our performance is inter-dependent with others. Preparation and practice helps to build confidence and minimise unproductive fear as we learn from mistakes and build on our successes. That is why the transfer of authority to *self-responsible teams* takes time—it requires the laying of foundations and the practice of new skills. The multiplication effect and adaptability of *self-responsible teams* is very similar to the synergy created by a well practiced and confident relay team.

The other day I witnessed a good example of this which was shared by Yves Morieux during his TED talk[58] about co-operation and reducing over-complicated rules that inhibit success. Morieux used the example of a relay team to illustrate the synergy that can be created by the multiplication effect of four 'silver level' runners working together in perfect sync to achieve a gold medal performance, versus a team that had the best individual times on the track but failed to get their act together on the day of the relay final. His example was the French 4 x 100 Women's Relay Team which upset the heavy favourites, the USA, to win the Gold Medal at the *2003 World Championships* in Paris. The French anchor runner, Christine Arron recovered from three metres behind the newly crowned, 100m *World Champion*, Torri Edwards, to give the home crowd at the *Stade de France* an unexpected joy.

On paper the USA should have won by 3-4 metres but the baton change and the teamwork between the four French runners made all the difference. When the vision of the race is slowed down, you can see how much more smoothly the baton moved between the French runners who obviously had a very high level of trust between them. If you watch the last baton change in particular, you will see how much the third runner 'ignites' her anchor team mate with energy, power and belief as she passes the baton and then screams into the back of her head with passionate encouragement, the likes of which I have rarely seen. The baton change for the USA team on the other hand was not as full of trust, confidence and fearlessness as the third runner bowed her head in exhaustion. This baton change made all the difference and inspired the last French runner to make an extra-ordinary effort to punch her chest through the finishing line first, despite being behind the World Champion. No doubt the roaring encouragement from the French home crowd would have also pushed her beyond her perceived limits.

So, whilst most managers may recognise the need for passing the baton and working together with their teams to achieve their personal best, a gold medal performance requires a high level of trust and a well practiced and confident sharing of responsibility within a flexible team environment.

> ***The real battle is not against competitors, it is against ourselves and our over-complicated approach to business.***
> Yves Morieux

Maslow's Hierarchy
Abraham Maslow's *Theory of Human Motivation* (1943), expressed in his *Needs Hierarchy Model* (Figure 23.1) could provide a clue as to why it is harder for some individuals to share power and authority, than it is for others, depending on their need for survival, security, belonging and esteem.

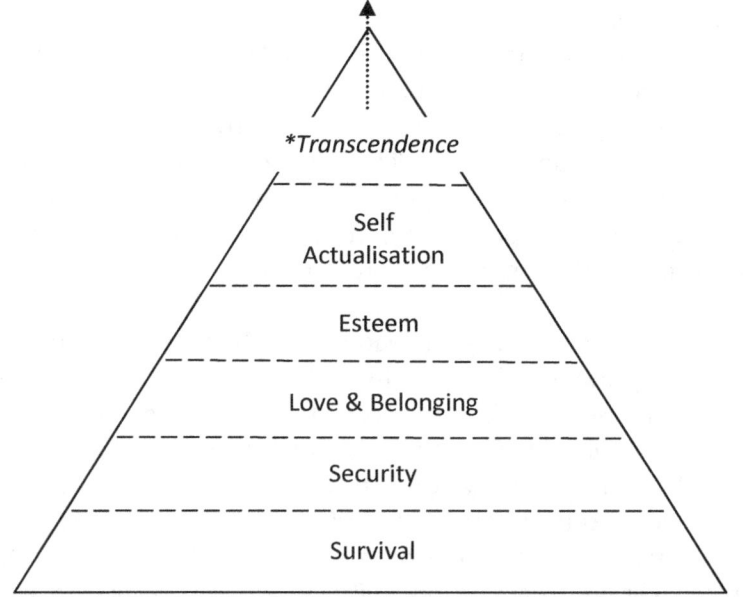

Figure 23.1 Adapted Maslow's Hierarchy—*The Theory of Human Motivation*, 1943

Maslow suggests that the most primary needs for human beings are *survival and security*, followed by *love, approval and belonging* which provide a foundation for healthy *self-esteem*. Once these more primary needs are met consistently, we can focus more on what Maslow calls *self-actualisation* (achievement, becoming the best we can be). Concentration Camp survivor and Author of *Man's Search for Meaning*, Victor Frankl, added *Transcendence* as the 'pinnacle need' beyond self, which is about service to others and transcending worldly needs in the pursuit of meaning and spiritual growth. In truth, this is not a *once-off* linear process—our needs oscillate daily.

Power Security and Self Worth
My theory is that those who have their psychological needs for security, approval and self-worth, met through their position, title and authority, will find it more challenging to let go of the sense of power and control that comes with their role. They may feel more threatened by the idea of transferring to, or at least sharing authority with, those they have previously been 'in charge' of. Their fear of losing power and control, or becoming redundant, can lead to resistance (consciously or unconsciously).

Sharing authority does not mean that those who were previously subordinate are now in charge. It simply means that team members can take charge of what they are responsible for and make decisions without necessarily defaulting to a supervisor. Of course they will still need guidance and expert advice when facing situations beyond their experience that may have critical consequences—this is where the manager's role as a coach and mentor is invaluable.

Some managers may fear that they will lose significance but instead, they will be freed up to do a number of things that they may not have had time for previously, such as: strategic level thinking and planning; co-ordinating team collaboration; facilitating group processes; coaching and mentoring less experienced people; and developing emerging leaders. So they still have a lot of responsibility, but it is expressed in a different way, requiring a broader skill-set and a more service-orientated relationship with the people they are leading.

Personal development of leaders can help them to move from a level of insecurity and ego-driven self-worth, to a place in *Maslow's Hierarchy* where their inner security is reinforced, they have less need for external validation, and their self-esteem is strengthened. From this more psychologically stable foundation, they can become more focused on personal growth, exploring their potential and helping others to learn and improve. Serving and developing others around them, becomes their core focus, which leverages team productivity as *Morieux's relay story* illustrates.

Leaders who can get to this place and let go of their attachment to being the 'authority,' can be much more powerful and can leverage their leadership through empowering others, thereby multiplying their influence dramatically.

> **When we act out of love rather than fear,
> we can go from the security to surrender in an instant!**

There are many organisations that are advocates for flatter structures, sharing authority, empowering their employees and changing their business model to be more like a *self-managed teams* model. They espouse the virtues of the new paradigm and some have even changed their structure to reflect this philosophy, but many of those in positions of authority have found it difficult to change their mindset.

Service Over Self-interest (SOS)

Structural change needs to be accompanied by a change in hearts and minds, a change in skill-sets and ultimately a change to ingrained habits of behaviour supported by a transformed culture. This change needs to be led from the top and to have the commitment of all leaders in the organisation. Organisations sink or stay afloat depending on the commitment of their leaders. The Captain is ultimately responsible for the condition of their ship and all of the 'souls' that sail it. Putting service over self-interest is a key character trait of leaders who wish to rely on their crew in rough seas. Perhaps the international distress signal SOS could mean something other than *Save Our Ship—Save our Souls*.

One of the books Mark introduced me to was *Flawless Consulting* written by Peter Block, a book for anyone who is trying to change or improve a situation but has no direct control over the implementation. This is often the challenge for a consultant who is asked to initiate an improvement process but is only engaged for a short time at the start and consequently, has no control over how things are implemented. Block explores how to have influence regardless of one's position in an organisation, and offers an alternative to the patriarchal beliefs that dominate our culture. He says that his work is about bringing change into the world through *consent and connectedness* rather than through mandate and force.

Block also wrote the book *Stewardship: Choosing Service Over Self-Interest*. Service over self-interest requires leaders to switch the traditional thinking about leadership upside down. Rather than thinking that staff are there to serve the leader, the leader is really there to serve his or her staff.

Letting go of the old 'Master-Servant' thinking is more challenging for those who are used to running a tightly controlled ship. This quote from the book *Stewardship* highlights the importance of how we distribute power within organisational structures and how some organisations are attempting to share control but finding it hard to let go.

We share control with the left hand and take it back with the right. One moment we are on the fast track toward participation and the next moment we are instituting more controls... Our task is to create organisations that work, but unless there is also a shift in how we distribute power, privilege, and the control of money; the efforts will be more cosmetic, than enduring.
Stewardship—Peter Block

The meaning of 'steward-ship' in the minds of most CEOs is about the responsibility they have, to handover 'the ship and her crew' to their successor in as good a shape as possible. This is not just about the shareholder value of the 'ship' but also the morale and performance of the crew. A crew that is content, engaged, self-responsible, inter-dependent and working together as a team with high levels of trust in themselves and their captain, can achieve extra-ordinary results.

One morning in September 1983

I remember sitting in a darkened room illuminated only by a small television set and the red tinge of an early morning sunrise peeping through the shutters of my modest student flat. I had been up all night and was transfixed to the television screen, as were millions of other Australians around the world.
We were witnessing the culmination of a titanic struggle to summit the only unclimbed Everest in the world of sport—to capture the America's Cup from the United States. This was a task that no other nation had ever come even remotely close to achieving in the 132 year history of this great international yachting contest. The USA held the longest winning streak in sporting history up until that day—26th of September, 1983.

I can still see Bob Hawke, the then Prime Minister of Australia, spilling a beer in his hand as he joyously cheered the now infamous words, 'Any boss who sacks anyone for not turning up today is a bum!'

On a white boat off the shore of Rhode Island Sound a crew of twelve men and their skipper John Bertrand had just wrestled the America's Cup from its pedestal in the New York Yacht Club where the certainty of 132 years of history had it firmly bolted to the floor.

Chapter 23—Loosening the Grip on Autocracy

Anyone who is familiar with the history knows that prior to the final showdown, the Australians had won only one race out of a best of seven final series and the Americans had won three. So the American Crew, skippered by Dennis Conner, only had one more race to win and they were the odds-on favourite to pull off another victory. Eventually the Australians clawed their way back from these impossible odds to put themselves in the final race and win it.

This unlikely victory has become legendary in Australian sport and John Bertrand's story of what transpired in his autobiography *Born to Win*, is one of the most inspiring stories I have ever read. In it, Bertrand gives a blow by blow description of each race and how the Australian crew dealt with their failures including breakages on the boat, unfavourable weather, bad luck and a number of other factors that didn't go their way. He shares his recollections of the psychological battle they were up against and how they learnt from their mistakes and strengthened their weaknesses without blame or excuses.

When asked to comment on what he saw as the key factors that contributed to this historical victory, Bertrand said: *The America's Cup was ultimately won by the team who sailed the boat. It had little to do with the famed 'winged keel', our crew outworked them, out sailed them and held our nerve under pressure. We worked for each other and for our commitment to our dream. Our morale, team spirit and sail improvements were better.*

Following the victory, Bertrand was also asked about the difference between his and Dennis Conner's leadership and how they performed as skippers. His answer highlights the importance of being a leader that multiplies the talents of the team, rather than limiting them.

> *Dennis Conner and I performed equally as well as each other but I think Dennis, being essentially an autocrat, did not get the same help and feedback from his crew that I received from mine... no one would have dared shout 'Shut up Conner and sail the boat,' as my crew had done with me. Dennis placed himself above other men... many of the American crew's decisions were made on his whim. When it came down to the winning and losing of the America's Cup I am afraid Dennis found himself a man alone... My boys on the other hand, would have died for me!*
>
> John Bertrand Skipper of *Australia II* - 1983

'Shut up and sail the boat.' These were not words from an autocratic captain to his crew. This crew loved their captain and felt trusted and respected enough to let him know that they wanted him to do his job and allow them to do theirs (of course Bertrand took it in the spirit intended).

Having been a part-time skipper of a yacht for a few years, I understand how challenging it is to sail a yacht by yourself and how much faster the boat will go when you have a crew that is in sync with each other and the skipper. The synergy of a well-oiled crew, of which the skipper is only one part, is powerful when they are all taking full responsibility for their roles and are contributing to decisions being made under pressure. A boat crew become the *eyes, ears, arms, legs and brain extension* of the skipper. These assets are multiplied by skippers who empower their crew to give feedback, to follow their intuition, and to be the best they can be.

Mark Auricht was a keen sailor too; he and his siblings spent many days restoring a boat with their father, Clive. The boat was named *Catharina*, after the ship that brought Mark's Great Great Grandfather Christian Auricht out to Australia from Germany in 1838. The journey took 4-5 months. The Auricht family would know very well, the laws of sailing, the importance of having a well-respected skipper, and a crew that is willing to go the distance for their leader and for each other. In my conversations with Clive, I've come to learn that he was and still is, a well-respected 'skipper' in his family, his community and in his field of medicine. Mark spoke fondly of his father's authenticity and integrity and was grateful for his example.

> *Authentic leadership is not about position or title.*
> *It is about being who you are with integrity and, through your honest actions, words and relationships, earning the right to lead.*

Grateful Leadership

Mark often used the phrase 'earning the right,' with regard to establishing credibility and respect as a leader. This is perhaps best summed up by an article titled *Grateful Leadership*, written by Travis Kemp—a consulting psychologist and fellow proponent of experiential learning. Travis was also a colleague and friend of Mark's. Here is some of what he had to say about authentic leadership and earning the right to lead.

> Leaders are granted the right to lead by those who choose to trust them and collaborate with them. The gifts of influence, engagement and respect are granted to them by those who choose to grant it to them, regardless of where they sit in the post-industrial hierarchy. Authentic leaders understand that they need to earn these gifts everyday through their actions, words, behaviours and interactions. They understand how valuable the gifts of trust, responsibility, honesty and openness are, to them being able to achieve what they are passionate about.

Excerpts from an article on *Grateful Leadership*[61] by Travis Kemp—March 2015.

Chapter 24   The Power of Leverage

Machu Picchu—April, 2010

 *After 4 days of stone steps, up and down over high mountain passes, surrounded by snow capped peaks and subtropical green valleys, punctuated with ancient archeological ruins we climbed the final steps to the end of the Inca Trail. This morning we emerged from the darkness of the early dawn into the mist, with the sun rising on our backs as we approached the 'Sun Gate'—the Threshold Guardian of one of the most magical places on earth. At first there was disappointment that the object of our desire was shrouded in fog. But after waiting patiently as the sun rose above the cloud forests below us, we were rewarded with the most spectacular view. As the clouds parted like curtains on a stage revealing the opening scene of a theatrical spectacle, we saw before us the awe-inspiring view of Machu Picchu for the first time. This moment will be etched in my mind forever!*

In 2010 Gabrielle and I took a group of clients on an adventure to Peru. We walked the Inca Trail and visited the ancient ruins of Machu Picchu which is one of my favourite places in the world. The architecture and engineering of this place is astounding apart from how inspiring it feels to be there. The Incas were amazing engineers who were able to move such large slabs of rock and position them in exactly the right place to build walls that were seamless and perfectly straight. This takes precision but also requires using the power of leverage. One of the most impressive examples of using the law of leverage is at a place called *Sacsayhuaman* on the outskirts of Cusco.

Cusco was the capital of the Incan Empire and is the gateway to the Sacred Valley where the Inca Trail starts. There are many ancient ruins along the Inca Trail and around Cusco. One of the largest group of ruins near Cusco is the fortress of *Sacsayhuaman* which is a vast area with stone walls and terraces made up of boulders as tall as 8.5 metres and weighing 360 tonnes. These huge boulders were apparently moved across country from another area about 2 kilometres away. It is remarkable to think about how the Incas moved such huge and heavy masses of rock over such a distance. There are many theories on how they did it but most historians agree that they applied the power of leverage using long levers to lift and move the rocks.

Sacsayhuaman, Cusco Peru—April, 2010

Team Leverage
The term leverage can also be used in the context of teamwork. It has been long understood that the multiplication effect of six people working together can achieve much more than adding together their individual efforts working solo. The end result is not 2+2+2 = 6. It is more likely to be closer to 2x2x2= 8. If we then add two more people to the equation, the multiplication effect doubles again to 16. This is the same principle as using a lever—when the lever gets longer, the power of leverage is multiplied many times.

If we apply this principle to leadership it works in the same way—the more people a leader can influence and then have them leverage that influence with others, the more the multiplication effect increases. So one person leading a group of followers is less powerful than a leader who develops other leaders and empowers them to do the same. The question is, how is this done?

Multiplier Leadership

In her book *Multipliers*, Liz Wiseman makes a distinction between what she calls *Multiplier Leaders* who empower those around them and are able to multiply the efforts of their team, versus those she refers to as *Diminishers* who drain the energy and capability of people around them. The *Multiplier Leader* is humble and is self-secure enough to empower others to excel, thus being able to leverage the potential of the people in their team.

The Diminishing Returns of Micro-Management

Diminisher Leaders as Liz Wiseman calls them, under-utilise the talent and potential of those they lead and in fact drain their energy by micro-managing, not allowing them enough space to think, speak or act, closing down debate and not investing in their people. Their ego's need for recognition and control gets in the way of them empowering others. They resist allowing others to have any level of authority and limit their input. Consequently *Diminishers* limit their own influence by not being able to leverage the talents of others.

Often, Wiseman says, people are *Accidental Diminishers*, they don't realise what they are doing, their diminishing behaviour is a blind spot unknown to them but probably quite obvious to those that they try to lead. This diminishing behaviour often leads to a lack of affinity between the *leader* and *follower* which compounds their ineffectiveness as a leader.

In my work with corporate leaders I often see this. The well-meaning leader who is oblivious to their diminishing behaviour and the effect it has on the team that they are wanting to lead. Unfortunately disrespect, disengagement, and lack of commitment are often the outcome and the team's results in terms of performance and job satisfaction suffer.

Team Democracy

John Bertrand's comments about Dennis Conner, lead me to believe that Conner, although a well-respected Olympic competitor and *America's Cup* skipper based on his racing results, was perhaps an *Accidental Diminisher* when it came to his leadership style. John Bertrand on the other hand displayed more of the typical *Multiplier Leadership* behaviours. Bertrand played a big part in choosing the talent for his crew and encouraging each of them to be the best they could be. He created what he refers to as a *great democracy* within the *Australia II* crew, thus liberating crew to think, speak and act self-reliantly. Bertrand challenged his crew to be brave, he listened to their feedback and invested in them as people, instilling in them many of the lessons that he had learned from his successes and failures at Olympic level. His formula for winning was embedded in his mind.

Bertrand's Winning Formula
Give me a boat that will make us equal, then let me harmonise the crew. Let me bring them together, thoughtfully, with respect for each other. Let me form a great democracy that a big racing-boat crew should be.

That is how I perceived the America's Cup being won—by a fantastically tight team. Men who would go to the wall for each other, inspiring, covering, supporting, helping out everywhere, each backing up the others, ready to jump in and help, to slave away at whatever was necessary, not because they had to but because they wanted to.

John Bertrand—Born to Win, p76

John Bertrand's philosophy is a great example of the benefits of *Multiplier Leadership* and highlights the power of leveraging the talents and input of all team members, working collaboratively toward a common goal.

Reflecting questions on Leadership

As we continue our exploration of what it takes to be a *New Frontier Leader,* let us take a moment to reflect on your experience of the leaders around you and, if you are involved in any kind of leadership (at work, at home or in the community), there is also an opportunity to reflect on your own leadership style.

1. Who do you look up to as a leadership role model (either someone you know or someone you've read about or seen leading in the public sphere)? What character traits or behaviours do they have that you see in yourself or would like to develop?

2. What would you say are your leadership strengths and areas for development? Are you more of a *Multiplier* or *Diminisher?*

3. Who would you choose as a mentor to help you to become the leader you would like to be (e.g. as a student, parent, on the sports field, in your community, family or at work)?

Chapter 25   Encouraging the Heart

I am often inspired by reading the biographies of courageous and inspiring people such as John Bertrand, Herb Elliot, Nelson Mandella, Mother Theresa, Richard Branson, and *Tae Kwon Do, Olympic Gold Medalist*—Lauren Burns, to name a few. Inspiring leaders, musicians, writers and sports people always play from the heart and instill courage in the hearts of others. This was one of Mark Auricht's biggest strengths, his ability to encourage the hearts of others, either through his words, his actions, his listening or just his presence. He used to say that *en-couragement* was about inspiring courage in another person. The root of the word courage is *cor*, which is the Latin word for heart. Mark was definitely an encourager of the heart.

 My most vivid memory of this was while climbing with Mark at Mount Arapiles which is considered a world renowned rock-climbing Mecca located near the Grampians in Australia. Apart from a few climbs indoors and at our local Morialta Falls, I was a novice. Up until then my only experience of rock climbing was as a ten year old, clinging to the vertical sandstone cliffs of North Head at the entrance to Sydney Harbour, while spying on the rock fishermen below us, who were gambling with the waves, as they held their long fishing rods out into the ocean.

This day at Arapiles, took me way out of my comfort zone. In the morning we did a climb called Agamemnon which required us to chimney up between two vertical rock faces, swapping from one wall to the other before making it to the top.

Agamemnon, Arapiles Australia, 1996
Photo taken by Mark Auricht

I wouldn't have even considered it possible if Mark hadn't encouraged me into it with such calm confidence.

Later in the day we commenced a longer multi-pitch climb, where you climb to the end of one length of rope and then start again with another until you get to the top. Mark lead the climb ahead of me, free climbing short sections until he could put an anchor into the rock face to protect him and me as I followed. If he were to fall, he would drop down past the last anchor point before swinging in his harness. For me being the following climber the fall wouldn't be so far but I was still shitting myself.

Being 'On Belay'—A Metaphor for Leadership
When the 'lead climber' gets to the top of each pitch, usually a ledge where they can anchor the top of the rope, they then belay the lower climber up to them by taking in the slack on the belay rope (safety line) which is attached to the climber ascending from below. This is called being 'on belay.' Belaying is a good metaphor for leadership, in that the more experienced leader (in Mark's case the lead climber) will often take on more risk and responsibility in the process of supporting and encouraging those that are less experienced, to climb to their potential. Each section of the climb between belay points is called a pitch.

Most of this technical jargon was not so familiar to me and I had never experienced a multi-pitch climb before, so it was exciting but also a bit nerve-racking. We'd left it a bit late in the day to start this climb, so the sun was starting to hide behind this big wall of rock, and shadows were beginning to form on the cliff face. I hadn't really noticed this until I got to the top of the first pitch. This is when I started to get a little anxious. The ledge we had climbed up to was under an overhang, so it was like being inside a cave.

Then Mark gave me the good news… "The next pitch starts under the outcrop which we need to climb out and around to get on to the next cliff face before continuing up to the top."

He then instructed me to wait on the ledge until he reached the top of the next pitch. There he could set himself up, ready to belay me as I climbed up to him, pulling the anchors that protected me, out of the cracks as I went.

"How will I know when you've reached the top?" I asked. "I'll yell out to you," he replied calmly. "What if I can't hear you for the wind?" I questioned… "it's picking up!"

"Well, how about you wait until you feel me tugging on the rope, then tug back and I'll confirm with two more tugs and then you'll know I am ready to roll," he said, without a hint of worry in his voice. "Sounds like a plan," I replied with butterflies in my stomach (they weren't flying in formation!).

Fear was coming up for me as I explored the 'What if's' in my anxious mind. Mark had obviously done this many times before and had a pool of confidence that I could only hope to dip my toe in, as I battled the wolf of fear within me.

"Remember the Cherokee Tale!" he said. "All you need to do is focus on the rock in front of you, the next foot and hand hold, breathe calmly and still your mind, observe the fear, then let it go... you'll be fine!" he said, as he disappeared above the overhang and left me standing there on the cold ledge.

As I looked out across to the Grampians on the horizon, taking in this spectacular view, the sun began to set and darkness washed around my feet. I waited patiently for half an hour or so, I think, but could hear nothing but the wind and feel nothing but silence on the end of the rope I was holding. I started to worry. "Had Mark already tugged the rope or yelled out to me? Perhaps I had missed it?"

Then after what seemed like an eternity, I felt a tug, then another. But after the initial feeling of relief, I started to second guess myself. "Was this an intentional tug to let me know that he was ready or was it an accidental tug as the rope got caught on something and was flung free. What if I start to climb and it turns out he is not ready to belay me?" Then I remembered a quote that I'd heard somewhere along the way.

> **Come to the edge, he said.**
> **Fear in me replied, I am afraid.**
> **Come to the edge, he said.**
> **Courage pulled me from the edge...**
> **And I flew.**
>
> Adapted from a quote by Christopher Lodgue

The next thing I know, I was climbing up this cliff in darkness, the rockface only illuminated by my head torch. In a strange way I was peaceful and calm knowing that all I had to do was focus on what I could see in the torch light. I just needed to take the next step and trust that Mark was on belay for me.

Mark and I eventually made it to the top as the moon was rising. Feeling relieved and elated, we then abseiled down into a dark abyss to safety. I am sure that Mark was well within his comfort zone and enjoyed taking me on an adventure out of mine. He did this often with me and others. I will always remember his encouragement of my heart.

~~~~~~~~~~~~~~~~~~~~~~~~~

The metaphor of being 'on belay for others' has always stuck with me and I have used it many times when leading people through fearful situations or telling them this story as an example of encouragement and support for those we lead. (When Allan Keogh made the first substantial donation to fund this book without wanting anything in return, he said to me: *I'll always be on belay for you.* I knew the sentiment behind his words).

The Heart of Leadership
There is much more talk about the 'heart of leadership' now, with such books as *The Heart of a Leader* by Ken Blanchard, *The Leader's Heart* by John Maxwell and *Approaching the Corporate Heart* by Margot Cairnes. In her book, Cairnes explains that the business world has typically rewarded competition, action and achievement; while thinking, self-awareness, self-reflection, emotional intelligence and empathy, are seen as less important and sometimes as wasting valuable time that could be spent on tasks.

Old style leaders leap from challenge to challenge running on adrenalin. They see their world as a competitive arena with stats and goals to be achieved at all costs, says Cairnes. She paints a picture that also echoes the sentiments of Dudley Lynch and Paul Kordis in another book introduced to me by Mark called *Strategy of the Dolphin,* where they describe highly competitive leaders as 'Sharks.' Business Sharks are often oblivious to their feelings and the feelings of others—so focussed on their goals they rarely notice the subtle impact of their actions on others, rarely tuning into their own physical state or into the health of the environment around them... until there is a crisis of course... and then they immediately fix it!

To be a healthy human being we need to listen to our head and our heart. Much of the business world unfortunately denies the heart and soul, but it is the heart and soul that is the essence of authentic leadership. Many more men have begun to embrace this, at least intellectually. Some, like me, have known its importance for a while but have not quite worked out how to bring this balance into the *head–dominant* culture of the business world where the heart and soul rarely get a look in. If *mindfulness* includes tuning into the feelings and guidance of the heart, perhaps we could instead, use the term *heartfulness,* to remind us that the mind is not just in the head?

I guess, leading with a balance of head and heart could be as challenging as a *right-hand or left-hand dominant* person, trying to become ambidextrous. They know they have two hands but naturally favour one. This is perhaps one of the benefits of having more balance in the boardroom. Two hands are better than one and it is generally accepted that 'psycho-emotional and social intelligences' differ somewhat between male and female. I use the terms 'male' and 'female' rather than men and women,

 because I believe, as Carl Jung did, that we all have a bit of *yin* and *yang* within us. Jung's Pyschological concept of Anima (femaleness with a man) and Animus (maleness within a women) reflects the ancient eastern philosophy of *yin* and *yang*.

Some of us, regardless of our physiological gender, have more *yang energy* and others, more *yin energy*. This may also fluctuate from day to day and at different stages in our life. That said, the majority of women, in my experience, seem to have a more natural appreciation for *yin qualities* (relationship orientated, intuitive and heart-centred) and most men that I know, have a tendency toward more *yang traits* (task/goal focussed and head-centred). Whether this is a hangover from our primal beginnings, hormonally driven, culturally driven or all three, I am not sure, but it seems to be generally true in most cultures that I have experienced.

These are of course generalisations and open to debate, however it is my belief that there is room for a little more heart in the boardroom. In Gabrielle's experience, coaching both men and women; she also observes more ambidexterity among women, when it comes to communicating both from the head and the heart. The *yin* and *yang* inequality in top positions of leadership at least, can be evidenced by the fact that less than 18% of Fortune 500 company board members are women[60]. This bias is also reflected in leadership positions within political and religious institutions where the stereo-typical strengths of women and men—the heart and the head, would both be of value if allowed to grow in equal measure.

Balancing the Yin and the Yang
As I Google searched for the top authors on leadership, I found lots of senior males who are considered the gurus on leadership but very few female authors on leadership who were born before the 1960s. What I did notice though, was that there are as many women as men who are considered influential leaders of their time such as Mother Theresa; Diana Princess of Wales; Oprah Winfrey; Margaret Thatcher; Eva Peron; Benazir Bhutto; Indira Ghandi; Ita Buttrose; Hillary Clinton; Julia Gillard; Rosa Parks; Cleopatra and Joan of Arc, to name just a few of the more famous examples. Whilst some of these women authored biographies or have become sought after speakers on leadership, generally speaking, they have been more doers than writers, when it comes to leadership. Perhaps this could also be why, up until recently, there have been few female authors on leadership apart from the more recent generation of women who are now not only doing, but also writing about their experiences and inspiring the next generation of women and men.

A notable example (in addition to the previously mentioned Liz Wiseman and Margot Cairnes) is Sheryl Sandberg, Author of *Lean In: Women, Work and the Will to Lead*. Sheryl Sandberg is married with two children and is presently the Chief Operating Officer at *Facebook*. Prior to working at *Facebook*, she was Vice President of Global Online Sales and Operations at *Google*, and Chief of Staff at the United States Treasury Department. Sheryl also currently serves on the boards of *Facebook*, the *Walt Disney Company*, *Women for Women International*, *V-Day* and *ONE*, she also Chairs the board of *Lean In*. Her leadership credentials in business have certainly earned her the right to be an authentic 'author-ity' on leadership.

Sheryl Sandberg offers a vital message for women and men. We need great leaders in key seats spread throughout society and we simply cannot afford to lose 50% of the smartest, most capable people.
Jim Collins—*Good to Great*

Ironically it is Sandberg's 'achievements' in the business world that back up her credibility as an author. However, it is not the results in themselves but the 'way' in which her results were achieved that is the difference worth reading about.

Presenting leadership as a list of carefully defined qualities (like strategic, analytical, and performance orientated) no longer holds true, says Sandberg. *Instead, true leadership stems from individuality that is honestly and sometimes imperfectly expressed. Leaders should strive for authenticity over perfection.*

In striving for authenticity over perfection, we must first become familiar with our *True Self* as opposed to the self we portray in our roles or our responses to the expectations of others. How many of us are really in tune with our truth and are resilient enough to resist the forces around us that take us off track and away from our authentic heart? This requires us to find, what I refer to as, our *True North*—the place within us which is consistent, reliable, honest and true to our values. From this place, we can be in a much stronger position to live in alignment with our authentic selves and be *on belay* for others from a position of strength, integrity and reliability.

Courage is to speak one's truth from the heart.

Summing up the Evolution to a New Way of Leading

In this part of our journey we have looked at the evolution of leadership, the challenges of the new frontier we are entering, and the journey we will need to take to make the transition to a new way of leading as globalisation, technological disruption, and cultural change make some of our old ways of living, learning and leading somewhat obsolete.

So is there a simple way of summing up the key character traits of leaders who are the *mountains of gold in a silver landscape*; the *John Bertrands* and *Sheryl Sandburgs* of the world; the *multipliers* and *encouragers of the heart*; and *those that are granted the gifts of influence, engagement and respect* that Travis Kemp talks about?

I like to refer to these examples of leadership as *True North Leaders* —people of solid character, integrity, authenticity and courage; people who have clarity of purpose and guiding principles that others respect, trust and are inspired by. I have covered some of these attributes already, but in the process of getting to the business end of this book, I'd like to cut through the excess leadership jargon that complicates things, in order to define the simple basics of what it takes to lead people through the challenging terrain of the *New Frontier*.

> ***Mastery is not a matter of daily increase, but daily decrease.***
> ***Improvement is often as simple as to simplify.***
> Bruce Lee

The True North Leadership Compass

In Parts IV and V, I provide a summary, using a simple model that may serve as a leadership compass for those who do not have one of their own. I am almost certain that this model does not include anything that has not already been written by explorers of leadership such as Stephen Covey, Jim Collins, John Maxwell, Ken Blanchard, Sheryl Sandberg, Dudley Lynch and Bill George, but it is my attempt at illustrating a summary of the simple truths that Mark taught me together with those I have discovered on my leadership journey since his passing of the baton.

This model represents my *True North* when it comes to leadership, a simplified answer to the *Key Character Trait* question posed earlier. It has become my compass after a long time navigating through life without one. I call it the *True North Leadership Compass (TNL Compass)*, a reference to the idea that finding one's *True North* and following it, is the secret to navigating through all of life's mountains, valleys and turning points to arrive where you are destined to be.

Narrabeen Beach, 2013

 **Reflection Questions on Encouraging the Heart**
It has been a reasonably long journey to this point, so let us take a break for reflection before I tell you the story of how I found my compass.

1. If there was a 'yin/yang see-saw' with *yin qualities* (eg intuitive, relationship-orientated, heart-centred) at one end, and *yang qualities* (e.g. logical, task/goal focussed, head-centred) at the other, where would you sit most of the time on the see-saw?
   (This might vary for the different roles you play in life or at different times, so add some notes if you wish to elaborate).

2. Ask the same question above, for others with whom you are in a closer relationship (e.g. partner, children, parents, work colleagues, leaders you know, etc). How are they different to you and how does this influence your relationship?

3. Under what circumstances are you more likely to be ruled by your head or your heart?

4. How 'tuned in' are you to your authentic heart (your *True North*) and are you resilient enough to resist the forces around you that may take you off track? *(If you have a challenge with this question, read on and you will probably get more clarity by the time we finish our journey together!)*

5. Do you have a compass to guide you through life? *(Again, read on if you would like to calibrate your compass or to gain a greater understanding of this concept.)*

PART IV

The Spiral Journey
Rites of Passage

Ancient Agricultural Site—Inca Trail Peru, 2010

THE TRUE NORTH LEADERSHIP COMPASS

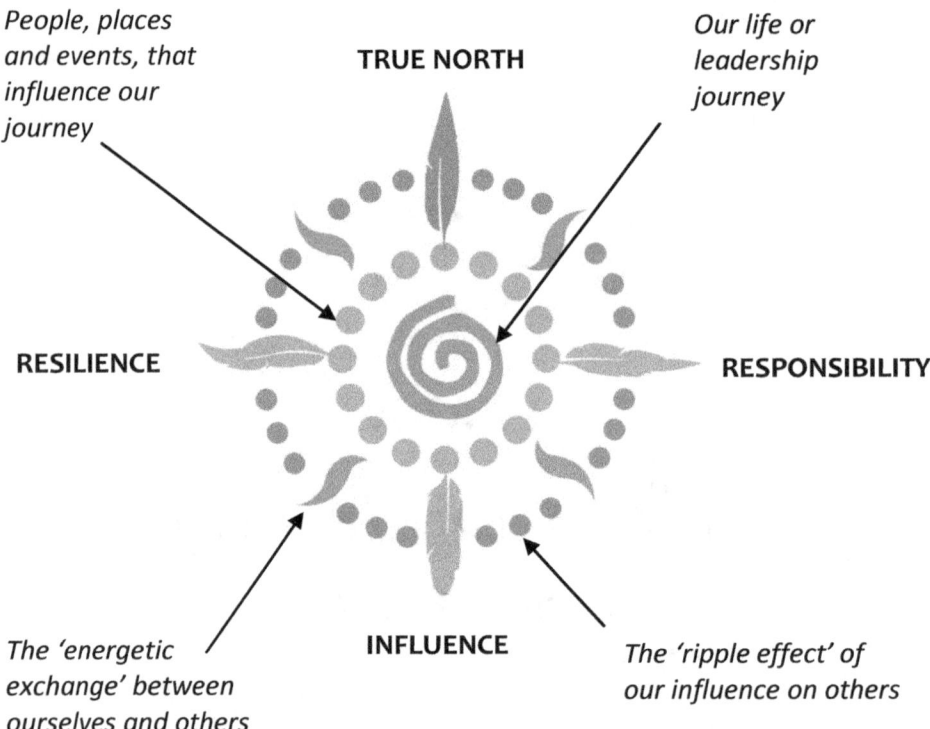

Figure 26.1 The True North Leadership Compass—W&G Enright © 2014

As you can see in *Figure 26* above, the *TNL Compass* layout is pretty basic. It includes *The Four Directions* of the compass, symbolised by feathers which relate to four key aspects of leadership (I will elaborate on these in Part V). The spiral at the centre represents the leader's journey, which I refer to as *The Spiral Journey*. The spiral is surrounded by *Circles of Influence*, which define the leader's values, character and competencies. The outer circles represent the *Ripple Effect* of the leader on those that they in turn influence. And the flames between the circles symbolise the *Energy Exchange* between the leader and those they interact with. In this part of the book I aim to tell you the story of how I found this compass and why I named it so. *True North* is not unique as a brand name, but for me it is a vital adjective that distinguishes a *unique brand of leader* from those with no compass.

Chapter 26   Finding True North

I've always had a fascination with those old World globes that spin on their brass fittings and find their homes on antique desk tops. If you take a good look at one, you'll notice that they have horizontal lines that wrap around them like belts from west to east which are called latitudes. The most recognisable latitude is the Equator. These global maps also have vertical lines or meridians that connect the south and north poles. These are called longitudes. The geographical term for the North Pole at the top where the longitudes meet is known as *True North*.

When I was lost in Mt Crawford Forest and a few times after that while navigating across trackless terrain in the Northern Flinders Ranges with *Operation Flinders*, I discovered that there is a difference between the direction of 'North' found by a magnetic red arrow on a compass and that of the actual physical North Pole. Compasses point to *Magnetic North* which varies depending on where you are on the planet, relative to the magnetic field of the Earth. So there is a variation between the north on a compass (*Magnetic North*) and the geographical position of the North Pole (*True North*) which is a constant.

True North is often used as a metaphor for the concept of integrity and authenticity (alignment with personal values, beliefs, truth) because it is seen as constant and 'true' compared with magnetic north which varies and is dependent on where you are. The direction of north on a compass may also be influenced by its surroundings if you hold it close to a metal belt buckle or fence post. We too can be affected by the energy of those around us. It is harder to live by one's truth in the absence of an inner compass.

So, *True North* can be thought of in terms of our *inner guidance system*—a *way* of living that is most aligned with what we feel is our *true mission* in life. Many of us wander through life following the direction of someone else's compass or with no compass at all. Some of us find a compass later in life which points us in the right direction. Whatever the timing, eventually we must find for ourselves, the truth of who we are and follow our own inner guidance if we are to feel fulfilled and well within. For me, this is the essence of what it means to live and lead with authenticity and integrity. Finding and following one's *True North* is one of the most pivotal challenges of leadership and in the grander scheme of life. The key question one might ask is—how do we find our *True North*? Is it something we know intuitively or is it somehow given to us on a stone tablet, like *The 10 Commandments*?

My belief is that some of us know from the day we are born, others have an inkling but may need to come into contact with the right teacher, mentor, coach, soul mate or 'enemy' to enlighten them. Some people are happy to follow someone else's doctrine, and many may not even care and are just happy to take each day as it comes. There is no 'right' way and everyone's way is different. For most of us though, we are shaped by our *Spiral Journey* and the *Circles of Influence* that impact us along the way.

The Spiral Journey
Like a Labyrinth, the spiral at the centre of the *TNL Compass* represents the journey we all take in life as we spiral around revisiting questions we thought we had answered, lessons we thought we had learned and challenges we thought we had overcome. It seems that most of us transform as we travel a continuous orbit around the sun of our life, revisiting familiar challenges but from a place of ever-evolving maturity like the rings of a tree. Some are conscious of this and some are oblivious to it.

> ***All journeys have secret destinations of which the traveller,
> in the beginning, is unaware.***
> Martin Buber

As I stop and reflect on how I came to find my *True North*, the quote above from Martin Buber keeps returning to me like a wave gently lapping at the shore of my thoughts. I remember the unfolding of my own leadership journey and the unexpected turning points that brought me to this page.

The *Circles of Influence* that surround the spiral symbolise the people, places and events that impact our life journey and therefore our leadership development. They influence our values, our beliefs, our character, and the development of our knowledge and skills. For some, these defining influences help us to find our *True North* and for others our direction may be forever obscure to us.

As I reflect on this, my memory drags me back to a number of people who have influenced my outlook on life; to places that have become sacred to me—now part of my 'Dreaming'—and to events that have offered valuable lessons along the way. Some of these random or intentional 'collisions' have changed my trajectory significantly.

The Meaning of 'Dreaming'
Dreaming and mythology can be considered as the same thing: the deep mental archetypes and images of wisdom which we take on and are guided by, when the conscious mind is in a state of quietness. In Aboriginal culture there is a much closer connection to the ancestral spirits of the land and stories from the past which are inadequately expressed by the English word 'Dreaming.'

> **What we draw on from our memories to think,
> imagine and create in our daily lives is our dreaming.**
> Djon Mundine, Bundjalung man and Aboriginal Curator, Campbelltown Arts Centre

It is with much respect that I use the word 'Dreaming' to express my connection to stories, places and people that have contributed to *my* identity and *my* truth. I too, feel a deep connection to the spirit of the land, especially around North Head in Sydney, Central Australia, Papua New Guinea, Japan and South America. My only regret is that I didn't get to meet most of my Grandparents, so I have little understanding of my ancestral stories apart from those shared by my parents. This book is not the place to tell my whole life story, but in the next few chapters, I will share some of my more challenging learning experiences to illustrate the concept of *The Spiral Journey*. These experiences have convinced me that it is not just the *lucky breaks* that provide us with opportunities to grow and become all we can be; it is often when we are most vulnerable.

I feel a little reticent to go off on too much of a tangent here, and yet I believe that the honest sharing of biographical stories where one gets to see behind the scenes in an author's life, is more powerful than a prescriptive manifesto preached from the pulpit of a book without the preacher's vulnerabilities and human foibles being shared.

I trust that these stories from parts of the *Spiral Journey* that I have experienced, will help you to see how the *turning points* in my path guided me here and how Mark's legacy unfolded in my life. I am sure, if you reflect on your own journey, you too will see the invisible threads that lead you to this page.

Daniel Goleman, the Author of *Emotional Intelligence*, places *self-awareness* as one of the most important competencies for emotionally intelligent leaders. Self-awareness comes from feedback and reflection. Investing time in reflection is an essential priority for leaders. During the process we come to understand ourselves more and can sift out the lessons from our experience that might be of value as we journey forward in life.

Sometimes in our more 'high gradient' personal development programs, we may ask participants to share some of their *Spiral Journey*. This can be a powerful affirmation for them and for those who identify with the stories being told. One way of doing this can be as simple as telling stories around a campfire about how we got our scars. This gives people the choice to share as much or as little as they are willing to.

Every scar has a story to tell.

The earliest meaning of the word courage was 'To speak one's truth from the heart.' Over time, this definition has become more associated with heroic deeds. I believe, this fails to recognise the inner strength required for us to speak honestly about who we are and about our experiences—good and bad.

Brene' Brown—CEO of *The Daring Way*[61]

 As I commence writing this morning, I take a bit of time to settle in. It's not very often that I am able to sit down and start tapping away without at first investing some time in quiet reflection. I might need to spend a moment meditating In the garden, taking a walk on the beach or sitting still in silence, waiting for inspiration. At times I'll be staring at a blank page, almost in a trance. Then, as if someone has tapped me on the shoulder or pressed the 'Play' button, I might hear a bird calling from the garden to wake me, or the words of a song or poem appear to lead me. Other times I have vivid memories and emotions that come unexpectedly. As I write this in *this* moment, I close my eyes and listen... like a water diviner... for memories and significant events that have shaped me. My subconscious takes me back to times when I was in the wilderness without a compass, and I follow the threads to try and make sense of how I got here from there.

Chapter 27   Waking Up in the Jungle

It started with darkness and pain as I woke confused from a broken sleep. I reached out to feel for my head torch and could hear the pitter patter of rain drops, dripping from the jungle canopy onto the roof of my tent. Others were groaning to life in the darkness outside. Were they drinking the same cocktail of excitement and anxiety as I was? My back and legs were aching after punishing my body up and down steep hills the day before. Against my will I got up, pulled on my wet clothes and soggy boots and did my best to get my mind focused for another challenging day. I illuminated my watch face and could just make out the numbers 5.00. After an hour of darkness the first rays of the sun filtered through the canopy as we farewelled the relative comfort of our campsite.

After numerous creek crossings our feet were soft and pulpy. Four hours of false peaks sapped the energy from our bones and tested our will before we were struck by the most awesome thunderstorm. We climbed what felt like a vertical wall, as water came down in torrents between the massive tree trunks, almost sweeping us off the mountain side. Then followed another 3 hours of climbing to the top of the Maguli Range through mud and torrential rain. The final steep descent into our overnight refuge, drew on scarce reserves of mental energy as we stumbled down into the darkness after 12 hours, head torch fading, comfort zone stretched to the absolute limit.

Yossi Ghinsberg's words echoed through my head: "Pain is in the body, misery is in the mind." Yossi was lost in an Amazon jungle after rafting over a waterfall. He survived after 22 days of torture.[62] My torture on the other hand, was self-inflicted but nothing compared with those who had battled through this terrain some 60 years before me.

After 8 days and over 90 kilometres of beautiful pristine rainforest, majestic views across jungle covered peaks, raging rivers and remote villages, we sat in silence at the steps of the Australian War Memorial at Isurava Battle[63] Site, overlooking the mist drenched mountains that dipped down through the clouds to the Yodda Valley below. No one spoke a word for at least 20 minutes.

The Zen Buddhists say "one cannot see their reflection in running water, only when it is still." This stillness and quiet, wrapped around us like a blanket of snow. The emotion was palpable in this place where so many had lost their lives or endured great suffering. After walking in their footsteps and gaining some small insight into the conditions they endured, I felt immense gratitude and respect for what they had done in the defence of our freedom.

From Wayne's Trek Journal—First Kokoda Trek, August 2003

Kokoda a Healing Journey

Walking the Kokoda Track[64] is a humbling experience. It is challenging beyond measure, but beyond the comfort zone is the growth zone and the universe of our potential, waiting to be discovered. When we succeed in life against all odds, we feel like we've conquered the world—the truth is, we have conquered our fear and doubt and our self-imposed limitations.

The Track works on people over time, until extraneous thoughts stop running and the mind becomes still. Then all of a sudden somewhere along the track, you 'wake up' and really see yourself for the first time in a long time. You reconnect with your heart, you see what's important and experience life, moment by moment, in the present. You are grateful to be alive and simplicity creeps in. The stillness of the jungle speaks to you. The pendulum swing of past and present, pleasure and pain, negative and positive; slows to a point of balance.

> *Like a wise craftsman, the track carves away at our facade, revealing the essence of who we are.*

Although I had lived the first sixteen years of my life in army camps as one of five sons to my mother (Jeanette) whose family had a strong military history, and my father (John) who was a Korean War veteran and served as a professional soldier for twenty five years, my first visit to the Kokoda Track was not motivated by the military connection or the physical challenge of 'conquering' one of the world's most torturous treks. For me it was a quest for healing, a journey back to a place of balance, a place that felt like home. At that time I was at a crossroad in my life, where I felt like I was out on a limb, hanging on for dear life, not knowing which way to jump or where I would land. I was no stranger to this feeling. I had been there before on more than one occasion. On this occasion I was called by the *Spirit of Adventure* to come to the jungle and re-discover myself.

Since 2003 I've made an annual pilgrimage across the Kokoda Track, often taking up to three groups each year and sometimes spending a month in the jungle when I've done back to back treks. After each trek, Gabrielle and I also continue to the coast where our porters and their families live.

Over the years, we have developed a strong bond with the people and culture of the village communities that inhabit this sacred place where so many young people lost their lives defending their homeland in World War II. Some of the Australian and Japanese soldiers were as young as 18. Even after so many treks, I still shed a tear for those who suffered so much and died too young. I remember back to when I was their age.

Death Sentence

I was in my last year of school, in the Riverland area SA, sitting in the back of my history class, discussing Napoleon's defeat at the Battle of Waterloo. The Deputy Principal interrupted my history teacher with a concerned whisper in his ear. What followed, replays in slow motion from my memory, as if I'm watching a movie.

My history teacher walked slowly down the aisle toward me, rows of heads turning to follow his path to the back of the room where I sat wondering who was in trouble? He put his hand gently on my shoulder and quietly requested that I pack up my books and make my way to the Principal's office.

I sat pensively in the dock waiting to hear the charges unjustly brought against me? The sentencing had already been decided and was one I had not remotely expected. The Principal was the messenger and the message was not negotiable: "You are sentenced to life without an older brother, a close friend and protector, whom you love so dearly." I heard the rest of the conditions ringing in my brain too: "There will be no parole, no good behaviour bond. The door is locked shut for ever and there is no key to free you from this prison."

My brother Peter had been killed in a winery accident just across the road from the school. We were only a year apart in age and we were inseparable... or so I thought!

Photo at Proof Range Beach, 1967

When I was given the news of his death and told to be strong for my younger brothers, I was confused and speechless. I wanted to piss my pants but this would not have been a good look for a teenage boy, so I stuttered the words, "C-can I g-go to the t-toilet?"

I remember walking across the assembly area to the toilet block like a soldier who'd just survived a relentless barrage of shelling from a hidden enemy. I was encircled by a silence that was deafening. I couldn't hear a thing and my peripheral vision had shut down. I stood at the urinal in shock, and took the longest piss for what seemed like an eternity. It felt like every cell had given up its last molecule of water and yet it kept pouring out of me until my body felt like an empty dehydrated shell.

The story of what happened over the next days, weeks, months and years is really the subject of another book, suffice it to say that this event was a turning point in my life and eventually pushed me down a challenging path of chronic depression, drug abuse and to a flirtation with the temptation of suicide. The only people who really knew about my secret despair were those closest to me—to the rest of the world, I probably looked okay.

Fortunately I met my wife Gabrielle at a crucial time. You could say, her smile, her positive outlook and her unconditional love 'saved' me. Rather than rescue me or buy into my darkness she instead provided a lantern of light that illuminated the tunnel I thought I was trapped in. She gave me the belief that I could dream again and led me toward the light.

> *If one dream should fall and break into a thousand pieces,*
> *never be afraid to pick one of them up and begin again.*
> From the children's book—*Flavia and the Dream Maker,* written by Flavia Weedn

Even after making the decision to live and to take responsibility for my life, I had only taken the first step on a long journey. During my journey through this labyrinth, I discovered resources deep within my being that I didn't know were there, I came across fellow travellers like Mark who inspired me to get better. Along the way I experienced joys, triumphs and summits that were equally as extreme as the dark valleys I searched to find my way back to my centre. Unlike *Humpty Dumpty* I had managed to put the fragments back together again with a little help from my friends, but my journey back to wellness was not the one way ticket that I thought it was.

Run Forest Run

When Mark died I was overwhelmed by the impact it had on me. It felt even more painful than my own brother's death. I can only guess that on top of the grief that I felt losing such a close friend, Mark's death may have also re-activated my unresolved *Post-Traumatic Stress*. I thought I had dealt with the grief of my brother Peter's death but when I reflect on it, I can see that I had just run away from it… I remember dealing with the pain of his unexpected loss through painting, martial arts and running. Like *Forest Gump*, I ran and I ran and I ran (all the way from the Riverland to Adelaide). I ran so much that I weighed only 56 kg when I was in my early twenties. Now my 'fighting weight' doesn't get much lower than 73 kg. When I stopped running, I took up Tae Kwon Do, windsurfing and triathlons. I've always needed to be active and at times it has been an addiction I guess, at least I am a healthy addict.

Honouring My Brother

I remember one morning in particular, running to my brother Peter's grave. As the sun rose through the flame trees and its laser beams of light filtered through the frosty morning mist, illuminating Peter's black marble headstone, I saw the gold lettering etched in its surface, sparkling in the early dawning light. I read again the words that I had read so many mornings before but they were bolder: **'The strength of his being will be remembered by all who knew him'.** *In that moment I distinctly remember a wave of energy rising in my chest and saying to myself: "The best way I can honour his life is to make the most of mine." I listened to the silence for a while before the quiet space was filled with the beautiful melodic warbling of a magpie. I smiled and breathed in her healing song, hoping it would stay with me as I jogged off towards the rising sun. Even today, the song of a magpie holds special significance for me.*

From that day forward I got on with my life but beneath my mask of humour, lay an ever-stalking depression. I really didn't make the connection between the depression and my unresolved grief until years later. I just thought I was a weak bastard, a typically melancholic artist, emotionally sensitive and overly focussed on worse-case scenarios. It wasn't until I met Gabrielle that I really started to unpack my mental torment through conversations with her and through the books I started to read and courses I studied. I underwent a lot of years of personal development including psycho-therapy, stress management, yoga, tai chi, meditation, relationship courses and leadership experiences. It was while travelling along this road to recovery that I studied counselling which is where I eventually crossed paths with Mark.

Follow Your Bliss

While reading a tribute to Mark, I was struck by his wife, Catherine's words when she said: *He took all of his dreams and passions and fashioned them into a life.* This reminded me of the promise I'd made to myself at my brother's grave and so, as if transported back to that morning at sunrise, I recommitted to honouring my *Blood Brother* Peter and my *Spirit Brother* Mark, by beginning a more concerted search for my truth and by following my 'bliss', as Joseph Campbell refers to it.

The Masters say that each life has a potentiality and the mission of life is to live that potentiality by finding your truth and following your bliss, there is something inside us that knows.
Joseph Campbell

Mark had already helped me to get a glimpse of what made my heart sing and now it was my responsibility to find the path to the horizon of my potential. I could choose to go through the gateway enlightened by his brief visit to my life or I could succumb to the self-pity I felt about my losses and be ruled by the *Grim Reaper* that I feared would never leave me alone.

So I began to design my life around my dreams and passions. After helping out with Mark's business for awhile, I began to focus on carving out my own path. This path was heavily influenced by the lessons I had learnt from Mark and the dreams he had kindled in me. The embers had nearly gone out in the immediate aftermath of his death, but the words that Catherine had shared in her tribute breathed new life into them, and they began to glow and burn again.

What happened in the following year is an interesting example of the *Spiral Journey*, history repeating itself, revisiting lessons I thought I had learnt and challenges I thought I had overcome. (If it sounds like I am going around in circles and continually repeating myself, it's because I am!).

> **Our life and leadership journey is a never-ending spiral of experiences which provide us with an opportunity to build on the lessons from the past and evolve into our future potential.**

Speechless

As mentioned in Chapter 13, a year after Mark's death, I started to have difficulty sounding words and my voice would drop out involuntarily during a presentation, or in the middle of a conversation. After months of frustration and trying to cover it up, I eventually received the diagnosis to explain this mystery and I came to accept that it wasn't temporary.

Having this condition in the prime of my life and being told there was no cure, required me to radically re-think my career options and financial security, not to mention the frustration and grief I felt at losing something that was so much a part of my identity. I started to worry about how I'd be perceived by others. I became silent in situations where I would normally be more vocal. I felt tentative rather than confident and I was anxious about whether I'd be able to articulate what I wanted to say. Without a voice it was more difficult to express my truth, I found it hard to break into group conversations and I was self-conscious about the way others interpreted my silence, embarrassment or apparent anxiety.

Although this time, I had not lost a loved one or dear friend, I did start to feel that I was losing the person that was me. And so the *Grim Reaper* visited me again, as if to test me once more! This time though, I had a way out. Like a hidden gate in a rodeo ring, I was desperate to find it.

Chapter 28   Kokoda – A Journey of the Spirit

While dealing with the frustration and grief associated with the loss of my voice, I happened to receive an email from a stranger, calling for people with an adventurous spirit to join a group walking the Kokoda Track. At first I dismissed this as a message for someone else. I couldn't afford it financially or timewise, and it seemed a bit risky based on what I had heard about Papua New Guinea (PNG). After forgetting about it for a few weeks I was clearing old emails and was about to delete this *call from the wild,* when I remembered the quote on the brass plaque that had been attached to the *Auricht Adventure Tower* in memory of Mark.

When the spirit of adventure calls to our heart, we must go.

These words flashed like a neon sign in my mind, urging me to remove my finger from the 'Delete' button and to click 'Reply' instead. It was in response to this *call to my heart* that I embarked on my first journey to the Kokoda Track. In hindsight, I now realise that this was my way of dealing with the grief of losing a friend and losing a part of myself that voiced who I thought I was. Walking the Kokoda Track was a way of getting out of my drama and getting some perspective on life, a way of renewing my confidence and affirming my resilience.

The Land of the Unexpected
Interestingly, it was Mark's birth, forty years earlier in August 1963, that brought his parents, Clive and Ruth Auricht, back from PNG after they had lived and worked there for two years with their first two sons Richard and Geoffrey. The history of Clive's time in PNG is well covered in his book *Medicine Beyond Kokoda,* which I touched on briefly in Chapter 6. Clive ended up working as a doctor at a place called Saiho in PNG's Northern Province (which is now called *Oro Province—Oro* means welcome). Saiho is near Awala, where Australian soldiers made their first contact with the Japanese during World War II. Clive moved to Saiho in February 1961 (a week after I was born as it turns out).

The local porters and guides that we use for our Kokoda treks come from the *Oro Province* and live in the villages along the northern beaches where the Japanese started their journey to the Kokoda Track and were defeated several months later, in January 1943.

I have travelled along the road from Kokoda past Saiho many times on my way to the coast to visit our porters' families and where Gabrielle and I now have a little house, thanks to our PNG friends. I didn't know until recently, about this uncanny connection with Mark's family. Clive says that PNG will always have a special place in his heart that time can never erase. Whenever I walk across the Kokoda Track now, I know that a piece of Mark's spirit walks with me. I feel it in certain places in the jungle, especially when I find myself alone.

Wayne on the Kokoda Track, 2004

Kokoda—A Journey of the Spirit

It has now been almost fifteen years since I first walked the Kokoda Track, a journey that took my spirit back to the wild places of my youth where I fell in love with nature and adventure. It felt like coming home. In this place I discovered answers to resolve the grief within me, I learned some valuable lessons about what really matters in life and I found my lost compass.

What started as a quest for healing turned into a business as I got more and more requests to take people there and realised that perhaps it could be a transforming place for others as well. Most people don't go there with the sole intention of experiencing a life changing journey... it is usually about walking in the footsteps of the young Australians who fought there against the Japanese in World War II. For some it's about the challenge and for others it's a 'bucket list' thing like Everest Base Camp. Whatever the initial intention, there is always a *secret destination* that people discover along the way.

After doing more than thirty Kokoda treks collectively, Gabrielle and I now know, that the tears we see in people's eyes as they complete the ninety six kilometre journey across the spine of Papua New Guinea, reflect a deeper journey of the spirit.

Like me, many others get more than they came for in this challenging but magical place. I came back a changed man, having found answers through that journey that reframed the way I thought about myself and the world in which I lived, and I wanted to share this profound experience with others.

Beyond the Jungle
It is this sharing of inspiring and transformative journeys with others that has taken Gabrielle and I back to the jungles of PNG and on to other places around the world including: Kilimanjaro and Serengetti in Africa; The Inca Trail, Salkantay Trail, Machu Picchu and the Amazon in Peru; Iguassu Falls in Brazil; Patagonia in Chile and Argentina; New Zealand's Fiorlands; Tasmania's Overland Track and Franklin River; the Kimberley in North-West Australia; and from the Larapinta Trail to Uluru in Australia's Red Centre. This year (2017), we will traverse Bhutan from west to east, where I'll no doubt send a *cooee* to Mark across the Himalayan sky.

I could not have imagined travelling to all of these places even once in my life, let alone visiting them a number of times and taking others with me. It is through the experience of taking people on these adventures that I have discovered the power of journeying, particularly journeys to wild and remote places that offer some uncertainty but leave people inspired and changed in some way. Gabrielle and I had no idea that this would happen and certainly not as a result of losing my voice. Blessings come from unexpected places and PNG has certainly lived up to its title—the *Land of the Unexpected*. I would have to say that, of all the places I've travelled around the world so far, the Kokoda Track and the northern beaches of the Oro Province in PNG have changed me the most. They always have a healing and rejuvenating effect on me. It's as if the jungle and the spirit of this place and its people are my most powerful medicine. They have become part of my *Dreaming*. I remain under their spell all these years later.

Family photo with sponsored daughter Elsie, 2012

Insights and Poems from Papua New Guinea

I have kept a journal during the years that I've been going to PNG. Here I share some of the lessons I have learned from this special place and some words that came to me in moments of poetic inspiration.

INITIATION – Some thoughts on the importance of initiation.

Where does a person go to learn their soul's name—a name that defines their true identity? This deep heart knowledge can only come from a process of initiation.
To know where we come from and who we are, we have to have taken a journey that challenges us.
Our modern world is full of uninitiated people.
Knowledge is taught in classrooms but for many there is a lack of initiation from wise elders or facing the challenges of the wilderness.
Emotional Intelligence is not learnt in classrooms but in the experience of living life's challenges, joys and lessons of the heart.
Adventures require more from us, they challenge our self-belief.
Although we may feel discomfort and fear; at a deeper level we yearn to know that we have what it takes to meet adventure's test.

Inspired by *Wild at Heart* – John Eldredge

BEYOND THE MEMORY OF WAR'S ENDLESS REACH – A poem I penned at Isurava.

Beyond the memory of war's endless reach,
in our hearts and our minds we came to find peace.
Walking slow in the jungle, watching our feet
and searching horizons from a mountain peak.
At the shore of the ocean, in the first light of dawn,
we find peace in the silence while in stillness we mourn.
In the rain and the thunder and each breath we take,
in the hearts of the people who inhabit this place.
Take time for the sunset, for an hour or minute;
take time for the moments that bring peace to your spirit.

ORO ORO – A greeting from the Oro (Welcome) Province.

Oro Oro (Welcome Welcome)
I offer you peace.
I offer you friendship.
I see your beauty.
I feel your need.
I honour the place in you where the Universal Spirit dwells.
When you and I are in that place, we are One.

A PNG version of Namaste

Chapter 28—Kokoda—A Journey of the Spirit

COMING HOME – Reflections at Buna Beach.

From my refuge under a palm tree on a volcanic sand beach, I hear 'plop... plop' raindrops creating circles on the sea.
Only dolphins and rain drops break the surface of the mill pond, so still you could see your reflection if you took a closer look.
Misty rain drips from the palm leaves onto the sand, sea-fog blankets the constant sound of swell lapping, crashing, caressing the shore; beckoning constantly at the edge, as if to tempt me in.
There is nothing more renewing after a long and challenging journey across mountains, valleys and rivers, than arriving at the water's edge where the journey ends... then stepping into the ocean, surrendering to the beckoning.
It feels like coming home.

RE-DISCOVERING Joy, Beauty and Balance – The healing nature of this place.

For too long I'd been playing someone else's game. A game that took me away from what was important and required me to play by rules I didn't want to live by.
I squandered time for the ones I loved and missed the beauty in the red, green and blue of our planet.
In this place, among these people, I have re-discovered the joy of play, the beauty in nature and the balance that comes with rest and reflection.

JOY IS IN THE HEART – Lessons from the villages.

The Koiari and Orokaiva people who live along the Kokoda Track, through to the Northern Beaches are predominantly subsistence farmers and hunters whose culture and traditions have changed very little over millennia.
How easy it is to think that we could help by teaching our 'civilised' ways to indigenous people who have been subsisting in the wild for thousands of years without our sophisticated technology.
Their physically challenging lifestyle creates resilient people. Their children run free, learning from their experience in the wild. Initiation into adulthood comes naturally with the help of traditional customs and wise elders who teach them how to live in balance with nature.
They have much to teach us about such things as simplicity, balance, love, joy, service, generosity, humility and family. Their singing teaches us that joy is not in things... it is in the heart.

Be grateful for the times that almost break you, and always remember those who shaped you.
Inspired by Sarah Haze

Gabrielle at Buna PNG, 2012

From Little Things Big Things Grow

As we ventured to other destinations beyond Kokoda, in response to requests from our clients, the business we now call *Free Spirit Adventures*, evolved. It was then that Gabrielle and I realised we were not just guiding people to some amazingly beautiful and inspiring places in the world; we were also leading them on a *journey within*. Through these adventures, we now endeavour to provide opportunities for people to appreciate the world round them, and to become more self-confident and self-aware, so that they can leave behind what they no longer need, and take forward that which is of value, to live life with renewed optimism, inspiration and belief in possibilities.

It was this concept of freeing people's spirit through adventure that I was first introduced to by Mark and that I have now come to know more intimately and to share with others. I often wonder whether the birth of *Free Spirit Adventures* (one of the unexpected destinations that I arrived at in response to the loss of my voice) was in some way a tree that grew out of the seeds he had planted in me through his encouragement of my gifts, his adventurous spirit and the example he set to live one's dreams.

> ***Some say God can be found in the wilderness***
> ***and adventure can be a deeply spiritual experience.***
> ***Whatever your concept of God, I believe this to be so.***

I've discovered that, like adventure, illness and crisis can be a spiritual experience too, in the way that they cause us to search within ourselves and stir our heart and soul. The Chinese meaning of the two characters that represent the word 'crisis' is *opportunity riding the dangerous wind*. Thus in every crisis or turning point in our lives, there is danger and opportunity. It is my hope you will embrace the turning points in your life, and discover the lessons and *secret destinations* that may be hidden in your *spiral journey*.

Wayne and Gabrielle—Kokoda Trail, 2012

Chapter 29   Vision Quest

True North is not only about our values, beliefs and sense of true-self, it is also about the vision we hold for ourselves, and how we use our gifts to live a meaningful life. Sometimes discovering this requires us to let go of the past and embrace the future. I was reminded of this on another adventure.

 I remember the sensation of floating as we hovered our way across the red earth to a secret location called 'Point X'. There beneath us I could see a steep-sided gorge that was the gateway to a hidden valley of palm-shaded waterways, winding their way through a maze of hills to Lake Argyle—four days walk from where we were about to land but in another sense, millions of miles away from anywhere I'd been before.

The rotor blades of our bumble bee swished above our heads as we were dropped near a solitary billabong at the opposite end of the gorge. This tranquil billabong surrounded by ancient boab trees and home to a family of fresh-water crocodiles, guarded the entrance to the water-filled gorge that was our only passage into the hidden valley and through to our ultimate destination.

Overnight we could see a whitewash of stars across the pitch black sky and the glowing eyes of the crocs peering across the billabong. In the morning the crocs were no-where to be seen but we knew they were in there somewhere. An orchestra of birds welcomed the sunrise as we had breakfast by the smouldering fire. Then came the 400 metre swim through the gorge as we pushed our floating packs through its narrow passage. The steep cliff walls of the gorge shaded its still cold waters and looked down upon us, as if we were ants swimming through a drain, struggling to keep afloat with our bundles of belongings.

After a near-hypothermic swim through this 'birth canal' of sorts, we thawed out and came to life as we took in the scenery of this spectacular place and felt its shy spirit for the first time.

Rite of Passage

This experience in the Kimberley reminded me of the concept of *Rites of Passage*[65] where we stand at the threshold to a new stage of life, sometimes fearing to let go as we prepare to enter an uncomfortable transformation. Then we plunge into the gorge which we must pass through to get from one world to the next.

Eventually we make it through this transition and embrace the next stage of life that we have entered into. Sometimes we get through on our own and other times we need a guide to help us.

It was while trekking through the Carr Boyd Ranges of the Kimberley that I connected with the idea of doing a Vision Quest. Vision Quests are perhaps not well known among the majority of the western population but are an integral part of the life journey among most indigenous cultures. They may be known by different names but most commonly they are part of the initiation process for young people as they transition into adulthood. They can also be used for other *rites of passage* during different life stages. *Rite of Passage* is the term used for passing from one stage of life to another or from one group or level of status to another.

Individual Indigenous cultures have their own names for their *rites of passage*. *Vision Quest* is an English umbrella term, and is not necessarily used by these cultures or reflective of their individual practices. Among Native American cultures it usually consists of a series of ceremonies led by Elders and supported by the community. The ritual of going on a *Vision Quest*, acknowledges that some truths are best learnt in solitude. This allows space for the individual to find a stronger connection with self and with nature's wisdom.

> **There comes a time when one must leave family, friends and work behind, to go off alone and find oneself. A 'Self' that isn't centred around the family, friend and work roles we play in life, but around the truth of who we are.**

Most *Vision Quests* involve a three-stage process of *separation, transition* and *re-integration*[66] that is based on the ancient rituals of their culture. In western cultures the typical ceremonies familiar to us are occasions such as birthdays (particularly 21st and 50th birthdays); Christenings; Bar mitzvahs, bachelor or hen's parties before marriage; weddings and funerals etc. Each country and faith has its own traditional ways of doing this—many religions have *rites of passage* to assist with transition (the 'Last Rites' for example). The *Vision Quests* of indigenous cultures tend to be more focussed on transformation than celebration (although during the *re-integration* stage, an individual's *return* from the wilderness is celebrated by their community).

Vision Quest rituals are uniquely challenging and transformative. They vary from culture to culture but essentially they focus on helping people to disconnect from old ways that no longer serve them, to move through the threshold between past and future and to return to a more authentic way of being in the world, with a renewed clarity of purpose and a stronger sense of their place in the circle of life.

Chapter 29—Vision Quest

When I turned fifty I was given a book titled: *The Art of Pilgrimage—The Seekers Guide to Making Travel Sacred,* written by Phil Cousineau. This book helped me to understand why my journeys to places like the Kokoda Track, Machu Picchu and Australia's outback were such powerfully transformative experiences. It also gave me some insight into how travel, adventure and even the leadership expeditions we facilitate now, can provide a *Vision Quest* type experience for those who seek it (and even for those who don't and are subtly taken to this secret destination by chance). In the words of Architect Anthony Lawlor, The Art of Pilgrimage *shows us how to travel outward to the edges of the world while simultaneously journeying to the depths of our soul.*

In a way, the desire of young adults to go on backpacking journeys to far off places when they finish school or university, is not just about seeing the world before they settle down to a life of work. It is perhaps also a subconscious drive to go on a *Vision Quest* which facilitates this *rite of passage.* In the absence of traditional rituals guided by Elders, as we see in indigenous cultures; many young people come up with their own initiation-like processes such as experimentation with drugs or other high-risk/adventurous behaviours. Youth-at-risk programs such as *Operation Flinders, True North Expeditions, Outward Bound,* and other activities such as scouting, martial arts and team sports, offer a healthy alternative to the destructive path that some young people find themselves following, and can support them through this challenging transition.

> *Where do we go to discover our true nature?*
> *The deep knowledge of the heart is not found in classrooms and books.*
> *To find it, we have to have taken a journey that tests and enlightens us.*

Even in midlife, some of us suddenly lose our footing on the ladder of life and realise its leaning against the wrong wall. We hear 'the call' and we feel the urge to go off on an adventure. I think that Mark intuitively knew this when he first named his business *Outbound Corporate Recharge* which later became *Venture Corporate Recharge.* He understood that business men and women also benefit from adventure experiences that help them to gain insights, clarity of purpose and a recharging of their spirit.

Like the transition from subordinate to supervisor or player to coach, *rites of passage* occur at a number of stages in our life as we transition from *childhood to adolescence—adolescence to adulthood—from single person to marriage and /or parenthood and from there to empty-nester or Elder.* Many go through these transitions without any ritual or support.

A *Vision Quest* can help us to navigate these *rites of passage* and to gain a clearer vision of our purpose, regardless of the context and where we are on our journey. Purpose is such an important ingredient when it comes to health, happiness and having a sense of meaning in our personal and professional lives, and yet many of us neglect it or are confused at times as to whether we are living 'on purpose' or drifting without a rudder.

It was during a time when I was confused about this that I decided to try a *Vision Quest* in the hope that it would help me to pick up my compass again and get back on track. My mood at this time of inner confusion was best summed up by the following journal entry a few days after returning from a month in the jungle.

Returning from the Wilderness

John Mayer's song Say what you need to say *is playing in the background, prompting me to write what's on my mind and in my heart. I feel a bit strange this morning, sitting at my desk, looking out into the garden. Part of me wants to be out there among the plants and the sunshine and fresh air, while I also want to be here writing. My desk is as close as you can get to being outdoors, especially if I open the wide French doors and let the outside in, but I still feel the 'tug of war' between these two worlds. I often notice this contrast more when I return from an adventure. My inner world has shifted and feels incongruent with the outer world I have come back to. The resulting perturbation causes me to change a little each time. I either have to change my outer world or the way I operate in it to match the shift inside of me, or allow the internal shift to dissipate and slip back into my comfort zone.*

I've just returned from another month in Papua New Guinea guiding a couple of groups across the Kokoda Track. The transition back to the 'civilised' world is always challenging but has been more difficult this time to say the least. A month of walking meditation in the jungle, pristine mountain air, beautiful waterfalls and rivers, inspiring cultural experiences and open-hearted people have taken me to a place in my consciousness that feels assaulted when it rubs up against the reality of city traffic, un-reality TV shows, news headlines, advertising and time deadlines. I feel the gravity of 'civilisation' pulling me away from the natural beauty and simplicity of where I feel a belonging.

The longer I spend in the wilderness with people of another time, the more I notice the disconnect between the inspiring qualities of things such as nature; adventure; beauty; love; joy; peace and balance, and the sometimes stressful world of media; technology; time constraints; money; noise; processed food; chairs; shoes; political correctness and over-regulation.

This contrast is sometimes overwhelming, confronting, painful, depressing and in conflict with my heart's truth and my more natural state of being. It jolts my senses, creates fog in my mind, perturbation in my soul and imbalance in my body. I feel a hint of sadness in my heart feeling this disconnect between my true nature and 'the sea of cars' (as Murray refers to it in his book My Life in a Sea of Cars). I wonder if others feel this distance from nature and their wild heart? Perhaps part of my purpose is to reconnect people with the inspiring qualities of nature, adventure, play, and journeying back to where they feel they belong; places that make their heart sing and where they feel most alive? I hear about 'Nature Deficit Disorder[67]' and often think that 'Adventure Therapy' is as important for 'adults at risk' as it is for young people at risk.

There is a pleasure in the pathless woods and rapture on the lonely shore; there is society, where none intrudes, by the deep sea, and music in its roar; I love not man the less, but Nature more.
Lord Byron

A Good Year

In 2012 I had what some would consider 'A Good Year.' I travelled to some amazing places:– trekking across the Overland Track and rafting down the Franklin River in Tasmania; exploring a remote maze of red-ochre ranges in the Kimberley; and reconnecting with my love of snow skiing in the white whipped cream of the Victorian Alps. I hadn't missed a year of walking the Kokoda Track since 2003, and this year was no different. I also managed to set aside a few weeks for writing and somehow kept up with training for my next karate grading despite the waxing and waning of my motivation. I was fit and healthy, had lots of new and interesting corporate clients and balanced this with leading another youth at risk group through the Flinders Ranges just to keep me humble.

I feel less than humble after writing the above paragraph as it sounds like a bit of a narcissistic brag worthy of a *Facebook* post! But I share this for good reason—to illustrate that, regardless of our *Facebook* posts, underneath all of the *apparent happiness* can lie a painful truth. For me that truth was that I was somewhat lost in the *wilderness of my mind* again. I was enjoying the adventure of it, the scenery and the variety of experiences I had manifested to match my dreams, but there was still something missing. I was wandering around among the trees without a clear destination or purpose that was aligned with my heart. I enjoyed what I was doing, don't get me wrong, but little by little I had disconnected from my heart again, free-falling into the clouds of my head. By September of that year I had become confusingly dissatisfied with where I had landed.

How ungrateful this seems now as I reflect on the blessings of 2012. Should I not have been happy with what I had created? Yes I was, and yet I was yearning for something more valuable. At the time I didn't really know what it was but there was another *unseen destination* yet to be revealed.

This disturbance within me is particularly noticeable when I have to re-enter the corporate world after returning from the mountains, the jungle and the peaceful coastal villages where life is so simple and uncomplicated compared with our 'apparently civilised' existence. Every time I go back *into the wild*, it wakes me up again. This time it woke me up from a deep sleep that I'd drifted into without knowing, finding myself lost in the labyrinth of my mind. This awakening that I experienced in the jungles of PNG and the red-ochre heartlands of Australia was frustratingly out of reach once I re-entered the corporate world where not all gigs make my heart sing.

Bull-Shift
Some of the corporate work that I had been doing in 2012 was in conjunction with a colleague of mine who asked me to assist with some leadership workshops interstate for a company that plays in the international playground of energy resources. I was grateful for the opportunity to work with and learn from my colleague but as the year ticked away I lost my 'mojo.' Most days I wore my corporate attire and spoke the appropriate corporate language, working in the comfort of an indoor venue looking out across the parklands beyond the Central Business District. On one level I felt good about the difference I might be making from inside the organisation and at the same time I wondered whether this was really where I should be?

The intention of the work was positive and constructive but I wasn't so sure that I was a good match for the client and their culture. I questioned whether my values were aligned with theirs and whether this was part of my personal mission. I was becoming tired of the Qantas Club, the safety briefings on all the aircraft that are subtly different and the hotel rooms full of opulence and spectacular city views but empty of warmth, homeliness and cherished loved ones. I also hungered for the fresh air and earthiness of the outdoors and the honesty of the conversations that nature evokes.

Then I met a guy who reminded me of who I was. At first this guy 'disturbed' me like a profound book. My head had been so full of intellectual understandings about organisational dynamics, psychological jargon and leadership theories, that I had started to find it hard to talk about leadership without wanting to include everything I'd ever read, listened to and experienced.

I am still challenged by the desire to over-explain and to include everything. I'm a bit of a hoarder of ideas if you hadn't noticed already... but at least I began to recognise my addiction and started to clear the attic and the cellar a little!

This 'disturbing guy' that I met while working interstate was a man named Andrew Horabin. He wrote a book titled *Bullshift*, a little book with a big message! After hearing him speak I felt a sense of 'coming home to my authentic self.' He challenged the audience to let go of the *bullshit* that we often see in corporate environments. He encouraged people to be more honest, more authentic and less caught up in political correctness and 'corporate speak.'

I really related to his style of presentation which was down to earth, funny and somewhat 'calling it as it is.' I liked his attitude, his lack of ego, his kind of 'Carl Baron on steroids' approach—seeing what others don't see and putting a magnifying glass up against it, as if to say:

> *See... look at this... can't you see it? Can't you see how you've been blind to it all this time... caught up in the games that everyone is playing... not seeing the subtext beneath people's words but feeling them and not knowing why they're not always pleasant feelings?*

Andrew Horabin is a brilliant mirror for those who buy into the *bullshit* too much and need a wakeup call, me included!

Let go of all the information, concepts, ideas and prejudices that your mind is stuffed with that stands between you and your true nature. Instead allow your mind to be silent, empty, open and ready... In the beginner's mind there are many possibilities, in the expert's mind there are few.
Sogyal Rinpoche—*The Tibetan Book of Living and Dying*

So I came home inspired to find my *True North* again, to recalibrate my compass, to find my way home, out of the labyrinth of my head and back into the high country of my heart and soul where I could reconnect to the awakening that called to me from the wild. It was here that I stood on the threshold of my *Vision Quest*.

To retrieve one's truth, one must head up into the high country of the soul, into wild and uncharted regions, where the heart dwells.
Inspired by John Eldredge—*Wild at Heart*

Reclaiming My Vision

Anyone who has experienced a *Vision Quest* will know that each individual's quest is deeply personal and all quests are different depending on who is guiding them and what questions the 'Quester' is grappling with as they approach, journey through, and reflect on their *Vision Quest* experience.

One of the key outcomes of a quest is to gain insights, answers to questions and clarity of vision. Most people go into the process with some sort of intention as to what they wish to get out of it and with one or more questions that they want to find answers to.

My key quest-ions were:
1. Should I continue doing the corporate work I was doing or just concentrate on adventure travel?
2. What was the cause of my chronic headaches and speech disability and what was the key to my healing?

It turns out that the answers to these questions were inter-connected. During my quest it became clear to me that it wasn't about choosing my audience, it was about focusing on the bigger picture of my purpose and my *medicine*. The term 'medicine' as mentioned early in our travels together, refers to how one uses their gifts and talents to serve the world in which they live, whether it be for other people, causes, or the environment. One of the insights I gained during my quest was: *To the extent to which I use my 'medicine' to help and heal others, I also help and heal myself. My job is not to drag people into a new way of being but to quietly go about what I know to be my purpose, and those with hearts to hear and vision to see, will connect with their part in it.*

It became clear to me that my purpose was: *To assist others to live a healthy, authentic and adventurous life aligned with their truth.* My medicine (the tools I'm good at using to assist others) was: *Taking people on journeys, whether it be through the use of experiential learning; storytelling (speaking and writing); coaching and mentoring; or through adventure travel.*

It doesn't matter whether I do this at a conference venue with corporate clients, in the jungles or the mountains with a group of adventurers or sitting in the red dust of the outback with youth at risk kids, as long as I am sharing my *medicine* and making a difference.

I also became aware that the more I moved away from my heart and held back on speaking my truth, the more pain I experienced and the more difficulty I had with my voice. I guess that's why I am sharing these personal truths with you as I write—I have made a promise to myself to speak and write from my heart without censoring what I believe to be true.

Some people will appreciate these words while others might find them boring, self-indulgent or irrelevant. Either way, I must simply write with honesty, despite the risk of being critiqued. I share these stories with you in the hope that you might relate to them and perhaps find some *fish beneath the surface*, for yourself.

Getting Back to Where I Once Belonged
After searching my heart to find what really made me come alive I received a strong message to turn my attention back to using *Adventure Based Experiential Learning* again. I had worked with it quite a bit while working with Mark and for a few years after his death as I helped his business transition into new hands, but in the five years leading up to 2012, I had used it less and less. Somehow I ended up doing less adventurous stuff in the corporate work we were doing. I still used experiential activities as metaphors for learning but they didn't include as many of the elements that I had learnt from Mark that took people on a journey and explored below the surface more adventurously. Unlike taking a glass bottom boat ride across the sea where one looks through to the ocean below but never ventures into the water to see the coral and the fish up close, Mark dove down to the unexplored depths beneath the surface. This opened up a much richer experience and was something I wanted to return to doing.

The Team Building Myth
I also questioned the effectiveness of the work I was doing in the area of team development. I was reasonably happy with the outcomes we were getting and the feedback was always good but I also knew from experience that what really makes the difference, is developing a critical mass of people who think and behave as leaders. In fact, I believe that one of the most important things an organisation can do to achieve greater resilience in their teams and long term success in their mission, is to invest in developing leadership mindsets and behaviours in all team members, not just the managers.

Team Building can be a misnomer, in that teams are often an ever-changing dynamic entity whose members come and go. It is more useful to focus on developing *team membership* skills and leadership attributes so that individuals can fulfill their potential in any team they work with. *Teamwork* is of course important but building a team and having it stay done is a bit like building a house of cards. It's more important to build within team members, the capacity to re-create their team as the landscape changes and to operate across teams, regardless of their job description.

I came back from my *Vision Quest* with some helpful answers to the riddles in my mind, much greater clarity about what I wanted to pay attention to in my work, and a greater understanding of how I wanted to go about it. This led to a name change from *Healthy Teams* to *True North Leadership* (TNL).

My eagerness to get back to a more adventure-based leadership program involving a journey experience, resulted in the development of what we now call the *True North Leadership Expedition (TNLXP)*[68]. This is not to be confused with Will Dobud's adventure therapy business—*True North Expeditions*. We just happened to register these business names at the same time, which was synchronistic but unplanned. Some of the proceeds of this book and our leadership program will be donated to Will's *youth at risk* programs in addition to our key recipient *Operation Flinders Foundation*.

The most unique feature of the *TNLXP*, is the journey component, which provokes in-depth discussions about leadership, provides opportunities for personal reflection and poses challenges that test one's leadership strengths and areas for development. This largely outdoor experience, simultaneously takes participants on an inward journey. It harks back to the experiences I was first introduced to by Mark and the processes he used to reveal the true nature of authentic leadership. This is where I feel most at home and where my 'medicine' comes alive.

During the year following my *Vision Quest*, Gabrielle and I agreed on the new name, *True North Leadership*, but had not yet settled on a design for its logo. We had lots of ideas but none of them really resonated with us strongly. We were after something which could also serve as a model for the leadership philosophy we wanted to convey. My usual method of finding answers to difficult questions is to go bush, so we ventured to the heart!

In 2014 we went back to the *Red Centre* of Australia to walk the *Larapinta Trail*, a spectacularly beautiful ochre and green path that snakes its way along the Western MacDonnell Ranges from Alice Springs to Mt Sonder near Redbank Gorge.

After completing the trek which takes you into some remote Aboriginal lands, cradling beautiful gorges and rugged red ridge tops with views as far as the eye can see, we continued on to *Kings Canyon* to explore her hidden treasures in the early dawn before journeying further to circumnavigate the inspiring indigenous landscapes of *Uluru* and *Kata Tjuta*.

It was while immersed in these sacred places, that we were inspired to create the logo for *True North Leadership*. (Hence the spiral, circles and feathers that give the *TNL Compass* its indigenous flavour). As we were finalising the *TNL* logo, we became aware of its strong metaphorical meaning and decided that it wasn't just a logo, but could also be used as a leadership model. (See Figure 26.1 on page 236)

This was the *Secret Destination* I arrived at while searching for a way to convey a simple summary of the enduring traits of outstanding leaders that we have explored in Part III of this book. When I first saw it in my mind, it explained everything that I had learnt from Mark and from my experiences over the years. It has now become the model we use to communicate our leadership philosophy.

The *True North Leadership* trading name reflects the evolution in our thinking and is a metaphor for the type of leadership required to navigate the unpredictable terrain of the future. This concept of a compass that provides direction and a commitment to guiding principles is a well-used metaphor. Peter Drucker, Author of *The Practice of Management,* has this to say about it: *If our business plans are centred on an overall purpose or vision and on a commitment to a set of principles, then the people who are closest to the action in the wilderness can use that compass and their own expertise and judgment to make decisions and take actions based on the realities of their own environment.*

In the same way that *True North* provides a reliable direction and guidance despite the changing environment and terrain one might face on a journey; *True North Leadership* is consistent with unwavering values and principles that provide guidance and direction when making decisions. *True North Leaders* live and lead more authentically, they are committed to and lead from their values and they empower those around them to rise to their potential, thus multiplying the influence of their leadership.

Acknowledging Bill George
During the process of registering the new business name, I did a domain name search to see whether the name was also available online. While doing this search I came across a book written by Bill George titled *True North – Discovering Your Authentic Leadership.* His work with leaders followed a similar philosophy which I also found affirming. George says:– *there are many leadership models out there that are credibly published in thousands of articles and books. Most offer a cure-all prescription of skills, competencies, strengths or intelligences. Few work to uncover the buried wisdom and defining stories of the person seeking greater leadership impact.*

George's words resonate a lot with me because I believe that finding our *True North* requires us to discover the treasure buried within the defining experiences of our *Spiral Journey*. This helps to establish our guiding principles and authentic leadership style. From this place, we can more effectively develop the leaders around us and help them to find their authentic leader within too.

For me, Mark's short-term collision with my orbit helped me to see things I couldn't see before or hadn't yet discovered. I have been fortunate enough to have had many mentors, co-conspirators and friends, together with one unconditionally loving soul-mate, who have helped me to find my buried treasure and who have led me to destinations I didn't expect to experience. I hope that some of these stories may have done the same for you.

> **We must never cease exploring, for at the end of all journeys
> we arrive where we began and come to know our self again.**
> Adapted from the writings of TS Elliot

I encourage you now to take a rest and reflect on your *Spiral Journey* before we take a more detailed tour of the *TNL Compass*. Consider what *True North* means for you and whether you are following the direction of your heart.

Reflection Questions

1. Who have been the most influential people in your life?
2. What have been your defining stories and have you arrived at any unexpected destinations, because of them?
3. Where do you feel most alive to your true nature?
4. How would you define your *True North*?
    - The Vision you hold for your life.
    - Your *Medicine*—gifts, talents that serve the world.
    - Guiding principles that you live by.

A POEM THAT CAME TO MIND TODAY
WB Enright 2.2.17

*To feel the love of family, to love, to laugh, to climb a tree.
To sing, to run, to swim in the sea.
To walk in Nature's beauty to see the vistas, the life, the energy.
To give to others and know they are me.
These are the things that set my heart free.*

What sets your heart free?

PART V

True North Leadership

A Compass for Leaders

True North Leadership Expedition—Adelaide Hills, 2015

TRUE NORTH
Guiding Principles
Integrity & Authenticity
Strategic Thinking
Prioritising

RESILIENCE
Strength & Flexibility
Emotional Intelligence
Patient Persistence
Adversity & Growth

RESPONSIBILITY
Responding by Choice
Mindfulness/Heartfulness
Creative Solutions
Life Balance

INFLUENCE
Trust & Respect
Understanding
Constructive Conflict
Empowerment

Figure 30.1 TNL Compass Headings—W&G Enright © 2014

Only the brave should lead, those whose integrity cannot be shaken, whose minds are enlightened enough to understand the high calling of the leader.
Adapted from Pearl S Buck

In this part of the book we will travel to the four cardinal points of the *TNL Compass*, exploring this model with a few thought-provoking stories to illustrate its relevance for future leaders and explorers of human potential. The *TNL Compass* in more about the character and emotional intelligence of a leader, than it is about task skills and leadership strategies. Here my intention is to provide a simple tool to help identify your strengths and areas for development, should you wish to improve your leadership effectiveness.

    As you come to the end of each chapter in this part of the book, I encourage you to return to this page and reflect on which aspects of the compass you see as your strengths and those that you'd like to improve. The key to improvement is self-awareness, intention, practice, feedback and applying what you learn along the way. Books, courses and coaches are helpful but there is no substitute for experience. Enjoy the challenge!

Chapter 30   The Four Directions

Lone Dingo

There is an outdoor shop in Alice Springs called the Lone Dingo. Whilst walking in there to get supplies for a recent Larapinta Trek, I saw a t-shirt with a picture of a small lone dingo, a boot print blazoned across the chest and the words *Tread Lightly*.

This took me back in time to an experience I had once during an Operation Flinders-Youth at Risk Program in the Northern Flinders Ranges. The location was at a place called Meriwee, which is a remote campsite about as far as you can get from the comfort and security of Base Camp. One of the roles of the Team Leader on an Operation Flinders exercise is to keep in radio communication with the Base Camp two or three times each day to provide grid reference updates as to the group's location, and abbreviated situational reports (SIT REP) on how things are going with the group.

So each night around sunset we radio Base to give them a SIT REP.
The problem with Meriwee is that it is a long way from Base, on the other side of the ranges which makes radio contact very difficult unless you climb to the top of a hill. Although hills require effort, they also have unexpected rewards.

So after making sure that everyone had their shelters up for the night and had cooked their evening meal, I disappeared up the nearest hill where I could still observe them and at the same time radio Base (not to mention getting a few minutes of peace and quiet and my only personal space for the day). These few minutes are so peaceful, rejuvenating and rare. After calling Base I sat for a minute to watch the setting sun, breathe in the fresh air of the bush at dusk and to listen to the silence. It was then that I heard him.

I remember hearing his ghostly howl, his cry of the heart reverberating into the pink sky at dusk... I searched the eastern horizon in the distance about 500m away. I couldn't see him at first because he blended into the landscape... and then I saw his head move and recognised his light coloured chest against the red and green of the hill as his pointed nose lifted high to the rising moon. Then silence... 10 minutes later to the north I heard him again and saw him on the northern horizon repeating his ritual... a further 10 minutes passed and he was doing the same on the western horizon and then again in the south.

It was as if he trotted around in a big circle from hill top to hill top at the four directions of the compass to announce the coming of the night and to voice his gratitude for the sun as it set on this beautiful day in the desert.

This memorable moment has always astounded me and stayed with me as a profound spiritual experience. In a way, I wonder if that dingo spoke to me that night and planted a seed for the *True North* image that later came to me while I was trekking in Australia's Red Centre? This may sound a bit far-fetched but I am somewhat of a believer in synchronicity.

Perhaps that lone dingo was in someway honouring what Native American India's call the *Four Directions*[69]. Although the ritual of honouring the *Four Directions* during native ceremonies has its roots in Native American culture, they are also referred to in other ancient cultures that have a close connection to nature (eg Mayan culture, the Incas and Australian Aborigines). The symbolism might differ slightly but it will usually represent nature's cycles of change such as the four seasons, often used as metaphors for times of personal transformation. (Child—Youth—Adult—Elder). They can also be referenced in conjunction with a more wholistic approach to healing (Body—Mind—Heart—Spirit).

> ***There is a season, a time for every purpose under heaven.***
> Ecclesiastes 3:1-8.

Following, is an example of how the *Four Directions* are referred to in some cultures. (The seasons in the northern and southern hemispheres are opposite, so the example in Figure 30.2 below is adapted for Australia.)

HONOURING THE FOUR DIRECTIONS

North: (Summer) the direction where the Elders dwell. From the north they receive their wisdom and inner guidance. The concept of *True North* consequently relates to guiding principles.

West: (Autumn) the direction of sunset, represents times in our life when things come to fruition and are completed. We honour the west by being grateful for what we have learned or achieved at the end of each day. In North America *Thanks Giving* is celebrated in Autumn after the harvest.

South: (Winter) is the direction of stillness and quiet reflection, where we take time to go inward for renewal and in preparation for transformation.

East: (Spring) the direction of sunrise and new beginnings, brings the opportunity to start afresh each day, providing new growth and renewed energy.

Figure 30.2 Honouring the 4 Directions—W Enright, adapted from *Vision Quest*, 2012

Chapter 30—The Four Directions

I am not a farmer of the land but I do aim to follow the principles of farming in my life and business, when I don't, it results in imbalance and stress. One of the principles I need to remind myself of, is to be grateful for each day and for the seasons in my life which have grown my character.

Some years ago when I was going through a long winter in my life, I wrote some words on a piece of card and stuck them on my bedside lamp. Even after all these years I still read them most nights before going to sleep, lest I forget to focus on the simple but profound principle of gratitude.

> ***Before going to bed each night I read something inspiring from a book,***
> ***I acknowledge my accomplishments, I give thanks for the lessons,***
> ***I let go of the day, I am at peace with my journey.***

We don't have to be a religious person to give thanks before a meal or for the blessings and lessons of each day. It's a matter of being mindful. Similarly, we don't have to be an indigenous person to honour the *Four Directions* or to recognise the passing of the seasons in nature or in our life, we are all connected to it on a deeper level than we sometimes realise. In my experience, it helps me to be mindful that life is cyclic, change is constant, there are times for sowing and times for reaping. These *Universal Principles* are part of Nature's laws. Stephen Covey refers to them as *The Laws of the Farm*, as opposed to the man-made laws of a particular society or culture that can sometimes conflict with Nature's laws.

I guess you could argue that we are all part of nature and therefore an expression of it, so that could complicate this oversimplified idea, but nonetheless I tend to agree with Covey, when our behaviour violates *Universal Principles* such as trust-worthiness, honesty, integrity, respect, love and forgiveness; there are always natural consequences.

When I work with young people at risk, I always prefer to allow natural consequences to prevail as a way of reinforcing the concept of making responsible choices. Communicating right and wrong with harsh words or punishment does not teach anything about personal responsibility or the concept of choices leading to natural consequences. With rights come responsibility and the same goes for freedom.

> **'Freedom' is the Braveheart's cry,**
> **but when we are as free as a bird in a stormy sky,**
> **will we then have the courage to be free?**
> Inspired by Nan Witcomb—*The Thoughts of Nanushka*

The Four Directions of the True North Compass

It is with the Four Directions in mind that I offer this compass for those who may not have one of their own. Below is a summary of the key attributes related to each of the four feathers of the compass and some questions to contemplate with regard to your leadership strengths.

The Four Directions of the True North Leadership Compass, point to key aspects of leadership that I think are most important aside from technical skills. In the next four chapters, I will take you on a tour of the *TNL Compass,* sharing stories, insights, lessons I have learned and some tips that may be of value. Of course none of this is new but remember, every journey has secret treasures. You just need to know where to look!

THE 4 DIRECTIONS OF THE TRUE NORTH LEADERSHIP COMPASS

True North
The ability to stay true to your mission, vision, and values while navigating your way through conflicting priorities, unexpected pressures, ethical dilemmas and tensions between your head and your heart. It is about living and speaking your truth, being authentic and acting always with integrity. **How well developed is your internal compass and do you listen to it and follow it courageously?**

Resilience
The ability to regulate your emotions when you are challenged; the level of patience and persistence you bring to the fore when things don't go to plan; your tolerance for failure and your ability to stay calm and respond mindfully under pressure. **How well do you deal with challenges, failure and conflict?**

Responsibility
The ability to respond to change and challenges with a solution-focused mindset. Being able to learn and adapt requires us to be able to reflect, be innovative and have the courage to take risks. Do you tend to think rigidly and become overwhelmed by problems or **can you maintain perspective, assess the situation with a clear head and creatively find solutions to difficult situations?**

Influence
The ability to leverage your relationships with others and thereby multiply your influence. This requires empathy, humility, trust, honesty, great communication skills and the ability to negotiate and manage conflict. **How well are you able to lead teams through challenging terrain and have them follow you with respect and confidence, knowing that you would trust them to do the same for others?**

Figure 30.3 The 4 Directions of the TNL Compass— W&G Enright © 2014

Chapter 31   True North – The Internal Compass

The world is changing and will continue to do so...
our work is a search for timeless principles that will remain true
no matter how the world changes around us.
Jim Collins—*Good to Great*

Guiding Principles
True North is an appropriate place to begin our walk through this model because leaders need to know themselves, their vision and their *personal guiding principles,* before they can successfully lead others; especially in uncertain territory where crucial decisions need to be made and integrity may often be tested. The essence of the *True North* aspect of the *TNL Model* (the North feather) therefore, is to have an inspiring vision and guiding values (a map and compass) to navigate to one's intended destination, and the integrity to remain committed to one's *True North* when pressured by resistance, obstacles and detours.

Thus, the first person we must learn to lead is ourselves. We need to have our own act together, including our ability to make good decisions in critical situations; to trust ourselves; to have integrity when others try to push us out of shape; and to be authentic despite sometimes being pressured by the world to be someone other than our true self. People may not always like our decisions but if we are respectful in the way we deliver them, respect will often be returned, despite disagreements on philosophy or resistance to uncomfortable decisions. *Integrity, authenticity, honesty* and *respect* are the hallmarks of a reliable and trustworthy character.

Return on Character
According to a new study that measured *Return on Character*,[70] published in the *Harvard Business Review* (April 2015), researchers found that:

CEOs whose employees gave them high marks for character traits such as integrity, responsibility, forgiveness and compassion, had an average return on assets nearly five times higher than those with low character ratings.
Fred Kiel—Co-founder of *KRW International*

Moral Intelligence

Among the types of intelligence required for highly functional leadership *Moral Intelligence* is considered one of the most crucial. The originators of the term were Fred Kiel and Doug Lennick, authors of *Moral Intelligence*. They identified four competencies for Moral Intelligence:

MORAL INTELLIGENCE COMPETENCIES

1. **Integrity:** Creating harmony between what we believe and how we act, doing what we know is right, always telling the truth.
2. **Responsibility:** Taking personal responsibility, admitting mistakes and failures, embracing responsibility for serving others.
3. **Forgiveness:** Letting go of one's own mistakes, letting go of others' mistakes.
4. **Compassion:** Actively caring about others.

Figure 31.1 *Moral Intelligence Competencies*—F Kiel and D Lennick, 2008

The *TNL Compass* includes Kiel and Lennick's *Moral Intelligence Competencies* and combines them with the *Emotional Intelligence Competencies* of Daniel Goleman (Self-Confidence, Self-Regulation, Self-Motivation, Empathy and People Skills) which I will refer to in the next three chapters.

Defining True North—The Values Compass

Perhaps one of the most important aspects of *Moral Intelligence* is having integrity to one's values. Values are the lines we will or will not cross to get where we want to go. Being clear about our personal values is very useful as a guide to good decision-making and essential to the concept of integrity. Values contribute to the *True North* part of our compass for life. When we stray too far off course we can use the compass to get back on track. This seems straight forward when it comes to making decisions in our personal life, but what about when it comes to leading others and participating as a member of a team at work or in the wider community?

Our personal values or a particular society's values may differ from what the majority of people in the world might consider to be *The Universal Values* that govern healthy human relationships. Defining a set of universally accepted guiding principles for everyone, is almost as hard as defining the 'Meaning of Life.' *True North* therefore, may be different for everyone depending on their personal beliefs and values.

I do believe however, that it is possible to at least define a personal mission or inspiring purpose for ourselves in life, guided by our passions, our gifted strengths and a set of value-based principles that may serve as our personal *True North* (our inner compass). We can do this for our families, our workplaces and our communities. Of course the more people there are involved, the harder it is to agree on commonly held values but there is always common ground at some level.

Relativity of Universal Principles

Ethics and morals are subject to variation all over the world and therefore are relative rather than absolute, but I like to think that there are some commonly held principles that are considered helpful if we want to get along with others in the world and live a well life. Following are some that Gabrielle and I strive to apply in our life.

Love
Respect
Compassion
Forgiveness
Responsibility
Doing One's Best
Service to Others
Clear Communication
Learning from Challenges
Integrity and Authenticity
Living in Balance with Nature
Mindful of the Needs of Others

Figure 31.2 Guiding Principles—W&G Enright

The Challenge of Commitment

One of the habits I have, which is driven by the principle of *integrity*, is persisting with a commitment to a course of action that I think is *the right thing to do*. This sometimes tests my resilience and my family's patience. Principles can be challenging to maintain a commitment to when there are conflicting priorities. A good metaphor for this is when we want to walk on a compass bearing for north but we have to change direction to get around obstacles or go off course for awhile in pursuit of higher priorities. As much as possible though, we will need to come back on course if we want to get to our desired destination. (I have more to say about this in Chapter 32.)

Stages of Morality

There is also the complication of what developmental psychologist Lawrence Kohlberg defines as the *Stages of Morality*[71] (Figure 31.3). His theory based on how people reason their way through moral dilemmas, concluded that, *as we widen the circle of diversity within which we have social contact, we mature in our ability to make complex moral decisions.*

STAGES OF MORALITY

6. **Universal Ethics**
   Universally accepted principles.
5. **Social Contract**
   What is best for society to function well.
4. **Authority and Social Order**
   Law and order.
3. **Interpersonal Conformity**
   Approval and social acceptance.
2. **Self-interest**
   What's in it for me?
1. **Obedience**
   Avoiding punishment.

Figure 31.3 *Stages of Moral Development*—L Kohlberg, 1958

Some people whose worldview is limited to their own interests and who have not experienced a *bigger picture*, may not go past the early stages, and end up being guided purely by obedience, self-interest or conformity. Others who are more community minded but perhaps have not experienced other cultures that are vastly different to their own, may live strictly by the law of the land or what's best for their society, but find it challenging to encompass culturally or religiously diverse views. Then there are some who have a much more universal viewpoint and will be more comfortable with complex moral reasoning, taking into account different points of view, different beliefs and specific circumstances.

Regardless of an individual's maturity with regard to moral reasoning, the key is to be clear about one's values and as much as possible, to live with integrity to one's guiding principles. Ideally, it is helpful if we are able to grow and develop an ever more mature view of the wider world and our place in it. This ability to consider a wider world-view will become increasingly more important as the inter-dependent global community in which we live is forced to tackle big challenges such as climate change, population growth, migration and pollution.

The idea of a *global code of ethics* sounds logical but there is more to life than logic, so I am not going to try and prescribe some definitive set of *Universal Laws*, as that will always be up for philosophical debate and is relative to particular circumstances and to our personal truth. The best we can do I believe, is to ask the questions:– *What are the key principles that guide my decisions and behaviour? How are they working for me and those I care about?* If they are leading to consequences that we are happy with, then it makes sense to abide by them and if not, then perhaps they need to be re-considered. Having a more universal view, expands the sphere of those we care about, which requires us to consider a bigger picture.

Adapting the Rules
One of the experiential learning games Gabrielle and I use with corporate groups (sometimes called the *Collaboration Game*), involves the objective of continuously improving the team score, while playing the game within a defined set of rules. Some of the rules are open to interpretation, so this game is also useful as a conversation starter about *moral dilemmas* and the challenges of decision-making when there is ambiguity about the 'right' course of action. Rules and laws are subject to negotiation, depending on the circumstances. This requires a more mature approach to moral reasoning which is not always black and white. For example, depending on where we are on *Maslow's Hierarchy of Needs*, the moral decisions we make can vary. If we are desperate to survive, we may break what is otherwise considered a straight forward law, or in the case of wanting to belong, we may do what we think will gain approval, even though the behaviour may go against our usual *moral code*. These considerations are much more complex in reality, than they are in theory. Hence, leaders of diverse groups in complex situations need to keep an open mind when making decisions.

Integrity – An Elastic Strength
Having the courage to live by and stand up for our values is the essence of integrity. Integrity literally means having 'wholeness of character,' just as an integer is a 'whole number' with no fractions. Having *integrity* means doing the right thing in a reliable way. It's a personal trait that we admire, since it means a person has a moral compass that doesn't waver. This unwavering reliability causes us to trust people in the same way as we would trust the structural integrity of a bridge, an aeroplane or a skyscraper.

*Integrity is based on strength of character
and the ability to withstand pressure from outside forces.*

Our eldest son Peter is a civil and structural engineer, now working in Boston, USA. He has an amazing mind for maths, physics, music and the complex arrangement of words. In fact he is such a lover of big words that we once considered getting him a t-shirt with the title *President of the Big Words Club* emblazoned on the chest. (I wonder where he gets his love of words and long-winded explanations, and then I see my reflection in the window beside me.) Despite my own infatuation with words, I struggle to understand some of the big words he uses when it comes to the physics of structural engineering but I do understand the simple concept of integrity.

Integrity, like resilience, is not about rigid strength, so much as an elastic strength like that of a tree with deep roots that bends without breaking, a skyscraper built to withstand the stresses of an earthquake, or a human being like Nelson Mandela whose integrity and resilience ended apartheid in South Africa. Despite having to endure 27 years in prison Nelson Mandela became the champion for anti-racial protests around the world. After being released from prison in 1990, he was awarded the *Nobel Peace Prize* and became the first democratically elected President of South Africa.

A symbol that is used to symbolise integrity is the tetrahedron, which has three triangle-shaped sides plus a fourth side which is its base (as opposed to a pyramid that has four sides and a base). The tetrahedron is the shape of a carbon atom that forms graphite and diamonds—the strongest shape in the world. It is a good symbol for integrity because it cannot be pushed out of shape. People with weak integrity are easily influenced to act against their personal values to gain public acceptance and approval. They may publicly declare a set of values that they have little loyalty to privately.

If you stand for nothing, you'll fall for anything.

A Test of Integrity is the ability to stay true to one's mission, vision and values while navigating through conflicting priorities, unexpected pressures, ethical dilemmas and tensions between head and heart. It is about living and speaking one's truth, being authentic and acting in alignment with one's moral compass. I am particularly impressed by young people who are able to maintain their integrity in the midst of powerful peer group pressure. It takes courage to be different and stand up for what you believe in. Our two sons Peter and Jesse are great examples of integrity.

The Parable of the Raft

The Parable of the Raft is probably one of the most famous parables taught by Buddha. He compared his own teachings to a raft that could be used to cross a river, but suggested that once one had made it safely to the other shore, there was no need to cling to the raft and worship it. His teachings, like those of other prophets such as Jesus and Muhammad, are considered a *Way* of living or a way to enlightenment, but the *Way* is not an end in itself. In the same sense, a compass is a tool that provides guidance by pointing us in the right direction, if we know where we are and where we want to go. It is important to understand that maps and compasses are only tools, they do not represent reality. We need to adapt to the realities of life along the way, including unexpected obstacles and variations between the *magnetic north* that gives us direction and the *True North* of our heart. In a changing world, our *Ways* may need to adapt also.

> *A true practitioner of one religion*
> *is a true follower of all religions.*
> Gyuto Monks of Tibet

Fear of the School Yard

When I was at school I did not have the strength of character and self-confidence to be the person I wanted to be. Instead I avoided the risk of expressing my true self for fear of disapproval, criticism and being picked on; especially when I was attending an all boys' school in Sydney. I had been to five different schools so I always felt like the new kid until I'd been there a few years. Then just as I'd get comfortable we would move again.

I guess the struggle to establish an identity and self-confidence is common for a lot of teenagers who haven't yet worked out who they are, what they stand for and what brand identity they want to express in the world. These things come from a few years of experimentation, trying on possible versions of oneself to see what feels true, and responding to the feedback of others. Now social media is making it even more challenging to get a handle on the true-self, as people often censor who they really are in favour of projecting an 'ideal self' online. But for those of us brave enough to risk the value judgements of others, we can eventually find our truth if we seek it. If it matters to us enough, we can work out what feels true. Over time we can clarify questions of purpose, values, identity and self-worth.

I felt unable to do this with much success while at school where the fish bowl was full of big bold gold fish swimming around filling the space, while the smaller less extroverted fish kept to the safety of the rocks, caves and plankton. My safe spaces at school were the art room where like-minded souls gathered to express their creativity, and the running track where I'd do lap after lap, connecting to the grass with my bare feet and listening to cheers of the magpies in the trees as I ran past. Everywhere else in the school yard I'd hang close to my big brother and one or two trusted friends.

When I was a young adult student-teacher, I would often notice a sense of fear and anxiety welling up within me whenever I re-entered a school yard. Consequently, even though I was trained to be a teacher, I ended up being too scared to stand up in front of kids and teach. Even though I wanted to teach, my lack of social confidence kept me imprisoned in situations where bolder personalities took the stage.

Some decades later I wanted to confront this fear and to help kids like me who started out being somewhat lacking in social confidence, self-esteem and mental strength. So I started to volunteer with *Operation Flinders Foundation* to learn the skills of being an adventure therapy team leader. It was through this process of confronting my inner demons while helping others to process theirs that I developed more confidence in staying true to my guiding principles, despite being confronted with some intimidating situations at times.

Gradually I found my *True North* through a variety of journeys that I took over the years after Mark's death as I have described in the chapters covering my *Spiral Journey*, but I would have to say that my *True North* was tested and strengthened most by my experiences with *Operation Flinders*.

> **The task of the leader is to get his people from where they are to where they have not been.**
> Henry A Kissinger

Navigating the Maze

It is June 2011, the beginning of winter and I am in the Northern Flinders Ranges resting in the shade of a gorge surrounded by red walls of rock. I have two other adults and eight teenage boys with me. Most of them are Wards of the State who have various physical and mental limitations which have either caused them to be abandoned at a young age or have developed as a result of trauma. Most of these boys were quite well natured once I got to know them, beyond their protective facade and initial reluctance to trust me. Trust is hard to establish when past experience teaches us not to rely on the world around us or within.

Night Move

Yesterday afternoon we got to our previous camp a bit early and considering that today we would need to travel a long distance to get to our next campsite (the most remote of the eight camps we would visit on our 100km circuit over the next week), I decided to do what is known as a 'night move'. This involves moving on past the usual established campsite and walking after dark to get closer to the next campsite, thus reducing the distance we have to walk the next day. I knew from looking at my map that today we'd have difficult terrain to navigate and a longer distance to cover if we stayed at the established camp. I didn't want to get lost in the dark in this maze of hills and gorges that we were about to enter with a group that already had more than enough fragility within its ranks.

So the compromise was to walk in the dark which also meant that we'd have to make camp in the middle of the bush without any of the usual comforts of an established camp. We'd have to carry food, water and some cooking gear. So after resting our weary legs, we topped up our water, distributed cans of food among the group and moved on into the setting sun.

Just on sunset we found a clearing to make a fire and after deciding not to carry cooking gear, we just punched a hole in each of the cans we carried and placed them in the hot coals. Then once cooked, we ate the contents straight out of the cans before burning them, crushing them and carrying them with us as we walked on into the night after a hearty feed. Kids hate washing up so they were happy with this but a little uncertain about what animals might be lurking in the darkness ahead of them.

After an hour or so walking in the dark, navigating by moonlight and compass, we found a reasonably flat space to put up a makeshift shelter and bed down for the night. Some of the boys had to stretch their comfort zone but for the most part, all seemed to enjoy the experience of walking at night.

Morning Has Broken

So here we are now, the next morning in the gorge where I started this story. The sun is up, we've had breakfast and found our way down into this gorge which enters a place called Goat Valley—an infamous maze of valleys heading in different directions. I now have two issues. One is a boy who has some slight intellectual and physical limitations and has lost his glasses, so his depth perception is limited and he is consequently going slow for fear of falling flat on his face or twisting his ankle. The other issue I have is another boy who has episodes of aggression when things don't go exactly to plan. The slow pace is frustrating him and he's starting to throw rocks to vent his frustration. I must now balance the needs of both of these boys and the rest of the group who are feeling the tension. Despite these distractions I need to keep a good eye on where I am in relation to the map and the direction I am wanting to go to find the next valley that will take us to the next and so on. If I take the wrong one, we will end up being taken in the wrong direction and in this place that's a sure fire way of getting totally lost.

Leading in these circumstances is challenging and at times I am confused about where I am as all the usual reference points of familiar hilltops and big creek lines are not easily visible among the maze. The sun's rays are dispersed by cloud cover and my compass is hardly useful apart from when I'm able to figure out exactly where I am, using landmarks, intuition and a bit of trigonometry with the map and compass. Having the time and mental space to work this out from minute to minute is continually hijacked by having to manage the challenging behaviours of the group who are perhaps just as uncertain about whether we were going to find our way out of here as I am. Fear and anxiety usually show up as anger, aggression or refusing to go on, so I am treading a fine line between keeping them moving and losing them.

The compass does give me one important bit of information however and that is the direction of north. The big red arrow always points north. This is a constant in much the same way that our personal 'North' can be used as a guiding reference for us in our life.

I can see the big red arrow pointing north, so I do my best to keep heading away from it to the south and a bit to the west where the campsite is marked on the map relative to the gorge where we started the day. I am also mentally correcting for detours using my intuition and a gut feel for the direction and distance that is constantly changing as we follow creek lines, goat tracks and ridges. I remember Mark using the moon on Makalu and so I take note of where the sun is in relation to the direction I want to go.

We keep moving forward like this, stopping every now and then to rest, eat, drink, explore caves and of course to put out emotional fires as we persist through the maze. Every hour or so, I climb to higher ground where I can see some recognisable features on the horizons around me. I am now grateful for the maths I managed to get my head around at school, as it helps me triangulate my position in relation to our ever-elusive campsite.

Eventually we made it to our campsite just on sunset after a few detours, back tracking and reluctantly climbing hills that we didn't want to climb because we'd come to a dead end in the maze. But these unwanted dead ends that forced us to climb, also had a blessing to offer us.

From up high we can get our bearings again and correct our course, to end up where we need to be before our light is extinguished.

It was a difficult day but we all felt pretty awesome as we sat around the campfire that night sharing stories about our challenging journey and speaking of the highs and lows that made us stronger, more confident and more connected to the landscape without and within.

~~~~~~~~~~~~~~~~~~~~~~~~~

Leading a trek is much easier if you have a local guide or at least a map indicating marked tracks that you can follow if they are clearly and accurately marked at regular intervals. Without these it is much more difficult to navigate and lead people safely across unfamiliar territory unless you have a good quality topographical map which is up-to-date and shows scale, landmarks and contours in the terrain. But even with a map one needs an accurate compass to stay orientated and a good sense of the surrounding environment and how it relates to the map, the wind, the sun, the moon and the stars.

Strategic plans, business plans, systems and processes provide such guidance but experienced leaders also have a clear sense of direction, a strong vision and an intuitive inner guidance based on sound values and guiding principles that help them to make decisions and to guide others, especially when the terrain is challenging, changing and sometimes confusing to read. Only the brave should lead in these circumstances; not just because navigation is challenging but also because fear can get the better of people in such circumstances and group dynamics can be more challenging when the pressure is on. Over time, highly effective leaders develop the confidence to lead decisively and with trust-worthy integrity and authenticity. *Operation Flinders* does a great job of training and mentoring its emerging leaders who work alongside more experienced leaders in the field and are supported until they have the confidence to take on the full responsibility of leadership.

Alignment of Private and Public Purpose
Before we can lead others in the pursuit of a common vision, I think it is not only important to be clear about our own personal purpose and vision but also, as far as possible, for there to be alignment between what is important to us personally and what we are committing to publicly.

I have come across many individuals in positions of leadership that have had a solid commitment to a cause or corporate vision but have lost themselves in the pursuit of it. They have ended up hacking their way through relentless vegetation, only to find themselves in the wrong jungle.

Unfortunately this can lead people to a place that eats away at their authenticity and integrity. I therefore think that it is crucial to have a good look at the alignment between one's personal purpose, vision and values and that of one's vocation or cause. Unfortunately if there is low alignment between what is important to us privately and publicly, then there is a high likelihood that either one or the other will be compromised or sacrificed.

> *There's something inside you that knows when you're in the centre,*
> *that knows when you're on the beam or off the beam.*
> *If you get off the beam to earn money, you've lost your life.*
> *If you stay in the centre and don't get any money, you still have your bliss.*
> Joseph Campbell

Gabrielle says that when you can stay in the centre of who you are, while you are earning a living, then the bliss is supreme! This comes from knowing who you are, what you stand for, what your personal purpose and values are and having the integrity to live by them authentically. Easy to say but challenging to do sometimes when we are trying to survive in a world of competing priorities such as relationships, parenthood, self-care, work and recreation etc.

> *To be yourself in a world that is constantly trying to make you something*
> *else is the greatest accomplishment.*
> Ralph Waldo Emerson

Being Respectfully Authentic

Being authentic is a major pillar of integrity and relies on us being self-aware enough to know our true self and brave enough to live in alignment with it. Knowing who we are, what we stand for and having the courage to follow our truth and live by our values, does not mean that we can't be flexible, take detours and be influenced by the feedback or needs of others. If we need to do this, we *can* do it consciously and in ways that do not compromise our principles.

If we look back at the *Self-Awareness Window* (Figure 15.1, page 153), it is the area of *awareness known to self and not others*, our 'Public Face,' that we can expand into by sharing more of who we truly are. When we reveal more of our authentic-self to others, including our strengths and vulnerabilities, they are more likely to understand us, have empathy and respect for us, and feel comfortable being themselves in our company.

As a leader though, we must also be careful not to disclose so much that we dilute our influence. This will depend on our relationship with those we are leading and whether they have earned our trust and respect.

Being authentic will usually enable a leader to build greater affinity, trust and engagement with those they lead, but only if their authenticity is relatable, respectful and adaptable to the needs of others. It is a mistake to use authenticity as an excuse for being a rude and arrogant bully or someone who uses humour to covertly erode another's self-worth e.g. "That's just who I am, so deal with it!" This kind of thing is just a cop out! Jim Rohn, one of my favourite business philosophers, said it better than I.

> *The challenge of leadership is*
> *to be strong but not rude;*
> *be kind but not weak;*
> *be bold but not bully;*
> *be thoughtful but not lazy;*
> *be humble but not timid;*
> *be proud but not arrogant;*
> *have humour but without folly.*
> Jim Rohn

Authenticity Evolution
Authentic leadership is about leading with your own unique style, rather than trying to be someone you are not. At the same time it is beneficial to pursue personal growth which will inevitably change who we are at heart. I am naturally more introverted so at first I tried to act more outgoing but this came at the cost of being genuine. Most people, particularly my children, have good bullshit detectors so my extroverted act wasn't very convincing. Over time I learned to embrace my introversion, to see it as part of my uniqueness instead of judging it as a liability. The irony now is that I have so stretched my comfort zone over many years of public speaking that people who don't know me very well, see me as an extrovert. This small part of me has now evolved into a stronger aspect of my genuine self.

Having experienced this change within me, I think that it is important to expand one's behavioural repertoire if we want to relate to more people or to encourage and inspire others. It doesn't mean we have to be fake, it just means that there will be occasions when we may be required to, or choose to, step up and stretch our comfort zone a little. An example of this would be when we're asked to speak in front of a crowd. If this is not something we're comfortable with, we might be full of fear at first and that's okay because people will generally empathise with our vulnerability, especially if we admit that we're nervous. If we do it enough though, our comfort zone will expand and what was at first unnatural for us can become part of our authentic self. The trick is to do this by choice, not out of obligation, fear or guilt. Acting contrary to our natural way of being for too long though, can be draining, stressful and unhealthy. I know myself that I can only turn up the volume on my extroverted self for so long before I need to retreat into my introverted cave for some rest and renewal.

The more I think about this, the more I realise that authenticity is a fluid thing. Sometimes we need to curb our unrelatable traits when we get feedback about our blindspots, other times we need to try on new behaviours to improve our relatability and social confidence. Perhaps it is not as simple as just 'being yourself' but I think it is a good place to start.

> ***True authenticity comes from the heart.***
> ***When we express ourselves from the heart while respecting the heart of others, we will always be on good terms.***

The Risk of Authenticity

I mentioned above that leaders need to be cautious about how much they use self-disclosure to build connection with people that they are leading. In some contexts it is important for people to earn trust first and to demonstrate that they will respect what personal information we might choose to share with them, especially with regard to confidentiality. Examples of this would be in the context of the medical, legal or political professions and also in relationships between teachers and students. In business, those in management positions may also sometimes be required to keep confidentiality about some aspects of what they are privy to.

Too much authenticity can be counter-productive if one expresses what they really think and feel, especially if it is not going to be helpful to the demands of the situation. A classic example of this for me, is when I work with young people at risk, where the leader needs to be respectfully firm and is required to keep a professional distance but still be able to make a connection. Our intention is to influence a participant's personal growth. To this end, we are as authentic as we can be, without compromising our influence.

It was Will Dobud, the founder of the adventure therapy program *True North Expeditions,* who first shared with me the phrase, *Connection before Correction.* My interpretation of this is that it is important to have a good rapport or connection with the young people we are trying to help, before they will be open to the feedback we give them. It is also important for them to understand that we give them feedback, not to pass judgement or to criticise, but to help them become more aware of their behaviour and its consequences. Our job is to guide, coach, mentor, teach and to keep them safe and to encourage their courage.

In the process of building this *connection* the team leaders of *youth at risk* programs such as *Operation Flinders* or Will's program, tread the fine line between maintaining authority and approachability. When I use the word 'authority' I don't mean being 'authoritarian,' I mean being the one who is responsible for keeping them safe, setting and maintaining reasonable boundaries and making crucial decisions that will affect the outcome of their experience.

Adventure therapy team leaders must establish firm boundaries from the start in order to set expectations for appropriate behaviour but this doesn't have to be done in an authoritarian manner. It can be done in a respectful and friendly manner together with reasonable explanations as to why certain behaviours are helpful or unacceptable. Participants will generally accept expectations that are reasonable and delivered in a respectful way. Team leaders must quickly establish a strong level of credibility and a degree of authority that participants will respect and follow before a more naturally evolved trust and respect can be established as the relationship develops and initial resistance dissipates. This is not always easy to do, especially if participants have an established bias against authority figures.

I try to do this by empathising with them first, acknowledging that they may feel resistant to the idea of having rules and boundaries but I keep it simple by saying, *I only have one expectation (or rule if you want to call it that) and that is RESPECT. This includes respect for others, for the environment, and most of all, for yourself; by giving yourself the opportunity to try a different way of doing things so that you get better outcomes in your life. When I observe you doing things that I think are disrespectful or unsafe, I will let you know but I'll always do it respectfully. Is that fair enough?*

Over a few days, as we get to know each other and the initial aggression and oppositional behaviours dissipate, I will begin to share more of my authentic self with them and start to build a more genuine connection as we overcome obstacles together, share personal stories around the campfire and have a bit of fun along the way. Humour is a great leveler and giving feedback is much easier once I have established a genuinely respectful connection with them. If that trust is broken at any time or respect is not maintained, my approach is to wait for the 'seizure of emotion' to settle before having a calm chat about it in private (with another adult present). After a few well crafted questions, some empathic listening and an opportunity to get back on track without further consequence, we usually come away from the 'peace talk' with a renewed commitment to our mutual agreement to make the most of the journey we are taking together. Being authentic and respectful makes this relationship a lot easier, as we do our best to role model the idea that they can be an author of their own life.

To be authentic is literally to be the author of your own life, to discover your native energies and desires, and then find your own way of acting on them, rather than simply living up to an image posited by cultural or family tradition. When you write your own life, you have played the game that was natural for you to play. You have kept a covenant with your own promise.
Warren Bennis & Joan Goldsmith—*Learning to Lead*

Adaptive Authenticity
A leader's personality traits, values, vulnerabilities, competencies and strengths are not set in stone. We are constantly evolving, becoming aware of our blind spots with regard to behaviours we may have tried that don't work for us, and discovering strengths yet to be developed. So, appropriate and mindful sharing of who we truly are, needs to be balanced with stretching our comfort zone, embracing the learning zone, and practising new behaviours that may not come naturally to us at first. This *adaptive authenticity* is akin to a sculpture which takes shape over time as the artist reveals the form within the stone or adds clay. All leaders are a work in progress, so being your authentic self, and speaking and living your truth is always a challenge requiring you, as the author of your true story, to do some editing from time to time or to write some new chapters.

True North for Organisations
Applying the concept of *True North* in an organisational context is not a new idea; business, government, community organisations and sporting teams, have been doing it for centuries. It is only the terminology that has changed. It is well understood that strategic plans, provide a map and compass to guide teams working together toward a common goal. Thus we have the usual Mission, Vision and Values Statements that leadership groups come up with. The key is, not only to have the statements, but also to invest time in discussing how they will be practically implemented in the day to day workings of your organisation. This requires input from everyone who understands the *playing field* and can help put together a well structured plan with clearly defined, roles, responsibilities, resourcing requirements, timelines, action steps and contingencies. On the following page (Figure 31.4), we provide some key considerations for strategic planning.

KEY CONSIDERATIONS FOR STRATEGIC PLANNING

Consider the Future Environment—Conduct a *STEEP Survey*
Skate to where the puck is going to be! What is currently happening in your environment? (**S**ocial, **T**echnological, **E**nvironmental, **E**conomic, **P**olitical). How steep is the terrain you need to be fit for? What are the future trends? Is your current strategy appropriate?

Take SDOC of Your Current Reality
Take SDOC of where you, your family, organisation, team are currently. The old *SWOT Analysis* can be framed in more positive language and used to identify growth priorities: – **S**trengths, **D**evelopment needs, **O**pportunities, **C**hallenges.

Consult Everyone for Input
Consultation is a crucial step in achieving a plan that will be workable. So draft a plan with the input of those who are to implement its details. If the 'troops' are not consulted about the finer practicalities of strategy implementation, the management will struggle to get them onboard and fail to gain their full commitment. All input is valuable. Allow people to question assumptions.

Inspiration is the Best Incentive
A mission and vision both need to be inspiring enough to 'pull' people towards them, like a rubber band pulling people out of their *comfort zone* into the *growth zone*. Inspiration is a more powerful incentive than 'push factors' such as authority, security, approval and fear.

Provide Specifics with SMART Goals
Tangible goals serve as checkpoints on the map and as a measure of progress. Make them **S**pecific, **M**easurable, **A**chievable, **R**esponsible and **T**ime defined.

Failure *is* an Option—When It Is Non-Critical and We Learn From It
Planning should always include a discussion about challenges, risks and worst-case scenarios. This provides useful contingency plans that are less reactive when things don't go as expected. It is helpful to have a culture where failure is viewed as a temporary event that offers opportunities to learn and improve. Tap into 'Black Hat' thinking to identify potential risks, then identify solutions.

Stay connected
During the implementation of a strategic plan, it is also important to have continuous communication about progress, including *review checkpoints* and *feedback loops* for continuous learning, improvement and correcting direction.

The team values are the rudder that steers decisions during the journey.

Figure 31.4 *Considerations for Strategic Planning*—W&G Enright © 2010

> *A 'Nav Plan' provides clear direction, and a context within which team members can be free to make responsible decisions.*

NAVIGATION PLAN—Map and Compass

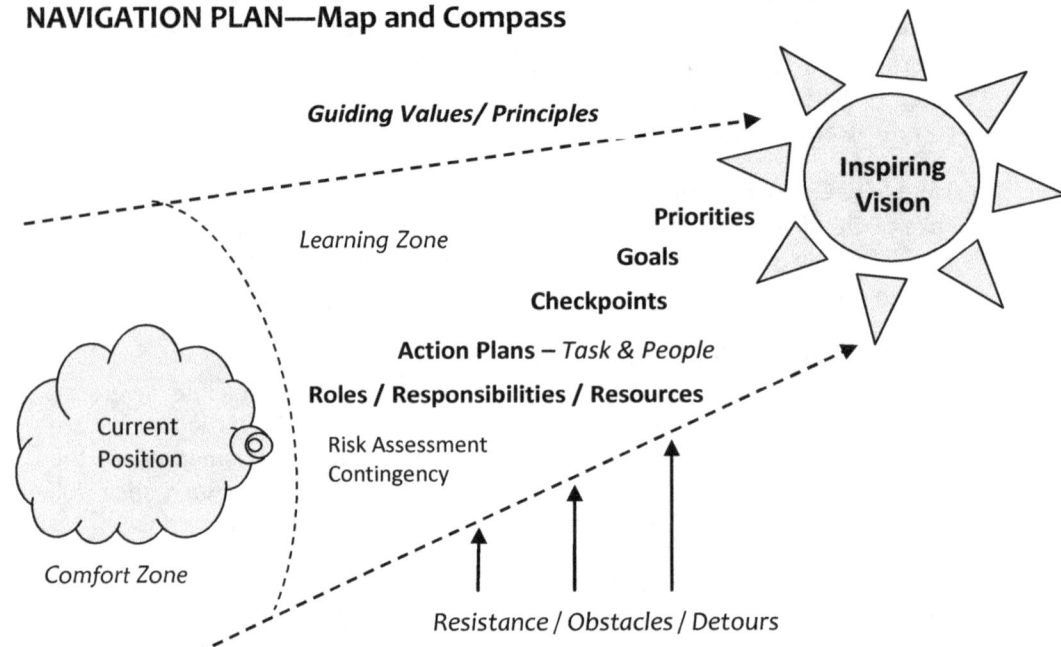

Figure 31.5 Strategic Planning Map—W Enright © 2004

Guiding Principles

In addition to a well articulated plan which maps the course to follow, it is also crucial to have a compass to help with decision making along the route. This is where clearly defined guiding principles (Team Agreements) come into play. We have already explored the concept of *Team Agreements* a number of times. In Chapter 21, we looked at the *Foundations of Change*, one of which is to establish *Agreements* (p195), and on page 210, I suggest *5 steps for Developing Team Agreements*. I will also touch on the importance of agreements again in Chapter 33, when we look at shared responsibility.

    It is worth re-enforcing that these guiding principles help individuals and teams to navigate conflicting priorities, moral dilemmas, self-interest and other obstacles that may need to be negotiated as we follow a theoretical plan. Decision making within the context of agreements, is much clearer, although there will be times when one may have to climb a hill for a higher perspective on the realities of the landscape before deciding which route to take. Leaders need to be the first to follow their compass.

> *A value preached but not practised, is not an authentic value.*

Focus Management
One of the most challenging aspects of having a strategic plan is managing the time it takes to implement it within a realistic timeframe. Typically most strategic plans, span a timeline of 2-5 years. In some countries like Japan, they focus on more long-term planning over as much as 20 years or more.

In reality there is no such thing as time management; we can't really manage time, only what we do with it. The best we can do is manage our focus if we are clear about our priorities. Investing some time in thinking about what is really important to us in life and clearly defining our priorities based on our purpose and values, will make decision making much easier.

Time management is dead... the true challenge is focus management.
Dave Crenshaw

A good example of 'Focus Management' is the concept of *'triage'*, which is the process of determining the priority of patients' treatments based on the severity of their conditions. *Triage* rations patient treatment efficiently when resources are insufficient for all to be treated immediately. I experienced this on the Kokoda Track a couple of years ago when I experienced my first medical evacuation after ten years of successfully getting all clients across the track, despite some more minor non-life-threatening illness and injuries that I've had to deal with over the years.

Wilderness First Aid training for Adventure Guides is very thorough. We are taught to focus on assessing the patient using quite a thorough checklist and assessment procedure, and to make decisions about priorities for treatment and long-term patient management for remote conditions where help may be days away. Wilderness First Aid places a big emphasis on being able to make good decisions when it comes to evacuation for potentially life-threatening circumstances. So it was with reluctance, yet clarity, that I decided to organise an evacuation for a critically ill young man after assessing that his condition was deteriorating and not recoverable without serious medical intervention.

After waiting all night for a chopper and then another 4 hours after it was scheduled to pick up the patient, I had to get quite assertive on the satellite phone after coming to the conclusion that they had not prioritised his evacuation. My exact words were: *I have had a sick patient for 48 hours now, the medivac helicopter was due to pick him up this morning at 7 am. It is now 11am, my sat phone battery is almost flat, the clouds are coming in. If the chopper does not get here within the hour it may not be able to land today and he will most probably die overnight.*

Within 15 minutes of sending this message I could hear a chopper circling above. A sight for sore eyes and a big relief for me and my fading patient.

The *triage* system does not always work well if there is not good quality communication to back it up. *Wilderness First Aid* qualifications do not necessarily equate to good patient outcomes. It depends on regular practical experience, the discipline to follow protocols and sometimes assertive communication when needed. One thing I do know though, is that having a clear protocol to follow can help a leader to remain calm and make better decisions about priorities when they are under pressure. Ambulance officers and emergency medicine staff are masters at this.

TIPS FOR PERSONAL PRIORITISING

Typically, most people prioritise their job or business tasks with more diligence than they do for their health and family. Following are some basic tips for personal prioritising.

1. From head to paper
Take time at the end of each day or at the beginning of the next, to write down a 'to do list' and tick off the things completed. This provides a sense of achievement and helps us to stay on track with our priorities.

2. Be clear about what is really important
I prioritise my list by putting an 'A' next to those items of highest importance and urgency. Importance should take precedence over urgency. I list my 'A's in order of priority, then I put a 'B' next to those items that are important but not as urgent. These items, though important, can be delayed but will eventually become urgent if I don't attend to them. All other items on my list are considered 'C' priorities and are usually delayed, delegated or deleted (refer to the 4 D's in *Figure 31.7* on page 292).

3. Schedule for success
I like to schedule specific time slots for my 'A' priorities first and also allow some time each day to do the things that help me to perform at my peak such as time for:
- **Self-improvement**: reading, reflecting, spending time with a mentor or attending a course.
- **Recharging my batteries:** relaxing, exercising, gardening.
- **Relationships**: family time, communication with colleagues or clients.

Figure 31.6 Tips for Personal Prioritising—W Enright © 2005

To Be or Not to Be

'B' priorities are just as important as 'A' priorities, the only difference is urgency. The 'B' priorities may not have urgent deadlines but they are like assets that depreciate if we don't invest in them. When we build our assets, we get a greater *return on investment* by being more effective and efficient.

> **'B' priorities help us to 'Be' better people.**
> Gabrielle Enright

Sharpening the Saw

On page 287 of Stephen Covey's classic 7 *Habits of Highly Effective People*, he tells the story of a wood cutter who is too busy sawing, to stop and sharpen his saw. This is part of what Covey calls the 'Private Victory'. Mark's business *Venture Corporate Recharge* was based on this principle of taking time out to 'sharpen one's saw' which can involve personal development and reflection, team development or leadership development. All of these are investments in sharpening the tools that make an individual or organisation more effective and to perform at their best.

Some years ago I remember doing a course with Master Trainer, Stephanie Burns, called *Skills for Training Mastery*. This was her advice.

If you want to be a Master teacher, facilitator, coach or guide, then you must invest time in three key areas:-
1. *Continuous learning about your craft.*
2. *Practising your craft.*
3. *Renewing the energy you need to do your craft with quality.*

> **There is no point in being technically brilliant if you're not learning, improving and renewing, so that you can deliver with quality.**
> Stephanie Burns

This advice applies to anything in life that we want to excel at and emphasises the need for prioritising some balance in how we invest our time. Stephen Covey also emphasises this in his *Time Management Matrix* (7 *Habits of Highly Effective People*), which I have since adapted into a simple model, which I call a *Priority Map*, as it can be a helpful tool to map out and navigate the day or week ahead. Like any map though, it is not the real terrain. We must adapt to reality as we do our best to follow the map. Once we become familiar with the terrain, we can use the map less often, but it is still useful to have one, should we get dis-orientated. I like to check it before I head off into the wilderness each morning!

Using the Priority Map

The *Priority Map* provides a guide for prioritising one's focus, and allowing time for self care, relationships, planning and learning. The 4Ds (Figure 31.7) help us to make a *mindful choice* when unexpected interruptions pop up. Refer to Figure 34.5 on p351 for tips on delegation, which is perhaps the most powerful way to save time. Reduce time-debt by deleting *time-wasters* and improving responses to unexpected urgencies from a mindset of choice. Savings can then be re-invested into building assets in Quadrant B. The return on investment helps us to be happier, healthier and more productive in Quadrant A. These principles can also be applied to money and energy.

PRIORITY MAP

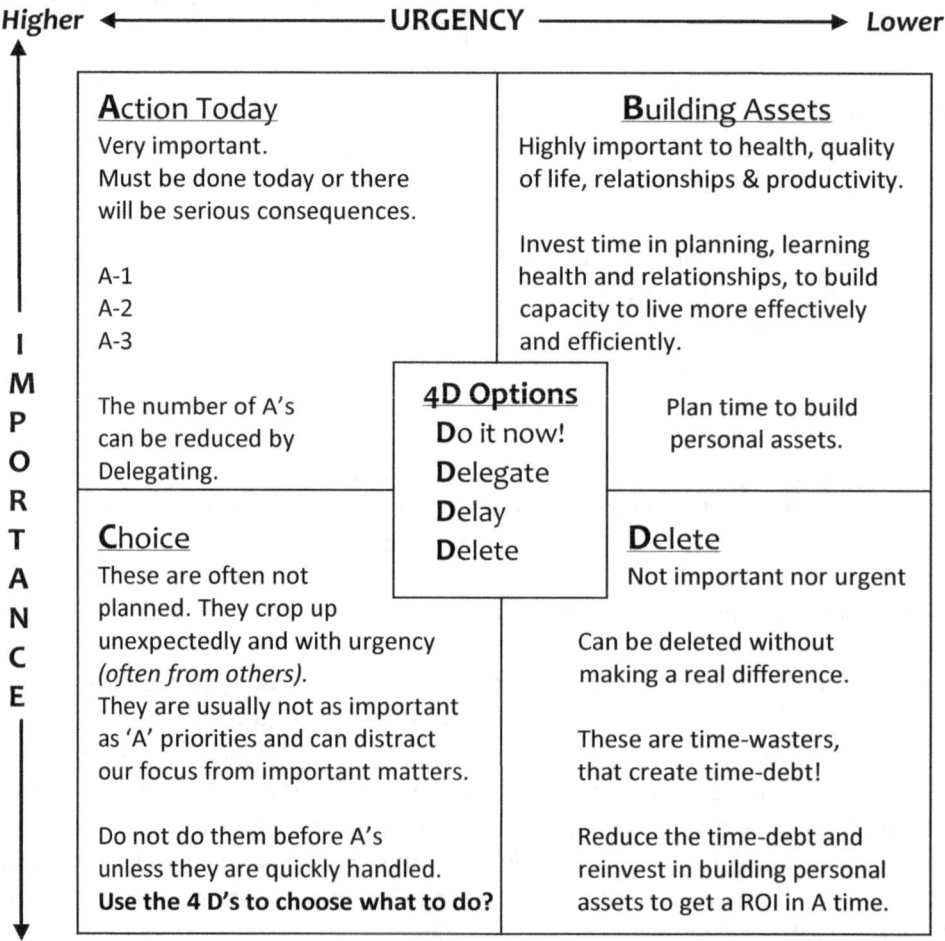

Figure 31.7 Priority Map—W Enright © 2005

Chapter 32   Resilience

So, we've defined our *True North*, sorted our priorities around our purpose and values, and we have a map and compass to guide us toward our inspiring vision. Then what? The challenge really begins when we take off on our journey toward our dreams and find that it is perhaps more challenging than we expected. This is where *the rubber meets the road,* and where our resilience is tested. Will our tyres be durable enough to last the distance, or will we end up on the side of the road despondently holding our map, as we search deep within ourselves for the inner resources to get us to our desired destination. This is where we discover our resilience!

A Flexible, Patient Strength
Often we hold up great political figures, sporting heroes, celebrities and business entrepreneurs as examples of resilience. People like Abraham Lincoln, Victor Frankyl, Yossi Ginsberg, Oprah Winfrey, Nelson Mandela, Mahatma Ghandi, to name a few who have earned the title. In my world though; one of the most resilient people I know, is my mother. However, I wouldn't describe her as tough, in fact I would have to say that she is the opposite. My mother is empathic and kind, vulnerable and anxious at times but she is adaptable to the fiercest of storms and bounces back again and again. These qualities remind me of the resilience of a tree that has enough flexibility to bend in gale-force winds without breaking and possesses the patience and persistence required to grow in the most adverse conditions.

For me, resilience is not about being tough, it's about having deep and strong foundations that give us the flexibility to adapt and grow in response to our environment like the tallest of trees. I have been fortunate enough to walk among some amazingly beautiful and imposingly gigantic trees in places such as the Kokoda Track, the Overland Track in Tasmania, the Amazon Rainforest, the Kauri forests of Western Australia and Boab trees of the Kimberley. These trees are ancient and they ooze resilience.

Resilient trees grow in the most exposed places
The height of a tree will often be mirrored underground with a similar, if not larger mass of roots that feed it and give it stability as it grows out into the world. On a recent trip to Ormiston Gorge and Kings Canyon in Central Australia I noticed a number of Ghost Gum trees growing among the red rocky outcrops of this beautiful landscape, some growing out at unusual angles from impossibly small cracks in the walls of a canyon, reaching out

into the void between the canyon walls, 100s of metres up from water holes that reflect the red ochre walls of the cliffs surrounding them. These distinct trees stand out from the crowd as resilient specimens, risking the elements, while finding their unique niche among the beauty of these sacred places, despite the sometimes harsh environment that tests their resilience.

For every tree the root system will look similar but will be as unique as a finger print, as unique as every individual who is born into this world and must find their way, not only to survive but also to grow in the direction of their potential. Like tree roots we all face obstacles, unfavourable conditions and sometimes injury or life-threatening circumstances. Many of us are fortunate enough to be nurtured and cared for, fertilised, sheltered and loved while others may be neglected or have to compete for scarce resources along the way. And so we become the product of nature and nurture, growing through our life experiences which become contributors to the strength of our foundations. It seems that those who are most resilient have often been exposed to significant adversity which builds within them a strength and flexibility much like that which is developed from years of physical and mental conditioning. They have chosen to take strength from their experiences, rather than be weakened by them.

> *I treasure the memory of past misfortunes.*
> *They have added to my bank of fortitude.*
> Bruce Lee

It is often said that fire is transforming and that there is fortune in misfortune. Last year Gabrielle, Jesse and I were watching Jim Carey give a speech to University graduates. He finished his speech with these words.

In the midst of fire, I remind myself that it is actually a light that God sent to enlighten my way to evolve, to grow and to actualise my true self and become a better human being. This is when I understand that life happens for me, not to me and that it is always for a reason and purpose that serves me.

It is sometimes difficult to remember this philosophy when we are under fire but I have found it useful to at least reflect on this, once I've gotten over the initial emotional reaction that I occasionally have when *Life happens*. Staying calm under pressure comes naturally to some, and for others it is more challenging. The key thing though is to be able to regulate our emotions enough to reflect on the lessons our challenges bring, so that we can grow from adversity, rather than be defeated by it. This is the essence of experiential learning—experience is not as valuable without reflection.

Resilience is Sometimes Fragile

In my experience, there can be a paradox when it comes to resilience; in that we can often experience trauma that makes us more resilient in some circumstances and more vulnerable in others. Resilience can sometimes be as fragile as a frozen lake that is able to take the load of a truck one day, and on another, unable to bear the burden of a single step when cracks appear and the heat of a blazing sun weakens its resolve.

This next story comes with a warning... *it includes a story about suicide...* not because I want to share the drama of it, but because I feel the need to share the reality of this sometimes taboo subject that touches many lives but is not talked about openly. So, if you are suffering depression and need support, please seek help, talk, walk, cry, write, paint or whatever you need to do, to get perspective. Instead of reading this story, ring Lifeline.

Lifeline 131114

I remember seriously thinking about ending my own life when I was in my late teens and more fleetingly on a few other occasions when I felt that the pain I was experiencing was unbearable, problems were unsolvable and it wasn't worth persisting. When I was a teenager I relied on the resilience of my mother to see it in my eyes and to hug me hard enough without words, to tell me that my life was worth living. Mothers know intuitively when we are hurting. Their love surrounds us even when they are not with us.

Laurice and Jeanette—Mother's Day, 2002

In later years I relied on the inner resilience I had developed through the experience of fighting back when I was down, and when that wasn't enough, I relied on the love of my wife to bring me back from quitting. Love conquers fear, always!

Find the love inside yourself.
Every heart has a story to tell.
Songwriter—Sarah Haze

Falling Through the Ice

On a Friday night in April 1999 I am sitting in the back of an ambulance looking back through its rear window as the cars, street lights and footpaths flash backwards away from me and I bounce from side to side along a bumpy street while the reflection of a red flashing light flicks in my face and the muted sound of a siren wails out into the night sky.

It is just after sunset and we (myself and a pair of 'ambos') have been tasked with attending a vehicle accident (car vs. electricity pole). It's not long before we arrive, the first ones on the scene to survey the damage and take the necessary action to stabilise a badly injured driver who is trapped in the front seat, steering wheel against his chest, legs wedged under a dashboard which has caved in on the lower half of his body under the impact of a head-on collision with a steel reinforced concrete pole. It appeared that the weight and mass of the whole front end of the car, including engine parts and body work were crushing his legs as they lay in his lap and wrap around his waist. I was tasked with the job of holding an oxygen mask on his face and trying to keep him calm and re-assured while the paramedics worked on him from the back seat.

Fortunately he survived. After an hour or more looking at close range into eyes full of fear, that were pleading for a second chance at life, I took my seat in the back of the ambulance feeling a lot more respectful and grateful for the life I had chosen to live.

After 3 hours we were back on the road and about to take a meal break when we received a call to attend a suspected suicide. On the way there, one of the paramedics asked: "Have you ever seen a deceased person?" "No, I don't think so, not in real life anyway," I replied. I was thirty eight years of age and had attended a few funerals but had never seen a lifeless body. I wondered what the point of his question was as my mind started to comprehend that perhaps this suspected suicide might involve actual death and what I was about to witness would not be a pretend scene from a movie. "You might want to prepare yourself," said the paramedic as he rolled a pair of latex gloves over his fingers and took a deep breath, easing out a calming sigh, as if to model for me, the process of putting on one's emotional armour.

It is interesting how this experience affected the people on the scene, including me. The police were matter of fact about it, for the most part, but showed a great deal of empathy to the children involved. The ambos were a little more sensitive and seemed emotionally impacted by the circumstances.

Chapter 32—Resilience

I found myself being angry with the man who hung himself, sad for the kids who were about the same age as mine and could not stop seeing the vision of the man hanging there in the shed. I can still see now as I write this—his slumped and lifeless body hanging lazily from a rough wooden rafter like a drooping wooden puppet with all its strings cut, except for one that held its weight off the cold concrete floor. It was a cold, grey figure hanging in the half dark—heavy with sadness, despair and helplessness. I can still see vividly his bare feet with dirty heels, a brown wallet bulking out the back pocket of his tattered denim jeans. His back to me as if embarrassed. I did not look at his face, he wasn't a person, he was a drooping form hanging from the rafters, devoid of any life or humanity. This sounds harsh and insensitive but that's my honest uncensored recollection.

~~~~~~~~~~~~~~~~~

It has been over ten years now since this happened and I still remember the details. For a number of weeks I found myself being angry, upset for his children and in grief over my own losses in life that I judged unfair. It re-activated the grief I still held onto over my brother's sudden, unfair and premature death... the pain of my family that was left in the wake of his loss. The circumstances were different but the emotions similar. I had to get some help from the SA Ambulance Service Peer Support people to unravel my thoughts and feelings around this. I didn't realise that there was also a subtle connection with my own brush with suicidal thoughts when I was younger. Perhaps I had been in some way shown through this experience the reality of what happens when one takes one's own life, leaving others behind who struggle to make sense of it. I was surprised that my dominant feeling was anger, rather than empathy for the man who obviously had come to the end of his coping limits and could not bear whatever pain he was going through any longer. After unpacking and processing all of my thoughts and feelings about it I was able to make sense of them and move on. That could have been me, had it not been for faith, hope and love. I had judged him too quickly and didn't see his pain, only the pain he inflicted on his kids. My judgements and consequent emotions were filtered through my own life experiences. The power of the mind leads us sometimes to growth or dysfunction. Unfortunately this man's mind must have been riddled with pain and stress. He lacked the hope and will to overcome his circumstances.

I guess this is an example of the complexities of trauma and stress, for there seems to be an unpredictable relationship between post-traumatic stress and the growth that can come from adversity. We can be vulnerable and yet resilient at the same time.

Some of us are more adept than others, at managing this tension between vulnerability and resilience, depending on the circumstances and what state we are in at the time. From my sailing days I learned that when the storm gets wild enough, the best we can do is drop our sails, find a safe harbour, batten down the hatches and ride it out until the sun comes out. I trust that when the inevitable storms of life come your way, you will know that the candle inside you burns for a reason and that it is precious and worth protecting from winds that would extinguish its light.

> **You will have wonderful surges forward.**
> **Then there must be a time of consolidating before the next forward surge.**
> **Accept this as part of the process and never be downhearted.**
> Eileen Caddy—*God Spoke to Me*

Emotional Intelligence

Our ability to remain calm under pressure and choose our response rather than reacting, which often goes hand in hand with the fight/flight response, is somewhat determined by our *emotional intelligence. (If you are interested in doing a quick self-assessment refer to the Appendix.)*

One of the hallmarks of 'emotional intelligence' is the ability to maintain one's composure and positivity when things don't go the way one expects. It is normal to react initially with frustration, disappointment or anger when things go wrong, but when we get stuck in these feelings and they inhibit our ability to respond with solutions or acceptance, we can become a victim of our emotions.

Even now when things go wrong for me, I can still have a gut reaction initially, but then I do what I know to calm down and endeavour to see it as an opportunity to practise responding from a place of choice, rather than reacting with fear. This might mean that I need to allow my emotions to flow for a few minutes before I can respond constructively. Gabrielle taught me that e-motions are *'energy-in-motion'* and that it is better to let them move, than to hold the energy in my body which often leads to pain and illness. After taking a few deep breaths I can mentally step away from the issue and put it into perspective. Perspective opens the mind to possibilities that we can't see when our emotionally driven *tunnel vision* shuts down our creativity.

> **You must learn to be still in the midst of activity**
> **and vibrantly alive in repose.**
> Indira Gandhi

Trauma's Impact on Emotional Regulation

Trauma has an interesting impact on the brain's ability to regulate emotion and its consequent responses to stressful situations, especially in young boys whose frontal lobe does not develop fully until well into their 20s. The frontal lobe is the part of the brain responsible for impulse control, empathy, ability to problem-solve, concentrate, persist and make critical decisions under pressure.

The effects of trauma on the brain were best described to me recently by an indigenous youth worker named Louie with whom I struck up a good friendship while working in the Northern Territory on a 'youth diversion program' helping participants to map out a more constructive pathway through life. We aimed to achieve this by exposing them to the inherent lessons that become available during the process of journeying through their natural environment and navigating around the obstacles along the way. Even though we were leading them through their own backyard—a place where many of them had ancestral connections to the land, most of them had become disconnected from it culturally and spiritually.

Our challenge was to help them reconnect with the land and with their inner guidance system. One of the biggest obstacles to us achieving this aim was not the external environment that we had to walk through but the internal environment between their ears. Louie's explanation of this was perhaps the simplest but most memorable way that I have had this explained to me. He described his understanding of what trauma does to the brain by holding up his right forearm, making a fist on top of it to represent the brain stem (the most primal part of the brain that is responsible for most of our survival functions such as breathing, heart rate and the fight/flight reactions we experience when we face perceived threats). With his other hand he wrapped it over the top of the fist that he had made. This represented the frontal lobe of the brain that can override some of the unconstructive reactions we have to stressful situations when our primal brain perceives a threat and over reacts to it based on conditioning from previous trauma.

A well-developed frontal lobe in most mature adults who have learnt to control their primal impulses will, in most circumstances, be able to self-regulate. However, people who have experienced severe or chronic traumatic situations, especially young people, will not have the same ability to self-regulate and it will only take small triggers to result in them 'flipping their lid' as Louie put it (as he said this, the hand wrapped around the fist pops up, to reveal the un-regulated primal fist beneath it). The symbolism of this was so obvious to me that I have never forgotten it.

Jack in the box

When I see young people losing the plot now, I see the open palm of Louie's hand like the lid of a 'Jack in the box', flipped open and allowing Jack to jump out, a little scary at first until you get used to it.

Understanding what is happening and being able to assist young people by being a temporary substitute for their frontal lobe, such as asking critical questions at the right time, calming them down and helping them to make better choices, is a crucial skill for those engaged in helping them.

The hard skills of navigating through the bush, using a radio, setting up camp, implementing wilderness first aid and all the other practical skills needed to survive in remote places are not really the hardest skills for an Adventure Therapist. Navigating the inner landscape of a troubled mind is much harder. Thus a leader not only needs to be personally resilient but may from time to time be called upon to support the resilience of others when they are feeling fragile or "flipping their lid".

The Power of One Choice

I thought I'd journeyed through some hard places in life, both metaphorically and on a number of treks in places like the Kokoda Track, until I decided to take on a different kind of challenge;- the multi-dimensional and often less predictable world of leading an *Operation Flinders* Team. The 100km walk through the rugged Flinders Ranges is difficult enough, but that's just the external challenge. The real test is the inner terrain we must cross. *Operation Flinders* is both rewarding and physically and mentally demanding, with the added dimension of social and emotional challenges that are unpredictable and sometimes out of one's control. For the young people participating, it's uncomfortable, intimidating and unknown territory. For most apprentice team leaders I would say it's similar. Even for the most seasoned Team Leader, there is still a mixture of anticipation and anxiety. You never know what you're going to have to deal with and every experience is different.

On my first exercise as an apprentice to the Team Leader, I had what some have called a 'baptism of fire.' I'm sure my experience is just a glowing ember compared with some of the challenges others might have experienced over the years, so the details of the story are not important. It is perhaps just another war story in the journal of *Operation Flinders* history. Nonetheless it was a valuable learning experience for me. My interest in sharing a small part of the story is to highlight something magical that happened as a result of it, a moment of inspiration that I will always remember. In the interests of keeping confidentiality I will share with you a somewhat metaphorical summary of the story.

A Rock in a Hard Place

 When I first saw them standing there on the red Martian landscape, looking lost and far from home. I couldn't hope to understand what they were feeling, I had anxiety of my own. I didn't know much about them, they looked tough and scared at the same time, hiding their discomfort beneath a well-oiled amour, ready to do battle. For some of us it's difficult to observe without judging, to have empathy for a fearful child masked by a battled hardened dragon.

At first, they seemed suspect, especially if I judged them by my well-conditioned intellect. I tried to open up to what I didn't know about them, because my own history suggested that I should have died years ago. I saw my past mirrored in their faces and their body language. Low on esteem, high on bravado, hanging in there, trying to make something of their life.

When I was in that scary space between the trapeze bars as a youth, I felt more pain than I thought a heart could bear, more loss than a soul could possibly grieve. The child within me was full of fear and anger, frayed at the edges and questioning whether he could survive. He was in a hard place where he would lose his life if he didn't make the right choice. He had to make friends with his courage or live in constant fear. I wondered if this were true for some of them or whether I was the only one?

This fear from my past, confronted me in a flash as I stepped onto the playing field, having to let go of my ego and be there for them in the same way that significant individuals had for me when I landed in some hard places in my own life, not knowing what was ahead and what demons I would have to face.

My empathy was tested some hours later when fear and anger took hold, stirring a sleeping dragon as he tried to protect one of his own. Survival instincts kick in when the pressure is on. Fear shows up as anger and a lack of understanding leads to conflict. This was my first experience of violence from people at such a young age. It really took me by surprise and tested my compassion.

After two days and a night of drama, most of the dragons ran out of steam and returned to their comfortable caves, except for one who made a choice to confront his fear and set himself free. On the third day of our journey, this one boy had an opportunity to join another team and continue what he started. He wanted so badly to go home, to surrender to his comfort zone, to quit and not challenge the inner rules he had lived by up until this day.

The word en-courage means to engender courage. This was all we could do with our words and our eyes. It was his choice to make, not ours, but we hoped that he would make the choice that could change his life.

He eventually decided to pick up a rock and mark it with a scratch on one side. "If the rock lands scratch side up I will stay and finish this thing...

If it lands scratch side down, I'm going home with the others," he said as he threw the rock into the sky. As the rock spun through the air for what seemed like an eternity, we crossed our fingers and our toes and hoped that grace would prevail.

When the rock fell back to earth, the dust rose through the early morning sunbeams as if to create a curtain of suspense. When the dust particles settled our hearts lifted as we saw the faint line of the scratch.

"Yes!" we said out loud, and without hesitation he threw his pack on his back and started walking toward his future where he would join another team and continue his journey.

Five days later, we approached his new team in the early hours of the morning as they received their dog tags in recognition of what they had achieved. He smiled as he saw us walking toward him. We had one more presentation to make to him for what he had endured and for the choice that he made.

"My rock!" he said as we placed the rock in his strong hands. The date of his decision was scratched beneath the line he'd marked for himself that day. We thought... 'stuff the protocol, surely taking home one rock from this rock infested place is not going to upset the geological ecosystem. This rock could quite possibly have saved his life?'

~~~~~~~~~~~~~~~~~~~~~

Magic Happens

As many Operation Flinders staff will attest to—freedom from fear and anger is a choice. A choice that every person, child or adult can make, especially when they discover over eight days in a hard place, that fear is often an illusion. And when one person makes that choice and sets them self free, it's a magical thing to witness.

Life often pulls at the strings of our fears, playing puppeteer over us until someone or some experience speaks to us: *Get up on your feet, stand up tall and free. Look at your reflection, don't you see what we see?*

Now he knows that he can choose where he goes and his destiny is in his own hands. We wish him well on his future journey and thank him for reminding us that, despite the fact that *shit happens, magic happens* too. My hope is, that one day in twenty years time, when his life is on track and he's sharing his blessings with others, he will remember the rock he found in that hard but magical place we call Operation Flinders.

Written by Wayne Enright © 2009
Operation Flinders Foundation magazine—*Thinking of Eagles*

Practice and Persistence pays off

One of the most common characteristics of successful people is their ability to persist in the face of adversity—to have patience when life's timing does not align with theirs. This can be hard to do in our fast-paced world. Goals and plans often set us up for the challenge of dealing with 'failure' if we are not flexible enough to deal with the mis-match between our expectations and life's reality. If we try to force things, pushing against the flow, and allow our impatience to fill us with desperation and frustration, we can be left exhausted, frustrated and stressed to the point of giving up.

Gabrielle often says *Everything will turn out okay in the end and if it doesn't, it's not the end!* Be patient, she encourages me. This is a habit I've yet to master on the small stuff. *Big stuff* (matters of greater long-term importance), I handle with patience and persistence for the most part, especially in my professional roles as a guide and facilitator. Funnily enough it is usually the *small stuff* that I allow under my skin of patience. (Perhaps there's a psycho-somatic link with my claustrophobia, a fear of being stuck?)

Failure is an Option

People who have a higher tolerance for failure often 'fail their way to success.' Abraham Lincoln and Thomas Edison are notable examples.

Abraham Lincoln was a failure in business and as a lawyer before turning to politics where his first try for the legislature was unsuccessful. He was defeated again in his first attempt to be nominated for congress, defeated in his application to be commissioner of the General Land Office, defeated in the senatorial election of 1854, defeated in his efforts for the vice-presidency in 1856, and defeated again in the senatorial election of 1858. This chronic record of failure would normally defeat a person's spirit.

However, he was persistent enough to eventually succeed at becoming one of the greatest, if not *the* greatest President of the United States of America. Despite having to lead during the Civil War, a time of great challenge, he was able to demonstrate *strategic patience*, preserving the Union; abolishing slavery; and modernising the American economy.

> **Happy is the man who can endure the highest and lowest fortune.**
> **He who has endured such vicissitudes with equanimity**
> **has deprived misfortune of its power.**
> Seneca—Roman Philosopher

Thomas Edison is also referred to as someone who failed his way to success. Even though his teachers said he was *too stupid to learn anything* he became the inventor of one of the most life changing technologies of our age.

Edison made 1,000 unsuccessful attempts at inventing the electric light bulb. When a reporter asked, *How did it feel to fail 1,000 times?* Edison replied, *I didn't fail 1,000 times. The light bulb was an invention with 1,000 steps.*

Apparent setbacks often lead to learning or to the planting of seeds that bear fruit after a harsh winter. Learning from failure is a key ingredient of success, nothing teaches like experience. Some of my most memorable lessons in karate were underlined when I had the wind knocked out of me. I certainly became more innovative when sparring with silver foxes wearing black belts. They teach more by surprise than through sermons; calm and observant, reaching back into the memory of their failures and the lessons therein, before executing a subtle move to pass the lessons forward.

Mountaineers, marathon runners, writers, artists and gardeners are just a few who know this truth; that setbacks are part of any worthwhile endeavour. The *seeds of greatness* are planted long before they bear fruit and often require a long period of focussed effort sprinkled with failure, obstacles and unexpected circumstances.

Winning or Learning—Either way we succeed

In his book *Failing Forward*, John Maxwell encourages us to look at failures as stepping-stones rather than stop signs. When I feel like giving up on a goal, I take time out to reflect on what I've learnt and how I can apply it to get closer to my goal. I only fail when I quit or fail to learn something from my mistakes, so I'm either winning or learning. Either way I'm succeeding, for success is not only about achieving goals, it is also about who we become on the journey towards them.

> **In the struggle between the river and the rock, the river always wins, not by strength and power, but by perseverance.**
> Zen Saying

A personal story of persistence

During the months that my father was dying in 2009, I remember training for a karate grading to earn my Brown Belt. Nearly thirty years earlier I was introduced to Tae Kwon Do and within a few years I had reached Red Belt which is usually followed by Brown and then Black. I then finished university, moved house and consequently changed clubs. After discovering that prior learning is not always recognized in a new Dojo, I started back at White Belt. It took a couple of years to work my way back up to Red Belt. I then changed jobs, moved again and discontinued Tae Kwon Do.

About 15 years later I took up karate, starting at White Belt yet again. After another 4 years of inconsistent training I was back up to Red Belt. This was becoming a habit! It took another two years until my Sensei said I was being looked at for a Brown Belt Grading, which means you have to train at least three times every week consistently for six months and attend all senior classes where the Sensei can observe your skills and more importantly, your attitude. What would normally take an average of five years with consistent training, took me more than 25 years (10 if I only count the years that I was actually turning up). I remember trying to train three times each week in those last few months before the grading. I was frustrated and impatient, waiting for permission to grade. I was also travelling six hours up and back to South Australia's Riverland, to see my father, in between trainings. I remember two weeks before Dad died, I let go of my addiction to my goal and surrendered, saying to myself, "This is not important in the scheme of things." I was about to quit when my Sensei said, "You are ready." I graded that weekend, got my Brown Belt and then took the long drive home to see my Dad and tell him the good news. He died a week later. This became a memorable lesson about patience, persistence and surrender. Always persist when it matters to you.

Spiritual Character is a Powerful Force
My understanding of pure martial arts, is that it is more about self-mastery than it is about aggression, violence and achieving belts. While the ancient arts were used as a form of self-defence, there was a deeper spiritual purpose that was more important than the physical skills. The self-discipline and mindfulness developed through practice teaches us how to flow with the challenges of life, with confidence and grace. Spiritual character is more powerful than physical force. Belts are useful milestones and serve as a recognition of progression but as in life the basics must be re-mastered every day.

Challenge Stimulates Growth
Stress and change are essential elements of what it means to be alive and yet most people try to avoid them, staying within their comfort zone or a predictable range of outcomes. The reality is that we actually need stress and change to stimulate our physiology, our mind and our emotions. Stress helps us grow in much the same way as a tree is strengthened by the wind and new born chicks are fortified by breaking out of their own shell. If we substitute the word 'challenge' for the word 'stress,' this helps us to reframe stress into something more constructive. An optimal level of challenge strengthens us; helps us to be motivated, stimulated and fulfilled; and ultimately causes us to grow.

If we don't experience enough challenge in our days we become bored, unmotivated and under-stimulated by life. This can lead to apathy and depression. On the other hand if we have too much stress or challenge we can become overwhelmed and start to experience what are commonly called 'stress symptoms.' These symptoms can be physical, mental, emotional and behavioural.

Fight, Flight, Freeze or Flow

An *acute stress reaction* is usually short term and in response to a threat that may be real or imagined. It is embedded in our physiology as a 'survival reflex' that protects us from danger. The body will automatically go into a *Fight/Flight/Freeze Response* when we perceive a threat. Some of us are able to regulate this quickly and can go with the flow more easily than others. Those who have experienced trauma or have been impacted by others around them who are hyper-vigilant, easily angered or tense all of the time; can unconsciously develop an exaggerated *reactivity* which makes it harder for them to control their responses to perceived threats.

> **The Fight/Flight/Freeze Response** is driven by physiological changes such as increases in:
> - Adrenalin
> - Heart rate
> - Blood pressure
> - Muscle tension
> - Circulation to limbs and brain
> - Sweating
> - State of alertness
>
> These changes can be helpful to avoid threats in the short-term but can also be detrimental to our health if prolonged. Relaxation has the opposite effect.
>
> **Figure 32.1** Stress Response Symptoms—H Benson *The Relaxation Response,* 1975

These stress responses vary among individuals, depending on a person's *internal wiring* which may be part of their natural temperament or, as I have said, can be influenced by conditioning from past experiences. Some people are more edgy and anxious; others are more comfortable with pressure, less fearful and more resilient. Gabrielle has a naturally sunny disposition and recovers from stress with more ease, whereas I have had to learn to walk in the rain and embrace the winters in my life.

> ***If you only walk on sunny days, you'll never reach your destination.***
> Paul Coelho—*Walk Through the Darkness*

The Balance Zone

There is a fine line between stress and success depending on the level of challenge we face and our ability to respond it. To use a surfing analogy, we need a certain level of challenge (sizeable waves) to make life interesting but if we don't make any commitment, the waves will pass us by and we will eventually become bored, frustrated or disinterested in life. On the other hand if we paddle on to a wave and it picks up too much momentum and dumps us, we can wipeout. So, the key is to develop enough skill (mental and physical) to handle the waves and to only tackle those that we know we can handle or that stretch us enough to learn and improve, without wiping out too severely. As we tackle more challenging waves and develop our skills and confidence, our comfort zone expands and we can handle more.

In the same way, there is *Constructive Stress* that is stimulating and helps us to grow, and *Destructive Stress* which we experience when we are either under-challenged (resulting in apathy or depression), or over-challenged to the point where we experience unhealthy stress symptoms, leading to pain, illness or destructive coping mechanisms. Short-term stress or the occasional wipeout is okay, but if our symptoms become chronic and severe, we need to do something about it.

As illustrated in *Figure 32.2*, there is an optimum level of challenge for each of us, where our quality of life and performance rises. If the level of challenge is too high or too low, these things deteriorate. As we expand our ability to respond to challenges, our *comfort zone* expands. Maintaining a balance between boredom and burnout is a continuous learning process. We are most well and perform at our best when we're in the *Balance Zone*.

THE BALANCE ZONE MODEL

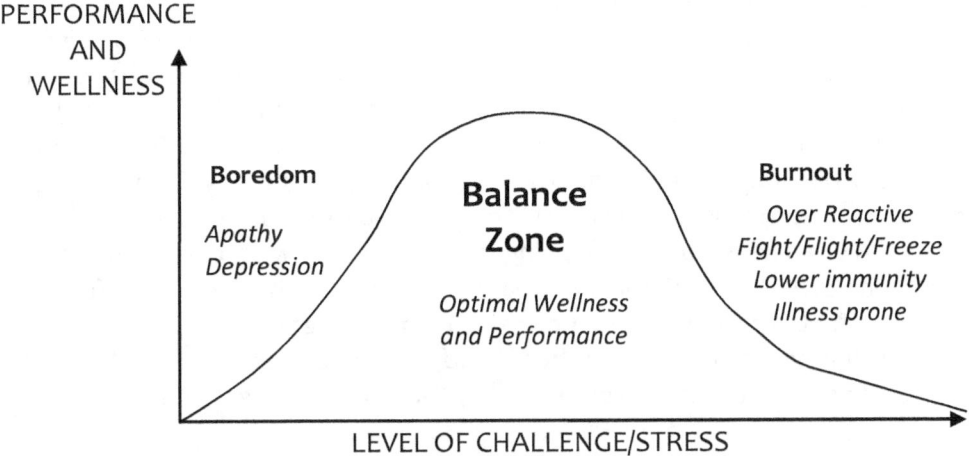

Figure 32.2 The Balance Zone—W Enright © 2005

Beyond the Wall

Challenges which require us to go beyond our perceived limits to test the resilience of our mind, body and spirit can be a powerful catalyst for building strength and flexibility within us. The challenge of Kokoda is a good example. Most people have to confront their fear somewhere along the way. One of these places comes after the flattest section on the track if you're heading south to north. This place is called *The Wall*. It sounds very intimidating and it is when you first look up at it from the flats that you've been trudging along for the previous hour or so. In reality, its near-vertical wall only lasts for about 20 minutes before tapering off to a more manageable slope which takes about an hour to climb before you come to a false peak for a breather. Then there is perhaps another hour before you reach the top and start heading down the other side to Menari Village some 1-2 hours walk down hill to a restful guesthouse.

Some years ago I borrowed a book from my sister-in-law Jennie, titled *The Critical Journey—Stages in the Life of Faith*, written by Janet Hagberg and Robert Guelich. The title grabbed me, as you could say, I was going through a bit of a crisis of faith at the time. In this book there is a chapter called *The Wall* (Chapter 7, page 113), which describes the places in our life when we hit rock bottom, have our backs against the wall or are forced to confront our demons. Hagberg and Guelich say.

The Wall is often a dark place, but in some ways sacred in that it forces us to be vulnerable enough to listen to the messages from our wise self. It can also be a transforming place where we are not necessarily cured of our pain but we can learn how to embrace it and learn from it.

I remember the first few times that I faced *The Wall* on the Kokoda Track and other times going the opposite way, having to walk down it with painful knees. I used to approach it with fear and trepidation as I did with other challenges in my life that I was reluctant to confront. But I've learned that the letters in the word 'fear' reveal its illusionary nature: FEAR = *False Evidence Appearing Real*. I've discovered that the *Walls* in my life are places where I can learn how to look fear in the face and move ahead in spite of it.

We can have our most freeing moments when we confront the walls in our life. *The Wall* on the Kokoda Trail is one such place—painful yet empowering at the same time. It can also be a healing place as it was for me, a place that can transform the heart and soul. I still recall the first time I walked down it without pain in my knees. *The fear has gone,* I said to myself.

At the *walls* in our life we begin to see things for what they are and start to feel gratitude for everything, good and bad. It is here that we learn to embrace our whole story with forgiveness and detachment. In *The Critical Journey*, *The Wall* is also referred to as *'a place of revelation'* that helps us to *see and hear more clearly what it is that we are supposed to do with our life, a place where God melts, heals and captivates us most profoundly*. The following quote stood out boldly for me as I read one page.

At the Wall, God said to me:
For what I'm preparing you for in the world, you will need prolonged courage and strength, the kind that takes more than half a life time to develop.

When I read these words, I felt an affirming rush of emotion as I thought to myself:– *perhaps this explains some of the pain we all encounter in life that can at times seem so unreasonable. If it is indeed preparation for a greater purpose yet to be revealed, then perhaps the struggle is worth it.* I must say that I *have* become more aware of my purpose since turning 50, over five years ago, and it seems true, for me at least, that life's *walls* have prepared me for it. At *The Wall* on a muddy track in the mountains of Papua New Guinea I found my resilient and quiet centre, the place where my spirit dwells. I am now learning how to live from this place more.

The Wall is where grace and suffering meet to transform us.

The Wall on the Kokoda Track, 2009

Reflection Stop

We have journeyed a reasonably long way in the last two chapters, as we have travelled to the North and the West of the *TNL Compass,* so let us rest awhile and reflect on a few questions that relate to the *True North* and *Resilience* aspects of the compass, before we continue.

1. Are you able to live your life in alignment with your True North (with *integrity* and *authenticity*) or do you feel that there are some adjustments you'd like to make?

2. Do you invest your time and energy wisely or is there room for improvement in your *focus management* or your use of the 4Ds when unexpected interruptions come?

3. How well do you regulate your reactions to stress—do you *flip your lid* easily or are you calm in a crisis?

4. What are your most common stress symptoms and do you heed their feedback or push on to the point of illness or burnout?

5. What *Walls* have you faced in your life and how have they strengthened you?

6. What are the most memorable lessons that you have learnt from failure?

Chapter 33 Responsibility

Typically *responsibility* is defined as an individual's or group's obligation to follow through on commitments. Most people would consider this to include *accountability* for the consequences of a decision or action. When things go wrong, there is a tendency to say, *someone needs to take responsibility for this.* Often when we say this, we are not asking, *who is going to respond to the problem with a creative solution?* What we really mean is, *who can we blame?* Unfortunately playing the *Blame Game* is rarely constructive, unless that someone is response-able enough to not just be accountable but also to focus on finding a solution to the problem.

In truth, responsibility is somewhat linked to having some level of ownership in terms of *authority* and *accountability* but the most important distinction I would like to emphasise about the concept of responsibility (as it is expressed in the *True North Leadership Model*), is that it is more about one's ability to respond to life, hence the competency we call 'Response-Ability.' This is a concept I learned from Mark. It was a key value of his (and his organisation) that was emphasised in all of his leadership and team development programs. I have continued to hold this value and have endeavoured to demonstrate it in my own life, as well as including it as a key piece of our professional message.

Self-Responsible Teams
In Chapter 21 I wrote about *the journey to self-management* being part of what I referred to as the *New Frontier* for leaders and teams, whether they be sporting teams, organisations or project teams. I prefer to use the term *self-responsible* rather than *self-managing*, as the ultimate aim is for leaders or teams to be able to *respond* to changing conditions without needing to defer their decision-making to a higher power all of the time. Thus leadership can be informally shared by all team members.

Leaders, whether they be appointed or informal, will benefit from having clearly defined strategic objectives and action plans to follow in the pursuit of achieving a mission or vision, but they also need to have the ability to respond to unexpected detours, obstacles and other potential barriers that will inevitably challenge the successful achievement of their goals. Despite having a plan, we must still adapt along the way, not only to external factors but also to the sometimes demanding needs of those we may be leading during the journey. Group dynamics can have an unpredictable influence on the best laid plans.

Choosing Our Response

Response-Ability starts with our mental and emotional response to problems and crisis. Potentially stressful events can be considered 'good' or 'bad' depending on how we view them or how we choose to respond to them with our thoughts, emotions and behaviours. Often we don't choose at first, we just react out of our conditioning or temperament, but if we are mindful enough, we can cease reacting, step back from our circumstances and choose what we think, how we express our feelings as e-motions (*energy in motion*), and what we can do to deal with our uninvited circumstances. *It's not what happens; it's how we respond that counts.* Cliché but true! Our *Response-Ability* makes the difference between whether a crisis is good or bad in the end.

Opportunity Riding the Dangerous Wind

The Chinese characters for the word crisis translate to the words *danger* and *opportunity*. Thus one could say that stressful events can initially feel unpleasant but ultimate outcomes may be beneficial, including the opportunity to grow as a person, family, team, organisation or country. Many of the crises I have experienced have had blessings attached that were not obvious at first. This does not mean they weren't painful or wounding in some way but over time, we heal somewhat and the clouds part to reveal the blessings that are often unseen beyond the fog.

Of course our natural human reaction to crisis is to experience the stages of grief such as shock, denial, wishing that things could be different, blame, anger and depression. The later stages of the grieving process usually bring a level of acceptance. Sometimes this acceptance is solid and sometimes it can be fragile like a thin veil of ice.

Grief—Nature's Way of Healing

When I reflect on my personal experiences of grief, together with what I've learnt professionally, I have come to the conclusion that it is most constructive when we allow ourselves to go through the stages of grief by acknowledging our feelings without guilt, expressing our thoughts and emotions, and then gradually moving toward acceptance. This can be done by talking it out, walking it out, writing about it, crying, breathing, seeking counselling or psychological support. Acceptance comes when we allow ourselves to process the grief and are then able to focus on what we can learn from the crisis and any opportunities that have come with it. This allows us to re-calibrate, and is a part of being *response-able*.

Unfortunately some people get stuck in denial, blame, anger or depression and become 'victims' of their circumstances. People who 'master' their circumstances on the other hand, might have the same feelings of disappointment, frustration or grief but are able to process their feelings more constructively. This helps them to look for the opportunities in a crisis. Often this is harder to do alone and may require an empathic ear and support from others.

A set back is a setup for a comeback.
Willie Jolley

Growing Consciously
Growing from adversity often happens unconsciously but we also have the opportunity to grow consciously if we choose to be mindful when responding to and learning from stressful times in our lives. This is the essence of *Response-Ability*... it is our *ability to respond* to life's challenges with creative solutions from within our 'circle of influence' or at least to learn and grow from them. This helps us to be the master of our life circumstances, rather than giving our power away to them.

THE RESPONSIBILITY MODEL

Mastering Life's Challenges
Choosing to respond to life's challenges with solutions and learning

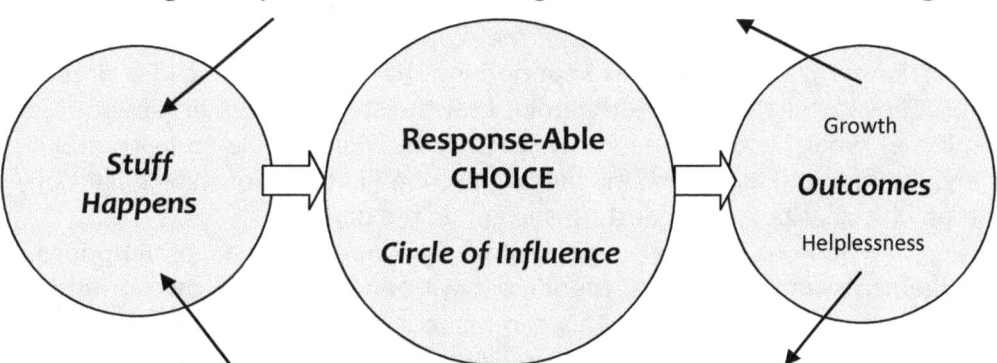

Becoming a victim of one's circumstances
Reacting with blame, excuses and justification
gives power to our circumstances.

Figure 33.1 The Responsibility Model—W Enright © 1991

Master or Victim—Your Choice

Becoming the Master or the Victim can be a default or a choice. Victims see failure as a label. Masters see it as an event and a learning opportunity. Victims learn helplessness. Masters learn to master their circumstances and emotional responses. Victims get stuck in anger, resentment, bitterness and depression. Masters may experience these same emotions and gradually transform them constructively. Victim behaviour typically includes *Below the Line* responses such as blame, excuses, justification or covert hostility.

The Mindfulness Paradox

Our ability to respond to life is significantly constrained or free, depending on how mindful we are. Being mindful is not a new concept; monks and meditators have been practising it for thousands of years, although they would probably describe it as being 'Mind–Empty.' (ie less attached to our mind). Gabrielle and I had been speaking about and practising the concept of mindfulness for years before it became a popular buzz word. We prefer to use the term *living consciously*, making a *conscious choice* or *being heartful*. The word 'Mindfulness' could be considered paradoxical if we were to be pedantic and split hairs about its literal meaning.

Mind Emptiness—The Way to Enlightenment

A popular story that illustrates the paradoxical nature of the word *mindfulness* involves a spiritual seeker who visits a Wise Master to learn about enlightenment. The Master pours the student a cup of tea and continues to pour even though the cup is overflowing. The student questions why the Master has kept pouring the tea when the cup is already full. The Master then makes the point that the student must first empty his mind of what he thinks he knows, before he will be able to learn about enlightenment. Enlightenment can be described in terms of shining light on that which has been previously unseen or 'in the dark.'

When our mind is already full of preconceived ideas, assumptions, judgements and intellectual theories, it will tend to run its own program based on past conditioning. This can make it difficult to be open to new ways of looking at the world, new ways of doing things or new ways of *being*. Perhaps *heartfulness* is a more appropriate term, in that our heart sees beyond the rational mind. For now I will continue to use the term *mindfulness*, having clarified its intended meaning.

> **The beginner's mind sees many possibilities
> the expert's mind sees few.**
> Sogyal Rinpoche

Being mindful, simply means being more tuned into our present thoughts, feelings, body sensations, and our surrounding environment. Often we are so caught up in tasks, random thoughts and emotional reactions that we are not fully conscious of what we are doing, thinking and feeling. Our body, mind and emotions can end up dictating our enjoyment of life and our ability to deal with stress. Mindfulness helps us to live more in the present moment. When we are more mindful, we have a greater capacity to detach from stressful events. We can instead, observe them without attachment in much the same way as we observe passing traffic or a leaf floating down a stream. We are then in a better position to choose our response with greater awareness. Mindfulness is a psychological skill that can be mastered with practice first in easy situations then in more challenging circumstances. Figure 33.2 is based on *Acceptance & Commitment Therapy (ACT).*[72]

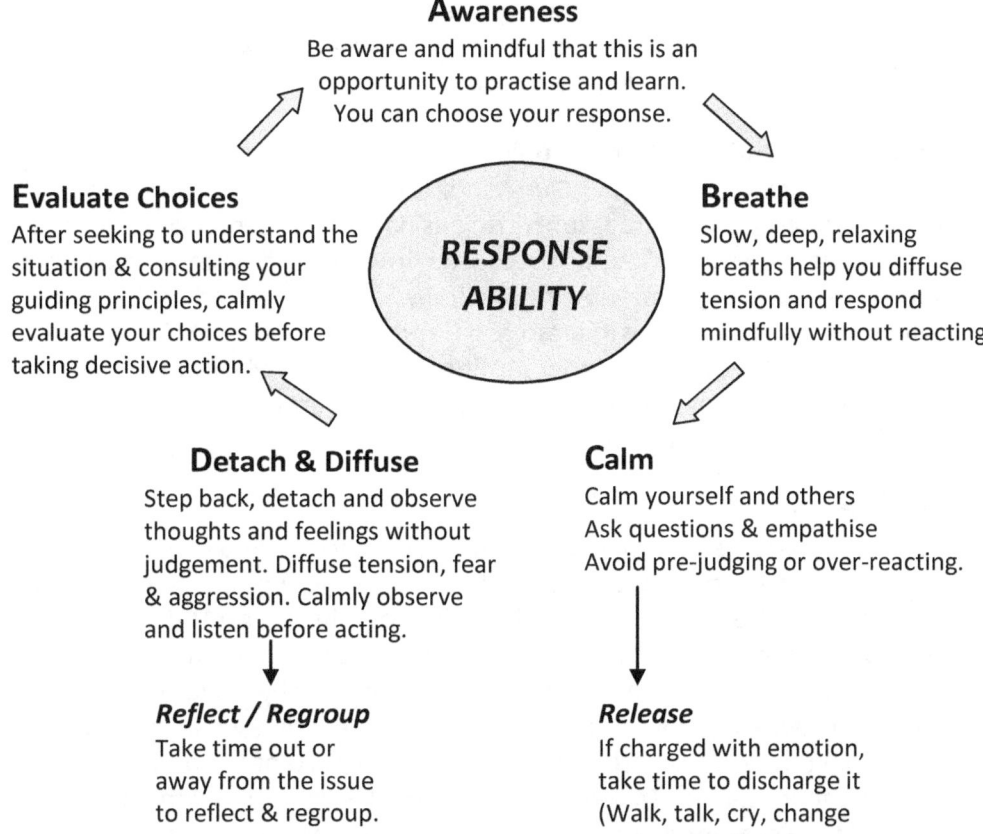

Figure 33.2 Mindful Responsibility—W&G Enright © 2014

Key Steps to Responding Mindfully

When we train ourselves to breath consciously, we are then more easily able to regulate our physiological, psycho-emotional and behavioural responses to challenging events. We may still experience fearful thoughts, unsettling feelings and physical sensations of stress, but we can observe them more calmly in the present moment, without judgement or attachment. This non-judgemental detachment is one of the key aspects of ACT, which Gabrielle and I were first introduced to in our counsellor training with Mark and which we have practised with meditation and yoga teachers for a number of years.

Once one masters this skill (which starts with the breath and training the mind to detach and observe under pressure) one can then consider options and take decisive action from a place of conscious choice, rather than being reactive. This can sometimes happen in a split second. To the observer there is no noticeable time to think, but when we master this skill of being present in the moment (often referred to as *presence of mind*), it feels like there is plenty of time. I have noticed this while sparring in a karate class or sailing down a wave while windsurfing in rough seas. It is amazing how quickly our mind can process information when we train it not to think, but to notice and respond in a split second.

The mind has a 'mind of its own' unless we train it!

Sounds strange but it is true. Our mind, like our body and emotions, will tend to run based on habitual subconscious patterns that may or may not be constructive unless we learn to master the art of calm detachment, allowing, letting go, and flowing skillfully with the river of life. Every challenge is an opportunity to learn and to practise these 'mindful response' skills in much the same way that surfing, sailing and whitewater skills are developed by entering unpredictable waters and learning to flow with them skillfully. The key word here is *skillfully*.

Going with the flow

There is a place close to my heart where I once lived called *Manly*, the most famous surf beach of Sydney's North Shore. Manly is unique in that it has a surf beach on the coastal side and a calm cove beach on the harbor side (perhaps a metaphor for the two sides of our nature now that I think of it). Manly Primary School is located halfway between the cove and the surf beach. Consequently, half of our class would go missing when the surf was up. Learning the art of mindful flow was more important to some of us than learning the *Three Rs*. The key foundation of surfing is learning how to operate in the present moment, reading the ocean and adapting to its flow.

Some years later, after moving to the relatively flat waters of Adelaide's beaches, I became addicted to windsurfing. It was then that I learnt to be present to the wind as well as the waves. I recall too, the lessons I learned from kayaking in the freezing cold rivers of New Zealand's Southern Alps and whitewater rafting down Tasmania's awesome Franklin River a number of times. I learnt to read the river, to flow with it, and use its power for progress, rather than fight against its raging strength. On occasions, as a beginner when I capsized, I learnt very quickly what not to do. I came to trust my ability to *read the flow* and to automatically respond with the right move to work with the rapids, rather than tense up in fear. I learnt too, when to get out of the river when it was not safe to continue.

We can't always predict what the river and the ocean of life will do, but we can learn to read it somewhat and to improve our ability to respond mindfully. As we go through different stages in our life, the prevailing conditions change. Consequently I am still in the process of learning the art of flow. It is one of my areas of continuous improvement.

> *Zen practice in the midst of activity is superior to that pursued within tranquility.*
> Hakuin

The Art of Allowing

Going with the flow is not just a question of surrender, we still need to respond with a few mindfully executed paddle strokes at the right moment, but we do so with an attitude of allowing rather than resisting and we learn to observe rather than be too attached to thoughts and feelings that may drown us if we were to simply surrender. The trick is to *stay in present time,* rather than get anxious about the future outcome of a situation. When it comes down to it, we can only do, what we can do, in the present moment.

In some ways the art of allowing and observing in stressful situations is a bit like responding to a seizure. Twice on *Operation Flinders* exercises I have experienced young people having a significant seizure; one was about an hour away from any paramedic support, and the other at the top of a steep climb. There wasn't much I could do except stand back and observe until their bodies had done their thing, but I still had to keep them safe, help them recover and then arrange for them to be medically assessed.

I remember too, being at my niece's wedding when her husband was giving his speech and had a minor seizure (one that was hardly noticeable to anyone else except him). He had brain cancer and was familiar with the daily disturbance of a seizure that caused his face to go numb and lose function temporarily. He would remain conscious but just stop talking, turn his face away and wait for it to pass.

Some of his seizures were more dramatic but this one during his wedding speech was a temporary interruption. I remember him stopping mid-sentence, turning his head and waiting before saying *Don't worry, I was just having a seizure* and then he carried on. This is a beautiful example of mindfulness, being in the present moment, maintaining composure and a sense of humour in what would normally be a frustrating circumstance. He and his wife Carrie lived with an amazing attitude and resilience. The celebration of Greg's life after his funeral was equally astonishing. It is the first time I have ever been to a *Wake* where every individual attending, ended up dancing in a swimming pool in whatever they wore to the funeral, suits and expensive dresses included. He certainly left some joy in his wake. Greg Lange was a beautiful and witty man who I remember with fondness.

Circle of Influence
One of the key skills associated with mindfulness is developing the mental habit of focusing on *our circle of influence,* a term written about by Stephen Covey in his book, *7 Habits of Highly Effective People.*

Our *circle of influence* is dependent on what we think we can control and this is often based on how clear we are about our strengths and weaknesses; our goals and values; and how well organised we are. Most of us can usually control our attitude, our actions and our effort, but we can't always control (nor should we) other people's attitudes, actions and effort, or their feelings, opinions and mistakes. Adversity comes in all shapes and sizes, and all we can ever do is respond within our *circle of influence,* whether it be large or small in that moment.

Too often we focus on our wider *circle of concerns*; things that we cannot control or influence immediately. This can generate frustration, anger, anxiety, fear, depression or a feeling of helplessness which can paralyse our ability to respond, even in the sphere of what we can change. Sometimes the only thing we can influence is how we choose to think and feel about events. If we begin within our *circle of influence,* our internal power expands to a point where we can start to impact our broader world.

Think Globally—Act Locally

The above slogan, often used by environmental groups, applies equally to our internal environment. If we act locally at first by taking charge of our tendency to react to situations, then we can be open to possible solutions to wider problems.

There are no problems, only solutions. Stop winging and start solving.
Leigh Farnell

Creative Solutions

Some of my most memorable moments working with indigenous guides along the Kokoda Track have been when we have had to get creative. I am always astounded at how quickly a group of our *PNG Brothers* can build a bridge across a raging river or make a shelter at an unscheduled bush camp in the pouring rain with nothing but resources from nature, their bare hands and one machete. They are geniuses at problem-solving and can teach us a thing or two about creative thinking.

Being creative requires us to be open to more than one way of thinking. In the past I would typically worry about everything that could go wrong but at the same time I am a very creative thinker. This seems paradoxical but worry is only worry when we are trapped by it. I used to think that worry was a bad thing but I've since discovered that it is only a negative when it stops us from doing things out of fear and aversion to failure. It can be constructive to consider potential risks, as long as we also think of creative ways to mitigate them. One of the best ways I have found to do this is to consider things from different points of view using a process such as Edward de Bono's *Six Thinking Hats*[73] method. (Figure 33.3 below)

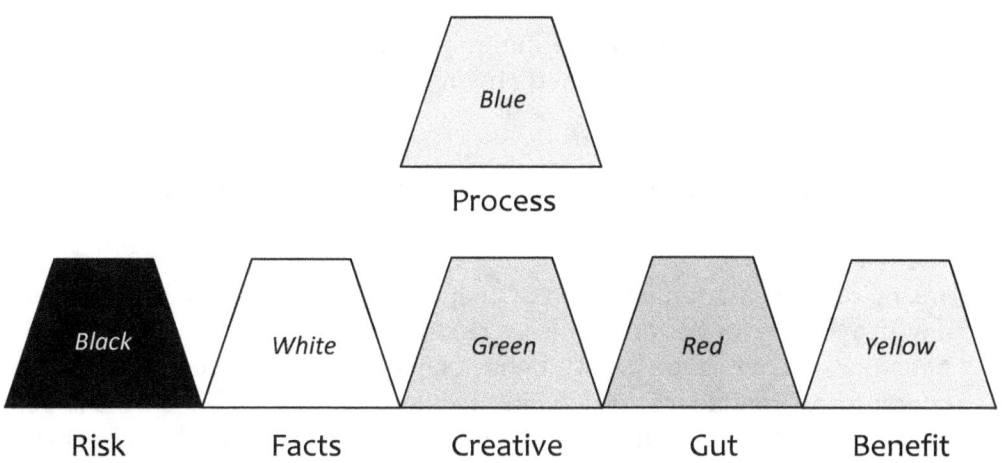

Figure 33.3 De Bono's Six Thinking Hats—Edward de Bono, 1999

Problem-Solving with de Bono's Hats
De Bono's *Six Thinking Hats* are a useful way of looking at problems from different angles that we might otherwise miss if we were to apply our default way of thinking. Each of us tends to have a habitual way of thinking, whether it be predominantly *optimistic* or *pessimistic* (*Yellow* and *Black Hat*); based on *facts* or *feelings* (*White* and *Red Hat*); coming up with lots of *creative ideas* (*Green Hat*); or few ideas but more focussed on *facilitating* the input of others (*process* or *Blue Hat* thinking).

Leaders in the past have mostly been promoted based on their expertise with task-based skills (usually founded on *White* and *Black Hat* thinking). A few have been the entrepreneurs with creative (*Green Hat* thinking) or those that are enthusiastically optimistic and inspirational (*Yellow Hatters*). Then there are those who wear the *Red Hat* and solve problems with their in-tuition (inner teacher); their gut feeling for possible solutions. The *Blue Hat,* or process thinkers on the other hand, are generally a rare species, in my experience.

Leading self-responsible teams in the more testing climate of the *New Frontier*, where we need as much input as possible and a wide range of perspectives, will require leaders to use all of the hats and also to wear the *Blue Hat* more often. This is a hat that is not that familiar to some leaders, who find it difficult to step back and facilitate the input of others while they assert their own view. Their view might be quite valid based on their experience, but it is not the only view, and less assertive people don't get a look in when the leader forgets to wear the blue 'Process Hat' while searching for solutions to a team's challenges. There is a link in the notes at the end of this book[73] for anyone interested in learning more about *de Bono's Hats* and how to use them in corporate teams or in teaching students.

Wear a black hat to explore risks... a green hat to explore possibilities.

The Art of Risk
Taking risks, as Mark mentioned in Chapter 14, is a big part of learning and anything we do for the first time is a risk. Young people, as we know having been one, often engage in risky behaviour to test themselves, to build their courage and confidence for life, and to develop their self-esteem and self-belief. Unfortunately the way they choose to do this is not always constructive in the absence of positive pathways for risk-taking.

On the other hand, many adults have become *risk-averse* as they learn to conform, get along, and to avoid failure and criticism. When we take a risk, we enter the zone where possibilities are explored and limits tested.

I think this is why so many adults are now looking for more adventure in their life. Many *Baby Boomers* in particular are somewhat tired of sipping cocktails by the pool at a resort. They want to venture out into the real world to test their *self-reliance wings*, like an eaglet that ventures out of the safety of its nest high on a cliff top.

An essential ingredient in the recipe for being a creative problem-solver is risk-taking, otherwise we are limited to the bank of choices we have available in our comfort zone. Taking risks requires us to trust ourselves enough to be daring and to befriend frustration and failure. As Maxwell says *failing forward* can be a stepping stone towards eventual success. *Resilience Responsibility* and *Risk-taking* underpin our ability to grow. Perhaps these 'three Rs' are just as important, if not more so, than those taught in school.

Resilient Balance
I've learnt to think that resilience and responsibility work together like the wings of a bird. To stay in flight and be in command of the flight path, balance is required, and resilience allows us to maintain our balance enough to be able to respond to life's challenges effectively and sustainably, from a point of resilient balance. This is well illustrated through the example of martial arts. The importance of balance is a key foundation of karate as it is in other martial arts or any athletic endeavour. Drawing on my roots as a physical educator once more, I recall many karate classes where our balance was tested as a key component of practising the basics.

On Tuesdays I would train with less experienced students at my local Do Jo. I found this more relaxing and fun, a chance to train with less intensity, teach others and be more playful but well within my comfort zone. On Thursdays I would attend senior classes with Brown Belts and Black Belts. Thursdays were always more challenging, sometimes in subtle ways as the Senior Sensei, who had a keen sense of humour, tested our balance while practising basic stances. Stances are different ways that one plants the body on the ground while executing the basics of punching, kicking, striking, blocking and moving toward or away from an opponent. The effectiveness of a technique flows from the quality of the stance.

In the real-world of self-defence, one is often rushed by an attacker and thus not afforded much space to do anything other than wrestle. This is very different to the good sportsmanship arena of Do Jo sparring or a Karate tournament where two opponents dance around each other and duck in and out of the combat zone in a more mindful manner.

There is one particular stance called *Sanchin Dachi* or 'Pigeon-toe stance,' which looks less stable, but happens to be one of the most effective stances when grappling with an opponent in real-life defensive situations.

When standing in *Sanchin Dachi* stance, the torso is facing forward, feet are set shoulder width apart, one slightly more forward of the other with feet turned inward at 45 degrees and heels out. The feet grip the floor tightly and the knees are bent, hips locked in place with core muscles tensed and arms ready to block, grapple or strike at close range.

When practising this stance in the Do Jo at senior classes, you'll see lines of Black Belts standing like statues fixed to the floor, unmoved by the playful nudges, punches, kicks from the Sensei as he walks up and down the rows of statues testing the stability of their stance.

 *I remember seeing him with my peripheral vision and feeling his energy as it came closer to my turn to be tested. My feet grip the floor as if my life depended on it. I tense my thighs and lock my hips into an unmovable position, as though I am about to compete in a tug-of-war. With my abdomen tight, ready to take a punch or kick, and my arms in a blocking position, eyes fixed straight ahead, my calm facade hides a serious resolve not to be moved.*

Sensei playfully pushes me from the sides to test my balance. No movement at first. Then as if to respond to my defiance he delivers a quick short-punch to my abdomen to put me off balance and then pushes me again without notice. I've learned this trick from past experience and so I again manage not to be put off balance. He then moves away as if disappointed that he couldn't catch me out. Just as I relax, thinking that I've won the game this time, he gives me a parting nudge from behind my left shoulder as he moves away. Despite my resolve, the right foot reflexively steps out of line to save me from falling sideways into the space between the perfect lines. A feeling of embarrassment confirms my ego's lack of humility. Stay vigilant and stay humble Sensei comments under his breath with a smile only I can see, as he walks on to the next victim of his humour.

It is this type of core stability and balance that often determines the strength and flexibility of our resilience. When we get to a point where we can respond from a point of relaxed and self-confident balance, knowing that we have the strength and flexibility within us to handle life's challenges without getting all tense and determined about it, it is then that our ability to stand strong and tall while responding with grace and effectiveness is most powerful. Thus self-management, life balance, mindfulness and the self-regulation that comes with emotional intelligence are all ingredients for becoming a resilient and responsible leader.

Red Bull and *Nike*, two of the most recognised and respected brands on the planet and particularly popular with those who dare to excel and go beyond the ordinary, both have wings and flight associated with their brand. *Nike* was the *Goddess* of Victory in Greek mythology, and the slogan *Red Bull gives you wings* is well-known. I would add that *Resilience* and *Responsibility* give the *True North Leader* wings. The first three feathers of the *TNL Compass* that we have covered so far, provide a strong foundation from which leadership can be most influential. It is this last feather of the model that represents the art of *Influence*, which we will explore in Chapter 34.

Self Mastery before Public Mastery

Before we explore the art of *Influence* which is more associated with what Stephen Covey refers to as the 'Public Victory,' I would like to finish this part of the book with a brief look at self-management and life balance—this is what Covey calls the 'Private Victory.' It is Covey's mantra and my belief too, that if we are to sustain success in the public arena, we must first master ourselves in the way we manage our mind, body, emotions and spirit. This requires us to become aware of these aspects of self, how healthy and balanced they are, how we treat them and what impact this is having on our well-being, quality of life and personal effectiveness. All of this underpins our performance as a leader, as it influences the *Energetic Exchange* we have with others and our ability to respond to the challenges of our environment.

> **First and foremost, the job of a leader is to take charge of their own energy and then to orchestrate the energy of those around them.**
> Peter Drucker

Medicine Wheels

At the beginning of Chapter 11 on *Organisational Wellness*, I introduced you to a book I discovered in 1988. The *Wellness Workbook* (Travis and Ryan) revolved around a 'Wellness Wheel' with twelve segments. Based on my studies in physical education, biology, psychotherapy and stress management; together with my own personal experience, I was inspired to develop a simplified version of the *Wellness Wheel* which I trialled during a stress management course that I had developed for members of the health and fitness centre I was managing back then. I initially called it the *'Wheel of Health'* and later *'The Life Balance Profile.'* The original version had six segments which I later increased to eight while working as a corporate health consultant. I developed various versions of this wheel as my thinking evolved about the key areas that influence our well-being and quality of life.

For many years I presented a 90 minute seminar on the wheel and then started running retreats for the *South Australian Ambulance Welfare Fund* based on the eight areas of this *Medicine Wheel*. Mark and I collaborated on this program back in the nineties and later became involved in an organisation-wide strategic planning process for the *SA Ambulance Service*, together with delivering other team and personal development programs for emergency service organisations such as the *Metropolitan Fire Service* and *SA Police*. During those years, I learnt much about stress and the importance of self-management to mental health.

Our ability to respond to life's challenges and live our best life, depends on how well balanced we are in key areas that affect our wellness, and how consciously we are able to adjust this balance to sail favourably into shifting winds, through occasional storms and the changing seasons of our life.

Living Balance
In 2005 Gabrielle and I developed a behaviour change program called *Living Balance*—a 12 week program which covered each area of the wheel of health, plus some introductory information on goal setting and the principles of behaviour change, together with some extra explorations into mindfulness, the meaning of life and dying well.

The program involved a pre- and post-assessment to get a baseline for comparison at the end of the program. It also involved pre- and post-life-coaching sessions and I wrote a book to go with it, titled *Living Balance—A Journey to Wellness*. The book at this time is only available in e-copy or printed specifically for our *Life Balance and Well-Being Retreats* which are held in Adelaide and in other relaxing getaways such as Lombok and Bali. Gabrielle has also developed a new 5 weekend course—*The Unfolding Self*, which explores one's life journey and expanding one's tool kit for living well.

I am convinced that leaders who are good self-managers have more energy, higher levels of wellness, and less stress. This state of being then helps them to perform at their optimum and to be a good role model for those they lead. The resilience of a leader and their ability to respond to stress favourably, is significantly improved by sustaining a good life balance. This is not always possible but the ability to adjust one's sails for the wind will contribute to a reasonable baseline of wellness.

On the following page you will see the current version of the *Life Balance Profile* (Figure 33.4). Gabrielle and I have amended it over the years to reflect current Well-Be-ing concerns we witness. I encourage you to use it as a tool for gauging how balanced you are in different areas of your life and for setting goals to improve your quality of life and wellness.

THE LIFE BALANCE PROFILE

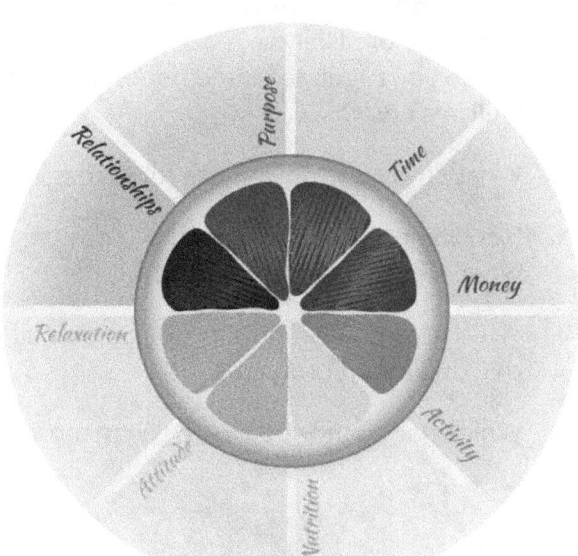

Figure 33.4 The Life Balance Profile—W&G Enright © 2005

*Health and motivation goes beyond 'do-ing' courses
to the way we are 'be-ing' as a result of our 'know-ing.'*
Gabrielle Enright

How Balanced are you?
How would you rate yourself on a scale from 1-10 for each of the areas of the Life Balance Profile? (Figure 33.4) If the centre is zero and the outside edge of each spoke is 10, put a dot on the line to reflect your ratings. Then join the dots to see how well balanced your wheel is.

Do-ing Becomes Be-ing
Achieving a 10 in each area is not necessarily the goal and is rarely sustainable. It is about being aware of when you are out of balance and knowing how to get back to your optimum level. Reading a book or doing a course to gain intellectual knowledge about a subject helps us to become more self-aware and educated. The most important step though, is to set some self-improvement goals and take action until it becomes part of your lifestyle. It has taken me many years to master some parts of this wheel and some I still have a challenge with despite my knowledge.

Reflection on Responsibility

1. Are you more likely to react without being mindful or can you regulate your emotional reactions quite well in a crisis?

2. What strategies do you use for managing stress?

3. How mindful are you on a day to day basis and when things don't go to plan?

4. Which *de Bono* hat or hats do you default to when thinking about problems?

5. Which hat would you like to try on more often?

Windsurfing at Glenelg, 1984

We are the captains of our soul, adjusting our sails for the winds of change, learning to live more consciously and remembering how to be all we can be.

Chapter 34   The Art of Influence

Before you are a leader, success is all about growing yourself.
When you become a leader, success is all about growing others.
Jack Welch, former GE chairman and CEO

Land It
I agree with the above quote in principle but would have to say that personal growth is even more important as we focus on helping others to grow. The more I lead, the more I realise that I need to keep growing, especially in the area of communication. I've also learnt that leadership deals with emotion, energy and spirit and that my words have the power to encourage or break a person's spirit. If I am not mindful of my speech and daily deeds, I may have the title of *Leader* without influencing constructively.

After losing my voice I became much more mindful about what I was trying to say as words became a scarce commodity for me. *Did I speak too much, too arrogantly or without enough empathy?* After this epiphany I began to choose my words more wisely, realising that every single word and the energy behind it, counted. In some ways the pauses between our words, like the spaces between musical notes, are even more potent.

Silence is often the supreme voice of truth.

Now that I have learnt to steer my voice more often than not, I sometimes forget that the power of silence is just as significant, as the words I speak. I was reminded of this during a feedback session last year. We were sitting around a fire, sharing what we'd learned from each other over the days we'd journeyed together. One participant described my tendency to be overly wordy, *as if he was watching a plane circling around and around above an airfield and wondering if it was ever going to land.* I now have a new affirmation that I say to myself when doing a presentation or summarising a debrief, which is simply this. *Land It!* (Perhaps it would have been good to know this one before I started writing the second half of this book!).

Earning the Right
Mark often talked about the concept of *Earning the Right*. Most of us would agree that our leadership is only supported by those who grant us the right to lead them. This right must be earned through our daily actions, well chosen words and respectful relationships. When we are humble, empathic,

trustworthy and respectful on a consistent basis, our ability to influence others is strengthened. To be trusted we need to be trust-worthy and to be respected we need to be respect-ful in our relations with others. There is a fine line between confidence and arrogance—it's called *Humility*.

Self-confidence is a healthy strength to have but few people respect arrogance. I notice in my dealings with indigenous elders of different cultures, that the *True Chiefs* are often not obvious until they are introduced. They don't dress in royal robes unless there is a ceremony, and they talk the least of everyone in a village unless they have some official task to perform.

Characteristics of a True Chief

In 2011, I was made an Honourary Chief of a community called Saroda, on the north coast of Papua New Guinea. This was very unexpected and very humbling, a memory I will cherish.
I recall being chaired into the village surrounded by people drumming, singing, dancing and then having a headdress with beautiful feathers placed on my head as the real Chief said a few words. I did my best to speak some words of gratitude in the local language, as my voice failed me. It was very overwhelming and cannot be described adequately in words. After the ceremony the Chief smiled at me and said quietly, 'The Chief has no ego, so don't let it go to your head.' This reminded me of a Chuang Tzu quote.

> **The perfect man has no self,**
> **the spiritual man has no achievement,**
> **the sage has no name.**

Chief with Elders at Saroda—Oro Province PNG, 2011

TRADITIONAL AMERICAN INDIAN LEADERSHIP

- All leadership possesses spiritual significance and is guided by spirit.
- Leaders demonstrate generosity and kindness, and honour all living things.
- Elders cultivate the leadership of future generations.
- Leaders are humble servants to the community. Individuals do not seek leadership, instead leaders emerge from their contributions to the community and the people recognise and select those considered most able to lead.
- The community can cease to recognise leaders who do not lead with integrity, by simply choosing to not follow them.
- Leaders lead by example rather than by authority or command.
- Leaders take their time when making a decision.
- When tribal leaders meet to deliberate on a matter they seek understanding and consensus through mutual inquiry. There is no debate, just sharing ideas.
- Methods of resolving social conflict are based on the concept of restitution that is focused on restoring respectful personal and social relations.

www.navajocourts.org/Harmonization/TraditionalAmericanIndianLeadership

Figure 34.1 Traditional American Indian Leadership—Navajo Courts, 1997

The summary above captures the qualities of Chiefs that I know in PNG. Observing these *True Chiefs* has helped me to understand humility, which is one of the characteristics I admired about Mark. I, on the other hand, have had to learn about humility after being a bit cocky at times when I was younger. Becoming a parent and working with youth at risk groups has humbled me on many occasions. Every now and then I still get reminded that I am not the bullet proof adventurer that some people might think I am.

Lessons on Humility from Kilimanjaro

On a recent trip to climb Kilimanjaro I learnt a significant lesson on humility. the word humiliation comes to mind when I reflect on this experience. In *Kiswahili*, the dominant language of Tanzania, the word *Kilima* means 'small hill,' and the word *njaro* means 'greatness.' In theory, the name *Kilimanjaro* could therefore mean 'great, small hill.' One thing is for sure, Kilimanjaro is no small hill. At the roof of Africa its summit sits at 5895m, which is more than 500 metres higher than Everest Base Camp. 500 metres doesn't sound like much but can add another 3 hours to the climb and for some, could make the difference between life and death.

Kilimanjaro is more of a trek than a true climb. However it is a mountain to be respected like all mountains above 5000m. The effects of altitude on the body can be significant even at relatively low elevations around 3000m above sea level and the risks for some are not to be underestimated. Approximately 1000 people are evacuated from Kilimanjaro every year and the average annual death toll is up to ten, mostly related to severe altitude sickness. Even seasoned Everest climbers can get quite sick because of the aggressive acclimatisation schedule (a very short few days compared with a number of weeks that would be spent acclimatising for an Everest summit).

I have twice trekked at altitude before in South America:– 4200m over *Dead Woman's Pass* on the Inca Trail, and as high as 4800m on the *Salkantay (Savage Mountain) Trail.* Each time I have experienced symptoms from 3000m onward, so it seems my body is not designed for altitude.

Tanzania September, 2015

On Kilimanjaro I started to experience mild altitude sickness at the first overnight camp (3000m) and on Day 3 (4600m) I struggled for an hour with nausea while climbing up to a place called the Lava Tower where I promptly threw up as we neared the highest elevation for the day. While others tucked into lunch I couldn't stand the thought of food but I knew I would feel better if I had another chuck, so I grabbed a jam sandwich from my lunch box and found a suitable boulder to lean against while I took a bite and suffered the discomfort of another vomit until I dry-retched my insides out. By then our clients had finished lunch and were ready to descend to our overnight camp (climb higher, sleep lower is the mantra for acclimatisation). Off I went smiling on the outside but suffering on the inside.

As I walked like a ghostly-faced zombie, while others enjoyed the post-lunch euphoria of descending; our head guide Julius shouldered my 10kg pack and told me assertively that I should not argue the point. He would carry my pathetically light-weight pack as I walked down into the more oxygenated air. My ego wrestled with the incongruence between his decision and my sense of self. Here I was, the so-called leader of this group with over 25 Kokoda treks in my legs and I wasn't even strong enough to carry a measly 10kg downhill. I understood enough about altitude to know that it does not discriminate and that any individual no matter how fit, can suffer its wrath on any given day for no particular reason, but I was embarrassed that I had to give in to it.

Pain is in the body, misery is in the mind—I kept telling myself.
A mantra borrowed from Yosi Ginsberg

Humility is a Gift Born From Humiliation

Over the next two days I faired a little better but still suffered with headaches and lethargy, particularly on day 6 as we climbed to our high camp (4662m), trudging in at lunchtime with a pumping headache and nausea again. I struggled to eat lunch and have an afternoon rest in my tent before forcing down yet more food at 5 pm to maximise my reserves for the summit push later that night.

At this time I remember feeling as sick as a dog and shaking my head, holding back tears as I contemplated not going with the others for the summit. I really couldn't see how I would make it given that I was already suffering badly and had no energy. I made the decision to re-assess in 5hrs time when I had to be ready to go or stay. Rightly or wrongly, I took some medications as a last resort and tossed and turned through a broken sleep until 11 pm when it was time to get ready.

I was now feeling a little better, so decided to make a start and see how things panned out. At midnight we were all suited up and ready to go. It was freezing cold, so with 2 pairs of socks, 3 layers on the legs, 5 layers on the torso, 2 sets of gloves and 2 beanies; we moved in slow motion like lunar astronauts across the rock strewn campsite to the trail which lead up the mountain another 1200m+ to the top (a roughly 10km round trip that would take about 12 hours if things went to plan).

Kilimanjaro—Barafu Campsite (4662m) September, 2015

Never under-estimate a 'Small Hill.'

Pole Pole to the Summit

We followed the lines of head torches beaming ahead of us and looked back occasionally to see more white dots following behind us. The mountain was bathed in darkness as the full moon had already crossed its horizon to the west, illuminating Kili's profile as we gained elevation above our high camp. Despite the extra layers my nose, fingers and toes felt the pain from the sub zero temperature and the hose on my hydration bladder began to freeze up.

"Pole pole" (slowly slowly) is the key mantra as we take each step, breathe and take the next, following in the footsteps of those in front of us. Our guide sets the tempo and sings us all the way to the top as we settle into a rhythm hour after cold and dark hour. All I remember is breathing as I inched my way upward behind the others, battling nausea, headache and thoughts of nothing, trying to stay conscious and focussed but losing the battle to sleep occasionally as I 'meditated' out of my body through the rhythm of the breath. At times I lost contact with the train and wondered whether I would fall by the way side. After 5hrs we stopped for a cuppa and I downed a liquid shot of glucose to keep me going, despite the impending vomit rising in my chest. An hour later I felt I could go no further as I dozed off three times, staggering to stay on my feet and keep moving slowly forward.

And then a dim glow of light rising from the eastern horizon heralded the first hint of dawn. The landscape below became silhouetted against a red and yellow tinge growing bolder as the seconds passed. Tears welled in my eyes as I felt a renewed hope of making it to the top. I looked to Gabrielle and others who were feeling similar emotions as the sunrise began to warm us and recharge our hearts.

We paused to witness the most magnificent sunrise over the Mawenzi peaks in the distance and turned to the west to see the light bouncing off the Rebmann Glacier near the top of Kili. We could now see our ultimate destination in the distance but knew that it would take at least another hour or so of patient and persistent plodding to get there. This last hour to Stella Point was probably the hardest physical challenge I have ever had to overcome, more than any of my Kokoda treks, or carrying 20+kgs over alpine passes in New Zealand or the trackless rocky hills in the heat of the Northern Flinders Ranges or the Kimberley. I feared that even if I could make it to the horizon it would be a false peak like those I have experienced on the Kokoda Trail after 2 hours of climbing, only to see another horizon pop up as we crest the top of what looks like the summit. It was all I could do to stay on my feet and keep moving forward between breaths as we finally reached Stella Point (5756m), the rim of the Kibo Crater which leads around to the true summit 150 metres or so higher.

Reaching Stella Point feels like the top at an altitude 300m higher the Everest Base Camp but if you want to stand on the true summit you need to walk for another 45mins around the rim of the Kibo Glacier past this point. In my case, I was too wasted to take another step and only got this far with the assistance of Gabrielle who basically reached out her hand and pulled me up the last few metres to the top of the ridge. My brain was suffering and I knew I needed to get down as soon as possible to alleviate the pressure lest I suffer more severe damage.

All nine of us made it to this point (5756m) and there were many tears and hugs shared as we congratulated and thanked each other. I don't remember much more.

Kilimanjaro—September, 2015

Six of our party continued on for another 150m around the crater rim to Uhuru Peak, while three of us descended to more welcome air. It took about three hours to descend back to camp down the steep scree slope before we staggered back into camp with nothing left in the tank. After a two hour rest we then continued down the mountain side to a lower camp at 3100m. From there we could see in the far distance the ice capped Kibo Glacier at the top of Kilimanjaro. It was hard to believe that just six hours earlier, we were standing on the top!

I remember thinking of Mark and how much more he must have put himself through in his desire to reach the summit of Everest. I also thought about how difficult it must have been for him to turn around when he was so close, and the disappointment he must have felt as he descended. Kilimanjaro is nowhere near as difficult as Everest but on this day it stripped me bare and humbled me beyond words. I take my hat off to anyone who has a go at climbing a high altitude mountain, especially those peaks in the stratosphere above 8000 metres.

Dare to Be Courageous and Vulnerable

The Kili experience taught me a lot about humility, to never be arrogant enough to think that we conquer mountains or that we are bullet proof or beyond requiring the help, support and feedback of others. Just because Gabrielle and I get up in front of people and talk about self-improvement or lead people on adventurous journeys, doesn't mean that we always have our act together and aren't sometimes dealing with our own fear, doubt, conflict or pain. It is in daring to be adventurous while being vulnerable and human, that we hope to set an example for our children and to help others.

To be truly authentic requires a willingness to embrace our weaknesses, to be honest about our shortcomings, to live without pretence or false bravado. Humility engenders trust, empathy and respect. These are essential qualities for a leader, perhaps contrary to the belief that a leader must be strong, brave, courageous and unwavering in the face of adversity or personal fear and doubt.

> *Through authentic speech, action and relationships,*
> *we earn the right to lead.*

Inner Mastery Proceeds Outer Mastery

I heard Mark say once that *public success is an inside job*. I know this is true for public speaking, and is reinforced by the master trainer, Stephanie Burns, and speaking coach David Griggs, when they say *If you want to get better at teaching, facilitating, guiding, leading or public speaking, go and do things in other parts of your life that stretch your comfort zone and build your repertoire of behaviours.* I found this to be true with martial arts such as Tae Kwon Do, Tai Chi and Karate that taught me things about myself and how to interact confidently in the world, that I wouldn't have learnt elsewhere.

The 'Public Victory' Stephen Covey talks about, is our ability to impact the world around us and to make a difference in the lives of others but as I have emphasised already, the 'Private Victory' must come first. Our ability to self-manage, re-balance and live our 'personal best' life puts us in a stronger position to be effective in our outer world, particularly in the world of relationships and leadership.

The quality of our relationships with self and others is determined by our self-esteem, attitudes, beliefs, past experiences and our communication skills. We can't change other people but we can choose how we respond to them and we can develop our people skills to improve the quality of our relationships whether it be as a leader, team member, parent or in the community.

Associate with Positive

I've heard that we become like the people we most associate with. My father was always on about choosing my friends wisely and not hanging around people who were, in his words, *No-hopers*. I've tried to follow this rule generally but I also think it is important not to be prejudiced about anyone who might be different, anti-social or struggling in life to survive or belong. There is always a reason why people behave the way they do, so I think it is good to be curious and to seek to understand others. I can't remember where I heard it but someone said to me once, *I don't like that bloke, I better get to know him.* I have often used this phrase when running workshops on relationships and conflict resolution. Perhaps the best we can do for *No-Hopers* is to give them hope and understanding!

> ***In the garden of our life we need to weed out that which chokes the life out of us, while planting and nurturing that which we want to grow abundantly.***

Culture is a Reflection of Leadership

As in our personal life, work cultures generally stem from the mindsets, conversations and behaviours of the critical mass. The responsibility of the leader is to be a *thermostat* who sets the atmosphere and environment for the culture, rather than be a *thermometer* at the affect of the environment around them. Culture is thus, a reflection of leadership, not just the person who has the title of *Boss*, but also the team of leaders they surround themselves with and others who they seek as mentors. This is why I liked to associate with Mark and his team at *Venture Corporate Recharge*. They were good mentors and associates for me and I will always value their influence.

Empathy and Diversity

Biological diversity is a core ingredient in the health of any eco-system, including human societies that are more likely to grow and thrive when diversity is embraced and used to advantage. At the same time, diversity does have its challenges when it results in prejudice and conflict. People differ in personality style, gender, culture, life experience, values, beliefs and priorities, so one of the biggest challenges for some people is to get along with people who are different to them. Embracing differences doesn't mean that we need to agree with others who have a different point of view. However, it is helpful if we can seek to understand their perspective. Having empathy for others, no matter how different they are to us, helps us to build bridges of understanding that lead to less conflict and more co-operation. Sometimes we discover that we are not that different after all.

Understanding is More Important than Agreement

When we are dealing with someone we haven't gotten to know yet, or even when we are in a relationship with someone we like, it is common to have mis-understandings. Most conflict is born from mis-understanding. To use an archery analogy:– if 'understanding' is the 'bulls-eye' and we miss our intended objective, we can either get upset and quit or we can try again. With coaching we can get some feedback to fine tune our aim or our technique. Then with practise we will eventually get more accurate with our communication and our ability to relate to people. Often when there is a difference of opinion, we can still find common ground, build trust, respect and rapport and come to an understanding. Too much time and energy is wasted arguing for agreement or *making stuff up* because of a lack of communication. Understanding is more important than agreement.

The 'Understanding Triangle'

The model below shows the inter-relationship between three things that contribute to the quality of relationship and understanding between people.

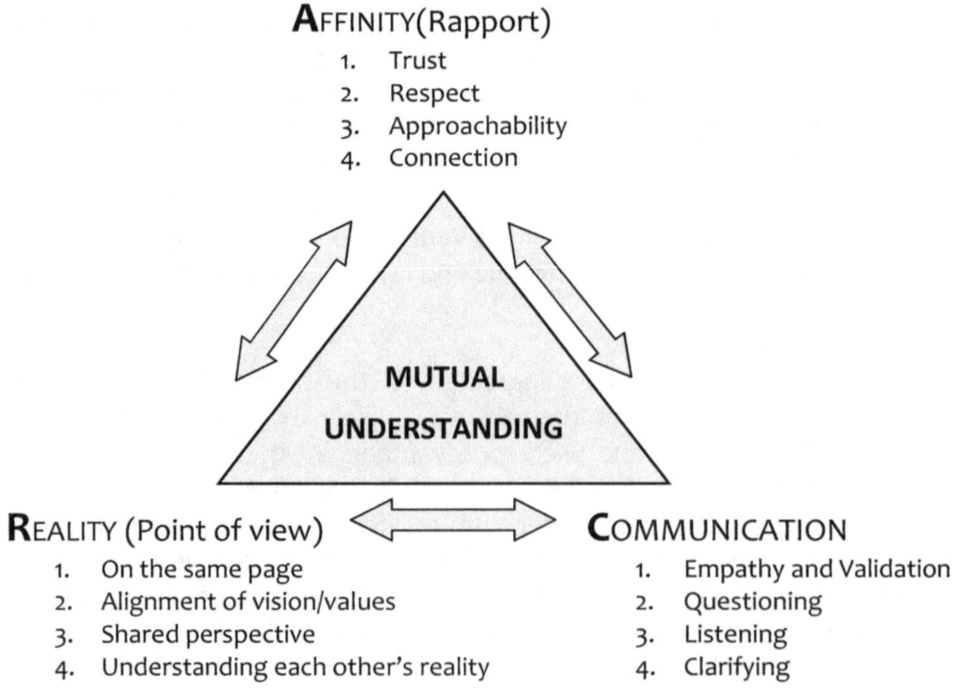

AFFINITY(Rapport)
1. Trust
2. Respect
3. Approachability
4. Connection

MUTUAL UNDERSTANDING

REALITY (Point of view)
1. On the same page
2. Alignment of vision/values
3. Shared perspective
4. Understanding each other's reality

COMMUNICATION
1. Empathy and Validation
2. Questioning
3. Listening
4. Clarifying

Figure 34.2 Understanding Triangle (Adapted *ARC Triangle*—Hubbard, 1950)

If any of the three parts of the triangle are limited, mutual understanding will be affected. Lack of communication leads people to make assumptions about reality (aka *'Making stuff up'*) which can have a damaging impact on affinity, leading to further problems with communication and more misunderstandings. All three parts of the triangle are inter-dependent.

AFFINITY is the degree to which we feel aligned with each other and how much we like each other or have a rapport between us. Affinity is underpinned by trust and respect, so to have a healthy connection and an understanding relationship between us, there must be trust, respect and rapport. When Gabrielle and I facilitate conversations about trust, we often use the example of what we call the 'Trust Bridge.' This idea came from an image we use of Gabrielle crossing a log bridge during her first trek along the Kokoda Trail in 2004 (when we didn't have the well-equipped river-safety teams we use today). In this photo she is crossing a bridge without a rope, having to trust herself, the log and the guide, while not being distracted by the raging torrent beneath her.

Gabrielle on the Kokoda Trail—August, 2004

Trust Bridges
Trust bridges sometimes take a long time to build, they must have good integrity, and we are more likely to cross them confidently if we trust the person on the other side. On the other hand, weak trust bridges can break in an instant and are difficult to repair. Trust therefore, can be fragile or strong depending on the relationship. Affinity is built when we cross the trust bridge and know that it will be reliable. Often leaders over-rely on the authority of their position to influence those they lead. If they have not *earned the right* by being trust- and respect-worthy, then affinity will be low, they will be less approachable, and communication will become difficult.

This results in a lack of understanding which diminishes affinity further and further. People don't leave organisations as much as they leave managers with whom they have low affinity, respect and trust.

Trusting the Inner Guide
Sometimes as leaders we will find ourselves in situations where we have no one else to turn to but ourselves and we have to trust our decision making.

I mentioned earlier in Chapter 31 that I had my first medivac from the Kokoda Track a year or so ago, after successfully getting 100% of our clients across the track for over a decade. On this trek, one of my clients had an allergic reaction to his malaria medication and had been vomiting chronically enough to be critically dehydrated. After following all of the wilderness first aid protocols and using all of the medical resources at my disposal, I made the decision to evacuate him. The chopper was supposed to arrive at first light, so after delaying our departure, I sent the rest of the group ahead with guides and porters to the next camp which was a day's walk away. Alone with my critically ill friend and two guides I waited impatiently, eyes fixed on the sky.

By the time the chopper came and our patient was finally on his way to hospital, I was 5 hours behind my trekking group and had to catch up to meet them at the next overnight location before dark. This section of the track is one of the most difficult and can take in excess of 8 hours to walk, depending on the condition of the track. I had about 6 hours to make the journey before sunset.

My guides decided to hang back for a swim at a place called Ofi Creek and because I knew the way and had some distance to make up, I ended up powering along by myself up over the imposing Maguli Range to Naoro Village and then down across the Naoro Valley to the Brown River where I would cross its fast flowing waters and continue on for another hour to my destination at a place called Agulolo.

When I got to the Brown River which is about 50 metres wide at best (100+ metres wide when in flood), I realised that the river safety team was ahead of me and surprisingly, my normally speedy guides were still behind me. For a moment I hesitated with a hint of fear in my chest. "Should I cross the river by myself or wait for the guides?" (I thought they would have caught up to me by now and perhaps they might have taken a short-cut and were somehow ahead of me).

Rather than wait and be caught out in the swampy jungle after dark, I decided to cross the river alone (not normally a wise thing to do but considering my circumstances I thought it was my best option). Fortunately I knew the river pretty well after crossing it many times over the past ten years but it was always changing enough to be unpredictable.

Then, as I settled my urge to panic, I experienced an uncanny feeling that someone was with me with outstretched hand, leading me into the water from the safety of the sandy shore. An unusual calm came over me and I walked into the fast flowing river with confidence; wading across at just the right angle and in the right section of the river so that the current carried me across to the opposite bank without incident. It reminded me of the time I went climbing with Mark at Arapiles, without being able to see him above me, I trusted that he would be on belay for me as I climbed out and around a rocky outcrop to make my way up a cliff face in the dark. I felt his spirit and trusted his presence again as I crossed the river to safe shores on the other side. I eventually arrived at camp just on dark with my guides about 10 minutes behind me. This experience tested my trust on a lot of levels but most of all it tested my ability to trust my inner guide.

~~~~~~~~~~~~~~~~~~~~

Trust is about believing that our expectations will be met and that the person we are in relationship with will be able to be relied upon, whether it be ourselves, our partner, a guide or a leader in the workplace. Trust is developed incrementally and becomes an essential part of maintaining respect and rapport. All of these are aspects of *Affinity* which is at the top of the *Understanding Triangle*. When *Affinity* is diminished, we are less likely to understand each other's reality as a result of a reluctance to engage in open and honest communication. Building *bridges of trust* is crucial to *Affinity*.

REALITY is the point of view or perspective that each of us has. This can sometimes be the same but most often it will be different unless we can communicate clearly enough to clarify each other's point of view and come to some common understanding. If we see things from a totally different perspective or we lack common ground and alignment of vision and values, then we won't have mutual understanding. Every person's truth is true for them. Our challenge is to be able to acknowledge each other's truth without judgement. This is a choice available to all of us, to *hear* another's reality.

I can only say that I have come to know a truth,
not the truth, for truth has many faces.

Developing a Shared Reality

One of the major challenges in all relationships, particularly in organisations, is to come to an agreement on the type of workplace culture everyone wants and what behaviours are considered acceptable or unacceptable in achieving it. This requires agreement on team values which provide the foundation for what I have referred to as *Team Agreements*. Developing agreements sounds easy to do, but because everyone has a different *reality* when it comes to personally held beliefs and what they think constitutes acceptable behaviour, it can take quite a bit of communication before individual points of view are shaped into a *Shared Reality*. Once there is alignment with regard to the *shared reality* about where the team is heading and how they are going to get there within the context of their agreements, people can then take responsibility for their role. Shared reality makes shared responsibility more workable with less misunderstanding.

Shared Responsibility

Figure 34.3 below, provides examples of behaviours that either help or hinder healthy relationships in a team or family environment. This is a simple way of identifying which behaviours are acceptable (*above the line*) or unacceptable (*below the line*). Sometimes there will be grey areas influenced by personal priorities and assumptions. These behaviours can also be referred to as *Master* or *Victim Responses* in relation to how team members respond to problems. (Refer back to the *Responsibility Model*—Figure 33.1 in Chapter 33.)

Above the Line Behaviours—Master Responses
Focused on solutions rather than problems/ positive expectations
Affirming and supportive behaviours, attitudes and words
Constructive feedback delivered in a supportive manner
Open and honest communication
Learning and 'continuous improvement' focus

Below the Line Behaviours—Victim Responses
Blame, justification, denial, excuses or quitting
Passive / aggressive communication
Defensive behaviour
Critical and judgemental / gossiping

Figure 34.3 Lines of Responsibility—Adapted from M Auricht, 2000

COMMUNICATION is perhaps the most essential part of the *Understanding Triangle*, for without effective communication it is difficult to have mutual understanding of each other's reality or to have high levels of affinity. Asking questions to seek or clarify understanding, communicating with empathy and respect, giving feedback without invalidation; all of these aspects of communication contribute to mutual understanding and affinity.

> *Communication is the code that opens the combination lock to understanding.*

Whenever there is conflict or mis-understanding it is usually as a result of communication barriers, a difference in point of view or lack of *affinity* between people or groups. We call this an *ARC Break*. Like a break in a circuit, we can fix it by figuring out where the break is and doing our best to mend it. This often starts with communication, for example: expressing empathy; asking questions to seek understanding of the other's point of view; listening for their reality; clarifying assumptions; and acknowledging the other's perspective which helps to re-build rapport and trust. Once affinity is strengthened, the communication will usually start to flow and agreement/mutual understanding can be achieved. This becomes a self-reinforcing spiral. If we don't communicate as above, it leads to a downward spiral.

Gabrielle and I now use the term *ARC Break* quite regularly when we notice our affinity dropping, confusion about each other's reality, or communication becoming more difficult between us. This gives us a common language to alert each other to the fact that we need to identify where the *break* is in the circuit, and to fix it before it gets too hard. It also reminds us that most misunderstandings can be resolved by clarifying each other's reality, re-establishing affinity and improving our communication.

The Art of Communication—Lessons from the Martial Arts
I have often thought about why sometimes I still struggle to implement the basics of relating to others in a healthy way, when I'm feeling defensive, misunderstood or angry. Upon reflection, I think it is similar to the principles I've learnt through the martial arts. I have noticed that if one is tense, angry, fearful or lacking in confidence when sparring in a tournament, this often leads to an over-emphasis on attacking too aggressively in an attempt to score points through force. This results in an ineffective application of skills. If the opponent is also inexperienced, they will often escalate their level of aggression too, in an attempt to match energies. This can lead to a flurry of aggression where both parties get hurt.

I now see that martial arts can be a good metaphor for life and relationships. If we are good at the art of communication and conflict management, we are less likely to get hurt or to hurt others. These skills don't come easily to all of us, especially when we are under pressure. It is much easier to deal with conflict constructively if both parties are reasonably well practised at it and are playing by fair rules in a controlled way.

I'd rather spar with a master than a novice any day. Novices are often full of aggression and little control. Masters on the other hand are more focused on teaching than winning. They spar in a more controlled and mindful manner, remaining calm, while they closely observe the intentions of their opponent. They seek to dissipate the opponent's aggression by allowing it, flowing with it, deflecting it or stepping out of reach. Ultimately their patience allows them to disarm their opponent with a simple technique delivered with minimal aggression but maximum effect. This requires emotional regulation, patience and mindfulness, as well as masterful technique.

Sparring with Black Belts, 2008

Non-violence is the summit of bravery.
Mahatma Gandhi

Mark trained in the martial arts of *Tae Kwon Do* and *Judo*, while my experience has been in *Tae Kwon Do*, *Karate* and the more gentle art of *Tai Chi*. In martial arts, as in relationships, it is helpful to know your strengths and weaknesses and those of your opponent. This can often minimise the escalation of conflict.

If I was ever sparring a tall person with a good kick, I would always move in very close to remove the space they had to execute an effective kick. This doesn't work so well with a *Tae Kwon Do* Black Belt who will easily push you back with a short *push-kick* first, followed quickly by a *jumping side-kick* that has more power. Fortunately one of the rules of *Tae Kwon Do* is 'control.'

Knowing yourself and your opponent, and controlling the tendency toward aggression in a conflict is crucial to minimising injury to self and other. Mark's art, *Judo*, focuses on flowing with the opponent's aggression and using their momentum to put them off balance. *Ju-do* comes from the throwing and grappling techniques of *Ju-jitsu* which was created by warriors for the battlefield and was more concerned with defeating an opponent. '*Do*' styles are concerned with defeating one's self and therefore have a greater emphasis on philosophy with moral and spiritual connotations; the ultimate aim being enlightenment and personal improvement.

> ***Meeting physical force with soul force is the key to peace.***
> Adapted from the words of Dr Martin Luther King

I trust that you'll see the metaphors in martial arts that relate to conflict resolution in less physical circumstances. Through the use of questions, empathic listening, seeking to understand and respecting others, we can often avoid escalating conflict and instead create rapport and increased affinity. Once affinity is strong, then open and honest communication flows more easily. We can't do this without first mastering ourselves, including our ability to stay calm and mindful so that we can diffuse conflict and build respect. Being dictated to by another person's aggression is to be avoided.

Constructive Conflict
Navigating conflict while maintaining affinity is one of the more difficult challenges of leadership. Conflict, like stress, is neither good nor bad; it can lead to destruction or creativity, depending on how we view it and handle it. Fortunately or unfortunately, I grew up in a family of five boys where there was regular sibling sparring and a strong mix of triumph and tragedy, love and conflict, change and challenge. By my late teens I was over my internal conflict and wanted to make more of my life. But I still tended to avoid anything that challenged me to assert myself.

It wasn't until I learned from Master Lee, my *Tae Kwon Do* teacher, how to stand tall and assert myself confidently despite my fear, that I became comfortable asserting myself in life generally. This meant learning how to engage in what I call 'constructive conflict,' where two or more people can have a different opinion or approach but still be able to negotiate an outcome that is acceptable to both, and perhaps even create something that neither could conceive of alone, nor think possible.

> ***Conflict doesn't have to result in war. If only we could sit around a fire, break bread, listen to each other's story and choose to respect our differences.***

Because we all have different personalities, different values and beliefs, different past experiences and points of view, it is not surprising that there will be an *understanding gap* between two or more people at any given time. Constructive conflict is based on the premise that *everyone is right based on their perception* and that the most constructive thing we can do is to seek understanding first and then move in the direction of a win-win if possible.

Assertiveness and Response-Ability
Being assertive requires us to be 'response-able.' In other words, it is a *proactive choice* rather than a reaction based on fear which can often lead to aggression or becoming passive and powerless. There is a continuum between these two extremes. Being *assertive* is the *Middle Way*.

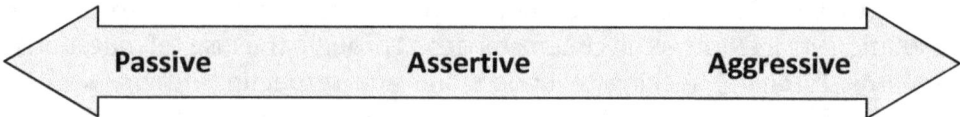

Reacting aggressively to conflict is not necessarily defined by violence. It just means that we are focusing on our own needs and dismissing the needs of the other person.

Conversely, **reacting passively** usually involves dismissing our own needs and allowing the other person's needs to dictate. (This could be a habit or in some circumstances a survival choice.)

Responding assertively is much more likely to take the needs of both parties into account. We won't always get what we want but we will have acknowledged the other person's point of view, expressed how we feel and what our preferred outcomes are. When we do this, a *win-win* solution is more likely. Of course it is more challenging to be assertive when others are playing the *passive/aggressive game*. In this case, we perhaps need to disarm them first with empathy and acknowledgement, then attempt to walk alongside them rather than in front or behind. *Power plays* are often founded on fear. When we remove the fear, the dynamics change.

Applying the Art of Conflict
As we have learnt from our short excursion into the martial arts, when faced with a confrontation, an angry outburst or a difficult person, the key is to choose a constructive response rather than be sucked into matching the other person's behaviour, becoming defensive or going on the attack.

In *Figure 34.4* below, I provide *Six Steps to Constructive Conflict,* based on a number of courses we have participated in over the years, together with lessons from my own experiences. Gabrielle and I now teach these as part of a customer service course that we run for one of our major clients. It is surprising how many people find it challenging to put these steps into practice. I encourage you to welcome conflict as an opportunity to practise these skills. After awhile they become second nature.

SIX STEPS TO CONSTRUCTIVE CONFLICT

1. The first key skill is to remain calm and in control of your emotional response. If you can't do this, it might be best to take some time out before you are ready to respond. (Refer to Figure 33.2 on page 315.)

2. The second priority is to 'seek to understand' the other person by asking questions, acknowledging their feelings and listening to their point of view.

3. Check the accuracy of your understanding by reflecting back to the other person what you think they might be feeling and what you think they said. This demonstrates that you are listening and is much more powerful than just saying "I understand."

4. Never assume that the other person thinks the same way you do. Always ask questions and clarify before jumping to conclusions. Find out what their needs are and seek to fulfil them or at least acknowledge them. Be willing to co-operate.

5. Never blame, judge, criticise or demand. Always be calmly assertive, rather than aggressive. Use "I" statements to express how you feel, why you feel that way and what you'd prefer to happen now or next time.

6. Go for the win-win. Try to find some common ground or to figure out a way that both parties can benefit or at least feel that their point of view has been acknowledged and respected.

Figure 34.4 Six Steps to Constructive Conflict—W&G Enright © 2005

These skills might seem like common sense, but common sense is not very common when it comes to conflict resolution, because we either haven't developed effective skills or our emotions get in the way. Aside from practising the communication skills, emotional regulation is essential to the effective application of skills under pressure.

We can improve our ability to regulate emotion in conflict situations by practising the *art of mindfulness* (see page 315). When we are more mindful, we have a greater capacity to detach, observe and respond from a place of considered choice. We are also less likely to be clouded by our prejudices. We can instead, observe our reactions and the actions of others without attachment and judgement. It is also helpful to be conscious of our intentions, so that we are mindful of any hidden agendas we might have that cloud our judgement.

When we practise mindfulness, our ability to respond is set free, the boundaries we construct about the world and about ourselves and others, are more permeable or disintegrate altogether. Without these illusionary boundaries manufactured by the mind, we can see that we are all of *equal value* as human beings. It is only the boundaries and limitations we put on ourselves and others that create inequality.

A Dream of Equality
In Martin Luther King's *I Have a Dream* speech, he refers to the words of the United States Declaration of Independence. The second paragraph of the declaration starts as follows:

We hold these truths to be self-evident, that all men are created equal, that they are endowed by their Creator with certain unalienable Rights, that among these are Life, Liberty and the Pursuit of Happiness... to secure these rights, Governments are instituted among Men, deriving their just powers from the consent of the governed.

My understanding of this, is that in a democracy, a leader's power is reliant on the consent of the people and that human rights are sacred and undeniable. The right to be *equally valued* being among them.

I HAVE A DREAM
I have a dream that one day this nation will rise up and live out the true meaning of its creed: We hold these truths to be self-evident, that all men are created equal.
I have a dream that one day... the sons of former slaves and the sons of former slave owners will be able to sit down together at the table of brotherhood.
I have a dream that my four little children will one day live in a nation where they will not be judged by the colour of their skin but by the content of their character.   Dr Martin Luther King

Source: Wikipedia

This ideal of *Equal Value* was a principal that Mark focussed on in his workshops. I recall discussing the concept of *Equal Value Communication* during one of Mark's professional development sessions. We spent quite some time exploring what it meant for the way we communicate with our loved ones, with clients and with ourselves. Following this session I wrote some notes (summarised under the heading of *Equal Value Communication* below), that I still use today in our programs and workshops. I again acknowledge Mark for leading me to contemplate more deeply, the meaning of *Equality*. My belief now is that, philosophically, we could all have equal rights as human beings, and yet the reality is that we don't all end up being equal in a practical sense. This doesn't mean though, that we shouldn't treat each other with *equal value*.

> *All creatures are the same life, the same essence,*
> *the same power, the same one and nothing less.*
> Henry Suso

***Equal Value* Communication**
One of our greatest needs as human beings is to feel valued by others. Our sense of self-worth is both internally and externally determined. On the list of things that motivate people, recognition comes higher than money. Recognition is very empowering. Most of us at a basic level, at least want to be acknowledged equally regardless of our social status. We all want mutual respect.

Equal value does not mean that we all need to value the same things or that we all have the same net worth monetarily. The reality is, we are all different. We have different personalities, different strengths and weaknesses and different opinions based on our past experiences. Our values however, are at the core of who we are. They are the foundation of our identity. When someone criticises our values or does not even appear to respect that we have values that are different to theirs, we can feel invalidated as a person.

> *I see you, I hear you.*
> *We validate people by 'hearing' and 'seeing' them*
> *for who they are in all their human-ness.*

Acknowledging another person's opinion or respecting their differences, does not mean we have to agree with their opinion or even like them necessarily. Acknowledging them validates their value as a fellow human.

Assertive communication, where we express our own feelings and needs as well as considering the needs and feelings of the other person, is a good example of *equal value communication*. Communicating 'adult to adult' rather than 'parent to child' is another form of *equal value communication*.

Sometimes we are unaware that we have de-valued someone's words when we say "*Yes, but…* ." This essentially negates what they have said and in a sense invalidates it. Try using "*and*" as the joining word between your statement and theirs. This validates their statement *and* yours.

Equal value communication may be as simple as a smile, saying hello, listening attentively, letting someone into the traffic, making eye contact or just showing interest. Often we as leaders, teachers or parents are unaware of the impact of our actions and words. Our every action, thought and word strengthens or weakens our identity and that of those we interact with.

In 1927 W. Livingston Larned wrote a poem called *Father Forgets*, which featured in the classic Dale Carnegie book *How to Win Friends and Influence People*. Being a father of two boys, his words struck a chord with me and led me to write a modern day version to remind me of the power of words, especially between parents and children.

The Power of Words
As the moonlight filters through the shutters into your room, I sit watching you while you sleep. Your little fingers squashed up under the soft skin of your cheek and your cherub lips accentuate the innocence on your face. I feel a pang of guilt flowing through me as I reflect on how I treated you today. I wish I could take back the words I fired at you, like arrows through your heart.

I thought about how, instead of wishing you a good morning and giving you a hug, I commented on how scruffy you looked and the fact that you were running late for school. Then without needing to, I reminded you to wash your face and clean your teeth. In my hurry to get to work on time, I forgot to give you a hug and a goodbye kiss. As I reversed out of the driveway you rushed to the car window to say goodbye and I impatiently wound the window down and grumbled at you to hurry up.

Coming home from work I saw you playing in the park and embarrassed you in front of your friends when I yelled at you to get home and change out of your school clothes. At dinner time I found fault too when you talked with your mouth full and chatted with your brother while I was trying to watch the news. As if the news was more important than my son's day!

Later in the evening I was catching up on some work that I brought home from the office. You came in sheepishly, with a fearful and sad look in your eyes. I glanced up from my computer, impatient at the interruption.

You hesitated at the door. "What is it?" I snapped. You said nothing, but spontaneously took the risk to race across the room and throw your arms around my neck. I felt your small but strong arms tighten with an affection that came straight from your heart; a heart that not even my neglect could weaken. And then, suddenly you were gone, tip-toeing off to bed.

It was shortly afterward that tears rolled down my face as I realised what I'd done. Where had I been all day? In a world of criticism and fault-finding? It was not that I didn't love you; it was that I expected too much of youth. I was measuring you by my adult yardstick and focusing on what was wrong rather than what was right with you.

There is so much that is good and true in your character. Your little heart is as big as the moon. Your spontaneous impulse to rush in and kiss me good night, after the way I treated you this day has taught me a great lesson about unconditional love. I have come to your bedside in the darkness and sat here ashamed of myself.

Of all the millions of children who are born in to this world every day, I was truly blessed with you. I am truly sorry my son, for the way I have treated you. As I look at you asleep in your bed, I wish that I could take back the day and start over. All I can do is strive to be a better father tomorrow and trust that you will forgive my thoughtless actions and remind me by your example, what it is to be truly human.

A modern day version of W Livingston Larned's *Father Forgets*—W Enright, 2005

Encouragement
Unfortunately for some people, the only recognition they get is for when they do something wrong. Parents and teachers need to be especially mindful of this duty of care. We can make a huge difference to our environment by being positive and encouraging in the way we interact with others, especially those we lead and influence. People will do much more than they ever thought they could when they are encouraged and supported. We add to the self-efficacy of others by catching them doing their best and affirming them through our words and actions.

Leaders don't realise that by being negative in the way they speak with people or in the way they communicate through their body language, they can develop a self-replicating pattern in the people they lead. It's important for leaders to be tuned into the power of words and conversations.
Grant Donovan

Parenting and Leadership

Parenting is a form of leadership, requiring us to have our own 'act together' somewhat and to have the skills to guide, coach/mentor and empower others to be the best they can be. It can be a tough gig sometimes but the rewards outweigh the fatigue, the doubt and fear we sometimes experience, and the times when we stuff up. We must remember that *we* are the adult in the room and that everything we do and say is noticed by young hearts watching and listening, building a picture for themselves of how to 'be' in this world... at least until they become a teenager! Then they have to break free to establish their own identity and work out for themselves, which bits of us they want to keep and make their own and which bits they want to 'not be like.' Hopefully somewhere along the line we are able to instill in them some guiding principles and resilience to help them navigate their own way through life.

   Parenting requires us to face our own shortcomings and in spite of ourselves, to be there for a fragile human being who depends on us to love and care for them, to teach them, to be there for them when they fall, to pick them up and encourage them, to listen, to empathise, to cheer them on whatever they choose to do or become.

> ***Children belong not to us
> but to the universe.
> We are but the archers that
> launch them forth to their potential.***

Jesse and Pete with Gabrielle—Tassie, 2007

The Art of Delegation

Delegation is possibly the least well-practised aspect of leadership in my experience, and yet it is the key to saving time, especially when we are a parent, teaching young adults to be more responsible at home. Not only do we save time by transferring responsibility for a task, but we also empower others to take responsibility and leadership, so it is in fact, an investment in the long term development of emerging adults or leaders which results in leverage.

The most common reasons for not delegating include:
- It takes more time to delegate than to do it myself.
- It won't be done the way I would like and when I need it to be done.
- It will reflect badly on me if it isn't the result I would have achieved.

Despite these concerns there is usually long-term gain for short-term pain.

TIPS FOR EFFECTIVE DELEGATION

1. **Know Your Players**
   Ask the person you are delegating to, to let you know how they best learn. Do they need verbal instructions, more or less detail, visual diagrams, practical experience, coaching, feedback, the opportunity to practise in a non-critical environment. What can you do to pass on what they need to know, in a way that works best for them?

2. **Clear Expectations**
   Be really clear and specific about the tasks you want them to do:– what, how, when, and to what standard. Ask them to repeat back to you what they understand from your communication, to check for accuracy. Two-way responsibility applies to communication, following through with commitments, meeting at scheduled checkpoints and letting each other know the best way to check in and ask questions if anything is unclear. Agreements will minimise mis-understandings.

3. **Start Small and Gradually Transfer Responsibility**
   To build trust in those that you are delegating to, start with small appropriate chunks according to their capacity and reliability. Then gradually increase the amount of responsibility by giving them more as they prove their reliability.

4. **Feedback**
   Coaching and feedback is particularly important to delegation and is best done early on, and at regular intervals along the way. It is easier to correct small deviations from the expectations early, than to wait until it's too late and have to make more significant adjustments, which can be costly in time, money, energy and confidence. Feedback can be framed as a normal part of the process of delegation, so that the person you are delegating to sees it as a standard part of the mentoring process and not as personal criticism or judgement.

5. **Checkpoints**
   Scheduling regular checkpoints along the way (not just at the end point) to monitor progress provides an opportunity to check for quality, give feedback, address any questions, clarify that expectations are understood and are being met.

6. **Gratitude and Appreciation**
   Early and continuous acknowledgement and validation for their efforts will keep them motivated and focused. If you set them up for success, they will become more competent and confident, which leads to a positive association with delegation for them and for you.

Figure 34.5 Tips for Effective Delegation—Gabrielle Enright © 2015

The Gift of Feedback

One of the more challenging skills of leadership and parenting is providing corrective feedback while at the same time being able to maintain trust, respect and affinity (connection/rapport). Feedback is an essential part of delegation as we empower those that we lead to take on more responsibility.

We can gain valuable insights from the feedback of others, if it is done with empathy, sensitivity and with the intention to help us improve. We can become aware of *blindspots* that might be hindering our performance or relationships. Constructive feedback delivered respectfully, helps us to become self-aware and to self-correct our behaviour without feeling invalidated. The skills for giving helpful feedback are similar to those used for negotiating misunderstanding; essentially it helps us to understand ourselves more.

5 Steps for Giving the Gift of Feedback

1. Ask questions to seek understanding.
2. Actively listen to their reality.
3. Empathise with and acknowledge their point of view.
4. Give feedback about observed behaviour that could be a *blindspot*.
5. Provide some guidance and encourage the person to improve.

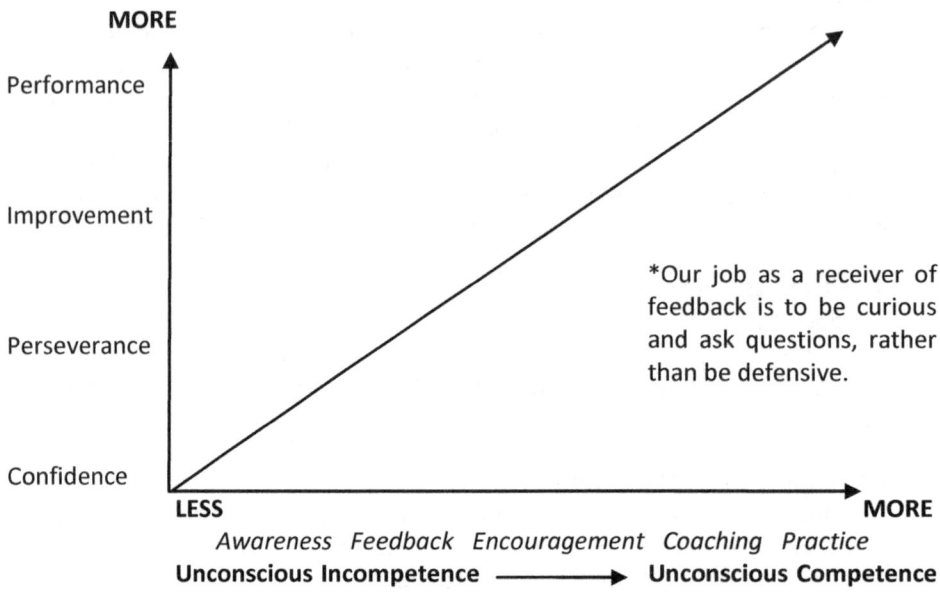

Figure 34.6 The Role of Feedback in Performance Improvement—W Enright © 2005

Positive Reinforcement

When we catch people doing *constructive behaviours* and provide reinforcing feedback, it is powerful because it has positive emotions associated with it.

Feedback that is delivered in a respectful, supportive and encouraging manner leads to awareness, confidence and perseverance, which ultimately results in improved performance. Once people become *unconsciously competent* (that is, they have reached a skill level which becomes habitual), they will automatically self-correct.

Know yourself and know your players

Of course the way we deliver feedback will also need to be adjusted, depending on the temperament of the person we are leading or coaching. It also helps to be mindful of how we come across to others. This self-awareness, so crucial to leadership, is developed through the process of self-reflection and being open to feedback from others about our own *blindspots*. If we are in a role of influence it is important to know ourselves as well as those we are leading.

> ***The difference between love and hate is understanding.***
> Ivory Dorsey

Personality Profiles

One aspect of knowing yourself and your players is understanding the basic temperaments that make up one's personality and influence behaviour. Mark introduced me to a personality profile called the *Tick Profile*, developed by Des Hunt. The *Tick Profile* refers to four personality types using the names of birds:– Eagle, Peacock, Dove and Owl. Hunt's *Tick Profile* is very similar to the more well know *DISC Profile* which has evolved from the theories of Dr William Marston in the late 1920s. Many of the current day personality assessment tools have origins that can be traced as far back as the Ancient Greek physician Aelius Galenus who coined the terms:- *sanguine, choleric, melancholic and phlegmatic* to describe four temperaments that were associated with pre-dispositions to different types of illness when they were too dominant or out of balance. Mark used the *Tick Profile* and the *Myers Briggs Type Indicator (MBTI)* with teams and leaders to help them become more aware of their natural tendencies for processing information, dealing with people, solving problems and handling stress. *Temperament* or *personality profiles* measure our innate psychological preferences and how they are expressed in our life. This is useful in terms of identifying our strengths and being aware of the areas that challenge us more. We can then play to our strengths, develop the areas we're not so strong in and broaden our repertoire of responses to life.

A Simple Approach to Personality Awareness.
Gabrielle and I use a simple approach to explore aspects of personality by focusing on *four easy-to-remember temperaments* which are determined by the interaction of two continuums of behaviour.

On the *Animal Instincts Model* (Figure 34.7—opposite page), you can see a vertical continuum with OUTWARD at the top and INWARD at the bottom. This relates to our tendency towards *Extroversion* or *Introversion*, which is not just about our social tendency to be more *outgoing* or *reserved*, but it is also to do with how we think, solve problems and express ideas. Introverts for example will have a tendency to be more contemplative when thinking through a solution to a problem. Extroverts on the other hand are more likely to voice ideas as they think of them. If you're in the middle of the continuum you might do both or it might depend on who you're with or your team role. The horizontal continuum relates to preference for getting *TASKS* done versus interacting with *PEOPLE*.

You could fill out a lengthy questionnaire to get a scientific score for this, but most people have a feel for their natural preferences. Assessments are most useful when we want to go into more depth about how the mix of the four aspects might interact with each other to be expressed in a helpful or unhelpful way.

Animal Instincts
In 2005 Gabrielle and I came up with our own simplified and user-friendly version of *the four temperaments* described by researchers and theorists such as Galenus, Marston and Hunt. Ours is based on a subjective self-assessment and is used to raise awareness and a general understanding of temperaments. We named the four types after familiar animals that displayed instinctive qualities typical of the four temperaments. Hence the name *Animal Instincts*. (Refer to the *Animal Instincts Map (Figure 34.7)* and *Table of Tendencies (Figure 34.8)* on the following pages.) These preferred ways of operating are instinctively part of our nature but as we mature, environmental factors and experience can change the way our natural mix of temperaments are expressed.

With greater awareness of how the interaction of our personality preferences play out when we're under pressure, and how they influence our relationships and performance, we can learn to adjust the volume of our default behaviours up or down, so that they are more appropriate for a particular situation or interaction with another person.

I believe that it is important not to label people based on one aspect of their being and it is not constructive to use our natural temperament as an excuse for living below our potential or not confronting things that we are unhappy about in our life. On the contrary, we all have the power to develop our non-preferred ways of operating by stretching our comfort zone and trying on different ways of being.

To provide a personal example: As a twenty-year-old I would have been down at the more *Inward focussed* end of the vertical axis on the model below and across to the left at the *Task* end of the horizontal axis. When you draw a dotted line between those two points (Figure 34.7), you can see that where they intersect is well inside the *Beaver* quadrant. In reality our personalities are actually a multi-dimensional mix of all four quadrants but for the purpose of this simple explanation I have provided a one-dimensional example.

The *Extreme Beaver* was my default position most of the time in my late teens and early twenties (unless I was intoxicated, in which case I could move into the *Monkey* quadrant a little more easily). At that time in my life I walked around with my head down, felt uncomfortable confronting certain circumstances in my life and was not socially confident enough to take charge of my life. I would often just follow the lead of others and feel sorry for myself when things didn't flow my way. One day I will never forget is the day a close friend said the words: *You can do more with your life*. I remember thinking about her comment all day. The next day I quit my dead-end job and left home to seek my dreams.

ANIMAL INSTINCTS MAP

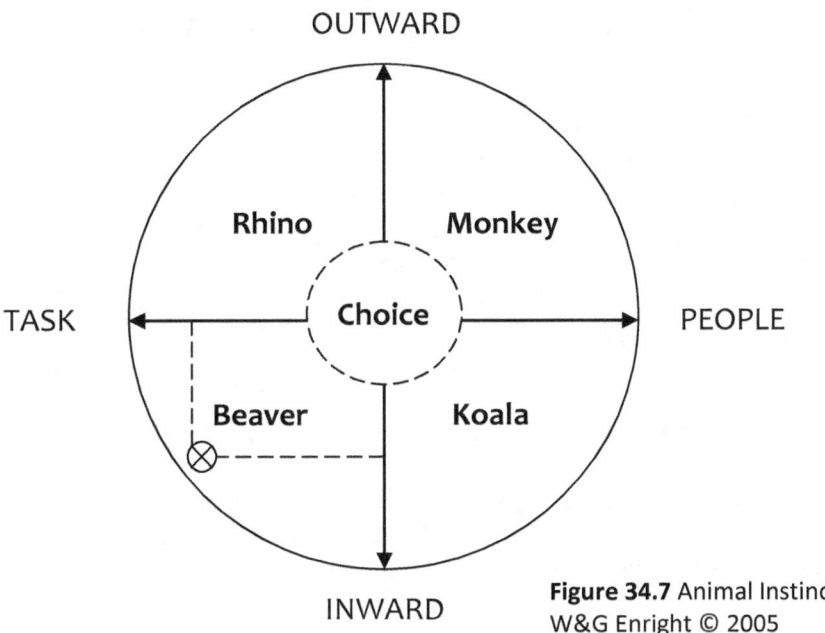

Figure 34.7 Animal Instincts
W&G Enright © 2005

Years later I have learned that my behaviour was not just determined by temperament but also influenced by fear and low self-confidence. Traits that were part of my temperament were expressed unconstructively in response to the circumstances of my life. Those same traits and others that I developed through personal growth experiences have now changed the way I express myself in the world. I now dwell in the *Circle of Choice*.

This means I am more comfortable operating in any of the four quadrants when I need to and can choose which part of my personality to use in certain situations or with certain people. For example, if I have to handle a crisis in an emergency situation I will move into *Rhino* mode. If things are a little tense and I need to lighten people's attitudes, I can move into *Monkey* mode and tap into my sense of humour. If one of my children or my wife is hurting I will choose to be more of a nurturing, supportive *Koala*; and when I am planning an event or doing a risk assessment for a trek I will use my strengths in the *Beaver* quadrant, where I am most comfortable planning, organising and thinking through the details.

Sometimes people display traits that reflect a particular quadrant's typical behaviours but it happens as a way of coping or masking fear, rather than being that person's natural way of being. As I mentioned earlier when discussing authenticity, if we operate outside of our preferred comfort zone for too long, it can get too stressful or exhausting, so knowing your strengths is valuable, as is expanding your comfort zone and adaptability.

ANIMAL INSTINCTS – TABLE OF TENDENCIES[74]

Animal	RHINO	MONKEY	KOALA	BEAVER
Strengths	Decisive Achiever Focused Determined	People focus Creative Influence Fun	Empathy Support Calm Considerate	Details Structure Organisation Accuracy
Challenges	Too fast Low empathy	Miss detail Lack focus	Sensitivity Self-neglect	Perfectionist Being rushed
Stress Response	Bull dozer Force v Think	Humour Distraction	Withdraw Avoidance	Overwhelm OCD
Greatest Need	Respect In charge	Fun Attention	Peace Stability	Order Detail

Figure 34.8 Animal Instincts Table of Tendencies—W&G Enright © 2005

See the Appendix to find out your scores for each quadrant.
Please note: The *Animal Instincts* Self-Assessment in the Appendix is a subjective snapshot that provides a general indication of your mix of personality preferences.

The Elasticity of Personality

The truth is, that we humans are very adaptive, so this snapshot only provides an overview map of our personality. Like any map though, it does not represent the full reality of our internal terrain. If we think of it like an x-ray of our skeletal structure it only shows an aspect of one's self. On top of that there are many other layers interacting with our skeletal system. Not to mention the fact that our physiology is changing and evolving from minute to minute. Physiology is also influenced by the mind, emotions, spirit and our wider environment... need I say more.

The way our personality makeup is expressed is also very dependent on the context within which we are operating. Context can include things such as the people we are interacting with (family, friends, work colleagues, strangers). It can also depend on how we are feeling on a particular day (relaxed, happy, sad, mad, stressed or intoxicated). If you ask someone else to complete the same assessment for you, they may give you a different score. There is often a difference between how we perceive ourselves and how others see us, so it can be useful feedback.

Strengths Taken to Extreme Become Weaknesses

Despite contextual variations, there are certain trends in our behaviour which become more pronounced when we're under pressure. Our strengths may come to the fore more strongly in a crisis or can become so extreme that they turn into weaknesses. Following are some examples:

The Rhino Strengths: of *faster pace, determination, goal orientation,* and *focus*, if taken to extreme can come across as arrogant, bullish and insensitive. Koalas can find them intimidating and impatient.

The Monkey Strengths: of *faster pace, social fun orientation, creativity,* and *spontaneity*, if taken to extreme can lead to skipping details, and losing focus on completion of tasks. Beavers can get frustrated with the Monkey's lack of attention to detail.

The Koala Strengths: of *slower pace, empathy, sensitivity* and *support*, if taken to extreme can result in self-neglect and being overly sensitive. Rhinos can see Koalas as too sensitive and not bold enough.

The Beaver Strengths: of *slower pace, attention to detail, need for structure and accuracy*, if taken to extreme can lead to perfectionism, obsession over details and painfully slow decision-making, especially frustrating for Rhinos. Monkeys get bored listening to Beavers like me who over-explain details. Beavers need to *land it* or lose people!

It is useful to be aware of our *blind spots* with regard to strengths and weaknesses and to be able to modify our behaviour to suit the situation or the person we are needing to relate to. We always have a choice and with practise and a more mindful intention we can improve our ability to relate to people who may have the opposite tendencies to us. We are after all, a combination of all types which are simply a set of naturally preferred behaviours that can be regulated, at least temporarily.

Of course people are more complex than this simplified theory suggests. If we take into account other needs outlined by Abraham Maslow, such as our needs for survival, love and belonging, esteem, self-actualisation and service to others; these needs can also influence the way our temperament is expressed from day to day. Our introversion or extroversion is also influenced by our fears, our self-esteem and by the dynamics of the relationships we navigate during a typical day. So the stereotypes we have in our heads about different personalities do not always play out the way we expect in reality.

The key thing to be aware of is that everyone is different and we all have strengths. Teams that have a lot of diversity will tend to perform better because of their combined strengths. At the same time differences can cause conflict if we are not prepared to be flexible or to seek to understand each other and embrace our different communication styles. Leaders need to be acutely aware of this.

Quiet Influence
A couple of years ago our son Jesse who is a less talkative and wiser soul than me, introduced us to a book called *Quiet: The Power of Introverts in a World that Can't Stop Talking*, written by Susan Cain. Jesse found the book very affirming of his quieter temperament. He used to think that his quiet way was not socially acceptable and that people felt uncomfortable with his lack of talkativeness. Now he sees it as a strength and knows that he can choose to talk when it matters and remain quiet when he feels it is appropriate. While he understands that stretching his comfort zone and expanding his social repertoire is important for some situations it is not a mandated requirement for leadership or for personal happiness.

When most of us think of great leaders, we typically think of people with confidence and charisma, strong voices and bold extroverted personalities. Contrary to the popular myth, introverts actually make good leaders. They just *lead with quiet confidence,* says Jennifer Kahnweiler author of *The Introverted Leader: Building On Your Quiet Strength*. If we set aside our misconceptions about introverts, we can see that they have many attributes that are helpful when it comes to leadership.

I came across the following list of introvert strengths, while preparing for a presentation I was giving at a leadership breakfast recently:

STRENGTHS OF INTROVERTED LEADERS

1. **The one who speaks does not always know and the one who knows does not always speak.**
   Introverted leaders are generally considered to be better listeners.
   A study conducted by Francesca Gino, Associate Professor at Harvard Business School, reveals that *quiet bosses with proactive teams can be highly successful, because introverted leaders carefully listen to what their followers have to say. Extroverted leaders are more comfortable with passive subordinates who go along with being told what to do.*

2. **Quiet reflection time is a valuable investment.**
   While everyone is busy talking in a meeting, introverts are busy processing their thoughts. Clinical psychologist Laurie Helgoe suggests that introverts have an *internal power—the power to birth fully formed ideas, insights, and solutions. An introvert who sits back in a meeting, taking in the arguments, reflecting on the big picture, may appear to be not contributing, until they find a solution that others missed.* Solitude provides opportunities for self-reflection, thinking, observing, planning or imagining, not to mention reading, researching and writing.

3. **Humble leaders serve and realise the potential of others.**
   A 2006 Servant Leadership study, conducted by Jane T. Waddell of Regent University, suggests that *some of the virtues of servant leadership that we all admire are also attributes that are more likely to be found in those who have a preference for introversion.* One of these virtues is humility. Servant leadership is characterised by a primary desire to be of service to others and to empower followers to grow.

4. **Introverts can be a calm and steady influence.**
   Introverts are generally cool, calm and collected. As Beth Buelow, author of *Insight: Reflections on the Gifts of Being an Introvert*, notes: *My energy tends to be a calming presence, which means I don't take up too much space in a room or conversation. I have a greater influence when I am intentional and deliberate in my speech and presence.*

A summary of book reviews and articles published on PsychCentral.com.[75]

THE FOUR P'S PROCESS—INTROVERT STRENGTHS

Preparation
Introverts don't wing it, they spend time thinking through their goals and preparing for questions, which gives them an edge.

Presentation
When introverts are with you, they're *with* you; because they prepare extensively, they are able to go with the flow, and stay in the present moment.

Push Themselves
Introverts challenge themselves. They are conscious about stretching and growing.

Practice
Introverts capitalise on their quiet time. They use it to reflect on their work and restore their energy. Introverts who are good leaders, adapt and adjust to their environment, but they don't change the essence of who they are.

The Introverted Leader: Building On Your Quiet Strength—J Kahnweiler, 2013

Jesse blending into the forest in Tasmania's Wilderness

Individuals who live in alignment with their strengths and passions are more fulfilled than those who are restrained by the pots we put them in.

> *True leaders don't create followers, they create more leaders.*
> Tom Peters—*In Search of Excellence*

The Ripple Effect

The final part of the *True North Leadership Compass*, that I'd like to touch on briefly, is the outer circumference which is made up of a number of smaller circles which represent the people we influence in our lives. Just as the circles around the centre spiral represent the people, places and events that influence our leadership journey, so too do *we* become one of those circles for the people we influence. John Maxwell, author of *Developing the Leaders Around You*, says *organisations rise and fall based on the quality of their long-range leadership, and that is why companies must develop new generations of leaders.*

This ripple effect is something that can happen by accident or by intention. A leader's influence continues to ripple out in ever widening circles to the edges of their *circle of influence* and beyond. This represents the legacy of the leader who develops other leaders around them and continues to pass the baton. I trust that the *TNL Compass* has provided you with an easy-reference to the key attributes of influential leaders whose legacy, like Mark Auricht's, will continue to have an impact for generations to come.

> *Our leadership journey is a never-ending learning spiral,*
> *influenced by the people and experiences we surround ourselves with.*
> *Our intentions, actions and words create a ripple effect that leaves a legacy,*
> *the impact of which we will never be fully aware, but which will continue on*
> *without us to the distant shores of the future.*

Ripples—Lombok, 2011

Completion

It has been a long journey around the *TNL Compass* where we've looked at the *Spiral Journey*; the *Circles of Influence* that impact our *True North* and our direction in life; and the *4 Directions* of *True North, Resilience, Responsibility* and *Influence*. We have also looked at the importance of *Life Balance* as it affects the *Energy Exchange* within and around us, and we've touched on the importance of understanding the *Ripple Effect* of our influence into the future. I trust that this compass will be of value to you personally or to those you may be leading, coaching, nurturing or guiding. May you come back to it again and again, as a reference and a reflection tool.

Before we complete our travels together, we have one more territory to visit. The last part of this book deals with *fulfilling your significance,* and is a final salute to Mark. It is intended to complete the circle we have travelled together and to leave you with some inspiration. As we leave this part of the book, let us reflect on a few questions relating to influence.

Reflection Questions

1. How often do you have *ARC breaks* in your relationships and what do you usually do to fix them?

2. What are your strengths and areas for improvement? with regard to the following:
   - Ability to build trust and rapport
   - Communication
   - Constructive conflict
   - Knowing self and others
   - Giving and receiving feedback

3. What would you say is your predominant temperament and which of the personality *Animals* do you find most challenging to deal with?

4. What legacy would you like to be remembered for?

Have a rest now and prepare for the last leg of our journey...
We head off at first light...

PART VI

Apogee
Reaching the Summit of Your Potential

Wayne—Salkantay Trail, Peru 2013

Apogee

One of the first programs I worked on with Mark after leaving my full-time job in the Year 2000, was in the Snowy Mountains for a company called Lou Miranda Estate. In 2001 they released a wine called *Apogee* which was dedicated to Mark's memory. On the label it describes the wine thus: *Apogee is the pinnacle of high country and exemplifies our ultimate expression of winemaking.* The dictionary definition of *Apogee* is:- *the peak or summit, the pinnacle, the culmination, highest point in the development of something.*

Mark climbed as high as he could climb and he lived to the highest level he aspired to in the time that he was here. His life's work exemplified the ultimate expression of who he was and what he had to share with the world. He showed us how to follow the path of one's happiness, living as authentically as he could, with humility, courage and generosity. He helped others to find their truth and develop their potential.

The final part of this tribute to Mark explores this idea of living out the ultimate expression of one's life, no matter how short-lived it may be. My hope is that you will be able to discover *your Apogee* and allow it to guide you across the horizons of *your* life, leading you along the path of *your* happiness to the highest point of *your* potential.

I tried alcohol, drugs and co-dependent relationships.
I studied faiths and philosophy in search of the answers to happiness.
Again and again I fell into fear and depression...
but every now and again joy would break through the ice, like the sun bursting through the clouds on a stormy day. It was during one of these elusive 'break through' moments that I seized the day and;
after finding the path of my happiness; walked back into my life.

Chapter 35   Renovating the Inner Landscape

 It is now late November 2015 and I am finding time to write again. It is a beautiful spring morning, the sun filtering through the leaves of the Chinese Elm in our backyard; highlighting the rocks and under story of our little sanctuary. My office looks out into this little piece of paradise with its Japanese bridge inviting me into the tea house, a small waterfall that looks like it could be hundreds of feet high relative to its surroundings in the garden. The Japanese perfected the art of replicating nature's scale in miniature so that one feels that they are immersed in a beautiful wilderness of grand scale, even though they may be sitting in a small courtyard.

This idea of the microcosm being a reflection of the macrocosm underpins ancient philosophies and is demonstrated in art, literature, music, theatre, landscaped gardens and travel experiences. Each of these take us on a journey to other places in our minds and hearts. We may be transported to another time and place, sometimes familiar, sometimes never before experienced.

Whenever I travel somewhere different I have a tendency to come home and construct something in the backyard that is a reflection of where I have been. Our backyard is an interesting place. One year I built a fire pit which when we sit around it, feels like I am out camping in the bush. Fire has been used ceremonially by many cultures for millennia and signifies transformation. Even just sitting around a fire can have a transforming effect on the mind and soul. I've lost count of the number of campfires I've sat around with people, sharing stories, singing, laughing, contemplating.

For the last five years or so, I have been visualising a deck overlooking the garden, almost like a lookout or boardwalk where you can take in the vista or lie in the shade or sun, stretch, do yoga or tai chi in the morning. For me I almost want to do a little bow of the head as if entering a *Dojo* with its timber floor, space for movement, sacred feeling. When I was doing *Karate* regularly I would often have the tendency to bow as I entered a sacred space. In Japan this is a sign of respect for the place you are entering or the person you are meeting or about to do battle with. I like the feeling of sacred spaces and places, they have an immediate effect on my heart.

So this deck that I have been visualising has finally come to fruition. At this time of year when most of our travel adventures are completed and our corporate work is slowing down, I usually start to write again, get into the garden or start some construction project. This year it was the long-awaited deck. In hindsight it was not as easy as I had imagined. Building a deck is a great metaphor for personal development. It's interesting how when we clean out the closet or garage, spring clean the house, change our garden or renovate our house, it often reflects what is going on for us on the inside. It's as if we change our outer landscape to be congruent with our inner landscape. Often we need to start first by excavating deep enough to uncover things we need to clear or repair or workaround. We need to dig sometimes deeper than we thought to allow space for the new scaffolding we need to build to support our new structure. Our foundations need to be strong and well put together to have longevity. The levels have to be right in order to deal with the rain and storms when they eventually come. There are always unexpected little problems that we didn't know were going to present themselves, problems we have to work around in order to keep the project on track. Good planning is required to get where we want to go. The decking itself is the easy part, the icing on the cake so to speak. Then there is the lighting and the finishing touches. All of this takes time and patience and an investment of energy and concentration. While building the deck it was at times difficult not to become despondent, frustrated and impatient. In the end though it, was all worth it.

The deck will make an amazing difference to the space in our garden and how people feel when they enter it. In much the same way, when we work on developing ourselves and become the best person we can be, this makes an amazing difference to our quality of life and the quality of our relationships with people who share our space.

~~~~~~~~~~~~~~~~~~

Stephen Covey in his book *7 Habits of Highly Effective People* suggests that before we can influence others in our external environment, we must take a journey inward and begin the process of self-mastery. In this chapter I'd like to take a look at how we can begin this process of internal change, first for ourselves and also to help others.

The Myth of Self-Mastery
Self-mastery, like life balance is perhaps an *ideal* to strive for but a reality that requires constant adjustment to the ever-changing matrix of life. When we see a person standing on one leg in a perfect yoga pose or karate stance, it looks like they are perfectly still but the truth is that the muscles of the leg and core are constantly making micro-adjustments to maintain the balance. Quantum physics reveals to us too, that solid matter is not what it seems, in reality it is not a static state; put simply, a solid is made up of constantly vibrating sub-atomic particles and more space than we would imagine. So perhaps self-mastery is either a myth or a moment to moment proposition?

I'm not sure that it's possible to achieve ultimate self-mastery and have it stay done (unless of course you are an enlightened guru who has achieved *Nirvana*). My belief is that mastery is an ongoing process of practice, learning, self-discipline and growth. I have a habit of referring to martial arts to illustrate ideas because it is a good metaphor for so many aspects of life. I now understand after many years of dedication to the Dojo, that one only becomes a *Black Belt* for a moment, and must then continue to practise daily to maintain and improve their skills and most importantly their attitude and approach to life. Mastery is fleeting if we don't continue to dedicate ourselves to it. I've found this to be true in anything that I've gotten good at and especially in trying to master my mind, body and emotions. These I am still working on!

Living Consciously
If we want to achieve at least some level of self-mastery, we must first begin to master the ability to live more consciously. I believe for the most part that I am able to do this but a lot of the time I get caught napping and realise that even though I am awake, thinking, making decisions, holding conversations and doing tasks; I am not always aware enough 'in the moment,' to manage my thoughts, emotions and behaviours as much as I would like to. They sometimes run on autopilot as I wade through the day, in much the same way as one does when they arrive somewhere and can't remember how they got there. Habits can be helpful or a hindrance. Although they provide comfortable patterns that support us to live with less

effort, by their very nature they are automatic and often reactive. Living more proactively sometimes requires us to question these habitual ways of living. It's not so much a matter of judging our habits as good or bad but a matter of whether they are useful, constructive and working for us.

One of my mentors would often reserve judgement about my attitudes and behaviour. He would only ask the question: *How is it working for you?* The first step in behaviour change therefore, is to become conscious of the need for change and to then be prepared to move out of our comfort zone. This requires us to be motivated. The word 'motiv-ated' literally means to be in a state of motion, so we need to take action if we want things to change.

The Dog and the Nail

I once visited a friend who lived in a log cabin in the hills. It was the middle of winter so we sat by the warmth of his open fire place, drinking hot chocolate while we chatted. I noticed over time, that his big old Labrador dog, who was lying by the open fire half asleep, would open one eye and whimper every now and then. I became curious as to why he was doing this and asked my friend whether there was something wrong with his dog.

I found his explanation quite amusing. He chuckled and said "Oh he's probably complaining about the fact that there are a few nail heads sticking up through the floor boards and irritating his backside. It happens every time he lies next to the fire." The dog turned his head and looked at me with one eye brow raised and whimpered again for effect. "Why doesn't he just get up and move if it's so uncomfortable?" I asked. "Probably because it's not quite uncomfortable enough to motivate him to move; besides he likes the warmth of the fire, he's a bit lazy and he likes to complain," my friend replied.

How true this is for many of us who live in a comfort zone, putting up with things we are uncomfortable with but not quite willing to change. It's a challenge to change habits which have been formed over a lifetime or to trade things that we find temporarily satisfying for ways of being that require more apparent effort but can reap broad-reaching rewards. Unfortunately too many people don't 'move off the nails' until they are faced with a crisis, whether it be a major illness, marriage breakdown, financial crisis or burn out. It is often then, too late to turn the tide and prevent it from reaching the shore of regret.

We either step forward into growth or back into safety.
Abraham Maslow

Understanding our ingrained patterns of behaviour and how to change them, often requires us to look a little deeper, to explore the thoughts, emotions and beliefs that support these habits. As we have said before, our *Inner Landscape* needs to change before our outer world can.

Beneath the Iceberg

In *The Wellness Workbook*, Dr John Travis suggests that illness represents only the tip of the iceberg. It is, in his words, *a surface indication of underlying human needs.* Much of the western medical system is involved with chipping away at the surface symptoms. If we don't take responsibility to look deeper and to challenge the habits that run our lives, symptoms will continue to 'bob up' out of the water, no matter how much we 'bandaid' them. These symptoms may be physical, mental, emotional, behavioural or a crisis of the spirit. Our surface state of health therefore mirrors the health of our underlying habits.

The results we get in life, whether they be in the area of our health, relationships, work or community; are generally highly dependent on our behaviour, which is inexplicably linked to our mind, heart and soul. This can be represented by the metaphor of the iceberg where the results observed at the surface are supported by what lies beneath.

THE ICEBERG MODEL

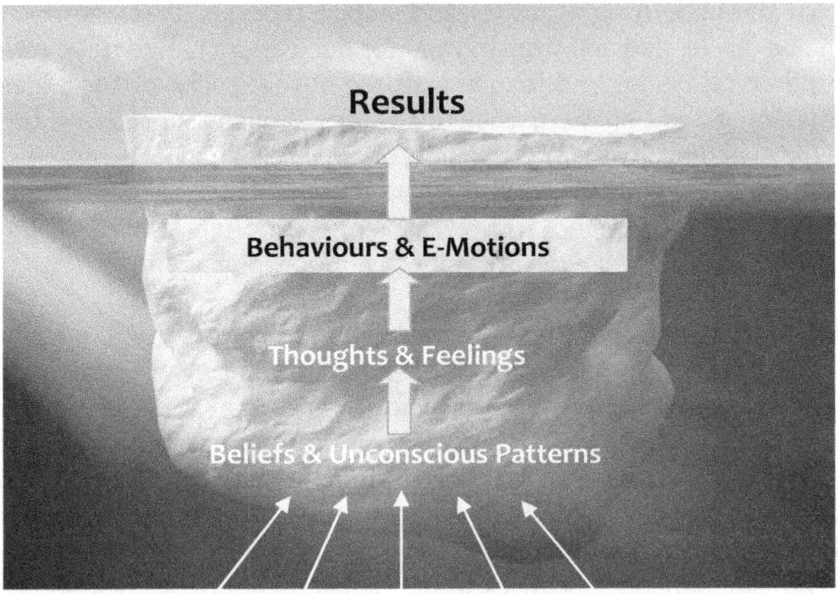

Our experiences influence the INNER RULES that we live by

Figure 35.1 The Iceberg Model—Adapted from Travis and Ryan, 1988

Challenging the Inner Rules

Understanding what lies beneath the surface is the first step in mastering oneself or at the very least, mastering the process of changing behaviour so that we can move in the direction of wellness, improved performance and an optimum quality of life. An experienced coach or mentor can be very helpful in assisting us to navigate our inner landscape, helping us to drill down beneath the surface to discover the inter-relationships between our thoughts, feelings, behaviour and personal effectiveness. Our thoughts and feelings may be somewhat part of our natural make-up but tend to be programmed by our life experiences which influence the 'inner rules' that we live by. These 'inner rules' are the subconscious beliefs and conditioned response patterns that run our thoughts, feelings and behaviours—all of which extend from the bottom of this metaphorical iceberg to the surface of our life. We can try to make cosmetic changes to the tip of the iceberg but unless we start with re-programming the lower realms of the iceberg, any changes we make at the surface will be difficult to sustain for very long. If you chop off the top of an iceberg, the submerged part of the iceberg will pop up to the surface. This is a force of nature not to be denied and is as true for our health, as it is for our performance at work, or in our relationships at home.

As Mark referred to in his article on *Adventure Based Experiential Learning (Chapter 14)*, one of the principles of sustainable behaviour change is that the underlying attitudes and 'action theories' that one holds onto, must be challenged and transformed for behaviour change to be more than temporary. If beliefs and fears are stored at the *feeling* or *heart* level, then our learning and behaviour change strategies must connect with the heart. We may become aware of our beliefs on an intellectual level but not be able to transform them unless we have a literal *change of heart.* This is why learning that involves adventure, challenge, emotion and a shifting of the heart, is much more powerful as a behaviour change agent.

From Story to Possibility

Our *Inner Rules* are significantly influenced by what I like to call our 'Story.' The story we tell ourselves about who we are, what we're capable of, how much we are worth, what our strengths and weaknesses are, etc. The *Turning Points* activity that Mark facilitated on my first *ABEL* program helped me to have an objective look at my *Story* and how it influenced my self-talk, self-image, efficacy and esteem. I can now see where I've attached meaning to events and made subconscious decisions about how to respond to them. These may have helped me to cope in the past but are no longer valid or constructive in my life now.

Bringing our *Inner Rules* into the light, re-framing our stories and embracing new possibilities can be a powerful and life-changing process. Adventure experiences are a powerful agent for change in this area because they confront us on a more challenging level than a book or a chat or a reflection exercise can do alone. Challenging experiences, even when they are controlled within the context of a safely facilitated adventure learning program, can often shift our perception of ourselves in the world, in much the same way as a life crisis can. I've seen evidence of this many times during *youth at risk* wilderness therapy programs where young people arrive full of anger, low self-esteem and anti-social behaviour, then, after eight days in the wilderness, they leave with a stronger self-image, more calm in their heart, improved social skills and a more positive expectation for their future. This change occurs first in their *inner landscape* as they re-frame the story they've told themselves for so many years. Then eventually, it manifests in the way they end up living their lives and perceiving the world and their place in it. Often for those who have felt disempowered or have perhaps lived a life of false bravado, these kinds of powerful learning experiences change the way they see themselves, enough to find a new sense of genuine self-confidence that was not there previously.

Reframing My Story

I remember when I was a teenager, I had long hair and a slumped posture, I wasn't particularly confident and found it difficult to make eye contact with people I didn't know and to break into a conversation with strangers.

As I mentioned previously, I was the skinny kid protected by my big brother but bullied when he wasn't there. I was passive rather than assertive, and consequently I didn't voice my needs or challenge things I wasn't happy with. I avoided conflict in exchange for peace, but internally I didn't have 'peace of mind.' It took years to change my self-image, to stand taller, to look people in the eye and assert my truth. I eventually learned to confront challenging situations and to discover a more authentic public confidence.

This slow transition was uncomfortable, sometimes even painful, but little by little I changed the 'story' that I had written in the past. Much of this I attribute to leaving home and having to fend for myself but also to the influence of Gabrielle as she encouraged me to let go of the old beliefs that no longer served me. By the time I met Mark when I was in my mid-twenties, I was a much stronger man than my former self but still had some attachments to my 'Story.' When I did the 'Turning Points' activity with Mark, it helped me to put my story into perspective and to begin to re-write it.

I still reflect on my evolution, even today, because it has been such a significant change for me. I now reflect on parts of my upbringing with humour. I remember a time when I was sixteen and had just got my driver's licence. I asked my father if I could borrow the car. He had just retired from the army and didn't care much for my long hair, so he pitched a proposition: "If you get ya hair cut, you can borrow the car any time you like," he barked in his best 'Sergeant-Major' voice. I quickly replied with what I thought was a winning rebuttal: "Hang on Dad, Jesus had long hair!" and quicker still, he matched my challenge with a check-mate move worthy of a chess master, "Yeh... and he walked everywhere he went too." 'Game over,' I conceded in my head with a smile.

Wayne, 1979

**In each of us there is a potential waiting patiently for us to discover it.
Sometimes even when it reaches out to us, saying "here I am"
we miss the chance to bring it out of the shadows into the light.
Stretching to the outer reaches of our perceived boundaries
is where we free ourselves from the shadows of our past.**

Chapter 36 Fulfilling Your Significance

When I was a kid I had no idea what my purpose was supposed to be or whether my life would have any significance but I had a feeling that there was something that I was here to do and I just had to keep looking until I found it. It wasn't until I met Mark that I started to get a feel for the direction I should take and I was perhaps fifty years of age by the time that I had a good sense of my purpose. After doing the *Vision Quest*, I was much clearer and I feel that since then I have started to 'fulfil my significance,' as I follow my inner compass, speak my truth and find fulfilment in sharing my gifts to help others. Fortunately I have a life partner who is very much on the same track as me and our mantra for our children is perhaps best summed up in the following words.

> *Be aware of that which has meaning for you and let it be your guide.*
> *Live your truth with kindness and authenticity and let it be a compass for your journey through life.*

It doesn't really matter what we think our purpose is, it doesn't have to be grandiose or unique necessarily. It could be to be a gardener, a handyman or cleaner. These may not seem like 'world famous' vocations but each of them can contribute significantly to the *quality of life* of others. If you have ever heard of the *Pike Place Fish Market* in Seattle, you'll know that they don't just sell fish, they *Make People's Day* while they are doing it. A purpose doesn't even have to be a vocation, it could just be the gift of listening to another, sharing art or being a loving parent, brother or sister. As long as we follow *the path of our happiness,* follow our *bliss*, and live from the heart, this will usually lead us to where we need to be.

> *Life is not only a process of discovery, but also a process of creation.*
> *Seek therefore, to not only discover your hidden treasures*
> *but also to create who you want to be, by becoming the author of your life.*
>
> Adapted from a quote by Neale Donald Walsch
> *Conversations with God*

Allowing Time for Reflection

Sometimes being aware of what has meaning for us, knowing our truth and being clear about the person we want to be and the purpose of our *being*, is not always easy to discover without reflecting on our life experience and contemplating these questions of purpose. Some people know from an early age and some, like me, have to wait patiently or be nudged by significant people or events.

In the *True North Leadership (TNL) Model* I have combined the *Turning Points* process introduced to me by Mark, together with a process called the *Circle of Stones* which I became familiar with on my Vision Quest. Gabrielle and I use this process during our *TNL Expeditions* and as a component of our *Free Spirit Wellbeing Retreats* (see Services p 415).

Participants are given time alone to reflect and write or draw in a personal journal. Journals are often used for daily reflections, especially in relation to one's journey through life. I would highly recommend taking time out on a regular basis for personal reflection. This can be done at the beginning of a New Year or significant milestone in your life, such as a birthday. In Figure 36.1 (page 375) I offer some questions for reflection.

Personal reflection can also become part of your daily routine. I can't say that I do it every day, but on the days that I make time to ride my bike to the beach for a walk or a swim, I sit for 10 minutes and breathe mindfully. On other days I enjoy some quiet time in our garden teahouse with a morning cup of tea; later in the day I take a few minutes before bed, to lie on the floor, stretch, relax, and breathe calmly while I review the day. There are two simple questions I ask myself: *What did I learn today and did I give my best to myself and others?*

Kaiezn Do – The Way of Continuous Improvement

I remember back to Tae Kwon Do classes with Master Choon Bong Lee in the early eighties. At the end of each class, while sitting in a kneeling position, back up straight and eyes closed, breathing silently and relaxed, Master Lee would ask us to reflect on our day... "Have you given your best today, for yourself and for others, what have you learnt about yourself and where can you improve?" It only took a few minutes to do this as our heart rate and breathing slowed back to a relaxed rhythm after a hard workout, but I always relished this short meditation and it was a good way of reminding us that Master Lee's classes were more about improving our inner self. His influence in my life, while not always obvious to those around me, has always stayed with me and is especially noticeable when I take the time to become still and tune into my calm spirit.

Solo Time

If you would like to experience this feeling and become more aware of your strengths, your truth, things to be grateful for, and your unfolding purpose; I would suggest going somewhere quiet and still, where you can be by yourself without interruption or distractions. You may wish to do this somewhere in nature, whether it is a garden, at the beach or somewhere more remote in the wilderness for a longer solo time. It doesn't really matter, as long as it is a place the helps you to feel relaxed, safe and contemplative.

Before pondering the questions I wish to reflect on, I find it helpful to take some time to settle my body, mind and emotions by sitting or lying in a relaxed position, closing my eyes, relaxing my breath, scanning my body for tension and breathing it away. Then imagining my mind is like a picture screen, I allow thoughts to drift past the screen without getting attached to them. I observe them calmly as if in slow motion and I focus on calming my emotions like ripples expanding out on a pond, losing their power. When I am calm and still, then I am ready to reflect on the questions.

QUESTIONS OF SIGNIFICANCE

1. **Have I given my best?** (to myself and others)

2. **What have I done well?** (strengths, achievements, giving to others)

3. **How can I improve?** (start, stop, less, more—things to learn)

4. **What have I learnt about myself?** (strengths, areas for development)

5. **Key influences/turning points in my life?** (people, places and events)

6. **What is my truth?** (beliefs, values, guiding principles, passions, gifts, mission in life, things that matter most to me)

7. **Do I live in alignment with my truth?** (if not, how can I do this more?)

8. **Where to from here?** (purpose/vision, unfinished business, action)

Figure 36.1 Questions of Significance—W Enright, 2014

These treasures remain unknown unless we search for them.
Sometimes we half-hear them in the stillness of a forest,
at sunset or between two waves in an ocean of noise.

Living Outside the Flags

Answering significant questions such as those in Figure 36.1 can help to point us in the direction of achieving our potential and yet to get there we may need to be like the caged bird that sees the open door and takes the risk to fly free. The biggest obstacle to *fulfilling our significance* is fear. Fear makes letting go difficult and can steal our freedom to be all that we can be.

> *I'm not living between the flags.*[76]
> *I'm not mucking around in the shore breaks.*
> *I'm out beyond the breakers, rising and falling with the swell*
> *It's quiet and peaceful... I feel a big wave coming and I'm ready for it.*
> James Murray—*My Life in the Sea of Cars*

Some years before I first walked the *Larapinta Trail* in the Red Centre of Australia, I took a road trip with my family from Adelaide to Darwin and back. It was while coming back though Mataranka Springs that I found a gem of a book called *My Life in the Sea of Cars: A Letter from Arnhem Land*, written by James Murray. He recounts nine days spent in the remote and beautiful landscapes of the Northern Territory. Sharing his journey of exploration and self-discovery, he passionately argues for a new way of living. As you can tell from the quote above, Murray is a non-conformist. His words struck a chord with me. I think that this quote from his book speaks to the heart of living with imagination and taking on life and all that it has in store for us, regardless of our fear. It's about having the courage to take risks, to adventure into the unknown, following your own inner compass to destinations beyond the horizon that require imagination and sometimes bravery.

> *A man with imagination has wings.*

I'm not sure who wrote this quote about imagination but it sounds like a good slogan for an energy drink advertisement. I was given a framed picture of a man hang gliding into the sunset, with this quote at the bottom and a plaque attached in appreciation for ten years service at *Corporate Health Group*. I'm guessing that I might have had a reputation for challenging boundaries and staring out of the window, day dreaming. In the end I gave up being an employee, not because I didn't like my job or the people I worked with, but perhaps because, like James Murray, I didn't want to *live between the flags* and I wanted to discover what was out there, if I went for it. I wanted to be free like a bird in the sky. What I didn't know though, was that with freedom comes responsibility.

Chapter 36—Fulfilling Your Significance

Taking the Leap of Faith

Fear is the dragon that guards the entrance to our greatest gifts.
Adapted from Ancient Mythology – WB Enright

My first experience of the more adventurous side of *Adventure Based Experiential Learning*, where I was challenged to face some fear and get out of my comfort zone, was in 1990 at the *Venture Corporate Recharge—High Ropes Course*. Although I had been learning incidentally from adventure experiences since I was a small child, exploring trackless bush land, camping in caves, climbing trees, descending cliffs and more; this was my first taste of a purposefully facilitated adventure activity where I would consciously reflect on the experience and what it had to teach me.

It was in actual fact, classed as 'soft adventure,' in that it was an artificially created adventure environment with most of the *actual risk* engineered out of it, and reasonably predictable variables compared with a 'real adventure' in the wilderness where nature calls the shots. Despite this, for those experiencing it for the first time with little knowledge of the engineering involved in building it and the high grade safety equipment used to keep participants safe, it had a high level of *perceived risk*. I knew intellectually that the equipment itself was over-engineered for its use, i.e. cables, pulleys, belay devices and climbing ropes were strong enough to hold the weight of a car, let alone a person. The only real risk was that my safety relied on fellow team members learning and correctly applying belay skills that should keep me safe while I performed a high wire balancing act fifty feet up in the canopy of a pine forest. This was the unpredictable variable, somewhat minimised by *hawk eye* instructors who supervised each belay team supporting the climber high up in the trees.

The finale of the high ropes course is the *Leap of Faith* where one climbs up to a platform attached to the top of a tree. I remember the first time as if it were now.

I feel the pounding of my heart in my chest as I straightened up on the platform, hugging the tree trunk before turning nervously to survey the scenery before me. I feel as if I am standing on a small rocky outcrop, suspended at the edge of a sheer cliff face. The platform is just over a foot wide and reaches out about two feet away from the tree into thin air. Fifty feet below me I can see eyes looking up at me with anticipation. In this moment I feel exceedingly exposed.

I am back there now, feeling a touch of vertigo and fear as I look across at a trapeze bar suspended on a cable between two trees. The bar is at eye level but seems an eternity away from me as I peer across the chasm.

The eyes below urge me to jump out and grab the bar which is about six feet out of reach. I know that when I jump… if I jump… I will fall like a stone towards the earth, but I must fly across the chasm and grab the bar before I fall out of its reach. I ask myself, "Is this possible, can I bring myself to do this, against the better judgement of my internal guidance system which is cautioning me against this 'suicidal' choice?"

I have to override these rationale thoughts and the fear rising in my throat. My legs start to shake with an overload of adrenalin. The battle between fear and courage has begun. Fear screams into my body "Turn back you fool, you will fall to your death." Courage counters, "Come to the edge and fly with me, I will keep you safe." Fear grabs me by the shoulder and warns me not to go against its better judgement.

Then with a rush of blood through my chest, courage pulls me into the void… and I fly… In a split second but what seems like an eternity, I cross the space between the platform and bar, falling as I touch the bar with my finger tips. Another rush of adrenalin courses through my limbs as gravity pulls me down toward the hard ground that awaits a crushing collision with my fragile body.

Then as if pulled up by a parachute opening, I come to the end of my belay rope which stretches as it prevents me from falling any further. I'm left swinging in mid-air, laughing and hollering at my miraculous escape from a painful meeting with the forest floor. "F… F… Far out, that was close."

Despite not holding on to the trapeze bar, I had taken a leap of faith and won. The bar was the bait, but the leap was what required me to win the battle with my fear, to en-courage myself to take a risk and in so doing, experience a sense of freedom in that split second that will last an eternity.

On the other side of fear is freedom.
Jamie Clarke—Canadian Adventurer

Sounds simple enough but when you're there on the edge it's difficult… it really does feel like life and death. The mind, body and emotions tap into something primal that one has to short-circuit in order to take control back and jump into the void. Whilst in reality this is only a *subjective risk*, a very real sense of fear comes up. When we feel the fear and jump into it, this leap into thin air has a visceral impact in our body—the memory of having taken a leap of faith and survived, stays in the cellular memory so to speak.

This, in my experience of taking many people through similar situations, whether it be on the *High Ropes Course* or completing the arduous challenge of crossing the Kokoda Track, is such a powerful metaphor that it stays with people and permeates their life into the future. There comes a time when we have to let go of the comfort and habits of what we know and feel safe with, a time when we take a risk and jump into the abyss not knowing whether we will succeed or fail. Beyond the fear, a leap of faith often brings with it great rewards for those who are prepared to let go of their attachment to safety. Since 1990 I have encouraged many others to take the leap, and on most occasions I will ask the first jumper for the day to read a poem before they jump into the void.

The Risk of Freedom

To express your dreams and ideals to the world is to risk ridicule.

To reach out to others is to risk commitment.

To love is to risk being vulnerable.

To hope is to risk disappointment.

To expose your emotions is to risk revealing your true heart.

To attempt success is to risk failure.

To live in full colour is to risk dying in the darkness.

Despite all of this, we must take risks, for the greatest tragedy in life is to risk nothing at all.

Those who avoid risk may minimise pain and penalty, but they simply cannot learn, feel, change, grow, love or live to their full potential.

Restrained by their fear, they become a prisoner, forfeiting their freedom.

Only those who are willing to risk can be truly free.

    Adapted by WB Enright, from a poem by William Arthur Ward (1921-1994)

The Leap of Faith—Woodhouse, 1990

If per chance someday you have the opportunity to visit the *Auricht Adventure Tower*, adjacent to the *High Ropes Course* at *Woodhouse Activity Centre* in the Adelaide Hills, you will find a small humble plaque put there on the west corner of the tower in memory of Mark Auricht who had the vision to build one of the best adventure facilities of its time in South Australia. You'll perhaps remember the quote on the plaque which inspired the title of this book.

When the Spirit of Adventure calls to our Heart, we must go.

Thousands of people have climbed the *Auricht Tower*, abseiled down its north face and taken the *Leap of Faith* from the pines within the forest, since Mark built these facilities over 25 years ago. Some came for fun, some to stretch their comfort zone, some had no inkling why, but for those who stood at the edge, fully present and aware of themselves in that moment of truth, they would often hear two voices battling for their attention:

Fear would say *Turn back, hold on to safety.*

Courage would say *Let go, be bold, jump into the void!*

Some allowed fear to hold them back but most took heart from the voice of courage and jumped through their fear to freedom. Forever after that moment, they knew that their limits were self-imposed. When the *Spirit of Adventure* calls to your heart, may you remember without reservation, that you too can choose to follow it rather than fear it. Freedom is waiting.

Chapter 37   The Journey Home

Our civilisation teaches us to take possession of things,
when it should rather initiate us in the art of letting go.
Marilyn Ferguson—*The Aquarian Conspiracy*

 This morning we attended a funeral for a young African boy who was our son Jesse's year ten school mate. The priest said: "In Africa, death only comes to the young. Old people just return home." I'd suggest that *returning home* is true for any person of any age if they have fulfilled their purpose, left a legacy or made an impact through the ripple effect of their life. After Mark died I questioned why his inspiring life had vanished too soon from this earth when he had so much more to give the world. The only answer I have found to be helpful is to be open to the possibility that we are spiritual beings with a divine purpose in life and when our purpose is fulfilled, some of us go home early.

We often refer to kind and generous people as angels. Some people define angels as *Messengers or Agents of God*. For me, I am agnostic about whether I'll ever see an angel with big wings flying through the air, but I do believe that some people are *Spiritual Messengers*, blessing us with their presence for however long they are in our lives. I think all of us can bless others as we go about our purpose and share our m*edicine* in the world. We just have to live 'on purpose' before we take the journey home, rather than waste *The Dash* between the dates of our physical birth and death.

The Catharina Sails On
I see him now, face to the wind, on the bow of the *Catharina*, as I stand watching her sails fade over the horizon. I feel a hand clutching mine and a voice saying, *They're gone… Gone where I wonder?*

Gone from our sight, that is all; they are just as magnificent as when we first saw them. The shrinking size and loss of sight is in us, not in them… At that moment I knew in my heart that there were others beyond the horizon watching them coming as they cheered with gladness, *Here they come!*

Adapted from a poem titled *What is Dying* by Bishop Brent (1862-1926)

I recall a version of this poem being read by Darren Williams at the *Auricht Adventure Tower* on the day of Mark's Memorial Service. It reminds me of how much of a blessing Mark's life was and still *is*, as his *Ship* sails on.

ANGELS

In the early hours of the morning when all is silent and still, the
first rays of the sun peep into my garden, reminding me of the Angels in my life.
As I think of them, tears come and love washes over me in silent waves,
gently caressing my heart and touching the core of my soul.

As a youth living in a hostile world, my big brother Angel watched over me.
Sooner or later he had to leave me to fend for myself,
pushing me out of the nest to test my self-reliance wings.

The sky was dark and scary for a while, I wanted to crash and burn.
But a gentle thermal lifted me from the darkness to see a bright blue sky.
I soared above the storm clouds and saw a beautiful vision,
a picture perfect world full of dreams and possibilities.

Along the way I fell in love with a fellow traveller,
She was like a freshly scented rose, full of laughter and love,
a singing voice that brings tears to your eyes,
a smile that captures everything that is beautiful and warm in this world,
a heart of unconditional love and giving, and as strong as a tree that bends
in the fiercest storm, a generous person of purpose.

Then I met another Angel along the road less travelled.
We had courageous dreams to change the world, to adventure together.
He encouraged others without fail, praised every risk,
celebrated every triumph, laughed with you, empowered you.
His soul was generous, caring, inspiring and loyal. I loved that about him.

This Angel fashioned his dreams into a life, inspiring others to follow their truth.
He shared a secret with me once:
"That girl with the beautiful smile, the one you're on the journey with;
she's an Angel you know!"

He helped me recognise the Angels around me and see the rainbows in every storm.
On days when the sky was clear blue, a warm breeze caressing our cheeks,
wild-flower scent intoxicating our minds, he would say "What a pearler of a day."

One day when his earthly purpose was fulfilled,
he became one with the snow and returned home.
The caterpillar had fulfilled its promise to the butterfly.

I miss his friendship and his 'you can do anything' whisper from the balcony.
He reminded me to be grateful for the Angels in my life.

Written by Wayne Enright in Memory of Mark Auricht, 2003

Chapter 37—The Journey Home

My Final Day of Writing—March 24, 2016

*It is now Maundy Thursday, the day before Easter.
I'm coming to the end of my writing now and I feel sad but joyous at the same time.*

I sit down to write but I feel compelled to take my time, to open the French doors that allow the outside world into my writing space. From here I can see, smell and feel the energy of the garden calling me. I sweep the deck that reaches out into the garden, like a Zen monk sweeps the temple floor, listening to the birds and soaking in the morning sun. I prune my bonsai tree and a few dead fronds of a fern nearby and then I make a cup of tea and sit by the fire pit listening to the waterfall as it cascades over ancient rocks into a pool under the Chinese Elm tree. I notice the Japanese maple leaves are turning red as Autumn is here now. The days are getting shorter and cooler. I notice the cool breeze as I stand on one of the large sandstone rocks that edge the dry river bed coming from the rock pool. I look up to the sky as it begins to cry with rain.

Tears well to the surface, as I suddenly remember that it is the 38th Anniversary of my brother Peter's death today. He would have been 57 years old. He died on the Thursday before Easter March 23, 1978. The actual date comes and goes now without much emotional charge but I always remember this Thursday before Easter. It was a time of mourning followed by a time of new beginning. I still feel my brother Peter's spirit like the tide feels the distant moon. I feel Mark's presence too, as he sits with me around the fire, comforting me. At times I've felt both of them with me, silently encouraging me as I have taken this writing journey. Though they are not with me now in my physical world, I give thanks for the continuing influence of my 'Brothers in Spirit.' I know as I come to the end of this fifteen year project, that it will also be a time of new beginning.

Brighton South Australia, 2016

Epilogue

The Circle of Stones
It is October 2012 and I find myself alone in a remote area of the Northern Flinders Ranges, sitting in the red dust under a blanket of black between the stars. I feel the dark chill of the night and sense the nocturnal beings watching me as I sit on the earth surrounded by a circle of stones… listening to the silence of the present while reflecting on the tracks of my past.

I have been alone now for 3 days and nights, just me, the wilderness and the raw reality of my body, mind and emotions. No music, books, people, time piece or food to distract me from myself. Only 12 litres of water and a tarp for shelter from the rain and sun, should I choose to escape their intensity.

This is the last night of 'Solo Time' on my Vision Quest. During this time I have been reflecting on my past and my future, keeping a journal, going for short walks in the cool of the morning and climbing some rocky outcrops at dusk to survey the view.

> **Solitude is the place of purification.**
> Martin Buber

On this last night before returning to a distant base camp to share my story, I am completing a ritual called the 'Circle of Stones,' where one chooses a number of rocks or stones to represent people, places or events in one's life that have had an impact or perhaps represent some unfinished business. This is an opportunity to see the path we have taken, the choices we have made, the people, places and events that have shaped us and to express gratitude, forgiveness or acknowledgement.

I have placed the rocks in a circle about 4 metres in diameter. At sunset I closed the circle with one last rock, making a commitment to stay within the circle until sunrise. I sacrifice sleep for quiet reflection while I take a nostalgic and sometimes confronting journey around my 'Circle of Stones.' During this night I have contemplated quietly, laughed loudly and cried with joy, rage, grief and gratitude. I have written letters to the living and the dead and among all of these things I have found peace and clarity.

For the last time this night I look at the moon as it creeps along its arc through the night sky towards the horizon in the west. Not wearing a watch, I imagine the increments of time that have passed from sunset through to now. Relying on my intuition more than my logic, I know that it's about half an hour before first light. As if on cue, I hear in the distance, the melodic song of a solitary bird searching for the dawn... that beautiful whistle one hears just before sunrise.

Words inspired by a song from my youth come to me...

**The songbirds sing to honour the dawn,
forever the sun will shine on your shore,
saying I love you, like never before.**
Inspired by Christine McVie

I only have a little while to go now before the sun comes up, then I will remove the most eastern stone from the circle and through this gate I will walk towards the sunrise of my future, taking with me the treasure from my past.

Vision Quest, 2012

Among the foundation stones of our life we find gems of immeasurable value. I asked myself that night: *Shall I leave them hidden in the dust of my past or reveal the beautiful light reflected through them for all to see?* I thank Mark for being one of the gems among my foundation stones, a friend whose legacy was too valuable to become lost treasure.

I encourage you, as Mark encouraged me, to explore your *Foundation Stones*, search within to find your treasure and share it generously.

THANK YOU

I thank you for hanging in there with me through the ups and downs of this journey. I thank you for your patience as I have taken detours along the way, and I thank you for taking the time to hear this story of how Mark's life and legacy influenced mine. I hope that you have found some treasures here and that you will be inspired to explore the frontiers of your inner and outer worlds to the edges of your potential and in so doing, fulfil *your* significance.

Gabrielle and Wayne with Peruvian Guide 'Effy'—Salkantay Trail Peru, 2013

Perhaps it's no coincidence that you've read this book.
Perhaps there is something about these adventures
that you and I came here to remember.
I choose to believe that Mark is sitting on a mountain
somewhere out in another dimension smiling on us.
Meeting again after many lifetimes
is certain for those who are sacred friends.
Inspired by Richard Bach
Author of *Illusions: The Adventures of a Reluctant Messiah*

If you found some treasure among these pages and would like to send me a message with your thoughts, I would appreciate your feedback. My contact details are on the last page at the back of this book.

I honour your spirit of adventure and wish you well on your journey

Appendices and References

APPENDIX A: Animal Instincts Profile

Please rate yourself on a **scale from 1 - 10**
to indicate how you see yourself most of the time, in most situations.

1 = not like me   5 = sometimes like me   10= very much like me

1. Nurturing
2. Supportive
3. Sensitive
4. Encouraging
5. More passive
6. Rather listen than talk
7. Take time to make decisions.
8. Peacemaker
9. Empathic
10. Quietly spoken
11. Analytical
12. Organised
13. Good planner
14. Attention to detail
15. 'Perfectionist' streak
16. Tidy
17. Like structure
18. Like to think things through.
19. Decisions based on logic rather than emotion.
20. Prefer to work alone
21. Fun loving
22. Talkative
23. Animated
24. Highly spirited
25. Like attention
26. Energetic
27. Not into details
28. Focused on people before tasks.
29. Spontaneous
30. Don't like to be too structured.
31. Driven
32. Like to get things done
33. Demanding of myself and others.
34. Focused
35. Strong willed
36. Like to be in charge, rather than follow.
37. More fast paced
38. Like to be right
39. Like to do things my own way.
40. Have a competitive streak

Add totals for each group of questions below

ANIMAL	RELATED QUESTIONS	TOTAL SCORES FOR EACH
Koala	1 – 10	
Beaver	11 - 20	
Monkey	21 – 30	
Rhino	31 - 40	

Please note: This self-assessment and the *AI Table of Tendencies*[74] (p356), was developed by W Enright based on practical experience, and the work of Galenus, Marston and Hunt.

APPENDIX B: Emotional Competency Profile

Rate yourself on a scale from 1 – 10 for each of the three aspects related to the five competencies. A rating toward the lower end of the scale means that you see yourself as deficient in this competency and need to significantly improve. A rating toward the upper end of the scale means that you see this trait as a strength of yours and would say that you feel quite competent in this area.

Self-Awareness
- Ability to tune into your feelings and use them to guide decisions [ ]
- A realistic assessment of your strengths and development needs [ ]
- A well-grounded sense of self-confidence [ ]

Self-Regulation
- Ability to handle your emotions under pressure [ ]
- Being able to handle ambiguity and uncertainty [ ]
- Recover well from emotional distress and disappointment [ ]

Motivation
- A strong drive to do what it takes to succeed [ ]
- Ability to persevere in the face of setbacks and frustration [ ]
- Optimistic attitude even when there are challenges to overcome [ ]

Empathy
- Having sensitivity for the feelings of others [ ]
- Ability to build rapport with a broad diversity of people [ ]
- Willingness to seek understanding & see things from another's perspective [ ]

Social Skills
- Skill in managing relationships and building connections [ ]
- Being able to negotiate and settle disputes or disagreements [ ]
- Ability to influence and lead others [ ]

Notes: Adding scores for the three aspects within each competency will give you a combined score for that competency. Competencies with a combined score higher than 20 are considered a strength. A total score of 100+, after aggregating all five competencies, indicates a 'healthy' level of Emotional Competency. Emotional competencies tend to increase as one matures with life experience. Emotional development can be accelerated by taking risks and expanding one's comfort zone.

Please note: This self-assessment was developed by W Enright based on the 5 Competencies outlined by Daniel Goleman in his book: *Working with Emotional Intelligence* (see References).

APPENDIX C: Developing Self-managed Teams
SMT Conference Notes, 2001 Dr Grant Donovan PhD

The Transition from Autocratic Leadership to Self-managed Teams

Command & Control Culture
Being watched & being told
Performance Appraisals
Attendance is #1 / Comfort Zone
Dependence – Helplessness & Blame

*SMTs don't survive in C & C Cultures

Behaviour follows culture & mindset

Self-managed Teams
Learning by experience
Influenced by culture
Agreements
Teamwork
Business literacy
Healthy Competition

The transition to Self-Managed Teams requires a number of ingredients
- Culture change & mindset shift.
- Agreements & KPIs to provide guiding parameters for behaviour and performance.
- Skill development & business literacy.
- Transfer of authority & responsibility.
- Inter-dependence & collaborative environment.
- Trust, validation, recognition & encouragement.
- Learning environment – take responsible risks, learn from mistakes, give and receive feedback.
- Coaches, mentors and guides (not managers).
- CEO support – change must be lead from the top.

Steps to Making the Transition
1. Get everyone working on a **project in a non-business critical** area.
   *The project can be work based or an Experiential Learning activity designed to reflect the work context.

2. Identify **Key Performance Indicators** (KPI's).

3. **List barriers to performance** (what stops us from achieving KPIs).

4. **Identify solutions to barriers and set boundaries** within which 'anything else goes'.

5. **Apply solutions and boundaries to the non-business-critical project.**

6. **Review progress and reflect on learning** – how can we implement it in our organisation?

7. Set **parameters within which people can self-manage in the workplace.**
8. Lay the **foundations for business literacy** (understanding every aspect of the business, including financial impact of all actions & consequences).
9. **Once people have competent business literacy, they can start managing business critical tasks.**
10. What are all the **functions required**? "We don't need managers but **all the functions need to be managed."**
11. **Transfer**—from *Managed* to *Shared* (semi-autonomous) to *Self-managed* over time. Don't transfer authority for *Business-criticals* until they have the required skills. ***Transfer skills before authority.***
12. **Develop leadership and team skills through individual learning plans.**

Individual Learning Plans
1. Technical skills.
2. Business literacy.
3. People skills – leadership, team membership and customer service (internal and external).
4. Career visioning (personal vision & values – alignment with business V&V).
5. Life balance skills – self-improvement plan.
6. Wealth creation literacy & plan.
7. Profit share incentives.

Often managers will recruit people they like and throw them into a team. The best way to improve team performance is to develop the culture, structures, systems and strategies that make teamwork come naturally.

Steps to Creating a High Performance Team Environment
1. A CEO who will drive the development of teamwork and self-management.
2. Choosing an effective structure.
3. Building effective support systems.
4. Developing business literacy.
5. Transferring skills before transferring authority.
6. Partnering and persistence.
7. Team leadership skills.

*Recruit first for attitude, then train and support staff with good systems.

Choosing a Structure

The structure chosen will depend on the functions involved in your business.

Generally, there will need to be a 'Strategic Team' that is more involved in strategy than task and a 'Resource Team' that supports all other teams with material resources, information, admin support, marketing & support systems.

The structure will then have a number of 'Self-Managed Teams' (SMTs) that take full responsibility for the functioning and outcomes of their teams. This structure looks similar to that of a typical organisation but the difference is that the teams are all autonomously self-managed by the team members and yet they are interdependent. 'Managers' are replaced by 'Coaches' and team members take total responsibility and authority for how they run their team and how they achieve their KPIs within the context of their agreements.

It is important to have systems in place to support effective functioning of SMTs

Macro Systems
- Business Development
- Financial Management
- Communication
- Learning
- Incentive
- Performance Management

Micro Systems / Processes
- Meetings
- Decision Making
- Conflict Resolution
- Recruitment
- Measurement
- Authority Transfer
- Function Rotation

Systems help people to follow processes that are mutually agreed to and that are proven to be effective. This also helps with transferring authority over time from being fully managed to shared management, and then finally to self-management.

Systems help people to develop the skills so that they can take full responsibility and authority within the context of agreed boundaries.

If you would like assistance to implement this process in your organisation,
Please contact wayne@freespirittruenorth.com.au

NOTES

1. **Operation Flinders Foundation** is a South Australian based charitable organisation that runs a world leading wilderness adventure program for young people at risk. The *Operation Flinders Project* was set up by Pamela Murray-White in 1991. http://www.operationflinders.org.au/ ...p11.
2. **True North Expeditions**, established in 2012 by Will Dobud offers a research supported adventure therapy program, together with other individual services for children, adolescents and parents. http://www.truenorthexpeditions.com.au/ ...p11.
3. **New World Chaos**, a term I use to express the chaotic nature of the world we are now experiencing as rapid changes in technology and global inter-dependence, disrupt the sense of order that we once felt when the pace of change was more manageable and communities were less impacted by global events ...p17.
4. **True North** is the direction along the Earth's surface towards the geographic North Pole. In this book I use *True North* as a metaphor to capture one's guiding vision and values, (Principles which provide true, constant and reliable guidance)...p17.
5. **Auricht House** was opened by *Centacare* in 2005 as a respite centre for children with intellectual disabilities. The House was named after Mark Auricht whose 2001 Everest Expedition was raising funds for the new respite service...p28.
6. Sogyal Rinpoche, *The Tibetan Book of Living & Dying* (United Kingdom: Rider, Random House Group, 2008),40 ...p34.
7. *On the other side of fear is freedom*, a quote by Jamie Clarke (Canadian mountaineer) http://jamieclarke.com/speaker/...p34.
8. **First Ascent of an Eight-Thousander** (Mt Annapurna - Herzog and Lachenal - June 3, 1950) https://en.wikipedia.org/wiki/Eight-thousander ...p35.
9. **Venture Corporate Recharge logo** depicts a person behind a desk, running to the top of a mountain to stand on top of its summit with hands outstretched to the sky...p40.
10. **Everest and Himalaya information** – https://en.wikipedia.org/wiki/Himalayas and https://en.wikipedia.org/wiki/Mount_Everest ...p51.
11. **The Cost of Climbing Everest**, Kraig Beckler, freelance adventure writer - Dec 8th, 2016. http://www.grindtv.com/travel/much-cost-climb-mt-everest ...p51.
12. **The Himalayan Data Base** (HDB), launched in 1993 but started many years earlier by Elizabeth Hawley. The HDB is the most historically comprehensive compilation of Himalayan expedition information available and thus the source of my statistics ...p52.
13. **Khumbu Icefall**, located at the head of the *Kumbu Glacier* at an altitude of 5485m on the Nepali slopes of Everest's south side, not far above Base Camp. The icefall is considered one of the most dangerous stages of the *South Col Route* to Everest's summit, due to the constantly moving and unpredictable ice. Most Sherpa deaths happen in this area due to the number of times they must pass through this zone as they ferry loads and set up ropes and ladders for expedition members ...p57.
14. **Everest North Face Map**, adapted to show *SA Everest Expedition North Col Route*, with Camp locations. Source of the original map: http://www.chinatrekking.com/maps/tibet-maps/mt-everest-map ...p57.
15. **Duncan Chessell Interview** conducted by Julian Burton in 2004, shared with permission from Duncan Chessell ...p72.
16. **Himex Sherpas who laid Mark Auricht to rest** – Duncan Chessell organised with Russell Brice, owner of *Himalayan Experience* (Himex), to use his Sherpas at SA Camp2 (7900m) to lay Mark's body to rest. Thank you to Russell for his assistance ...p78.

17. ***Above 8000m is not a place where people can afford morality,*** Japanese climber, Eisuke Shigekawa said after being asked to assist a trio of Indian climbers who were in need of rescue above 8000m on Everest's North-West Ridge. Source: Nick Heil, *Dark Summit – the true story of Everest's most controversial season* (Australia: Penguin Group, 2008),4. Heil explores the climbers and companies, the events and expeditions involved in the 2006 Everest season, to find answers to the question: *What is one man's responsibility to another in such extreme conditions?* ...p80.

18. **ATSIC** – *Aboriginal and Torres Strait Islander Commission* ...p85.

19. **Youth at Risk**. Helping young homeless people was a cause close to Mark's heart. It is with this in mind that I wish to continue his legacy by donating the proceeds of this book to programs assisting young people to achieve their potential ...p95.

20. ***Into the Wild*** is a 2007 American biographical drama survival film written and directed by Sean Penn. It is an adaptation of Jon Krakauer's 1996 non-fiction book of the same name, based on the travels of Christopher McCandless across North America and his life spent in the Alaskan wilderness in the early 1990s. Jon Krakauer also wrote *Into Thin Air*, his personal account of the 1996 Everest disaster ...p99.

21. **The Hero's Journey**, introduced by Joseph Campbell in *The Hero with a Thousand Faces* (USA: New World Library 1949), where he describes the narrative of a reluctant hero who ventures to extra-ordinary worlds, encountering obstacles and danger before winning a decisive victory, then returning to share boons with his fellow man. This *monomyth* has become a popular narrative in movies such as *Star Wars* and *Lord of the Rings* ...p104.

22. ***Medicine***, a term used to refer to one's unique gifts, passions or purpose, expressed in the world to serve others. My *Medicine* is to share stories and to take people on journeys of the spirit, whether it be through experiential learning, adventure travel or storytelling. I discovered and became clear about my *Medicine*, while on a Vision Quest with Rob Young in the Flinders Ranges of South Australia's outback. For more information go to: http://www.desertvisionquest.com/ ...p108.

23. ***Illusions:**The Adventures of a Reluctant Messiah (*USA: Dell Publishing Co, 1977*),* was written by Richard Bach, author of *Jonathon Livingston Seagull* and *Bridge Across Forever*. Bach is one of my favourite authors and his quotes are sprinkled throughout this book. He has since written *Illusions II*, after a near-death experience ...p113.

24. **Psychosynthesis**, developed by Italian psychiatrist Roberto Assagioli, a contemporary of Jung and Maslow, is an approach to psychotherapy which encompasses not only healing, but also supporting the growth of human potential into what Maslow termed self-actualisation and further still, into the spiritual or transpersonal dimensions of human experience. The methodologies of *Psychosynthesis* draw on both western and eastern philosophy, providing experiential processes which integrate the personality with the spiritual self and collective consciousness. See the reference section (Assagioli, Ferrucci and Young Brown). https://en.wikipedia.org/wiki/Psychosynthesis ...p113.

25. ***Experience and Education***, was written in 1938 by John Dewey, a pre-eminent educational theorist of the 20th century. Dewey continually emphasised experience, experiment, purposeful learning, freedom, and other concepts of progressive education. Dewey argues that the quality of an educational experience is critical and stresses the importance of the social and interactive processes of learning. Kurt Lewin and David Kolb later developed models to explain the process of experiential learning. For more information go to: https://rapidbi.com/learning-styles-kolb-lewin/ ...p115.

26. **The Treasure Challenge** is a metaphor for groups who need to work together to solve problems and overcome obstacles while pursuing a common goal. This activity can involve any number of activities and modes of transport including bushwalking, cycling, kayaking, dragon boats, motor vehicles, sailing etc. It can be designed to include adventure activities and orienteering depending on the level of challenge required and can be conducted over a few hours or days, with small or large groups. ...p118 (For more information, please see Services p415)

27. **The Illness/Wellness Continuum**, Travis & Ryan *Wellness Workbook 2nd edition* (California USA: Ten Speed Press, 1988),16 ...p119.

28. **Biofeedback**, includes the feedback we get from our biological responses to anything that impacts our mind, body, emotions and spirit. This could include lifestyle factors such as food, drink, smoking, drugs, exercise, rest, recreation, as well as the impact of our relationships, self-talk, stressors and life experiences. Thus we receive feedback from our mind, body, emotions and spirit that can help us to maintain equilibrium if we listen and adjust accordingly. Illness therefore serves to keep things in balance. If we ignore biofeedback, it can lead to a worsening state of health, but if we choose to learn from it, it can be a blessing that results in high level wellness ...p121.

29. **Wellness Advocates Network** was a workplace wellness program established in the early 90s that aimed to teach a critical mass of employees to become advocates for wellness in their workplaces. I was trained by Grant Donovan to be an advocate trainer. The concept was based on the principle of leverage and peer influence within workplaces, rather than over-relying on external wellness consultants ...p122.

30. **Self-Managed Work Teams Conference** was established in Australia by Grant Donovan as an evolution of the *National Wellness Conference* that he had been convening throughout the 1990s. Many of us who worked in the field of workplace wellness promotion, discovered that the health and performance of employees and the organisations they worked for, had more to do with workplace culture, relationships, purpose and leadership, than it did lifestyle. Health behaviours are often a reflection of mindset, self-worth and self-responsibility which is influenced by culture ...p122.

31. **Humourous Presenters** such as Dr John Tickell, Patricia Cameron-Hill, Don Ardell and Dr Patch Adams influenced me to add humour to my repertoire as a presenter and also to include it as a topic in our wellness retreats, life balance and stress management courses, as well as our leadership and team programs. Using humour is not about telling jokes; although sharing humourous anecdotes is fun, it is more about our attitude to life, particularly with regard to maintaining perspective in adversity ...p122.

32. *Silver Bullets: A Guide to Initiative Problems, Adventure Games and Trust Activities*, written by Karl Rohnke (Kendall Hunt, 1984). Karl has been an important 'player' in the field of experiential/adventure education, working with *Outward Bound*, before becoming one of the founders of the *Project Adventure* program and *The High 5 Adventure Learning Center* in Vermont ...p125.

33. **Accelerated Learning Principles**, include providing learning experiences which engage the head, heart and hands; that involve the learner creating their own meaning from experience; interacting with others; being challenged; having fun; and include engaging in learning that is relevant in the context of their life and work ...p126.
Dave Meier, Director of *The Centre for Accelerated Learning*, provides a good summary: http://www.ehs.ucr.edu/ehsacademy/presentations/trainingacceleratedlearning.doc.

34. **Venture Corporate Recharge Values** – Sourced from a handout circulated at a VCR professional development day, where we discussed how the values were demonstrated in daily behaviour with internal and external customers and in one's personal life ...p127.

Notes

35. **Ongoing Research into Learning and Teaching.** Russell Ackoff, *Turning Learning Right Side Up (*New Jersey: Prentice Hall, 2008) For more information about research into the effectiveness of education and how our minds learn, see the following websites:
http://www.oecd.org/site/educeri21st/40554299.pdf
http://news.mit.edu/2016/accelerate-learning-research-online-education-0202
http://www.ehs.ucr.edu/ehsacademy/presentations/trainingacceleratedlearning.doc.
http://www.abc.net.au/tv/programs/redesign-my-brain-with-todd-sampson/ ...p128

36. **Accelerated Learning Programs** ...p128
http://www.moneyandyouaustralia.com.au/
http://www.landmarkworldwide.com/the-landmark-forum
http://www.ca.thepacificinstitute.com/solutions/story/investment-in-excellence
https://www.peakpd.com/workshops_dr_stephanie_burns.html
http://content.becomeasuperlearner.com/tedxtalk/
*Gabrielle and I have designed a training program for those who would like to learn more about the art of facilitation and coaching, based on these programs (see Services p 415).

37. **Bloom's Learning Domains** include cognitive, affective, and psychomotor learning, sometimes referred to as *knowing(head), feeling(heart)* and *doing(hands)*. Blooms Taxonomy has been further researched by Harrow and Simpson to develop a more wholistic approach to education ...p129
http://www.maxvibrant.com/bloom-s-taxonomy/bloom-s-taxonomy

38. **The Law of Precession,** states that for every action we take, there is an *unintended side effect*, like the *ripple effect* of dropping a stone into water or honey bees that spend their lives flying from flower to flower to collect nectar to make honey (the side effect being that they pollinate flowers). Buckminster Fuller's theory of *Precession* states that our job is not to make money, but rather to add value to the lives others, the side effect of which is making money. He believed that it was unbalanced to work only for money, and only for yourself and your family. It is also unbalanced to NOT work for yourself and your family, while only working for others ...p130.

39. **Keogh Consulting** specialises in organisational development and transformation strategies, particularly for large scale projects. Keogh combines accelerated learning principles with their long term experience working with major international companies. http://www.keoghconsulting.com.au ...p130

40. **Connection before Correction**, a phrase with application for parents, teachers and leaders in any context, who need to give corrective feedback. This quote was shared with me by Will Dobud, Adventure Therapist and owner of *True North Expeditions* ...p133.
http://blog.positivediscipline.com/2007/11/connection-before-correction.html

41. **Metaphysical**, refers to a level of reality beyond scientific observation. In the context of *healing philosophy*, it helps me to understand the possible cause of my speech disability, beyond being a neurological disorder without a known cause. Although I don't understand it and can't prove it scientifically, my belief is that there is an inter-relationship between my mind, body, emotions and spirit. It feels intuitively true for me that my speech was affected by grief and not speaking my truth ...p136.

42. **You Will Have a Voice if You Find the Courage to Speak**, an article by Elizabeth Powell, an *Assistant Professor of Business Administration* at Darden School of Business (University of Virginia). Powell is co-author of *Women in Business: The Changing Face of Leadership* and is currently working on a new book, *Present: Leadership as Wise Practice* ...p136.
To read the full article (published in the *Washington Post* 2013) go to:
https://ideas.darden.virginia.edu/2014/01/a-leaders-speech-in-the-face-of-fear/

43. **A Research Summary for Corporate Adventure Training – Simon Priest**
    Link to Priest research: http://files.eric.ed.gov/fulltext/ED413127.pdf
    Despite a lack of evidence-based research since Priest's work in the 90s, the anecdotal evidence is overwhelming supportive of *ABEL* as a highly effective training tool. See the following link for the latest research on *Outdoor Learning* (focused mostly on schools). http://www.outdoorlearning.org/Portals/0/IOL%20Documents/Blagrave%20Report/outdoor-learning-giving-evidence-revised-final-report-nov-2015-etc-v21.pdf ...p139.
44. **Kurt Lewin's 12 Principles of Experiential Learning** was obtained from Johnson and Johnson, *Joining Together: Group Theory and Group Skills* (USA: Pearson 1987) ...p140.
45. **Kolb Learning Cycle.** David Kolb proposes a *4-stage Experiential Learning Cycle* (1974). https://www.simplypsychology.org/learning-kolb.html ...pp140 and 142.
46. **Simon Priest, *Effective Leadership in Adventure Programming*** (USA: Human Kinetics 2005) ...p147.
47. **The Business Game**, is a business simulation activity which requires participants to work collaboratively to achieve a profitable outcome, while navigating the usual challenges of business within a typical organisational structure. The game is designed in conjunction with the client, to replicate the team dynamics within their business and to highlight the key challenges they face ...p149. (see Services p415)
48. **Secrets of Experiential Learning,** a summary based on the research of corporate psychologists Relly Nadler & John Luckner, 2004. Permission from R Nadler ...p150.
49. **Johari Window**, conceived by Joseph Luft and Harrington Ingham in 1955, indicates four areas of awareness 1. *Open Arena* - That which is known to self and others, 2. *Public Facade* – known to self and not others (unless we choose to disclose it), 3. *Blind Spots* – known to others but not self (unless we receive feedback), and 4. The area of *Potential* which is unknown to self and others until we discover it ...p153.
50. **Coffee Conversations:** *The Simple Leadership Secret of High Performance Workplaces*, Donovan and Garland (Australia: Create Space Independent Publishing Platform, 2012) Eliminate complex and demotivating control systems, start treating people well, engage them in the decisions that affect their work and empower them to self-manage their own outcomes. http://coffeeconversations.com.au/ ...p155.
51. **Systems Theory** can be applied in physics, biology, sociology, organisational psychology, economics and politics. Systems are dynamic self-organising entities made up of interdependent parts which influence each other and self-correct via feedback loops that help to maintain balance so that they can survive and grow e.g. a biological ecosystem or the global economy. I recommend reading Capra & Luisi, *The Systems View of Life: A Unifying Vision* (USA, Cambridge University Press, 2014) ...p171.
52. **Systems Thinking in a business context,** was also pioneered by **Russell Ackoff**, an organisational theorist and consultant who developed the field of operations research, systems thinking, and management science: http://ackoffcenter.blogs.com/. **Peter Senge** wrote *The Fifth Discipline Fieldbook,* (New York: Currency Books, 1994), and more recently, *The Necessary Revolution: How Individuals and Organizations are Working Together to Create a Sustainable World,* (New York: Random House, 2008) ...p172.
53. **Gaia Theory** is the concept that Planet Earth is a living, breathing, self-regulating organism, that is constantly adapting. Developed in the late 1960's by British Scientist, James Lovelock, the theory posits that the organic and inorganic components of Planet Earth have evolved together as a single living, self-regulating system. It suggests that this living system has automatically controlled global temperature, atmospheric content, ocean salinity, and other factors, that maintain its own habitability. For more information, go to: http://www.gaiatheory.org/ ...p173.

54. ***Digital Disruption in the Professional Services Industry*** – an article by Peter Enright, (*Evolve Magazine* Parsons Brinckerhoff's client e-magazine: Feb 26, 2016) ...p173. https://issuu.com/wspparsonsbrinckerhoff/docs/evolve_firstquarter2016pdf/13
55. **The Butterfly Effect** is the concept that small causes can have large effects. Initially, it was used with weather prediction but later the term became a metaphor used in and out of science, see this link for more: https://en.wikipedia.org/wiki/Butterfly_effect ...p174.
56. ***Ingredients for the Best Workplaces on Earth***, Goffee and Jones (HBR May, 2013) https://hbr.org/2013/05/creating-the-best-workplace-on-earth ...p181.
57. **Netflix Slideshare** – *A Reference Guide to our Freedom and Responsibility Culture.* Netflix CEO Reed Hastings. https://www.slideshare.net/reed2001/culture-2009 ...p206.
58. **Yves Morieux TED talk** https://www.ted.com/talks/yves_morieux_how_too_many_rules_at_work_keep_you_from_getting_things_done
59. **Grateful Leadership – Travis Kemp** article posted on Linked In, March 26, 2015. https://www.linkedin.com/pulse/grateful-leadership-dr-travis-kemp ...p222.
60. **Gender Bias in the Board Room** – from a *Harvard Business Review* interview with Sheryl Sandberg, author of *Lean In: Women, Work and the Will to Lead* (UK: WH Allen, 2013). HBR Interview: https://hbr.org/2013/03/sheryl-sandberg-the-hbr-interv ...p231.
61. ***The Daring Way*** Brene' Brown http://thedaringway.com/about/ ...p240.
62. **Yosi Ginsberg,** *Heart of The Amazon* (Australia: Pan Macmillan, 1999)...p241.
63. **Isurava Battlefield Memorial**, is located at the northern end of the Kokoda Track, about one day's walk from Kokoda in Papua New Guinea. *Isurava* was the site of the first major battle along the Kokoda Track in August 1942, where Australian Militia fought alongside Regular Army soldiers, to defend Australia against the Japanese in World War 2. At the memorial site there are four marble pillars with the words *Courage, Endurance, Mateship* and *Sacrifice*. This is a sacred place where we hold a dawn service every year ...p241.
64. **Kokoda Track or Trail?** Both terms are used on the memorial arches at either end of the track. Officially the name is *Kokoda Trail,* but most Aussies and World War 2 Diggers prefer to call it the *Kokoda Track.* See Bill James' *Field Guide to the Kokoda Track* (Australia: Kokoda Press – revised edition 2008),32 ...p242.
65. **Rites of Passage** are a celebration of the transition which occurs when an individual leaves one group to enter another. It involves a significant change of status in society. In cultural anthropology the term is the Anglicisation of *rite de passage*, a French term innovated by the ethnographer Arnold van Gennep in his work *Les rites de passage.*
66. **Rites of Passage Stages –** *Stage 1: Separation*, one withdraws from their current status and prepares to move to another. *Stage 2: Transition,* the period between states, often spent alone. *Stage 3: Re-integration*, where, having completed the rite and assumed their 'new' identity, one re-enters society with one's new status. This stage is characterised by ceremonies and external symbols such as a wedding ring, particular coloured clothing or belts (in the case of martial arts) ...p254.
67. **Nature Deficit Disorder** is a phrase coined by Richard Louv in his book *Last Child in the Woods,*(North Carolina: Algonquin Books of Chapel Hill, 2008) in which he raises the concern that human beings, especially children, are spending less time outdoors, resulting in a wide range of behavioural problems. Louv states that *nature-deficit disorder is not meant to be a medical diagnosis but rather to serve as a description of the human costs of alienation from the natural world.* See: *Children's Nature Deficit: What We Know and Don't Know,* (September 2009) Charles & Louv ...p257. www.childrenandnature.org/wp-content/uploads/2015/04/CNNEvidenceoftheDeficit.pdf

68. **True North Leadership Expedition** is a multi-day leadership development journey, involving predominantly *adventure-based experiential learning,* and is based around the *True North Leadership Compass*. (see Services p 415 for more details) ...p262
69. **The Four Directions**, the summary I provide is just one way of articulating the *Four Directions* and their significance to indigenous cultures. My summary comes from a number of ceremonies that I've been involved with, together with personal experience on my Vision Quest. https://firstnationspedagogy.com/fourdirections.html ...p268.
70. **Return on Character** was researched by Fred Kiel and Doug Lennick. Their findings were published at https://hbr.org/2015/04/measuring-the-return-on-character ...p271.
71. **Stages of Morality – Lawrence Kohlberg** ...p274
    https://en.wikipedia.org/wiki/Lawrence_Kohlberg%27s_stages_of_moral_development
72. **Acceptance & Commitment Therapy (ACT) Cognitive-Behavioural Therapy (CBT)** ...p315. ACT is an innovative form of CBT that has built upon both the strengths and the weaknesses of traditional cognitive-behavioural therapy but moved away from the CBT's emphasis on changing or correcting one's thoughts in order to alleviate suffering. Instead, ACT incorporates acceptance strategies and mindfulness techniques to detach from judging thoughts as good or bad and emphasises reframing our experience. https://contextualscience.org/comparing_act_and_cbt
73. **Debono's Six Thinking Hats - A Resource Guide for teachers** ...p319.
    http://sisdtx.sharpschool.com/common/pages/DisplayFile.aspx?itemId=17274974
74. **Animal Instincts – Table of Tendencies,** is a brief synthesis of the theories expressed by Galenus, Marston and Hunt; combined with our personal experience of working with individuals and groups over the last 25 years, using the DISC and TICK Profiles ...p356.
75. **Strengths of Introverted leaders**, is a summary of book reviews and articles.
    See these sites:
    Jennifer Kahnweiler: https://www.forbes.com/2009/11/30/introverts-good-leaders-leadership-managing-personality.html
    Susan Cain: www.quietrev.com
    https://psychcentral.com/blog/archives/2013/09/28/4-things-introverts-do-that-makes-them-effective-leaders/
    www.geteverwise.com/leadership/strengths-of-introverted-leaders-and-how-to-empower-them/ ...p359
76. **Between the Flags** – In James Murray's book *My Life in a Sea of Cars*, (Australia: Transit Lounge Publishing, 2011)**,** he declares: "I am not swimming between the flags..." which is a metaphor for the 'comfort or safety zone'. In Australia, our surf beach conditions are very dangerous, so it is safest to swim between the yellow and red flags (a stretch of beach considered safe for swimmers and patrolled by Life Guards). I have changed this reference to 'Living between the flags', so as not to be mistaken for suggesting that people should disregard this important beach safety message. *Living outside the flags*, on the other hand, is a powerful metaphor for living beyond the safety of the comfort zone and embracing responsible risk-taking in life. ...p376
    *Always swim between the flags on surf beaches!

FIGURES

Part I

1.1	Makalu Camps—Mark Auricht, 1995	36
3.1	Mark's Successful Summits—Mark Auricht, 1998	55
3.2	SA Everest Expedition Climbing Route—SA Expedition Diaries, 2001	57

Part II

11.1	The Illness/Wellness Continuum—Adapted from John Travis, 1988	119
11.2	Task / People Model—Evolved from Mark Auricht, 1990	123
12.1	Venture Corporate Recharge—Core Values, 1996	127
13.1	The Spiral Journey—W&G Enright ©2015	138
14.1	Principles of Experiential Learning—Kurt Lewin, 1987	141
14.2	The Experiential Learning Cycle—Adapted from Kolb & Lewin, 1987	142
14.3	Key Ingredients for ABEL Program Success—Mark Auricht, 1996	144
14.4	The Training Bermuda Triangle—Don Ardell, 1991	146
14.5	Effectiveness of *ABEL* Corporate Training—Simon Priest, 1996	147
14.6	Secrets of Experiential Learning—Luckner & Nadler, 2004	150
15.1	Awareness Window, from *Johari Window*—Luft & Ingham, 1955	153
15.2	Essentials for *ABEL* Facilitators—Auricht & Enright, 2001	159
16.1	Foundations of Healthy Teams—W&G Enright ©2005	164
16.2	Team Foundations Defined—W&G Enright ©2005	165

Part III

19.1	High Performance Organisations—SMWT Conference, 1993	180
19.2	Ingredients for the Best Workplaces—Goffee & Jones: HBR May, 2013	181
20.1	Comparison of Leadership Paradigms—Donovan & Enright, 2001	190
20.2	The Journey to Self-Management—Adapted from G Donovan, 2001	191
21.1	The Self-Management Trilogy—W Enright © 2015	198
21.2	Operation Flinders Team Roles—W Enright, 2009	202
21.3	Qualities of an Ideal Team Member—Hastings: *Netflix* Slideshare, 2001	207
22.1	Developing Team Agreements—W&G Enright © 2004	210
23.1	Adapted Maslow's Hierarchy—*The Theory of Human Motivation*, 1943	217

Part IV

26.1	True North Leadership Compass—W&G Enright © 2014	236

Part V

30.1	TNL Compass Headings—W&G Enright ©2014	266
30.2	Honouring the 4 Directions—from Vision Quest W Enright, 2012	268
30.3	The 4 Directions of the TNL Compass—W&G Enright © 2014	270
31.1	Moral Intelligence Competencies— Kiel & Lennick, 2008	272
31.2	Guiding Principles—W&G Enright	273
31.3	Stages of Moral Development—L Kohlberg, 1958	274
31.4	Considerations for Strategic Planning—W&G Enright © 2010	287

Part V Figures Continued...

31.5	Strategic Planning Map—W Enright © 2004	288
31.6	Tips for Personal Prioritising—W Enright © 2005	290
31.7	Priority Map—W Enright © 2005	292
32.1	Stress Response Symptoms—Herbert Benson, 1975	306
32.2	The Balance Zone—W Enright © 2005	307
33.1	The Responsibility Model—W Enright © 1991	313
33.2	Mindful Responsibility—W&G Enright © 2014	315
33.3	De Bono's Six Thinking Hats—Edward de Bono, 1999	319
33.4	The Life Balance Profile—W&G Enright ©2005	325
34.1	Traditional American Indian Leadership—Navajo Courts, 1997	329
34.2	Understanding Triangle (Adapted *ARC Triangle*)—Hubbard, 1950	336
34.3	Lines of Responsibility—Adapted from Mark Auricht, 2000	340
34.4	Six Steps to Constructive Conflict—W&G Enright © 2005	345
34.5	Tips for Effective Delegation—Gabrielle Enright © 2015	351
34.6	The Role of Feedback in Performance Improvement—W Enright © 2005	352
34.7	Animal Instincts Model—W&G Enright © 2005	355
34.8	Animal Instincts Table of Tendencies—W&G Enright © 2005	356

Part VI

35.1	The Iceberg Model—Adapted from Travis & Ryan, 1988	369
36.1	Questions of Significance—W Enright, 2014	375

REFERENCES

AURICHT FAMILY
Auricht Family *From Persecution to Freedom – A History and Family Tree of Christian Auricht*, Australia: Self-published by Auricht Family.
Auricht, C (2011) *Medicine Beyond Kokoda*, Self-published in South Australia.

EVEREST
Boukreev & Weston DeWalt (1999) *The Climb: Tragic Ambitions on Everest*, New York: St Martin's Press.
Groom, M (1997) *Sheer Will- The Inspiring Life and Climbs of Michael Groom*, Australia: Random House Australia.
Heil, N (2008) *Dark Summit: The True Story of Everest's Most Controversial Season*, Australia: Penguin Group.
Krakauer, J (1998) *Into Thin Air*, New York: Anchor Books.
Maiden, P (2006) *Anzac Day on Mt Everest*, Queensland University.
Weathers, B (2005) *Left for Dead: My Journey Home from Everest*, USA: Sphere.

KOKODA
Enright, W (2010) *Kokoda: A Journey of the Spirit*, NSW: Momento.
James, Bill (2008) *Field Guide to the Kokoda Track*, Australia: Kokoda Press.

LEADERSHIP AND TEAMWORK
Blanchard, K (2001) *The Heart of a Leader*, Surrey: Eagle.
Bennis & Goldsmith (2010) *Learning to Lead: A Workbook on Becoming a leader*, New York: Basic Books.
Bertrand & Robinson (1985) *Born to Win*, Australia: Bantam Books.
Buelow, B (2012) *Insight: Reflections on the Gifts of Being an Introvert*, Kindle.
Cain, S (2012) *Quiet*, London: Penguin Books.
Cairnes, M (1998) *Approaching the Corporate Heart*, Sydney: Simon & Schuster.
Carnegie, D (1937) *How to Win Friends and Influence People*, New York: Simon & Schuster.
Collins, J (2001) *Good to Great*, New York: HarperCollins.
Covey, SR (1990) *The 7 Habits of Highly Effective People*, New York: Fireside.
Covey, SR (1991) *Principle Centred Leadership*, New York: Summit Books.
Donovan & Garland (2012) *Coffee Conversations: The Simple Leadership Secret of High Performance Workplaces*, Australia: Create Space.
Drucker, P (2007) *The Practice of Management*, New York: Harper.
George, Bill (2007) *True North: Discover Your Authentic Leadership*, San Francisco: Jossy Bass.
Johnson, D & Johnson, F (1987) *Joining Together: Group Theory and Group Skills*, USA: Pearson.
Kahnweiler, J (2013) *The Introverted Leader: Building on Your Quiet Strength*, San Francisco: Berrett-Koehler.
Kemp, T (2015) *Grateful Leadership*, LinkedIn March 26, 2015.
https://www.linkedin.com/pulse/grateful-leadership-dr-travis-kemp

Lynch & Kordis (1990) *Strategy of the Dolphin*, London: Arrow Books.
Maxwell, J (1995) *Developing the Leaders Around You*, Nashville: Thomas Nelson.
Patterson, Grenny, McMillan, Switzler (2005) *Crucial Conversations*, USA: Strand.
Powell, E (2007) *Women in Business: The Changing Face of Leadership*, USA: Praeger Publishing.
Sandberg, S (2013) *Lean In: Women, Work and the Will to Lead*, UK: WH Allen.
Senge, P with Kleiner, Roberts, Ross & Smith (1994) *The Fifth Discipline Fieldbook: Strategies and Tools for Building a Learning Organization*, New York: Currency Books.
Senge, P (2008) *The Necessary Revolution: How Individuals and Organizations are Working Together to Create a Sustainable World*, New York: Random House.
Wiseman & McKeown (2010) *The Multiplier: How the Best Leaders Make Everyone Smarter*, New York: Harper Collins.

LEARNING
Ackoff, R (2008) *Turning Learning Right Side Up*, New Jersey: Prentice Hall.
Dewey, J (1938) *Experience and Education*, USA: Touchstone.
Priest, S (2005) *Effective Leadership in Adventure Programming*, USA: Human Kinetics.
Rohnke, K (1984) *Silver Bullets: A Guide to Initiative Problems, Adventure Games and Trust Activities*, USA: Project Adventure, Kendall Hunt.
Rosenblatt, R (2011) *Unless it Moves the Human Heart: The Craft & Art of Writing*, New York: Harper Collins.

MARTIAL ARTS
Burns, Lauren (2003) *Fighting Spirit*, Victoria Australia: Claremont Books.
Chun, R Grand Master (2002) *Taekwondo Spirit & Practice: Beyond Self-Defense*, Massachusetts: YMAA
Hackney, C (2010) *Martial Virtues*, Vermont USA: Tuttle Publishing.
Millman, D (2000) *Way of the Peaceful Warrior: A Book that Changes Lives*, Tiburon: H.J. Kramer
Sun Tzu, (5th Century BC) *The Art of War*, (T. Cleary 1987) Boston: Shambhala.

MINDFULNESS
Benson, H (1975) *The Relaxation Response*, New York: Morrow and Company.
Sri Chinmoy (1997) *The Wings of Joy: Finding Your Path to Inner Peace*, New York: Fireside.
Tolle, E (2001) *The Power of Now: A Guide to Spiritual Enlightenment*, Sydney: Hodder.

MORALITY AND VALUES
Earl of Chesterfield (2014) *Letters to his Son*, Adelaide University e-books. https://ebooks.adelaide.edu.au/c/chesterfield/letters/
Keil & Lennick (2008) *Moral Intelligence*, University of Pennsylvania: Wharton School Publishing.

NATURE
Krakauer, J (1996) *Into the Wild*, New York: Villard Books.
Louv, R (2008) *Last Child in the Woods: Saving our Children from Nature-Deficit Disorder*, North Carolina: Algonquin Books of Chapel Hill.
Murray, J (2011) *My Life in the Sea of Cars: A letter from Arnhem Land*, Australia: Transit Lounge Publishing.

PSYCHOLOGY AND PERSONAL GROWTH
Assagioli, R (1975) *Psychosynthesis*, England: Turnstone Press.
Frankl, V (1959, 2006) *Man's Search for Meaning*, Boston: Beacon Press.
Ferrucci, P (1982) *What We May Be: Techniques for Psychological and Spiritual Growth through Psychosynthesis*, LA: JP Tarcher.
Maslow, A (1943) *A Theory of Human Motivation* (Reprinted by Martino Fine Books, 2013).
Young Brown, M (1983) *The Unfolding Self: Psychosynthesis and Counselling*, LA: Psychosynthesis Press.
Wilber, K (1979) *No Boundary: Eastern & Western Approaches to Personal Growth*, Boston: Shambhala.

PHILOSOPHY AND SPIRITUALITY
Bach, R (1973) *Jonathon Livingston Seagull*, London: Pan Books.
Bach, R (1977) *Illusions: The Adventures of a Reluctant Messiah*, USA: Dell Publishing.
Black Elk & Neihardt (2000) *Black Elk Speaks*, Lincoln: University of Nebraska Press.
Butler-Bowden, T (2005) *50 Spiritual Classics*, Boston: Nicholas Brealey Publishing.
Campbell, J (1949, 2008) *The Hero with a Thousand Faces*, USA: New World Library.
Campbell, J (1991) *Reflections on the Art of Living*, New York: HarperCollins.
Cousineau, P (1988) *The Art of Pilgrimage: The Seekers Guide to Making Travel Sacred*, San Francisco: Conari Press.
Eldredge, J (2001) *Wild at Heart: Discovering the Secret of a Man's Soul*, Nashville: Thomas Nelson.
Enright, G (2008) *Living the Light: Discovering Truth & Living in Spirit*, Adelaide South Australia: Peacock Publishing.
Hagberg, J & Guelich, R (2005) *The Critical Journey – Stages in the Life of Faith*, USA: Sheffield Publishing.
Moore, T (1994) *Care of the Soul: A Guide for Cultivating Depth and Sacredness in Everyday Life*, New York: Harper Perennial.
Mother Teresa (1995) *A Simple Path*, London: Rider.
Rinpoche, Sogyal (2008) *The Tibetan Book of Living & Dying*, London: Rider.
Walsch, ND (1997) *Conversations with God*, London: Hodder & Stoughton.

RESILIENCE AND EMOTIONAL INTELLIGENCE
Ginsberg, Y (1999) *Heart of The Amazon*, Australia: Pan Macmillan.
Goleman, D (1998) *Working with Emotional Intelligence*, London: Bloomsbury.
Jollie, W (1999) *A Setback is a Setup for a Comeback*, Sydney: Goko.
Maxwell, J (2000) *Failing Forward*, Nashville: Thomas Nelson.

SYSTEMS THINKING AND THE NEW FRONTIER
Capra & Luisi (2014) *The Systems View of Life: A Unifying Vision*, USA, Cambridge University Press.
Capra, F (1985) *The Turning Point: Science, Society and the Rising Culture*, London: Flamingo.
Capra, F (1989) *The Tao of Physics: An Exploration of the Parallels between Modern Physics and Eastern Mysticism*, London: Flamingo.
De Bono, E (1999) *Six Thinking Hats*, USA: Back Bay.
Enright, P (2016) *Digital Disruption in the Professional Services Industry*, Evolve Magazine, Parsons Brinckerhoff.
https://issuu.com/wspparsonsbrinckerhoff/docs/evolve_firstquarter2016pdf/13
Ferguson, M (1983) *The Aquarian Conspiracy: Personal and Social Transformation in the 1980's*, London: Granada Publishing.
Watson & Freeman (2012) *Future Vision: Scenarios for the World in 2040*, London: Scribe.
Wilber, K (2001) *A Theory of Everything: An Integral Vision for Business, Politics, Science and Spirituality*, Dublin: Gateway.

WELLNESS AND HEALING
Adams, Patch (1993) *Gesundheit*, Vermont: Healing Arts Press.
Ardell, D (1986) *High Level Wellness: An Alternative to Doctors, Drugs and Disease*, Berkeley: Ten Speed Press.
Enright, W (2005) *Living Balance: A Journey to Wellness*, (e-book) self published.
Travis & Ryan (1988) *Wellness Workbook* 2nd edition, Berkeley: Ten Speed Press.
Weedn, Flavia (1988) *Flavia and the Dream Maker*, Los Angeles: Innocent Age.

Additional Sources of Information
Army Alpine Association DVD: *Everest 2001 – Tragedy & Triumph* (2001).
South Australian Everest Expedition Diaries (2001).
Duncan Chessell Interviews—J. Burton (2004) W. Enright (2016/17).
Catherine Auricht-Crease Interviews—K. Webb (2004) W. Enright (2016/17).
Army Alpine Association Expedition Interviews—W. Enright (2017).
Alex Robey Interview with Mark Auricht on Everest (2001)
Edmund Hillary & Tenzing Norgay photograph, p50—Jamling Norgay (1953).
http://www.tenzing-norgay-trekking.de, CC BY-SA 3.0,
Source: https://commons.wikimedia.org/w/index.php?curid=11252058
Cover Photo of Mark Auricht on Lobuje East—Duncan Chessell (1998).

Thank you to Catherine Auricht-Crease, Duncan Chessell, Alex Robey, Katrina Webb, Julian Burton, Zac Zaharias, Brian Laursen, Tim Robathan and Bob Killop; for their valuable contributions to this publication.

INDEX

A
Above the Line, 211, 340
Accelerated Learning, 126, 128-132, 150
Acceptance & Commitment Therapy, 315-318
Acclimatisation, 36, 58, 62, 196, 330
Action Theories, 140 – 144,
Adults at Risk, 257
Adventure Based Experiential Learning 15, 29, 110, 115, 125, 139-160, 181-182, 261, 370, 375-378
Adversity, 293-309
Affinity, 124, 209-210, 283-285, 336-337, 339-341, 343-350, 352
AFL Football Analogy, 212
Agreements, 195, 209-212, 339-341
Altitude Sickness, 42, 50, 62-63, 72, 75, 330-333
Ambos, 122, 290, 296-297, 324
Angels, 78, 185, 381-382
Animal Instincts, 353-361, 391
Annapurna, 35, 58, 59
Anzac Day on Everest, 59, 73, 80
Apogee, 364-364
Aquarian Conspiracy, 186
Army Alpine Association (AAA), 58- 60, 72-82
Assertive, 344-345
Auricht, Clive, 90-92, 95, 179, 222, 247-248
Auricht Family History, 88-92
Authenticity, 112, 137, 222, 230, 232, 237, 240, 246, 251, 256-259, 263, 270-271, 276-277, 282-286
Autocracy / Authority, 170, 189-191, 198, 213, 218-222, 230, 285
Avalanche, 52, 58-60, 62
Awakening, 23, 25, 28, 241-242, 258
Awareness Window (Johari) 152-153, 282-284, 353-358

B
Balance, 123-124, 171-176, 230-232, 256-257,307, 321-326
Bertrand, John, 220-222, 225-226
Best Workplaces, 180-181
Blame, 198 -199, 311, 313-314, 345
Blind Lineup, 164, 415
Brave, 134, 266, 277, 281-282
Buckminster Fuller, 130
Bullshift, 258-259
Business Biology, 171, 212, 335
Business Game, 148-150, 214, 415
Butterfly Effect 174, 176

C
Call of Adventure, 49, 86, 99-101, 242, 247, 255
Campbell, Joseph, 89, 104, 245, 282
Character, 83-85, 166, 185, 219, 221-222, 226, 233, 269, 271
Chief, 328-329
Choice, 84, 144, 156, 269, 275, 292, 295-302, 304-305, 308-309, 312-316, 355-356, 371
Chomolungma, 49, 55, 78, 86
Chunk it Down, 47, 201-202, 206
Circles of Influence, 236, 238-239, 236-264, 313, 318, 361, 370-371, 385-386
Circle of Stones, 385-386
Coaching, 151-160, 158-160, 187, 191, 194, 197, 200,206-208, 212, 218, Part 5, 367-372, 415
Collaboration Game, 275, 415
Comfort Zone, 28, 29, 46, 48, 143, 156, 227-229, 242, 256, 283-284, 286, 321, 355-356, 368-372
Communication/Consultation, 165, 195, 199, 210-211, 270, 282-287, 335-337, 339-349, 415
Compass / Navigation, 16, 105, 108, 163, 233, 236-238, 259, 263, Part 5, 373
Compassion, 271-272
Conflict, 270, 336-350

Connection, 124, 219, 284-285, 287, 336-337, 339-341, 348-350, 352
Context/Framework, 195, 197, 200, 202-203, 206-208, 210-212, 357
Cost of Climbing Everest, 50, 51, 52
Courage, 33, 39, 227-234, 240, 270, 276-278, 285, 301, 334, 374-378
Crisis, 243, 252, 312
Critical Decisions, 39, 43-44, 65, 71, 74, 79-80, 244-245, 247, 275, 278-281, 288-292, 295-302, 304-305, 308-309, 338-339, 355, 371
Culture, 195, 335

D

Death Zone, 35, 36, 38, 50, 51, 52, 72, 76, 82
De Bono, 319-320
Debrief, Pre-framing, Freeze Frame, 154-159
Delegation, 2-1-202, 207, 289-292, 350-358
Democracy, 225
Digital Disruption, 173
Diminisher, 225
Diversity, 165, 230-232, 335, 345-348, 353-361
Dreams, Path of Happiness, Bliss, 29, 88-104, 175, 177, 244, 246, 282, 286, 345, 373-380
Dreaming, 239, 249

E

Earning the Right, 222, 327-334, 337
Emotional Intelligence, 240, 298-299, 322, 327-360, 392
Empathy, 270, 285, 327, 335, 341, 352
Empowerment, 169, 190, 218-222
Energy Exchange, 236, 323-325
Encouragement, 227-233, 285, 301, 348-350, 352-353
Enlightenment, 185, 242, 258-262, 277, 314
Equality, 230-232, 346-349

Everest (Peak 15), 26, 49-53, 57, 60-82, 193, 333
Excellence, 177-182
Experiential Learning, 114-115, 118, 139-160, 181-182, 213, 294

F

Facilitation Skills, 114, 125-126, 130, 142, 144-145, 150-160, 415
Failure, 100-102, 115-117, 179, 183, 193, 270, 287, 303-305, 308-309
Fear, 33, 34, 54, 78, 94, 134, 136, 175, 185, 215-219, 227-229, 242, 277-278, 294-309, 315-318, 334, 341-344, 356, 371, 374-378
Feedback, 124, 152-155, 157-160, 201, 203, 208-211, 214, 222, 282, 284-286, 287, 341, 344-345, 347-349, 351-358, 415
Fight/Flight/Freeze, 298-299, 301-302, 306-308
Fire, 203, 294, 365
Fit 4 Leadership, 214-215, 415
Flipping the Lid, 299
Flow, 305-307, 315-318
Focus Management, 288-992, 415
Forgiveness, 185, 271-272, 309, 385
Four D's for Managing Priorities, 292
Four Directions, 236, 266-270
Freedom, 34, 54, 91, 197, 205-208, 269, 302, 371-372, 374-378
Free Spirit Adventures, 249, 252, 415
Fulfilling Your Significance, 373-380

G

Gaia Theory, 173
Gender, 230-232
Global Garden, 174-176
Good to Great, 178, 194, 232, 271
Grateful Leadership, 222
Gratitude, 8-11, 27, 83, 86, 185, 249-251, 268-269, 351, 381-387
Grief, 27, 34, 73, 77-78, 82-83, 97, 135, 161, 243-247, 294-298, 312-314, 381-383

H

Healing, 119-122, 242, 247-251, 268, 312-313, 371-372, 381-387
Healthy Teams, 164-165, 262, 415
Heart, 16, 28, 86-87, 97-101, 131-132, 134, 163, 277-234, 247, 250-251, 257-260, 270, 284, 295, 308-309, 346-349, 369-370, 373
Heartbreaking News, 26, 68, 77, 243
Heartfulness, 230, 314, 346-350, 369-370
Hero's Journey, 89, 104
High Ropes Course, 143, 375-378
Himalaya, 49-53, 55, 249
Himalayan Data Base, 51, 52
Humility, 178, 270, 322, 327-334, 359
Humour/Fun/Joy, 129, 131, 144, 187-188, 251, 283, 285, 322, 372

I

Iceberg Model, 369-372
Identity, 277
Impermanence, 33, 34
Indigenous, 85, 239, 251, 254, 262, 267-268, 328-329
Influence, 169, 213, 264, 266, 270, 323, 327-362, 385-386
Initiation, 250 – 257
Inner Landscape/ Journey 29, 101-102, Part 2, 250-257, 262, 299-300, 334, 365-372
Inspiration, 83-86, 101-105, 110, 177, 183, 216-217, 220-221, 223, 225-226, 249, 287
Integrity, 237, 270-277
Intelligences (emotional, social, moral, spiritual) 123-124, 178, 201, 230, 240, 250, 270, 272, 298-299, 322, 342-346, 392
Into the Wild, 99, 101-102
Into Thin Air, 53
Introverted Leaders, 353-361
Isurava, 241, 250

K

Key Behavioural Indicators, 124, 211
Khumbu Icefall, 52, 57
Kilimanjaro, 53, 249, 329-334, 415
Kimberley, 249, 253, 257
Kings Speech, 136-137
Kokoda, 91-92, 162, 200, 241-242, 247-252, 255-257, 289, 308-309, 328, 337-339, 415

L

Land of the Unexpected, 247, 249
Larapinta Trail, 262, 415
Leadership, 48, 73, 94, 151, 165-166, 169-170, 176-179, 189-192, 197-201, 202-203, 206-212, 218-222, 228-233, 261-263, Part 5, 415
Leap of Faith / Trapeze, 43, 377-380
Learning Journey, Part 2, 184-189, 307-309, 313, 415
Learning Domains, 129
Learning from Failure, 303-305
Learning Organisation, 121, 393
Learning Zone / Growth Zone, 29, 125, 143, 156, 227-229, 242, 286
Legacy, 16, 25, 104-106, 108, 240
Lessons from Makalu, 47
Letting Go, 33-34, 43, 213, 215, 259
Leverage, 190-191, 216-226, 236, 270, 351, 361
Lewin's Principles, 140-142
Living the Light, 185, 405

M

Machu Picchu, 223
Magic Happens, 300-302
Makalu, 33-48, 54-55, 86
Mallory and Irvine, 49, 50, 57
Marshall Thurber, 129-130
Maslow, 217-218, 275, 358, 368
Master Gardener, 179, 367
Master vs Victim, 313-314, 340, 367
Martial Arts, 93, 213, 244, 255, 304-305, 321-322, 334, 341-346, 366-367

Medicine, 91, 108, 122, 249, 260, 262, 323-325, 381
Medivac, 63, 289-290, 337-339
Memorial, 83-98, 380-381
Mentoring, 151-160, 184-189, 191-192, 197, 212, 218, 281, Part 5, 370, 415
Metaphorical Learning, 109-112, 115, 118, 125, 129, 149
Metaphysical, 136, 357
Micro-management, 190-191, 197-198, 207-208, 225
Mind, 131, 196, 259, 367-372
Mindfulness / Meditation, 230, 269, 270, 314-320, 322-325, 338-339, 341-346, 367-372
Mixed Emotions, 38-40, 81-82
Money & You, 128-129
Morality, 80-81, 269, 271-274, 288
Multiplier, 190, 216, 221-226, 270

N

Nature, 29, 86, 101-104, 251, 255-258, 268-269
Netflix, 206-208
New Frontier, 166, 170-176, 181-184, 189-191, 215, 230, 233, 320
New World Chaos (Chaos Theory), 17, 174-176, 186, 190, 215

O

On Belay, 228-230, 339
Operation Flinders, 11, 200-206, 255, 267, 278-281, 284-286, 299-302
Organisational Wellness, 119-122, 146, 186-187, 286-288
Organisational Change, 193-208
Outdoor Education, 85, 94, 140-148, 201-206, 227-230, 250, 255-267

P

Parenting, 198, 209-212, 329, Part 5
Parables 99, 277
Passing the Baton, 216-217, 361
Patagonia, 103, 415
Patch Adams, 122, 187-188

Patience, 193, 270, 298, 303-305, 308-309, 332-333
Peace, 175, 250, 286, 336-349
People Skills, 123-124, 327-362
Persistence, 38-46, 70-71, 81-82, 183, 270, 273, 298, 300-305, 308-309, 330-333
Personality Profile, 353-361, 391
Philanthropy, 95
Pilgrimage, 241-242, 255
Planning, 195, 199-203, 206-207, 210-212, 281, 286-292, 366
Poetry, 185, 250-251, 264, 300-302, 377, 379, 382
Possibility, 319-320, 370-372
Post Traumatic Stress / Growth, 244, 294-297, 299, 300-302, 304-310
Precession, 130
Principle Centred, 181, 187, 269-292
Prioritising, 271-277, 288-292
Private Victory, 291, 323, 334, 343
Preparation, 47, 58, 194-197, 199-203, 206-207, 210-212, 286-292, 360, 366
Psychosynthesis, 113
Purpose/Mission, 238, 256, 270, 276-277, 281, 373-375, 385-386

R

Reflection, 19, 142, 153-155, 157-160, 359, 374-375, 385-386
Reframing, 369-372
Resilience, 251, 266, 270, 274-278, 293-310, 316-325
Respect, 166, 203, 210, 271, 282, 285-286, 328-329, 335-337, 346-350
Responsibility, 29, 165, 193, 197-209, 212, 228, 266, 269-272, 311-326, 340, 344, 350-351
Ripple Effect, 106, 236, 361-362
Risk, 30, 47, 50, 54, 86, 143, 176, 228, 270, 279-281, 284, 303, 319-321, 374-378
Rites of Passage, 248-256, 415
Routes to Climb Everest, 52, 57, 66

S

SA Everest Expedition, 56-57, 60-65
Sailing, 20-23, 156, 168, 219-222, 225-226, 298, 316-317, 324-326, 381
Samaritan, 45, 75
School, 131-132, 134, 277-278
SDOC Take (SWOT), 287
Secret Destinations, 161-166, 238, 247-249, 252, 255, 263
Secrets of Experiential Learning, 150
Self Care, 290-292, 322-326, 415
Self Disclosure, 239, 282-285
Self-Managed Work Teams, 180, 187, 189-212, 214-215, 393-395
Service, 7, 185, 218-220, 359, 415
Sherpa, 45, 50-52, 56, 62, 70, 78, 81,
Simplicity, 242
SMART Goals, 287
Solitude, 100-104, 374-375, 385-386
Solution Thinking, 270, 319-320
Soul Mates, 95-97
Spasmodic Dysphonia, 135
Spiral Journey, 138, 236-264, 385, 415
Spirituality, 16, 33-34, 45, 66, 78, 85, 95, 97, 131, 136, 185, 230, 247-248, 250-252, 259, 267-269, 305, 308-309, 328-329, 343, 369-370, 381-383
STEEP Survey (Business Analysis), 287
Stewardship, 219-220
Strategic Planning, 199, 207, 212, 281, 286-289, 393-395, 415
Strategy of the Dolphin, 230
Strengths, 164-165, 177-181, 185, 190-191, 207, 216-217, 221, 287, 355-361, 392
Stress, 293-299, 305-309, 318-325, 356, 415
Suicide, 293-310 (Lifeline 131114)
Summit, 38-39, 46, 55-57, 67, 70, 79-80, 95, 100-101, 193, 332-333, 364
Supplementary Oxygen, 35, 38, 50-51, 64, 69, 71-72, 75

Surfing, 307, 316-317
Self Survival vs Team, 38, 80-81
Systems Thinking, 171
Systems & Processes, 196, 206-207

T

Teaching 134, 151-160 155, 158-160, 200, 213, 278, Part 5, 415
Teamwork, 80, 163-166, 190-191, 193-208, 210-212, 221-222, 224-226, 261, 286, 336-337, 339-341, 343-345, 347-348, 393-395, 415
Temperament, (see - *Animal Instincts*) 353-361, 391
Tibetan Book of Living & Dying, 34, 259
Time Management, 289-292, 415
Todd Sampson, 5, 29, 104
Transfer of Authority, 190-191, 193, 197-226, 393-395
Transformation, 248-249, 253-256, 294, 301-302, 308-309, 312-313, 371-372, 393-395, 415
Trauma/Post-trauma Growth 299
Treasure & Sharing Boons, 16, 34, 99-102, 104-106, 385-386, 415
Treasure Challenge, 15-118, 415
Triage, 289-290
Tributes to Mark Auricht, 83-90, 93-98, 106
True North Expeditions, 11, 255, 284
True North Leadership, 262-362
True North Leadership Expedition, 374, 415
True North—Inner Compass, 17, 30, 163, 232, 233, 237, 253-288
Trust, 165, 215-219, 270, 278, 284-285, 317, 321, 337-339
Truth, 33-34, 102, 106, 108, 134, 136-137, 185, 213, 240, 253, 257-260, 277, 328-329, 339, 373
Turning Back, 37, 39, 50, 65, 71, 75, 79-80, 99-104, 193, 332-333
Turning Points (Influences), 161-189, 171-173, 186, 239-240, 370-372
Two Voices, 33, 42, 100, 215, 375-378

U

Understanding, 335-337, 339-341, 344-345
Unfolding Self, 324, 415
Universal Principles, 269, 272-277

V

Validation, 132, 345-353
Values, 81, 127, 165, 210-211, 270, 272-277, 286-292, 415
Value of Adventure, 28-29, 54, 130, 143, 248-252, 255, 377-380, 415
Venture Corporate Recharge, 28, 125-127, 335, 375-378
Vision, 47, 165, 253, 260-263, 270, 286-292, 415
Vision Quest, 253-264, 373, 385-386, 415
Voice, 134-137, 161-163, 240, 246-247, 249, 260, 327

W

Wall, 175, 308-309
Wellness, 119-122, 186-187, 322-326, 367-370, 415
Wild at Heart, 250, 256-257, 259
Wilderness Therapy, 200-206, 257-258, 242, 248-252, 255-257, 260, 262, 278-281, 284-286, 298-303, 308-309, 371
Women in Leadership, 214, 230-232

Y

Yin Yang 231
Youth at Risk, 11, 95, 200-206, 255, 267, 278-281, 284-286, 293-310
Yves Morieux TED Talk, 216-217

Z

Zac Zaharias, 58, 72-80

Reflection Questions

Adaptability 182
Adventure 30
Authenticity 138, 234, 310
Best Practice 182
Comfort Zone 48
Context, framework, systems, 208, 393
De Bono Hats (problem-solving) 326
Dreams, Passions 30, 375
Emotional Intelligence 310, 326, 362, 392
Feedback and Blindspots 118, 160, 362
Heart vs Head 234
High Performance 182
Inner Guidance / Compass 30, 234
Integrity 310
Leadership Character 177, 219, 221
Learning Journey / Failure 138, 160, 226
Legacy 118, 362
Medicine 138, 264, 375
Mentors 160, 192, 194, 226, 264
Micro-management 208
Mindfulness 326
Multiplier vs Diminisher 226
People Skills 124, 126, 362
Personality/ Temperament 362, 391
Preparation 47
Problem-solving 118, 310
Questions of Significance, 374-375
Reflection 160, 375
Responsibility 47
Risk taking 30, 47
Self-management 192
Strengths 182, 362, 392
Stress Management 310, 326
Team Behaviour 118, 166, 177
Time Management, Prioritising 310
True Nature 264
True North 264, 310, 375
Understanding 362
Spiral Journey / Adversity 264, 310
Values /Guiding Principles 264
Vision & Goals 47, 375
Yin Yang 234

SERVICES
www.freespirittruenorth.com.au

Experiential Learning Activities
- Team Alignment Challenge
- Treasure Challenge
- The Business Game
- Collaboration Game
- Team Communication Challenge

Inspiring Keynote Speakers (Leadership, Team, Wellness, Adventure)

True North Leadership Expedition (Multi-day Leadership Journey)

Unfolding Self Course (Renovating the Inner Landscape: 5 Week Course)
Nature Therapy
Life Coaching and Counselling

Retreats (2 or more days: Residential)
- Life Balance and Wellness
- Vision and Strategic Planning
- Team Values/Agreements and Feedback

True North Quest (Vision Quest Journey: 10 Days, Flinders Ranges)

Workshops & Training Programs
- Life Balance / Stress Management / Wellness & Resilience
- Focus Management & Mindful Living
- Animal Instincts (Leveraging Diversity)
- Dealing with Challenging People / Crucial Conversations
- Facilitator, Coach, Mentor (Skills Development for Leaders)

Adventures
- Kokoda (PNG), Kimberley, Litchfield & Nitmuluk (AUS)
- Inca or Salkantay Trail to Machu Picchu (Peru)
- Patagonia W Trek & Los Glaciers NP Treks (Chile/Argentina)
- Mt Kilimanjaro – Tanzanian Safari (Africa)
- Himalayan Journey (Bhutan) / Angkor Temples (Cambodia)
- Milford / Routeburn (NZ) / Camino (Spain)
- Overland Track and Franklin River Rafting (Tasmania)
- Larapinta Trail – Kings Canyon – Uluru Adventure (Central Australia)
- Flinders Ranges, Heysen Trail & Hills Coast Camino (South Australia)

CONTACT US

Website: www.freespirittruenorth.com.au

Book a Conference Speaker: wayne@freespirittruenorth.com.au

Sign up for our Newsletter: gabrielle@freespirittruenorth.com.au

 Follow us on Facebook

 Follow us on Instagram

To provide feedback about this publication, please contact wayne@freespirittruenorth.com.au

OTHER TITLES BY THIS AUTHOR

True North Quest - Reflection Journal

A beautifully presented Personal Reflection Journal - A companion to this publication.

www.ingramcontent.com/pod-product-compliance
Lightning Source LLC
Chambersburg PA
CBHW080049190426
43201CB00035B/2148